the *BEST* of
HOME ECONOMICS TEACHERS
BICENTENNIAL
COOKBOOK

Favorite Recipes® of
HOME ECONOMICS TEACHERS

©Favorite Recipes Press MCMLXXV   Post Office Box 3396, Montgomery, Alabama 36109

Library of Congress Cataloging in Publication Data
Main entry under title:
The Best of Home Economics Teachers Bicentennial
   Cookbook.

Includes index.
1. Cookery.
TX715.B4856   641.5   75-37511
ISBN 0-87197-103-8

Dear Homemaker

Home Economics Teachers throughout the Nation say, "Happy Birthday America" with this beautiful Bicentennial Cookbook! Home Economics Teachers have always been great contributors to the health and happiness of American homes. They teach us the *best way* to manage the homemaker's job . . . thus, homemakers have come a long, long way since the beginning of our Nation in 1776.

The Best of Home Economics Teachers Bicentennial Cookbook brings together all the splendid, traditional recipes which have been collected for many years in the Home Economics Teachers Cookbook series. Our Editors selected from this series recipes that are BASIC, easy-to-use, traditionally good for all occasions. We regret that we did not have space for the many more excellent recipes. Whatever the occasion, whether it is a traditional family holiday dinner or entertaining for special guests, you will find just the right recipe in this Bicentennial collection.

Much appreciation is due the Home Economics Teachers for all the many worthwhile projects they sponsor but a very special "thank you" is given for their fabulous cookbook series. Many vital school and community projects will be benefited by THE BEST OF HOME ECONOMICS TEACHERS BICENTENNIAL COOKBOOK.

Sincerely yours,

Nicky Beaulieu

Nicky Beaulieu

BOARD OF ADVISORS

RUTH STOVALL, Chairman
Branch Director, Program Services Branch
Division of Vocational-Technical
  and Higher Education
Alabama Department of Education

CATHERINE A. CARTER
Consultant, Consumer Homemaking
  Education
Illinois Division of Vocational
  and Technical Education

ANNE G. EIFLER
Senior Program Specialist
Home Economics Education
Pennsylvania Department of Education

JANET LATHAM
Supervisor, Home Economics Education
Idaho State Board of Vocational
  Education

BARBARA GAYLOR
Supervisor, Consumer and Homemaking
  Education
Michigan Department of Education

CHRISTINE E. NICKEL
Consultant, Home Economics Education
Wisconsin Board of Vocational Technical
  and Adult Education

FRANCES RUDD
Supervisor, Home Economics Education
Arkansas Department of Education

ODESSA N. SMITH
State Supervisor, Home Economics
  Education
Louisiana Department of Education

Preface

It's bicentennial year in America! And, people in every state throughout this great nation have been caught up in the "spirit of 76." As flags
are waving and bands are playing, there's a feeling of patriotism that
swells in the heart of every American. We are celebrating everything this
country stands for — freedom, peace and love. It's time to stop and
realize that this *is* a country that offers the very best to its citizens.

One of America's best is its cuisine — an art which began its development in the days of the Pilgrims. Home Economics Teachers across the
United States believe that this is the perfect year to focus on every
aspect of American cooking. And — that's exactly what we have done
in "The Best of Home Economics Teachers Bicentennial Cookbook."
This collection features the finest, typically American recipes found in
past editions. For over ten years, teachers have contributed their
favorite recipes in cookbooks ranging from the simplest, Quick and
Easy, to the fanciest, Holiday. The "best" of all thirteen categories have
come together now in this latest bicentennial edition.

Preserving recipes that have been American traditions is an excellent
way to perpetuate our country's heritage. We have taken the best of the
past, combined it with the best of the present and created a cookbook
that can be handed down to future generations with pride.

We ask you to join us in a salute to our nation and its cookery!

Contents

Regional Americana Favorites

Today America boasts of a truly dynamic and varied cuisine. There have been many changes in the American table since the earliest settlers landed at Jamestown. Leaving their homeland in search of a better life, these brave people began their journey with little knowledge of what awaited them on the land across the ocean. Soon after the Mayflower landed, the Pilgrims discovered they had arrived in a New World of plenty. Here, the woods and waters were filled with wild game of all kinds and the earth was unspoiled. Coming prepared to sustain themselves until crops could be planted and harvested, they brought the foods of the English.

The garden bounty of fresh artichokes, avocados, broccoli, grapes, peaches and oranges from California, apples and berries from Washington, Hawaiian bananas and pineapple, and Southern vegetables are readily available year round throughout the country. Beef from the Southwest and Midwest, wild game from the mountains and forests, dairy products from Wisconsin, king crab from Alaska and regional seafood from all of the coastlines are familiar foods available to cooks everywhere in the United States.

Regional food specialties are still, and probably always will be, dramatically evident across America despite the advent of the frozen, canned, premixed and "instant" foods that are so easy to find in all sections. The early colonists and pioneers, whether German, Oriental, Spanish, African, English or Scandinavian, brought with them the cooking and eating traditions of their own land. As they settled, they found that the land produced and offered a boundless supply of singularly American foodstuffs. So, although the settlers came with one tradition, and marveled at the abundance they found, they quickly learned to adapt their particular tradition to the bounty of America's natural resources. As the waves of pioneers and immigrants moved South and West, this tradition-adapting phenomena occurred again and again, and the result is that a truly regional, but purely American cuisine has developed.

Thanks to the Indians, the English Pilgrims were the first to learn how to adapt themselves to the natural bounty around them, after almost starving to death that first winter in their new land. They found a natural source of nourishment in the lobsters, clams, wild turkeys and berries in the surrounding forests and waters. They readily learned from the Indians how to cultivate corn, beans, squash and pumpkins. Notable New England dishes, still as delicious now as they were then, are clam chowder, succotash, brown bread, boiled dinners and pumpkin pie.

Pennsylvania Dutch cooking is one regional American cuisine still pure and unaffected by other national cuisines found in America today. It is hearty and rural, replete with the flavors and foods Germans most enjoy: savory soups; the flavor contrasts of sweet and sour; rich, sweet puddings and pies; and infinite varieties of delicious breads and cakes. An example of their ingenious frugality and probably their most famous contribution to American cuisine is scrapple (ponhaus). This is a delicious mixture of meat scraps and cornmeal which is simmered, then poured into molds to be eaten later, sliced or fried.

Southern Cooking is synonymous with Southern Hospitality. The long and fertile growing season produces an abundance of delicious garden vegetables — corn, yellow squash, sweet potatoes, tomatoes, peas and okra. Hot biscuits and corn bread, grits, Brunswick Stew, fried chicken and Smithfield Hams, pilau, pound cake and pecan pie are regional specialties of the Deep South.

Creole food, complex, rich and deliciously flavorful, is a tantalizing blend of French excellence, Spanish flair, and Indian and African inventiveness with spices and cooking. Again, the bounty of the land and waters in and around New Orleans provide the substance to Creole cuisine. Savory blends of fowl, rabbit, squirrel, fish, crab, oysters and shrimp, thickened with okra or file powder, all comprise famous Creole soups and stews such as Jambalaya, file gumbo and crawfish soup. Pralines, cafe brulot and sweet, tender yams are other famous foods from the Creole region.

The beef cattle industry has flourished in the Southwest for 150 years, and as a result, the best chili, perfect barbecue and the heartiest beef stews are trademarks of that region's cookery. Cowboy Stew, or Son-of-a-Gun Stew is a popularly known dish to which the marrow gut of a young calf adds the distinctive flavor. Mexican dishes such as tortillas, guacamole, frijoles, tamales and enchiladas are also Southwestern favorites. Influenced by the Deep South, southwesterners also enjoy okra, black-eyed peas and pecan pie.

The Midwest is acknowledged as one of the world's wealthiest food producing regions, most notably producing Iowa corn, Kansas wheat, Illinois beef and pork, and Wisconsin dairy products. It boasts of the best recipes of many peoples and countries, most significantly those of the Shaker, Scandinavian and European immigrants. Hungarian goulash, classic steak and potatoes, and Scandinavian pastries, cookies and sweet rolls are some of the perfections of Midwestern cuisine.

The abundance of West Coast gardens and fields has always been a source of amazement, and certainly shapes this region's cookery. Salmon, clams, oysters, crabs and lobster are served at waterfront restaurants, popular all along the West Coast. California produces a year round abundance of fresh fruits and vegetables — not to mention more than 3/4 of the wine consumed in the United States. Washington and Oregon grow a profusion of apples, pears, peaches and wild berries. Although Oriental and Spanish touches are common, sourdough bread, cioppino, abalone, green goddess dressing, avocados and nopal cactus are favorite West Coast foods.

Beyond the continental boundaries of the United States we have Hawaii with its very distinctive Polynesian and Oriental cuisine. The luau is an event we think of as most representative of Hawaiian cooking. A typical luau menu might include the smooth, thick porridge-like pulp of the taro root, or poi, a pit-roasted pig, with bananas, sweet potatoes, pork or salt fish buried and baked with it, coconut-arrowroot pudding and tropical fruits.

Alaska, the berry capital of America, boasts of the biggest and tastiest strawberries, cranberries, blueberries and raspberries (to mention only a few) to be found anywhere. While fiddlehead ferns and raw rosehips are popular, the abundance of wild game furnishes such unusual delights as ptarmigan pie, mooseburgers, and caribou stew. Sourdough bread, rolls and pancakes have been traditional fare since the Gold Rush Days, and some of the largest and tastiest vegetables ever seen grow near Anchorage in the Matanuska Valley. Large Alaska King Crab and deep-water scallops are delicious and plentiful.

It is very easy for a visitor to the United States to be misled about American cuisine. There are so many easy-stop and drive-in eating establishments sitting on roadsides all across America serving meals that look the same and taste the same — meals that can too easily be mistaken for "American Cuisine." But, luckily, this is not a true picture. An interested glance beneath the surface will reveal that American cooking could never really be so boring or lifeless. It is a bounteous and varied cookery, full of regional character. And, with all the regional flavors, it's still as different and exciting as each of its 50 states and its millions of inventive cooks.

Favorite Recipes of

FISH CHOWDER

BY MRS. BENJAMIN HARRISON
(Wife of the President)

ut a medium-sized shad or white-fish, three or four potatoes, one onion and a quarter of a pound of bacon into small pieces. Fry the bacon and onions a light brown. Put a layer of potatoes in the saucepan, over that a layer of the fish, then a sprinkling of onions and bacon, then a layer of tomatoes; sprinkle with pepper and salt, alternating the layers until all is in. Add enough water to cover, place over a moderate fire and let simmer twenty-five minutes. Boil one pint of milk, thickening it with cracker crumbs; let it stand a moment and then add to the chowder. Now stir for the first time, let boil an instant, season if not strong to taste, and serve hot.

Caroline S Harrison

A QUICKLY-MADE SOUP

BY MRS. HARRIET TAYLOR UPTON
(Daughter of Hon. E. B. Taylor, of Ohio, and author of "The Children of the White House")

othing perhaps is of more help to a house keeper than to be able to concoct at short notice a good soup. A meager lunch, or a light dinner is often turned into an attractive meal by the addition of a soup. Below is given one of the most simple of quickly-made soups:

Place one tablespoonful of butter in a stewpan till it boils but does not brown. Add two table-spoonfuls of flour; when all is thoroughly mixed add one teaspoonful of salt, one teaspoonful of celery salt, one saltspoonful of white pepper. Boil one quart of milk, and add the hot thickening. Remove the bone and skin from one small can of salmon; mince or chip it; add the fish to the milk, which, when once boiled, serve immediately.

Harriet T Upton

CURRIED MUTTON CHOPS

BY MRS. JOS. E. WASHINGTON
(Wife of Representative from Tennessee)

et the best rib chops, and have them cut about an inch thick. Put them in melted butter several hours before cooking. Half an hour before they are to be eaten slip the pan in which they are with the butter into the stove and melt the butter a second time. Then dip them into the following preparation: A loaf of stale bread rolled and sifted until it is like meal, the yellows of six hard-boiled eggs, three teaspoonfuls chopped parsley, two teaspoonfuls of grated onion, one teaspoonful of thyme, one teaspoonful of sweet marjoram, salt, pepper (black and red), etc., and two tablespoonfuls of curry powder. Mix this thoroughly together. When the chops have been rolled in this put them in a deep pan and add the melted butter and Port or Madeira wine enough to keep them from burning. Cook twenty minutes, basting frequently; cut heart-shaped papers; butter them well and wrap a chop in each, folding the edges carefully. Slip in the stove for two minutes, and serve very hot.

Mary B. Washington

STEWED CORN

BY MISS PHOEBE W. COUZINS, LL.B.
(Ex-United States Marshal, Eastern District of Missouri)

plit the kernels of corn before removing from the cob, and in cutting off cut them several times through, leaving a large part on the cob to be scraped off, so as to make a fine mass of the whole. Take a pint of milk or cream, bring it to a boil, and put the corn in and boil slowly in a closed porcelain kettle for fifteen or twenty minutes, with a very little salt and sugar. It is better still when steamed.

Phoebe W. Couzins L.L.B.
Ex. U. S. Marshal

Historical Statesmen

BEATEN BISCUIT

BY MRS. JAS. H. BLOUNT
(Wife of Representative from Georgia)

o a quart of flour take a large table-spoonful of lard and a teaspoonful of salt. Mix with cold sweet milk and water — half and half — into a stiff dough; lay it on a marble or wooden board, and beat it with a club of hickory or poplar wood till the dough becomes blistered and nearly as soft as yeast-powder dough. Roll it half an inch thick, cut out with a biscuit-cutter, prick with a kitchen fork three rows of holes clear through to the bottom. Bake in a moderate oven, and when done, allow them to remain a few moments longer, to brown a little more thoroughly. Break open and butter.

E. W. Blount

APPLE PAN DOWDY

BY MRS. MARCUS A. SMITH
(Wife of the Delegate from Arizona)

or a family of six, use two-quart pan. Pare and slice some good pie apples; place a layer of apples about an inch thick; season with sugar and a speck of salt. Put a layer of cracker crumbs half an inch thick; alternate apples and cracker till the pan is full. Bake one hour, and serve with cream or rich milk. Rhode Island greenings are best.

Elizabeth M. Smith

DIXIE PUDDING

BY MRS. W. H. F. LEE
(Wife of Representative from Virginia)

ne pint of bread crumbs, one quart of milk, yolks of four eggs, rind of one lemon, one cup of sugar. Bake in pudding-dish. When done spread over with some kind of jams; beat the whites of the eggs light, season with the juice of lemon; one cup of sugar; put on top of pudding; set in oven for a minute to brown.

Mrs W. H. F. Lee

BREAD TOTE

BY MRS. JOHN LIND
(Wife of Representative from Minnesota)

wo cups bread crumbs, sifted and evenly browned or roasted, eight eggs (yolks), one and a half cups of granulated sugar, one-half pound chocolate (grated), three-fourths pound almonds, one-half pound citron, one-half teaspoon cinnamon, one-half cloves, one-fourth teaspoon cardamon, one-fourth cup brandy, juice and grated rind of one lemon. Mix sugar and yolks until very light; then add all ingredients except bread crumbs and whites of eggs, and stir well; then wet or dampen the crumbs with white wine and add to the rest last whites of the eggs well beaten. For icing, chocolate or a white frosting. Bake one and a half hours slowly.

Alice A. Lind
New Ulm Minnesota

SPONGE CAKE

BY MRS. ISABELLA BEECHER HOOKER
(The noted Advocate of Women's Rights)

ne pound sugar, one-half pound flour, ten eggs, one lemon, salt. Beat the whites and yolks of the eggs separately and till very light; then mix the sugar with the yolks thoroughly; then add the grated lemon peel and the juice, and a little salt; then add the flour, cutting it with a large knife, moving the mass as lightly as possible and avoid beating entirely.

Isabella Beecher Hooker
Hartford Conn

New England

RED FLANNEL HASH

3 c. chopped cooked corned beef
2 c. coarsely chopped cooked potatoes
1 c. chopped cooked beets
1 sm. onion, finely chopped
2 tbsp. snipped parsley
1/2 tsp. salt
1/8 tsp. pepper
1 5 1/3-oz. can evaporated milk
2 tbsp. lard or drippings

Combine corned beef, potatoes, beets, onion, parsley, salt and pepper; stir in evaporated milk. Heat lard in large frying pan. Place corned beef mixture in frying pan, pressing down firmly. Cook, pressing together and turning, for 15 to 20 minutes. Press together; cook over low heat for 5 minutes or until crust forms on bottom. Loosen hash from pan with turner; invert onto platter. Cooked beef may be substituted for corned beef; add 1 teaspoon salt. Yield: 4 servings.

Photograph for this recipe on page 6.

OLD-FASHIONED SPLIT PEA SOUP

1 c. split peas
1 hambone or pieces of cubed ham
1 carrot, grated
2 med. onions, minced
1 potato, grated
1/4 c. diced celery
1/4 c. finely chopped green pepper
Salt and pepper to taste

Cover split peas with 6 cups boiling water; let soak for 1 hour. Add hambone, carrot, onions, potato, celery and green pepper. Season with salt and pepper. Simmer until peas are tender. Add water if needed; simmer for 5 to 10 minutes longer. Pour into soup bowls; garnish with diced ham. Yield: 4 servings.

Mrs. Shirley Leslie
Magazine, Arkansas

YANKEE POT ROAST

1 4-lb. beef pot roast
1 can beef broth
1 tsp. salt
1/4 tsp. pepper
1/4 tsp. crushed rosemary
4 sm. carrots, halved lengthwise
2 med. turnips, quartered
8 sm. white onions
Chopped parsley
1/4 c. flour

Brown beef on all sides in fat in large heavy pan. Pour in beef broth. Cover; cook over low heat for 2 hours and 30 minutes. Add salt, pepper, rosemary, carrots, turnips and onions. Cook, covered, for 1 hour longer or until beef and vegetables are tender. Remove beef and vegetables to heated platter; garnish with parsley. Blend 1/4 cup water into flour; stir flour mixture slowly into pan juices. Cook, stirring constantly, until gravy is thickened. Season with additional salt and pepper. Yield: 6 servings.

Mrs. Ned R. Mitchell
Charleston, South Carolina

SUCCOTASH

2 c. fresh lima or butter beans
2 c. fresh corn
1 c. milk
4 tsp. butter
Salt and pepper to taste

Combine beans, corn and milk in saucepan; simmer until vegetables are tender. Add butter and seasonings. Mix well; serve. Yield: 4 servings.

Mrs. Videllia M. Peters
Goodridge, Minnesota

BOSTON BAKED BEANS

2 c. navy or pea beans
1 onion, chopped
1/2 lb. salt pork
2 tsp. salt
1/4 tsp. dry mustard
Pinch of pepper
1/4 c. molasses

Soak beans for 2 hours in 2 quarts warm water in large kettle. Bring to a quick boil; simmer until tender. Drain beans, reserving water. Fill bean pot with half the beans; add onion and remaining beans. Remove and discard rind from salt pork; cut pork at intervals with knife. Press pork deep into beans until surface is level. Combine salt, mustard, pepper, molasses and 3/4 cup boiling water; pour over beans. Pour the reserved water to top of bean pot; cover. Bake at 300 degrees for 3 hours. Remove cover; bake for 1 hour longer. Yield: 6 servings.

Mrs. Alice L. Brooks
Carbon, Texas

NOR'EASTER BLUEBERRY MUFFINS

1 3/4 c. flour
2 1/2 tsp. baking powder
2 tbsp. sugar
3/4 tsp. salt
3/4 c. blueberries
1/3 c. shortening, melted
1 egg, well beaten
1/2 c. milk

Sift flour, baking powder, sugar and salt together into mixing bowl. Make well in center; add blueberries. Cool shortening. Combine egg and milk; add to shortening. Add shortening mixture to dry ingredients all at once, mixing well. Fill greased muffin pans 2/3 full with blueberry batter. Bake at 400 degrees for 25 minutes or until lightly browned. Yield: 12 muffins.

Mrs. B. Fred German
Copperhill, Tennessee

VERMONT MAPLE CAKE

2 c. sifted flour
3/4 c. sugar
3/4 c. (packed) brown sugar
3 tsp. baking powder
1 tsp. salt
1/2 c. vegetable oil
7 eggs, separated
2 tsp. maple flavoring
1/2 tsp. cream of tartar
1 c. chopped nuts

Sift flour, sugar, brown sugar, baking powder and salt together into mixing bowl; shape well in center. Add oil, egg yolks, 3/4 cup water and flavoring. Beat with electric mixer at medium speed until smooth. Combine egg whites and cream of tartar in separate bowl; beat with electric mixer until stiff peaks form. Pour batter over egg whites, folding in gently. Do not stir. Fold in nuts. Pour batter into ungreased 10-inch tube pan. Bake in preheated 325-degree oven for 55 minutes. Increase oven temperature to 350 degrees; bake for 10 to 15 minutes longer or until top springs back when lightly touched. Place tube pan upside down over neck of funnel to cool.

Mrs. Carolynn Helgren
Falfurrias, Texas

Pennsylvania Dutch

PENNSYLVANIA DUTCH STUFFING

6 med. potatoes
1 med. onion
3 slices bread
1/2 c. diced celery
2 tbsp. melted butter
1 1/2 c. warm milk
2 tsp. salt
1/8 tsp. pepper
2 tbsp. minced parsley
1/4 tsp. saffron
2 eggs, well beaten

Pare and cut up potatoes; boil in water until soft. Chop onion; cut bread into cubes. Saute onion, celery and bread cubes in melted butter. Drain and mash potatoes. Add onion, celery, bread cubes, milk, salt, pepper, parsley and saffron; beat well. Add eggs; blend thoroughly. Turn into greased casserole. Bake for 1 hour at 350 degrees. Serve immediately as accompaniment to meat or poultry. Yield: 6 servings.

Lucy M. Bamberger
Schaefferstown, Pennsylvania

WILTED GREENS

4 or 5 slices bacon
2 tbsp. butter
1/4 c. mild vinegar
1 tsp. grated onion
1 tsp. sugar
1 head lettuce, torn
Shredded cabbage
2 hard-cooked eggs, sliced

Saute bacon until crisp; remove from pan. Drain; crumble into small pieces. Melt butter in skillet; stir in vinegar, bacon, onion and sugar. Combine lettuce and cabbage in bowl. Pour hot dressing over greens; toss to coat evenly. Arrange servings on warm plates; garnish with eggs. Dandelion greens or young spinach leaves may be substituted for cabbage, if desired. Yield: 4 servings.

Janice Kindler
Grand Rapids, Ohio

SCRAPPLE

1 hog's head, cleaned
2 c. sifted cornmeal
Salt to taste
Sage to taste
Sausage seasoning to taste

Place hog's head in large kettle; cover with water. Cook until meat can be easily removed from bones. Remove and chop meat fine. Cook broth until reduced to 1/2 gallon. Add cornmeal; cook until thickened. Add finely chopped meat and seasoning to taste. Pour into four 5 x 10-inch loaf pans to 3-inch thickness; chill. Cut into 1/4 to 1/2-inch thick slices; fry quickly in small amount of hot fat until browned. Serve with sausage and eggs, if desired.

Mrs. Martha G. Akers
Riner, Virginia

PHILADELPHIA OYSTER STEW

1/4 lb. salt pork
1 qt. oysters
Salt and pepper to taste

Cut salt pork into small cubes; fry until crisp. Heat oysters slowly in their own liquor. Add pork and drippings; cook until oysters are plump and edges curled. Season with salt and pepper; serve immediately.

Alice I. Jett
Reedville, Virginia

SAUERKRAUT AND FISH CASSEROLE

3 tbsp. margarine
1 1/2 tbsp. flour
2/3 c. finely chopped onions
Salt
1/8 tsp. pepper
1/4 tsp. marjoram
1/2 tsp. dillseed
1 pt. sauerkraut
1 lb. halibut
Dash of paprika

Melt margarine in saucepan. Add flour; cook, stirring continuously, until delicately browned. Add onions, 1/4 teaspoon salt, pepper, marjoram, dillseed and sauerkraut. Mix thoroughly; turn into baking dish. Arrange halibut on top; cover. Bake at 350 degrees for 40 to 45 minutes. Sprinkle halibut with 1/8 teaspoon salt and paprika; place under broiler. Broil for 5 minutes or until browned. Yield: 4 servings.

Sister Mary Benedict
Crookston, Minnesota

MINIATURE SHOOFLY PIES

1 1/2 c. margarine
6 oz. cream cheese
3 1/2 c. flour
2 eggs
1 1/2 c. (packed) brown sugar
2 tbsp. melted butter
1/4 tsp. vanilla
1 c. sugar

Soften 1 cup margarine and cream cheese. Combine 2 cups flour, softened margarine and cream cheese to form a dough. Line muffin tins with dough, pressing evenly around sides and bottoms of tins. Combine eggs, brown sugar, melted butter and vanilla; pour into pastry-lined muffin tins. Cut remaining margarine and sugar into remaining flour; sprinkle over filling in muffin tins. Bake in preheated 400-degree oven for about 20 minutes or until golden brown. Yield: 16 servings.

Mrs. Mary Weaver
Schwenksville, Pennsylvania

Southern

MARYLAND CRAB CAKES

1 lb. crab meat
3 slices bread, cubed
3 tbsp. mayonnaise
1 tsp. mustard
1 tsp. vinegar
1 tsp. salt
1/8 tsp. red pepper
1 egg, beaten
Butter

Remove any bits of shell from crab meat. Combine crab meat, bread cubes, mayonnaise, mustard, vinegar, salt, red pepper and egg. Shape crab mixture into 6 cakes. Melt butter in heavy skillet. Fry crab cakes for about 5 minutes on each side or until lightly browned. Serve hot. Yield: 6 servings.

Mary S. Briscoe
Prince Frederick, Maryland

GRITS AND CHEESE

1/2 tsp. salt
2 1/2 c. water
1/2 c. grits
1/2 c. cubed sharp cheese
1/2 c. margarine
1 tbsp. Tabasco sauce
2 tbsp. Worcestershire sauce
2 cloves of garlic, minced
1 egg, beaten

Combine salt and water in medium saucepan; bring to a boil. Add grits, stirring constantly. Reduce heat; cook, stirring frequently, for about 15 minutes or until thick. Stir in cheese cubes, margarine, sauces, garlic

and egg; mix well. Turn into greased baking dish. Bake in preheated 350-degree oven for about 50 minutes or until set.

Mrs. Emely Sundbeck
Manor, Texas

FRIED OKRA

1 1/2 to 2 lb. small okra
1 c. cornmeal or cracker crumbs
1 c. bacon fat

Slice okra; coat well with cornmeal. Fry in hot fat in skillet until well browned and crisp. Drain on absorbent paper. Yield: 4 servings.

Mrs. Ruth Ragsdale
Richmond, Virginia

LANE CAKE

1 1/2 c. butter or margarine
4 c. sugar
3 1/2 c. sifted flour
3 tsp. baking powder
1 c. milk
2 tsp. vanilla
8 eggs, separated
1 c. chopped raisins
1 c. chopped nuts
1 c. coconut
1 c. wine or bourbon

Cream 1 cup butter and 2 cups sugar together until fluffy and light. Sift flour with baking powder. Add flour mixture to creamed mixture alternately with milk. Add 1 teaspoon vanilla. Fold in stiffly beaten egg whites. Spoon batter into three greased and floured 9-inch layer cake pans. Bake in preheated 350-degree oven for 20 to 30 minutes or until cakes test done. Beat egg yolks slightly; add remaining sugar and butter. Cook in double boiler until thick, stirring constantly. Add raisins, nuts and coconut. Stir in remaining vanilla and wine. Spread filling thickly between layers of cake; frost top and side.

Ruth Stovall
State Supervisor, Home Economics Education
State Dept. of Education
Montgomery, Alabama

SAUSAGE AND HOMINY SCRAMBLE

1 to 1 1/2 lb. pork sausage links
2 tbsp. water
1   15-oz. can hominy, drained
1 tsp. salt
1/8 tsp. pepper
4 eggs
1/3 c. milk

Place sausage and water in cold frying pan; cover tightly. Cook over low heat for 5 minutes. Remove cover; cook links until brown on all sides. Remove to hot platter; keep warm. Pour off all but 1/4 cup drippings in pan. Add hominy, salt and pepper; heat thoroughly. Beat eggs and milk; add to hominy. Cook over low heat just until eggs are set, stirring occasionally. Serve on platter with sausage. Yield: 6-8 servings.

SALLY LUNN

3/4 c. milk
2 tbsp. sugar
1 tsp. salt
2 tbsp. shortening
1 pkg. yeast
2 3/4 c. flour
1 egg

Scald milk in saucepan; add sugar, salt and shortening, stirring to dissolve. Pour into mixing bowl; cool to lukewarm. Dissolve yeast in 1/4 cup lukewarm water. Add 2 cups flour to milk mixture; beat until smooth. Stir in yeast. Add egg; beat for 1 minute. Add remaining flour; beat until smooth. Cover; let rise until doubled in bulk. Stir down; turn into greased layer or loaf pan. Let rise until doubled in bulk. Bake in preheated 350-degree oven for 45 minutes or until done.

Mrs. Lula S. Patrick
Monticello, Kentucky

CHEESE-STUFFED SQUASH

3 yellow crookneck squash
1 1/2 tbsp. butter
2 tbsp. flour
Salt and pepper
1/2 c. milk
1 tbsp. grated onion
4 slices cooked bacon, crumbled
1 c. grated cheese
1/2 c. buttered crumbs

Cook whole squash in boiling water until almost tender; drain well. Cut in half lengthwise; scoop out pulp, reserving pulp and shells. Mash pulp. Melt butter in saucepan over low heat; blend in flour, 1/4 teaspoon salt and a dash of pepper. Remove from heat; stir in milk gradually. Return to heat; cook, stirring constantly, until sauce is thickened. Combine sauce, reserved pulp, onion, 3/4 of the bacon and half the cheese; mix well. Season with salt and pepper to taste; spoon into reserved shells. Sprinkle with crumbs, remaining bacon and cheese. Garnish with paprika. Place in shallow baking pan; add small amount of water. Bake in preheated 375-degree oven for 25 to 30 minutes or until browned. Yield: 6 servings.

Mrs. Helen Loftin
Denton, North Carolina

Creole

CREAMY PRALINES

1 box light brown sugar
1 sm. can evaporated milk
2 tbsp. Karo syrup
2 tbsp. water
1/4 c. butter
1 tsp. vanilla
1 1/2 c. pecan halves

Combine brown sugar, milk, syrup and water in saucepan; bring to a boil. Boil until soft ball is formed when tested in cold water. Remove from heat. Add butter; let cool. Add vanilla; beat until creamy. Stir in pecans; drop by spoonfuls onto wax paper or greased marble.

Ruth Stovall, State Dept. of Ed.
Montgomery, Alabama

CREOLE CASSOULET

1   2-lb. boneless smoked pork butt
1 tbsp. mixed pickling spice
1/4 c. (packed) brown sugar
2   10-oz. packages frozen black-eyed
      peas
1 c. coarsely chopped onion
1 chicken bouillon cube
1 garlic clove, chopped
1 c. tomato juice
1 c. white wine or chicken bouillon
1 bay leaf
1/2 tsp. fines herbes
1/4 tsp. coarsely ground pepper
1 tsp. salt

Remove any casing from pork. Place pork, pickling spices and sugar in deep saucepan or kettle; add enough hot water to cover. Bring to a boil; reduce heat to low. Cook for about 1 hour or until just fork tender. Let stand in cooking liquid while preparing peas. Combine peas with 2 cups water and remaining ingredients; bring to a rapid boil. Reduce heat to low; simmer for 30 minutes. Turn peas into 2 1/2-quart casserole; place drained pork butt in peas. Cover. Bake in preheated 350-degree oven for 1 hour. Remove cover; bake for 30 minutes longer, adding more wine or tomato juice to peas, if necessary. Remove pork butt from casserole; slice. Arrange slices in center of casserole. Yield: 5-6 servings.

Photograph for this recipe below.

CREOLE GUMBO

1 lg. chicken
1 c. oil
1 c. sifted flour
8 stalks celery, chopped
3 lg. onions, chopped
1 green pepper, chopped
2 cloves of garlic, minced
1 lb. sliced okra
1/2 c. Worcestershire sauce
1/2 c. catsup
1/2 can tomatoes
2 tsp. salt
1 lg. slice ham, chopped

2 bay leaves
1/4 tsp. thyme
1/4 tsp. rosemary or red pepper
flakes
2 lb. crab meat
4 lb. peeled shrimp
Lemon juice to taste (opt.)
Hot cooked rice

Cook chicken in kettle in salted water to cover until tender; reserve 2 quarts stock. Remove meat from bones; cut into bite-size pieces. Set aside. Heat oil in large iron pot. Add flour slowly; cook until roux is medium to dark brown. Add celery, onions, green pepper and garlic to roux; cook over low heat, stirring constantly, until soft. Saute okra until brown; add to celery mixture. Stir well. Add chicken, reserved stock, 2 quarts water, Worcestershire sauce, catsup, tomatoes, salt, ham, bay leaves, thyme and rosemary. Simmer for about 3 hours. Add crab meat and shrimp; simmer for about 30 minutes longer. Stir in lemon juice. Serve hot gumbo over rice. Yield: 10 to 12 servings.

Mrs. Tharessa Walker
Saline, Louisiana

MIRLITON FARCI

4 mirlitons
1/2 c. butter
1/2 lb. ham, finely ground
1 lb. boiled shrimp, minced
1 sm. onion, ground
2 sprigs of thyme
2 bay leaves
3 tbsp. chopped parsley
1/2 loaf stale French bread
Salt and pepper to taste
Bread crumbs

Boil mirlitons in salted water to cover in saucepan until tender; drain. Cut in half; scoop out centers, reserving shells. Mash mirliton pulp. Melt butter in saucepan; add mirliton pulp. Stir in ham, shrimp, onion, thyme, bay leaves, parsley and small amount of liquid, if needed. Cover; simmer for 20 minutes, adding water as needed. Soak French bread in water; press out water. Add bread to mirliton mixture; season with salt

and pepper. Cook for 10 minutes longer over low heat, stirring constantly. Fill reserved shells with mirliton mixture. Sprinkle with bread crumbs; dot with additional butter. Place on baking sheet. Bake at 375 degrees until heated through and crumbs are brown. Yield: 4 servings.

Jo Ann Lewis
New Orleans, Louisiana

LOUISIANA YAM CROWN CAKE

2 c. sifted flour
1 1/2 tsp. soda
1/2 tsp. cloves
1 tsp. salt
1 1/2 tsp. cinnamon
1 tsp. nutmeg
2 c. sugar
1 1/4 c. cooking oil
4 eggs
2 tsp. vanilla
2 c. mashed cooked yams
1/2 c. chopped pecans

Sift flour with soda, cloves, salt, cinnamon and nutmeg. Combine sugar and oil in mixing bowl; mix thoroughly. Add eggs, one at a time, beating well after each addition. Add vanilla. Stir in flour mixture, yams and pecans; mix thoroughly. Spoon batter into greased tube or bundt pan. Bake in preheated 350-degree oven for 1 hour and 15 minutes or until done. Invert onto plate to cool. Remove cake from pan; slit horizontally. Spread filling between layers. Sprinkle confectioners' sugar on top, if desired.

Filling

1/4 c. butter, softened
1 3-oz. package cream cheese,
softened
1/2 box confectioners' sugar
1/2 tsp. vanilla
1/2 c. chopped nuts

Cream butter and cheese together. Stir in confectioners' sugar, vanilla and nuts; mix well.

Mrs. Vivian J. Ryland
Effie, Louisiana

Southwestern

CHILLED GAZPACHO

1 c. finely chopped peeled tomatoes
1/2 c. finely chopped celery
1/2 c. finely chopped cucumber
1/2 c. finely chopped green pepper
1/2 c. finely chopped onion
2 tsp. snipped parsley or chives
1 tsp. minced garlic
1/2 tsp. Worcestershire sauce
3 tbsp. wine vinegar
2 tbsp. salad oil or olive oil
2 1/2 c. tomato juice
1 tsp. salt
1/4 tsp. pepper

Combine tomatoes, celery, cucumber, green pepper and onion in large glass bowl. Sprinkle parsley and garlic over vegetables. Combine Worcestershire sauce, wine vinegar, salad oil and tomato juice in jar. Cover; shake to mix well. Pour over vegetables. Add salt and pepper; toss to mix well. Cover; place in refrigerator. Chill for at least 4 hours or overnight. Serve cold. Yield: 4 servings.

Mrs. Louanna Kirkpatrick
Frankfort, Indiana

BARBECUED SPARERIBS

4 lb. lean meaty spareribs
Salt
1/4 tsp. pepper
1 tsp. chili powder
1 tsp. celery seed
2 tbsp. brown sugar
1/4 c. vinegar
Few drops of hot sauce
1/4 c. Worcestershire sauce
1 c. catsup
1 c. water

Cut spareribs into serving pieces. Brown ribs on both sides in skillet. Season with 1 1/2 teaspoons salt and pepper. Remove from skillet; place in 4-quart roasting pan. Combine chili powder, celery seed, 1 teaspoon salt, brown sugar, vinegar, hot sauce and remaining ingredients in saucepan; bring to a boil. Cook for several minutes or until blended. Pour over browned ribs; cover. Bake at 325 degrees for 2 hours to 2 hours and 30 minutes or until tender, basting frequently. Remove cover. Increase oven temperature to 350 degrees; bake until ribs are brown. Remove to warm platter.

Mrs. Mary Carroll
Greenville, Texas

REFRIED BEANS

2 c. dried pinto beans
6 c. water
1/4 lb. salt pork, sliced
Salt to taste
2 cloves of garlic, chopped fine
2 tbsp. chili powder
2 tbsp. cooking oil

Wash beans; place in water. Let soak for several hours. Add salt pork. Place on stove; bring to a boil. Reduce heat; simmer until beans are tender. Mash beans until smooth. Add salt, garlic, chili powder and cooking oil. Fry in heavy frying pan over medium heat until mixture is heated through. Yield: 8 servings.

Louise Barnes
Teague, Texas

JALAPENO CORN BREAD

4 slices bacon
2 c. yellow cornmeal
1 tsp. salt
2 tbsp. sugar
1/2 tsp. soda
1 c. milk
2 eggs
2 tbsp. garlic salt
1 c. chopped onion
1/4 c. chopped pimento
4 jalapeno peppers, minced
1 c. whole kernel corn
2 tbsp. bacon fat
1/2 lb. Cheddar cheese, grated

Fry bacon until crisp; break up into small pieces. Combine cornmeal, salt, sugar and soda. Add milk and eggs; stir until well mixed. Add garlic salt, onion, pimento, peppers, corn and bacon pieces; beat well for 1 minute. Grease a 10-inch iron skillet with bacon fat. Pour 1/2 of the cornmeal mixture into pan; top with half the cheese. Spoon on remaining cornmeal mixture; top with remaining cheese. Bake in preheated 350-degree oven for 35 minutes. Yield: 8 servings.

Carla Sue Park
Dayton, Texas

FRESH PEACH-ALMOND UPSIDE-DOWN PIE

2 tbsp. soft butter
2/3 c. toasted sliced almonds
Brown sugar
Pastry for 2-crust 9-in. pie
3/4 c. sugar
5 c. sliced fresh peaches
2 tbsp. tapioca
1/2 tsp. nutmeg
1/4 tsp. cinnamon
Milk

Line 9-inch pie pan with 12-inch square of foil. Let excess foil overhang edge. Spread with butter. Press almonds and 1/3 cup packed brown sugar into butter. Fit bottom pastry crust into pie pan over almonds and brown sugar. Mix remaining ingredients except milk with 1/4 cup packed brown sugar. Pour into pastry shell. Cover with top crust. Seal and flute edge; prick top with fork. Brush lightly with milk. Bake in preheated 450-degree oven for 10 minutes. Reduce oven temperature to 375 degrees; bake for 35 to 40 minutes longer. Cool thoroughly. Turn upside down onto serving plate; remove foil. Yield: 6 servings.

Mrs. Marie Harlan
Corpus Christi, Texas

FRUIT EMPANADAS

1 1/2 c. flour
1 tsp. baking powder
1 tsp. salt
6 tbsp. shortening
2 c. minced cooked dried fruit
1 c. sugar

1 tsp. cinnamon
1/4 tsp. cloves

Sift flour with baking powder and salt; cut in shortening. Add enough water to make a dough easy to handle. Roll out dough 1/8 inch thick; cut in rounds about 3 inches in diameter. Combine fruit, sugar and spices. Place a small amount of fruit on half of each circle of dough. Fold dough over; press edges together. Pinch edges between thumb and forefinger, sealing well. Bake at 375 degrees until brown. Yield: 8-10 servings.

Fern S. Zimmerman
Clayton, New Mexico

Midwestern

MEAT LOAF WITH CHEESE STUFFING

3 lb. ground beef
3 c. fresh bread crumbs
1 c. minced onions
1/2 c. minced green pepper
4 eggs, slightly beaten
3 tbsp. horseradish
1 tbsp. salt
2 tbsp. prepared mustard
1/4 c. evaporated milk
1/4 c. catsup
2 8-oz. packages sharp cheese slices
Snipped parsley

Combine beef, bread crumbs, onions, green pepper, eggs, horseradish, salt, mustard, milk and catsup. Divide into 3 parts; pat 1 part into loaf pan. Cover with 5 overlapping cheese slices. Spread with second part of meat mixture. Cover with 6 cheese slices. Add remaining meat mixture. Invert loaf onto jelly roll pan or foil-covered cookie sheet. Turn up edges of foil to form rim. Bake at 350 degrees for 45 minutes or until done. Crumble 2 cheese slices over meat loaf; bake for 5 minutes longer. Cool for 15 minutes before serving. Garnish with parsley; slice to serve. Yield: 10-12 servings.

Patricia Irvin
Wells, Minnesota

ROCK LOBSTER PILAU

3   8-oz. packages frozen South African
rock lobster tails
4 slices bacon, chopped
1 1/2 c. converted rice
1/4 c. butter
1 sm. onion, chopped
1 sm. green pepper, chopped
1 c. chopped celery
4 c. (about) chicken broth
1 tsp. Worcestershire sauce
Salt and cayenne pepper to taste

Drop frozen lobster tails into boiling, salted water; bring to a boil. Boil for 1 minute. Drain; drench with cold water. Remove underside membrane with scissors. Remove lobster meat; cut into 1/2-inch slices. Fry bacon in large skillet until crisp; remove bacon pieces. Saute rice in bacon drippings in skillet until golden brown; add butter. Add onion, green pepper and celery; saute until soft. Stir in 4 cups chicken broth and Worcestershire sauce; cover. Simmer, stirring occasionally, until rice is tender, adding more chicken broth to prevent sticking, if needed. Add lobster pieces; simmer for 5 minutes longer. Add salt and cayenne pepper; stir well. Sprinkle with bacon pieces. Yield: 6 servings.

Photograph for this recipe above.

OLD-FASHIONED VEGETABLE SOUP

2 to 3 soupbones with meat
2 tbsp. fat
8 c. water
1/3 c. barley
1 med. onion, chopped
1 c. sliced carrots
1 c. chopped celery and leaves
2   1-lb. cans tomatoes
1 c. whole kernel corn
1 c. green peas
3 sprigs of parsley, minced
1 tbsp. salt
1/4 tsp. rosemary
1/4 tsp. marjoram
1/4 tsp. thyme
1/2 bay leaf, crushed
3 peppercorns

Cut meat from soupbones into small chunks. Brown in hot fat in large skillet or Dutch oven. Add water and soupbones; simmer, covered, for 1 hour and 30 minutes to 2 hours. Remove soupbones; skim fat from stock. Add barley; simmer for 45 minutes. Add onion, carrots, celery, tomatoes, corn, peas, parsley, salt, rosemary, marjoram and thyme. Tie bay leaf and peppercorns in cheesecloth bag; add to soup mixture. Cook for 25 to 35 minutes or until vegetables are tender. Remove cheesecloth bag before serving. Yield: 10-12 servings.

Mrs. Jan Erickson
White Bear Lake, Minnesota

HERBED ROASTING EARS

1/2 c. soft butter
1 tsp. dried rosemary
1/2 tsp. dried marjoram
6 ears of sweet corn, cleaned
1 head romaine

Blend butter with herbs; spread on corn. Wrap each ear of corn in 2 to 3 leaves of romaine; place in shallow baking dish. Cover tightly with foil. Bake at 450 degrees for 20 to 25 minutes. Serve immediately.

Betty Phillips
Scurry, Texas

CHICKEN CROQUETTES

1 1/2 c. finely chopped cooked
   chicken
2 tbsp. finely chopped onion
3/4 c. thick white sauce
1/8 tsp. pepper
1 tsp. salt
2 tbsp. water
1 egg, slightly beaten
1/2 c. finely chopped almonds
1 1/4 c. cracker crumbs

Combine chicken, onion, white sauce and seasonings. Shape into croquettes, using 1 rounded tablespoonful of mixture for each croquette. Add water to egg. Combine almonds and cracker crumbs. Roll croquettes in crumb mixture; dip into egg. Roll again in crumb mixture. Set aside for 10 minutes to dry. Fry in deep fat at 375-degrees for 2 minutes or until golden. Yield: 4 servings.

Mrs. Thyra K. Davis
Manhattan, Kansas

West Coast

TOSSED BROCCOLI SALAD

1 lb. broccoli
3 tbsp. olive oil
3 tbsp. lemon juice
1 med. clove of garlic, thinly sliced
1/4 tsp. salt
1/8 tsp. pepper

Cook broccoli in boiling salted water until just tender. Drain; place in refrigerator until thoroughly chilled. Sprinkle oil, lemon juice, garlic slices, salt and pepper over broccoli. Toss well; serve.

Mrs. Dan Ross
Oakdale, California

BARBECUED DUNGENESS CRAB

1 c. margarine
2 cans consomme
1 c. vinegar
1/2 c. (packed) brown sugar
1 c. catsup
1 tsp. pepper
1 tsp. chili powder
2 tsp. hot sauce
1 1/2 tsp. dry mustard
1/2 tsp. celery seed
1/2 tsp. allspice
1 tsp. salt
2 bay leaves
3 tbsp. Worcestershire sauce
1 clove of garlic, chopped
1 onion, chopped
1 sm. can tomato sauce
1 lg. dungeness crab, cooked

Melt margarine in large saucepan; add consomme, vinegar and brown sugar. Stir in catsup, pepper, chili powder, hot sauce, mustard, celery seed, allspice, salt and bay leaves. Add Worcestershire sauce, garlic, onion and tomato sauce. Simmer sauce for 4 hours. Clean and crack crab; remove meat from shell. Cut into coarse pieces; drain crab for 1 hour. Place in baking dish; pour sauce over crab meat. Bake at 350 degrees for 45 minutes to 1 hour or until heated through and bubbly. Yield: 6 servings.

Mrs. Alice M. Downs
Milwaukee, Oregon

BISQUE TORTONI

6 eggs, separated
3/4 c. sugar
24 macaroons, grated
1/2 tsp. almond extract
2 tbsp. maraschino cherry juice
1 pt. whipping cream, whipped
1/4 c. Grape Nuts

Beat egg whites until stiff. Beat egg yolks and sugar until creamy and thick. Add 3/4 of the macaroons, almond extract, cherry juice, whipped cream and Grape Nuts. Fold in egg whites. Pack in individual nut cups; freeze. Sprinkle with remaining macaroon crumbs just before serving. May add finely chopped nuts and fruits before freezing if desired. Yield: 12 servings.

Mrs. Ann Busey
White Swan, Washington

CHILLED ARTICHOKES WITH GARLIC MAYONNAISE

6 lg. artichokes
Lemon juice
1 c. mayonnaise
1 clove of garlic, mashed
Paprika

Cut off artichoke stems at base; remove small leaves. Trim tips of leaves; cut off about 1 inch from top of artichokes. Rub cut edges of leaves with lemon juice. Stand artichokes in 1 inch boiling salted water. Simmer, covered, for 30 minutes or until tender. Drain well. Spread leaves apart; remove chokes from centers of artichokes with spoon. Chill, covered, for 1 hour or longer. Combine mayonnaise and garlic; spoon into artichokes. Sprinkle with paprika. Yield: 6 servings.

Mrs. Elizabeth Hayton
Kelso, Washington

SWEET STUFFED SALMON

2 salmon fillets or steaks
Salt and pepper
2 c. small bread cubes
2 tbsp. chopped onion
1 tbsp. parsley
2 tbsp. chopped sweet pickle or pickle
    relish
1 tbsp. lemon juice
1/4 c. oil
3 slices bacon

Place fillets in greased baking dish; sprinkle each side with salt and pepper to taste. Combine bread cubes with 1/2 teaspoon salt, 1/8 teaspoon pepper, onion, parsley, pickle, lemon juice and enough water to moisten mixture. Place stuffing on 1 fillet; top with remaining fillet. Fasten with skewers; brush with oil. Place bacon on top. Bake at 350 degrees for 30 to 40 minutes or until salmon flakes easily. Remove skewers; lift off bacon slices. Remove salmon skin. Replace bacon; garnish as desired and serve. Yield: 4-6 servings.

Mrs. Irene Knudsen
Crescent City, California

BLACKBERRY BUCKLE

1/4 c. butter
1/2 c. sugar
1 egg, well beaten
1 c. flour
1 1/2 tsp. baking powder
1/8 tsp. salt
1/3 c. milk
1 tsp. vanilla
2 c. sweetened fresh blackberries
Crumb Topping

Cream butter and sugar together. Add egg; beat well. Sift flour, baking powder and salt together; add to creamed mixture alternately with milk and vanilla. Pour batter into greased and floured 7-inch pan; cover with blackberries. Sprinkle Crumb Topping over blackberries. Bake at 375 degrees for 45 minutes or until done. May be served with whipped cream.

Crumb Topping

1/2 c. sugar
1/4 c. butter
1/3 c. flour
1/2 tsp. cinnamon

Cream sugar and butter together. Stir in flour and cinnamon until mixture is crumbly.

Mrs. Agnes C. Huffman
Modesto, California

Hawaii

CHICKEN HAWAIIAN WITH HOOMALIMALI SAUCE

6 broilers
Salt and pepper to taste
1 1/2 c. pineapple juice
3 tbsp. soy sauce
2 tbsp. oil
2 tbsp. sugar
1 clove of garlic, minced
1 1/2 tsp. ginger
3/4 c. crushed pineapple
1/4 c. cornstarch
2 tsp. chicken instant bouillon

1/4 c. slivered almonds
1/4 c. shredded coconut

Split chickens; season with salt and pepper. Combine pineapple juice, soy sauce, oil, 1 tablespoon sugar, garlic and ginger for basting sauce. Place chickens on broiler pans. Bake in 375-degree oven for 50 to 60 minutes, basting at least 4 times with sauce. Combine pineapple, 2 1/2 cups water, cornstarch, bouillon, almonds, coconut and remaining sugar; bring to a boil. Reduce heat; simmer for 45 minutes. Serve 1/4 cup sauce with each chicken half. Yield: 12 servings.

Mrs. Janie Harris
Wilson, Texas

SHRIMP CURRY

1 1/2 lb. fresh shrimp
6 tbsp. butter
6 tbsp. flour
1 1/2 tsp. finely chopped onion
1 c. milk
2 c. coconut milk
1 1/4 tsp. salt
2 tsp. curry powder
2 tsp. finely chopped gingerroot
1 1/2 tbsp. lemon juice
Cooked rice

Shell and devein shrimp. Melt butter in saucepan; remove from heat. Stir in flour and onion, blending until smooth. Return to heat; add milk slowly. Bring to a boil, stirring until thickened. Stir in coconut milk, salt, curry powder, gingerroot, lemon juice and shrimp. Simmer, covered, for 30 minutes. Serve over rice. Yield: 6 servings.

Beverly Hite
Carey, Ohio

POLYNESIAN PORK

6 pork chops
Salt and pepper to taste
1 med. can pineapple chunks
1 lg. onion, chopped
1/4 c. minced celery leaves
1 clove of garlic, minced
12 cooked prunes, pitted
2 tbsp. soy sauce
1/2 tsp. crushed marjoram

1 c. diagonally sliced celery
1 c. rice
1 tsp. ginger

Trim excess fat from chops; lightly grease heavy skillet with fat from 1 chop. Brown chops on both sides; drain off excess fat. Season lightly with salt and pepper. Drain pineapple; combine pineapple juice, onion, celery leaves, garlic, prunes, soy sauce and marjoram. Pour over chops; simmer, covered, for 20 to 30 minutes. Add pineapple and celery; cook for 10 minutes longer or until celery is tender and pork is well done, adding a small amount of water, if needed. Prepare rice according to package directions; add ginger, stirring to blend. Serve pork mixture over rice. Yield: 6 servings.

Sharon A. Anderson
Fosston, Minnesota

TOASTED COCONUT CHIPS

1 coconut

Remove coconut meat from shell; slice thinly. Spread slices in shallow pan. Bake at 200 degrees for 2 hours, stirring frequently. Cool; store in airtight jars.

Kathleen Stephens
Compton, California

FRESH PINEAPPLE PIE

1/3 c. flour
2/3 to 1 c. sugar
1/8 tsp. salt
3 eggs, lightly beaten
1 tbsp. lemon juice
2 c. shredded fresh pineapple
Pastry for 2-crust pie
1 tbsp. margarine or butter

Combine flour, sugar and salt; stir in eggs. Add lemon juice and pineapple, mixing well. Pour into pastry-lined pie pan; dot with margarine. Top with remaining crust; cut slits in top crust. Bake for 10 minutes in preheated 450-degree oven. Reduce oven temperature to 350 degrees; bake for 35 minutes longer.

Winnifred Pearson
Bonanza, Oregon

Salad Favorites

One of the more recent additions to Americans' lists of favorite foods is the salad. Enjoyed many years ago on special occasions or family gatherings on Sunday, salads were hearty meals-in-themselves. Big bowls of lettuce garnished with meat, fish, cheese and eggs were quite a welcome sight on the pioneer's table. Those were the days when everyone had to depend on themselves for the food they ate. Food grown in the field and cultivated in the home garden was what the homemaker of yesterday prepared for meals.

An outstanding example of a man who realized the bounties our wonderful country had to offer was Thomas Jefferson. As author of the Declaration of Independence and the third president of the United States, he made many accomplishments in political life. However, he also did much for the development of what we consider American cuisine. Jefferson was an avid gardener, raising every kind of fruit and vegetable imaginable. In addition, he loved to cook what he grew. This he did magnificently, for everyone who ate at his table raved. One of his favorite dishes was salad.

Throughout the years salads have become quite a vital part of our diet. As the importance of a balanced diet and good nutrition are emphasized more and more everyday, the appearance of salad with a meal or as a meal becomes more common. The variety of salads that can be prepared make serving beautiful salads every week more satisfying than monotonous. There are fruit salads, vegetable salads, meat, poultry and seafood salads, as well as cereal, pasta, egg and cheese salads. Frozen salads, congealed salads, slaws — all offer many varieties of ways to prepare salads and just as many ingredients that can be put in them. Learning to make salads beautifully taste-tempting is not as difficult as it may seem. Using the right color combinations with other foods to be served and the table setting is the key. Take into consideration everything that is to be served with the salad, then coordinate taste and color.

Different meals call for different types of salads. A fresh, crisp, green salad is an ideal entree when served with a hearty meal of meat and vegetables, while fruit salads are perfect appetizers, accompaniments and even desserts. In pioneer days making a gelatin salad took hours, for the farmer's wife had to boil a calf's foot to get the gelatin she needed. Now, due to technological advancements, we can make the same congealed salad in a matter of minutes. Tart salads are always good with seafood and salads known as the Chef's Salad and Caesar's Salad make excellent main dishes. However, these are relative newcomers, the Caesar's Salad, only having made its debut in Southern California in the 1920's.

Ask any American on a diet what they prefer for a mid-day meal and their answer is bound to be salad. While counting calories is never fun, the salad has brought enjoyment to those persons watching their weight. It's something that can contain a number of ingredients, be delicious, and low in calories, yet filling. Who could ask for more from a food?

The success or failure of a salad depends to a large degree on the type of dressing used with it. Although this is usually left up to an individual's own taste, there *are* dressings which naturally go with meat, vegetable and fruit salads. Just think how proud you would be to serve a dressing which you had made yourself. Homemade dressings don't take a long time to prepare and the rewards in taste are marvelous. Be sure to achieve the perfect blend of salad and salad dressing — tangy French dressing for greens, cooked dressing with greens and vegetables, sour cream dressings for vegetables and fruits, tart or sweet dressings for fruit salads and mayonnaise for meat, seafood and egg salads. Make sure the finishing touch to your salad adds to the flavor rather than smothers it! Here is where the person trying to gain instead of lose weight can benefit. Mayonnaise or oil and vinegar added to a man-sized salad will provide nutrition as well as wanted calories.

To be sure, times have changed since our forefathers first came to the land we now call America. Then, the pace was slow and time was of little importance in comparison to today. Limited to only the foods they grew on their own land, our ancestors learned to make the best of what they had no matter what the season of the year. As we look back over this country's past 200 years, there is no doubt that our country's heritage is one of which we should be quite proud. Today, the hustle and bustle of modern living has influenced every phase of our lives — including cooking. Most women today do not have the time they once had to spend in the kitchen. This is another reason salads have become so popular. Easy to prepare, they provide a family with the vitamins and nutrition they require and a taste sensation that they love. Due to the development of refrigeration and transportation, we no longer have to depend only on our own gardens for fruits and vegetables.

Whether it is summer or winter, spring or fall, there is always a fresh supply of produce available.

Of course, you want only the best for your family — and, this is exactly what you will find in this section of favorite salads. From Home Economics Teachers across the nation we have selected from the very best salads and salad dressing recipes to share again with you in this bicentennial year.

COOKED SALAD DRESSING

1/2 c. vinegar
1/2 c. sugar
1 tbsp. dry mustard
1 tbsp. cornstarch
1 tsp. salt
Dash of cayenne pepper
2 eggs, beaten
1 c. milk
1 tbsp. butter

Heat vinegar in top of double boiler. Mix sugar, mustard, cornstarch, salt and cayenne pepper; stir in eggs and milk. Add to hot vinegar slowly, stirring constantly. Cook over boiling water for 20 to 25 minutes or until thick, stirring constantly. Remove from heat; add butter. Beat with egg beater until smooth. More milk may be added if thinner dressing is desired. Three tablespoons flour may be substituted for cornstarch. One small can evaporated milk, diluted, may be used instead of fresh milk.

Mrs. Thomas Lye
Halifax, Nova Scotia, Canada

FRENCH DRESSING

1/2 c. catsup
1/4 c. vinegar
2/3 c. sugar
1 onion, grated
1/2 tsp. paprika
1 c. oil
1 tsp. Worcestershire sauce
1/2 tsp. salt
1/8 tsp. pepper

Combine all ingredients in quart jar; cover. Shake until well mixed. Store in refrigerator. Yield: 1 quart.

Betty Rogers
Atkinson, Nebraska

BEST-YET BLENDER MAYONNAISE

2 eggs
1 tsp. sugar
3/4 tsp. dry mustard
1/2 tsp. salt
1/2 tsp. paprika
2 c. salad oil
1 tbsp. wine vinegar
2 tbsp. lemon juice

Place eggs in blender container; add sugar, mustard, salt and paprika. Cover; process at high speed for 30 seconds. Push ingredients down with rubber spatula. Add 1/4 cup oil, small amount at a time, blending at high speed. Add vinegar slowly, blending constantly, then add remaining oil alternately with lemon juice, blending at high speed and pushing ingredients down with spatula occasionally. Yield: 2 1/2 cups.

Barbara Knowlton
Wellman, Texas

SHIRLEY'S MAYONNAISE

1 tsp. mustard
1/2 tsp. salt
1/8 tsp. pepper
1/8 tsp. paprika
1/4 tsp. sugar
1 egg
2 c. salad oil
3 tbsp. vinegar

Place first 6 ingredients in bowl; beat well. Add 1/2 cup oil very slowly, beating constantly. Add vinegar alternately with remaining oil, beating constantly. Refrigerate until served. Yield: 2 1/2 cups.

Mrs. Shirley Newcombe
Bay City, Michigan

THOUSAND ISLAND DRESSING

1 c. mayonnaise
2 tsp. prepared mustard
2 tbsp. catsup
1 tsp. salt
1 tsp. pepper
1 tsp. seasoned salt
1 tsp. garlic salt
1 tsp. onion salt
1 tbsp. minced onion
2 boiled eggs, grated

Combine all ingredients; blend well. Chill before serving.

Mrs. Sharlott M. Valentine
Vicksburg, Mississippi

CONGEALED RICE SALAD

1 c. rice
1 3-oz. package lemon gelatin
1 c. drained crushed pineapple
1 c. whipped cream
1 c. confectioners' sugar
1/2 c. chopped walnuts
1/2 c. miniature marshmallows

Cook rice according to package directions; cool. Mix 2 cups boiling water with gelatin; chill until partially set. Add rice, pineapple, whipped cream, sugar, walnuts and marshmallows; mix well. Chill until firm. Yield: 10 servings.

Mrs. Evelyn Johnson
Bottineau, North Dakota

RICE AND EGG SALAD

2 c. cold cooked rice
4 hard-cooked eggs, grated
1 c. chopped celery
1/2 c. chopped sweet or dill pickles
Salt and pepper to taste
1 tbsp. chopped pimento
1 c. shredded Cheddar cheese
3/4 c. mayonnaise

Combine all ingredients in bowl in order listed; mix well. Yield: 6-8 servings.

Mrs. Viola Johnson
Karnes City, Texas

CURRIED RICE SALAD

3 c. cooked rice
1 c. minced celery
2 tbsp. minced onion
1 tsp. curry powder
1/2 tsp. dry mustard
1/4 tsp. pepper

Salt to taste
3/4 c. salad dressing
1 tbsp. lime or lemon juice
1 8-oz. can crushed pineapple, drained
1/2 c. chopped salted peanuts or almonds

Place all ingredients except peanuts in salad bowl; toss well. Garnish with peanuts. Yield: 6 servings.

Mrs. Ialeen S. Mode
Franklinton, North Carolina

LUNCHEON MACARONI

3 c. cooked macaroni
1/4 c. chopped green pepper
1/4 c. chopped celery
1/4 c. chopped pickles
2 hard-cooked eggs, chopped
1/4 c. salad dressing

Mix all ingredients; place on salad greens. Garnish with tomato wedges, sliced hard-cooked eggs or pickles. Yield: 6 servings.

Sara Thompson
Pineville, Kentucky

GEORGE RECTOR'S
SPAGHETTI-CHICKEN SALAD

1/2 lb. elbow spaghetti
2 c. diced cooked chicken
1 c. chopped celery
1 tbsp. grated onion
1 tsp. salt
1/2 c. mayonnaise or salad dressing
2 tbsp. chopped green pepper
1 tbsp. minced red pepper or pimento

Cook spaghetti in boiling, salted water until tender; drain and chill. Add remaining ingredients; mix lightly. Serve on watercress or lettuce; garnish with grated hard-boiled eggs, if desired. Yield: 6 servings.

Mrs. K. E. Sharp
Borger, Texas

HOT MACARONI SALAD

1 can button mushrooms
1/4 lb. sliced bacon, diced
1/2 c. sugar
2 tbsp. flour
1/2 tsp. salt
1/8 tsp. pepper
3/4 c. cider vinegar
1 7-oz. package elbow macaroni
1/2 c. chopped onion
1/2 c. chopped celery
1/2 c. sliced radishes (opt.)
2 tbsp. chopped parsley

Drain mushrooms; reserve liquid. Add enough water to reserved liquid to make 2/3 cup liquid. Fry bacon until crisp. Add mushrooms, sugar, flour, salt and pepper; stir until blended. Stir in vinegar and mushroom liquid gradually; cook until thickened, stirring constantly. Keep warm. Cook macaroni in boiling, salted water for 7 to 8 minutes or until tender but firm; drain. Add mushroom mixture, onion and celery; mix lightly. Garnish with radishes and parsley; serve hot.

Dorothy Campbell
Deer Park, Washington

EASY EGG SALAD

6 hard-cooked eggs, chopped
1/4 c. chopped green pepper
1/4 c. sliced green onions
1/4 c. chopped ripe olives
1/3 c. mayonnaise
1 tsp. salt
Dash of pepper

Combine first 4 ingredients in bowl. Mix mayonnaise with salt and pepper; add to egg mixture. Toss lightly; chill. Serve on lettuce.

Frances Rodriguez
Espanola, New Mexico

EGG SALAD IN TOMATO CUPS

4 med. tomatoes
Salt
1 3-oz. package cream cheese
Cream
2 tbsp. chopped green onion
1/4 c. chopped green pepper
1/2 med. cucumber, chopped
3 hard-boiled eggs, chopped
1/4 c. salad dressing

Peel tomatoes; cut slices from top of each tomato. Scoop out centers. Sprinkle tomato shells with salt; invert onto plate. Chill. Blend cream cheese with enough cream to soften; line tomato cups with cream cheese mixture. Combine remaining ingredients; fill tomato cups. Chill thoroughly. Serve on lettuce with additional salad dressing. Yield: 4 servings.

Mrs. Monna Smith Miller
Lake City, Tennessee

DEVILED EGG MOLD

1 env. unflavored gelatin
1/2 c. water
1 tsp. salt
2 tbsp. lemon juice
1 tsp. Worcestershire sauce
1/8 tsp. cayenne pepper
3/4 c. mayonnaise
1 1/2 tsp. grated onion
1/2 c. finely diced celery
1/4 c. finely diced green pepper
1/4 c. chopped pimento
4 hard-cooked eggs, chopped

Sprinkle gelatin on water in saucepan; let soften. Place over low heat; stir until gelatin is dissolved. Remove from heat. Add salt, lemon juice, Worcestershire sauce and cayenne pepper; mix well. Cool. Stir in mayonnaise; fold in remaining ingredients. Turn into 3-cup mold or individual molds; chill until firm. Loosen gelatin by dipping mold in warm water to depth of gelatin; loosen around edge with tip of paring knife. Place serving dish on top of mold; turn upside down. Shake, holding dish tightly to mold. Garnish with salad greens and green pepper rings; serve with salad dressing. Yield: 6 servings.

Mrs. Alice Hansberger
Canton, Illinois

Recipe on page 52.

Recipe on page 186.

CREAM CHEESE TOMATO SALAD

1 can tomato soup
1 8-oz. package cream cheese
2 env. unflavored gelatin
1/2 c. cold water
1 c. salad dressing
1 tsp. minced onion
1 tsp. minced green pepper
1 c. finely chopped celery
1 c. finely chopped pecans

Heat tomato soup in saucepan; stir in cream cheese until smooth. Soften gelatin in cold water. Add to soup mixture; stir until dissolved. Stir in remaining ingredients; place in mold. Refrigerate until firm.

Mrs. Raye King
Coleman, Texas

GRAPE-CANTALOUPE SALAD

1 c. pineapple chunks
1/2 cantaloupe, cut in 1/2 x 2-in. strips
1 1/2 c. seedless green grapes
1 banana, cut in cubes
1/2 c. miniature marshmallows
1/2 c. salad dressing

Mix all ingredients except salad dressing. Add salad dressing; toss until mixed.

Mrs. Mavis Menzies
Winnipeg, Manitoba, Canada

PIMENTO CHEESE MOLD

1 3-oz. package lemon gelatin
1/2 tsp. salt
1 c. boiling water
1 5-oz. jar pimento cheese spread
1/2 c. salad dressing or mayonnaise
3/4 c. cold water
1 tbsp. vinegar
3 dashes of Tabasco sauce
1/2 c. chopped celery
1/4 c. finely chopped onion
2 tbsp. finely chopped green pepper

Dissolve gelatin and salt in boiling water. Add cheese spread and salad dressing; beat with electric or rotary beater until smooth. Stir in cold water, vinegar and Tabasco sauce; chill until partially set. Add remaining ingredients. Pour into individual molds or 3-cup mold; chill until firm. Unmold onto lettuce-lined plate. Yield: 4-6 servings.

Ellen F. Dow
Windsor, Vermont

STUFFED APPLE RING SALAD

4 or 5 red apples
Lemon juice or pineapple juice
1 8-oz. package cream cheese
1/2 c. chopped dates
1/4 c. chopped nuts

Wash apples; do not pare. Cut apples into 1/2-inch slices. Remove core from apple slices; brush slices with lemon juice. Mash cream cheese; beat until smooth. Add dates, nuts and small amount of lemon juice; mix well. Place apple rings on flat surface; fill centers with cream cheese mixture, spreading smooth with spatula. Arrange slices on shredded lettuce; serve with French dressing.

Mrs. Thelma M. Ash
Hampton, Virginia

STUFFED PEACH SALAD

1 3-oz. package cream cheese
2 doz. salted almonds, finely chopped
1/8 tsp. salt
1/4 tsp. sugar
Dash of paprika
Grated rind of 1/2 orange
12 canned peach halves, drained
6 lettuce leaves

Mix cream cheese, almonds, salt, sugar, paprika and grated rind; form into small balls. Arrange 2 peach halves in each lettuce leaf; place cream cheese balls in hollow of each peach half. Serve with or without dressing. Cream or orange juice may be added to cream cheese if mixture is too dry.

Mrs. Leda Callahan
El Paso, Texas

Recipes on pages 42, 147 and 257.

Recipe on page 88.

HAWAIIAN APRICOT FRUIT BOATS

1   30-oz. can apricot halves
3/4 c. Miracle Whip salad dressing
1/2 tsp. grated lemon peel
1 tbsp. lime juice
1 tbsp. chopped crystallized ginger
1 lg. ripe pineapple
3 tbsp. light rum
2 tbsp. sugar
3 c. watermelon balls
Chopped macadamia nuts (opt.)
Lime slices (opt.)

Drain apricots; reserve syrup for future use. Process enough apricots in electric blender to measure 3/4 cup puree. Add Miracle Whip salad dressing, lemon peel, lime juice and ginger to blender; process until mixture is smooth. Chill until serving time. Apricots may be pressed through a sieve if blender is not available. Cut pineapple in half lengthwise through green top. Loosen and remove flesh from pineapple shell, using a sharp knife. Cut out and discard core; slice pineapple flesh into bite-sized wedges. Chill pineapple shells. Measure 2 1/2 cups pineapple wedges for salad; reserve remaining pineapple for future use. Cut remaining apricots in half lengthwise. Combine rum and sugar in large bowl. Add pineapple wedges, watermelon balls and apricot slices; toss gently just until fruits are coated. Chill salad for several hours. Spoon salad into pineapple shells; sprinkle with nuts and garnish with lime slices.

Photograph for this recipe above.

STRAWBERRY SALAD GLACE

1   3-oz. package strawberry gelatin
2   3-oz. packages cream cheese, softened
Milk
1/2 c. finely chopped nuts
1 pt. strawberries, sweetened

Prepare gelatin according to package directions; chill until partially set. Mix cream cheese with small amount of milk until smooth; shape into 12 balls. Roll in nuts. Arrange balls in 10-inch ring mold; cover with strawberries. Pour gelatin over cheese balls and strawberries; chill until firm. Unmold; serve over watercress or lettuce. Raspberry gelatin and raspberries may be used instead of strawberry gelatin and strawberries. Yield: 8-10 servings.

Arlene Maisel
Highland Park, New Jersey

LAYERED PINEAPPLE GELATIN SALAD

1 pkg. lime gelatin
2 c. boiling water
3/4 c. pineapple juice
1 c. drained crushed pineapple
1 pkg. lemon gelatin
3/4 c. cold water
1 3-oz. package cream cheese, softened
1/2 c. whipping cream, whipped

Dissolve lime gelatin in 1 cup boiling water; stir in pineapple juice and pineapple. Pour into 8 x 8 x 2-inch pan or large mold; chill until firm. Dissolve lemon gelatin in remaining boiling water in bowl. Stir in cold water; chill until thickened. Place bowl of lemon gelatin in larger bowl of ice; whip gelatin until fluffy and thick. Beat cream cheese until smooth; fold in whipped cream. Fold into lemon gelatin. Spoon over congealed pineapple layer; chill until firm. Serve on crisp salad greens. Yield: 9 servings.

Mrs. Janie A. Stahlecker
Idalia, Colorado

RED-WHITE AND BLUE SALAD

2 pkg. raspberry gelatin
2 c. boiling water
1 env. unflavored gelatin
1 c. cold water
1 c. half and half
1 c. sugar
1 8-oz. package cream cheese
1 tsp. vanilla extract
1/2 c. chopped nuts
1 can blueberries

Dissolve 1 package raspberry gelatin in boiling water; pour into 9 x 13-inch pan. Chill

until firm. Combine unflavored gelatin and cold water; set aside. Mix half and half and sugar in saucepan; bring to a boil. Remove from heat. Add cream cheese; beat until smooth. Add vanilla, nuts and unflavored gelatin; stir until gelatin is dissolved. Cool. Pour over chilled layer; chill until firm. Drain blueberries; add enough water to blueberry juice to make 2 cups liquid. Bring to boiling point. Add remaining raspberry gelatin; stir until dissolved. Cool. Stir in blueberries; pour over cheese layer. Chill until firm. Yield: 15 servings.

Mrs. Mary Eveland
Des Moines, Iowa

FROZEN GRAPEFRUIT SALAD

1 8-oz. package cream cheese
1 c. sour cream
1/4 tsp. salt
1/2 c. sugar
2 c. grapefruit sections
1 avocado, diced
1 c. halved seedless white grapes
1/2 c. chopped pecans

Soften cream cheese; blend in sour cream. Add salt and sugar; stir until blended. Stir in grapefruit, avocado, grapes and pecans. Spoon into 5 x 9-inch loaf pan; cover. Freeze until firm. Slice; serve on salad greens. Yield: 8 servings.

Sue Kidd
Odessa, Texas

EASY FROZEN PEAR SALAD

1 1-lb. can pear halves
1 8-oz. package cream cheese

Drain pears; reserve syrup. Combine reserved pear syrup and cream cheese in blender container; process until smooth. Slice pears; place in 4 x 8-inch loaf pan. Pour cream cheese mixture over pear slices; freeze until firm. Slice pear mixture; serve on salad greens. Yield: 6 servings.

Mrs. Robert Blatchley
Homer, New York

FROZEN STRAWBERRY-PINEAPPLE SALAD

30 lg. marshmallows, cut into sm.
  pieces
1 No. 2 1/2 can crushed pineapple
2 pkg. frozen strawberries, thawed
3 bananas, cut into cubes
1 c. cream, whipped

Mix marshmallows and pineapple in bowl; soak overnight. Add strawberries and bananas; mix thoroughly. Fold in whipped cream; place in pan or mold. Freeze until firm. Yield: 8-10 servings.

Virginia Curran
Reno, Nevada

FROZEN CRANBERRY SALAD

4 c. cranberries
1 1/2 c. water
2 c. sugar
2 to 3 tbsp. lemon juice
2 3-oz. packages cream cheese
1/3 c. mayonnaise
1/2 c. confectioners' sugar
1 c. chopped English walnuts
2 c. heavy cream, whipped

Cook cranberries in water in saucepan until skins pop; press through sieve. Return pulp to saucepan. Stir in sugar; cook for 5 minutes. Stir in lemon juice; cool. Spoon into 24 paper liners in muffin tins. Place in freezer to chill. Combine remaining ingredients; spread over cranberry mixture. Freeze. May be frozen several weeks. Yield: 24 servings.

Linda Lang
Spring Grove, Minnesota

CORNED BEEF DECEPTION SALAD

1 12-oz. can corned beef, chilled
1 env. unflavored gelatin
1/3 c. cold water
1 beef bouillon cube
1 c. boiling water
3 hard-cooked eggs, chopped
2 tbsp. coarsely chopped green pepper

2 tbsp. finely chopped onion
1 c. cooked salad dressing

Cut corned beef into cubes. Soften gelatin in cold water. Add bouillon cube to boiling water; stir until dissolved. Add gelatin; stir until dissolved. Cool. Add corned beef, eggs, vegetables and salad dressing; stir until mixed. Pour into 8-inch ring mold; refrigerate until firm. Unmold onto lettuce; garnish with radish roses. Yield: 8 servings.

Mrs. Barbara Potterton
Manchester, Connecticut

ORIENTAL BEEF SALAD

2 c. cubed cooked beef
2 c. cooked red kidney beans
1/4 c. diced pimentos
1 c. diced celery
1/2 c. minced onions
2 c. bean sprouts, marinated in French
  dressing
Soy sauce to taste
Salt and pepper to taste
1/2 c. mayonnaise

Combine all ingredients in salad bowl in order listed; mix thoroughly. Yield: 10 servings.

Mrs. Earl W. Ellis
New Summerfield, Texas

HAM MOUSSE

1 tbsp. unflavored gelatin
1/4 c. cold water
1/4 c. vinegar
2 c. cubed ham
1 c. finely chopped celery
1 tbsp. sugar
1 tbsp. pickle relish
1 tsp. mustard
1/2 c. heavy cream, whipped
Watercress
Easy Horseradish Sauce

Soften gelatin in cold water and vinegar; dissolve over boiling water. Stir in ham, celery, sugar, relish and mustard; cool. Fold in whipped cream. Turn into mold; chill until firm. Unmold onto watercress. Serve with Easy Horseradish Sauce. Yield: 6 servings.

Easy Horseradish Sauce

3 tbsp. well-drained horseradish
1/2 tsp. salt
1/2 c. heavy cream, whipped

Fold horseradish and salt into whipped cream.

Mrs. Elvi Salmela
Hudson, Massachusetts

SUPPER SALAD

1/2 c. cooked green beans
1 1/2 c. diced cooked pork
1/2 c. cooked diced potatoes
1/2 c. cooked sliced carrots
1/2 c. cooked peas
1/2 c. cooked lima beans
1 c. French dressing
1/2 c. chopped sweet pickles
2 hard-cooked eggs, chopped
3/4 c. mayonnaise
Salt and pepper to taste
Crisp salad greens
Paprika

Cut green beans into 1/2-inch pieces. Place pork, potatoes, carrrots, peas, lima beans and green beans in bowl. Pour French dressing over ham mixture; toss lightly. Chill for at least 1 hour. Add pickles, eggs, mayonnaise, salt and pepper just before serving; mix lightly. Serve on salad greens; sprinkle with paprika. Yield: 6 servings.

Mrs. Kathleen Barnes
Lawrence, Indiana

VEAL ASPIC

1 env. unflavored gelatin
1/4 c. cold water
1 1/2 c. heated seasoned consomme
1/2 c. cooked peas
1 c. cooked sliced beets
1 hard-cooked egg, sliced
1 1/2 c. cubed veal

Soften gelatin in cold water. Add to hot consomme; stir until dissolved. Pour thin layer into greased mold; chill until thickened. Arrange peas, beets and egg on thickened gelatin; cover with layer of gelatin. Chill until partially set. Mix veal with remaining gelatin; pour into mold. Chill until firm. Serve on lettuce. Yield: 4 servings.

Mrs. Elaine Petrik
Calmar, Iowa

CHICKEN SALAD FOR TWO

1 c. cooked chopped chicken
1/2 c. sliced celery
1 1/2 tsp. lemon juice
Salt and pepper to taste
1/4 c. mayonnaise
2 hard-cooked eggs, chopped
Salad greens
1/4 c. cooked crumbled bacon

Toss chicken with celery, lemon juice, salt and pepper; stir in mayonnaise. Fold in eggs carefully; chill thoroughly. Serve on salad greens; sprinkle with bacon. Yield: 2 servings.

Mrs. Nellie C. Shymko
Willingdon, Alta, Canada

TURKEY-WALNUT SALAD

1/2 c. mayonnaise
1 tbsp. lemon juice
1 tsp. prepared horseradish
1/2 tsp. grated onion
Salt and pepper to taste
1/2 c. chopped toasted walnuts
2 c. diced cooked turkey
2 c. sliced celery
3 tbsp. diced pimento or green pepper
Salad greens

Combine mayonnaise, lemon juice, horseradish, onion and seasonings. Add walnuts, turkey, celery and pimento; mix well. Chill; serve on salad greens. Yield: 4-6 servings.

Mrs. Myra Garrison
Omaha, Nebraska

CHICKEN AND SOUR CREAM MOLD

2 env. unflavored gelatin
2 1/2 c. chicken broth
2 tbsp. grated onion
1 tsp. salt
Dash of pepper
2 c. cooked diced chicken
1/2 c. toasted slivered almonds
1/2 c. sliced black olives
2 c. sour cream

Sprinkle gelatin on 1 cup chicken broth in saucepan; let soften. Place over low heat; stir until gelatin is dissolved. Remove from heat; stir in remaining chicken broth, onion, salt and pepper. Chill until consistency of unbeaten egg white. Fold in chicken, almonds, olives and sour cream. Turn into 6-cup mold; chill until firm. Unmold onto serving plate; garnish with salad greens. Yield: 8 servings.

Mrs. John L. Hansbrough
Magee, Mississippi

SOUTH AFRICAN SALAD

2 6-oz. frozen South African rock
   lobster tails
2 tart apples
4 c. cooked rice
1 c. sliced celery
1 1-lb. can cut green beans, drained
1 8-oz. can diced carrots, drained
1 c. mayonnaise
1/2 c. light cream
1 tsp. curry powder
Salt to taste
Sliced scallions to taste

Drop frozen lobster tails into boiling, salted water. Bring to a boil; boil for 8 minutes. Drain; drench with cold water. Cut away underside membrane with kitchen shears. Insert fingers between shell and lobster meat at heavy end of tail; work lobster meat loose from shell, pulling meat out in 1 piece. Cut lobster meat into 1/2-inch crosswise slices. Peel and core apples; dice. Mix lobster meat, rice, celery, green beans, carrots and apples in large bowl. Mix mayonnaise, cream, curry powder and salt. Add to salad; stir until mixed. Pile salad into serving bowl. Sprinkle top with scallions; cover. Chill until ready to serve. Yield: 6 servings.

Photograph for this recipe on page 35.

HOT CHICKEN SALAD SUPREME

2 c. cooked diced chicken
2 c. chopped celery
3 tbsp. minced onion
3 tbsp. lemon juice
1/2 tsp. salt
1/2 tsp. pepper
1/2 c. chopped pecans
3/4 c. mayonnaise
1 sm. can sliced mushrooms, drained
1 can cream of chicken soup
1 c. crushed potato chips

Mix all ingredients except soup and potato chips; place in 2-quart casserole. Spoon soup over top; sprinkle with potato chips. Bake in preheated 350-degree oven for 30 minutes. Yield: 6-8 servings.

Mrs. Nancy H. Shannon
Greenbrier, Tennessee

BAYLEY'S WEST INDIES SALAD

1 med. onion, finely chopped
1 lb. fresh lump crab meat
Salt and pepper to taste
1/2 c. salad oil
6 tbsp. cider vinegar
1/2 c. ice water

Place half the onion in serving bowl. Separate crab meat; arrange over onion. Spread remaining onion over crab meat; season with salt and pepper. Pour oil, vinegar and ice water over crab mixture. Cover; refrigerate for 2 to 12 hours. Toss lightly just before serving. Yield: 6 servings.

Grace Lunsford
Foley, Alabama

ROCK LOBSTER VEGETABLE SALAD

6   2-oz. frozen South African
     rock lobster tails
1   10-oz. package frozen mixed
     vegetables, cooked and drained
1 c. chopped celery
1/4 c. chopped red onion
1 c. mayonnaise
2 tbsp. Dijon mustard
Juice of 1/2 lemon

Drop frozen rock lobster tails into boiling salted water. Return water to a boil; boil for 2 minutes. Drain; drench with cold water. Cut away underside membrane with scissors; pull out meat in one piece. Reserve shells. Slice meat crosswise. Mix rock lobster meat with cooked vegetables, celery, onion, mayonnaise, mustard and lemon juice; chill until ready to serve. May serve as buffet salad over crisp lettuce leaves in large bowl, garnished with capers, or spooned into reserved shells for individual servings as a first course. Yield: 6 servings.

Photograph for this recipe above.

CRAB LUNCHEON SALAD

1   7 1/2-oz. can crab meat, well
     drained
1/2 c. sliced celery
2 tbsp. sliced ripe olives
1 tbsp. sliced green onion
Salt to taste
1/4 tsp. monosodium glutamate
Dash of pepper
1/2 c. mayonnaise or salad dressing
3 hard-boiled eggs, sliced
1 med. cantaloupe
Lemon juice

Flake crab meat; stir in celery, olives, onion, salt, monosodium glutamate and pepper. Fold in mayonnaise and 2 eggs; chill. Remove top third of cantaloupe, using sawtooth cut. Remove seeds from cantaloupe; remove cantaloupe from rind, using grapefruit knife or large sharp-edged spoon. Slice cantaloupe into sections for serving with salad. Sprinkle inside of cantaloupe shell with lemon juice; fill shell with crab salad. Garnish with remaining egg slices. Cut cantaloupe into quarters to serve; serve with sliced cantaloupe. Yield: 4 servings.

Cora Elizabeth Fairbanks
Rockport, Massachusetts

MAIN DISH SHRIMP SALAD

2 c. cold cooked macaroni
2 cans shrimp, drained
2 hard-cooked eggs, chopped
1 c. cold cooked peas
1/4 c. chopped green pepper
2 tbsp. chopped pimento
1 tbsp. minced onion
1/4 c. chopped ripe olives
Salad dressing
Salt and pepper to taste
Lettuce leaves
1 hard-cooked egg, sliced
Tomato wedges

Combine macaroni, shrimp, chopped eggs, peas, green pepper, pimento, onion and olives. Stir in enough salad dressing to moisten all ingredients; stir in salt and pepper. Serve on lettuce; garnish with egg slices and tomato wedges. Yield: 8 servings.

Mary H. Dyke
Gardiner, Maine

TUNA-POTATO SALAD

4 med. green peppers
2 6 1/2 or 7-oz. cans tuna, drained
3 c. diced cooked potatoes
1 c. chopped sweet gherkins
3/4 c. sliced celery
6 green onions, cut into 1-in. pieces
2 hard-cooked eggs, chopped
1 c. mayonnaise
2 tbsp. sweet gherkin pickle liquid
2 tbsp. prepared mustard
3/4 tsp. salt
1/4 tsp. pepper

Cut off tops of green peppers. Remove all seeds and membranes and discard. Cut around tops of peppers in Vandyke fashion; cook in boiling water for 3 to 5 minutes. Rinse in cold water; invert and refrigerate until ready to use. Break tuna into pieces. Combine potatoes, tuna, gherkins, celery, onions and eggs in large bowl; mix well. Mix mayonnaise, pickle liquid, mustard, salt and pepper together until smooth. Spoon over potato mixture; stir until well combined. Cover; refrigerate until serving time. Spoon salad into green pepper cups; garnish with sliced sweet gherkins and hard-cooked eggs, if desired.

Photograph for this recipe on page 44.

MEATLESS CHEF'S SALAD

1 16-oz. jar sweet mixed pickles
1 c. mayonnaise
1/3 c. chili sauce
2 tbsp. minced onion
1 tsp. salt
1/2 tsp. chili powder
2 hard-cooked eggs, chopped
1 20-oz. can chick peas or
    garbanzo beans, drained
1 16-oz. can cut green beans,
    drained
1 15 1/2-oz. can red kidney beans,
    drained
8 c. torn salad greens
1 8-oz. package Monterey Jack cheese
    slices, cut in julienne strips
2 tomatoes, cut into wedges
1 sm. avocado, sliced

Drain pickles; reserve liquid. Combine mayonnaise, chili sauce, 2 tablespoons reserved pickle liquid, onion, salt, chili powder and chopped eggs in small bowl. Set aside. Place peas and beans in 12 x 8-inch baking dish. Pour mayonnaise mixture over beans; cover and refrigerate for at least 4 hours, stirring occasionally. Place salad greens in large salad bowl. Remove peas and beans with slotted spoon; arrange on greens in spoke fashion, alternating with cheese strips, tomato wedges and avocado slices. Reserve dressing. Place pickles in center of salad. Pour on reserved mayonnaise mixture; toss lightly until well combined. Serve immediately. Yield: 6 servings.

Photograph for this recipe on page 26.

CHEF'S FRUIT SALAD

1 med. head lettuce
1 c. cottage cheese
1 c. canned pineapple chunks
1 unpared apple, diced
1/4 c. raisins
1/4 c. chopped nuts
3 to 4 tbsp. French dressing

Break lettuce into bite-size pieces; place in bowl. Add cottage cheese, fruits and nuts. Add dressing just before serving; toss lightly. Yield: 4-6 servings.

Mrs. Elizabeth M. Turner
Algood, Tennessee

CARROT-RAISIN AND NUT SALAD

4 lg. carrots, grated
1/2 c. seedless raisins
1/2 c. coarsely chopped pecans or peanuts
3/4 tsp. salt
Freshly ground pepper to taste
2 tsp. grated lemon rind
1 tbsp. lemon juice
1 c. sour cream

Combine all ingredients in bowl except sour cream. Spread sour cream over top; serve. Yield: 4 servings.

Mrs. Hilda Lee
Cedartown, Georgia

CAESAR SALAD

1 clove of garlic, pressed
1/2 c. salad oil
1 head lettuce
1 bunch endive
1 c. toasted croutons
1 2-oz. can anchovy fillets (opt.)
3 tomatoes, diced
1/4 c. lemon juice
1 egg, beaten
1/2 c. grated Parmesan cheese
1/4 c. finely crumbled bleu cheese
1 tsp. Worcestershire sauce
1/2 tsp. pepper
1/2 tsp. salt

Combine garlic and salad oil; let stand for several hours. Tear lettuce and endive into bite-sized pieces. Combine lettuce, endive, croutons, anchovy fillets and tomatoes in salad bowl. Strain oil; pour over vegetable mixture. Combine remaining ingredients; beat well. Pour over salad; toss lightly. Yield: 6 servings.

Shirley Ann Murray
Winchester, Virginia

RED HOT CABBAGE SLAW

1/4 c. butter
1/2 c. chopped onion
8 c. coarsely shredded red cabbage
1 tbsp. lemon juice
1 tbsp. caraway seed
1 tsp. salt
1 c. sour cream
1/4 c. white vinegar
1 c. orange sections

Melt butter in skillet; saute onion until tender. Stir in cabbage, lemon juice, caraway seed and salt. Heat, stirring occasionally, for 5 minutes. Cover; cook over low heat, stirring occasionally, for 10 minutes longer or until cabbage is tender. Combine sour cream and vinegar; stir into cabbage. Add orange sections; heat to serving temperature. Yield: 6 servings.

Photograph for this recipe on page 48.

CONGEALED ASPARAGUS RING

1 4-oz. jar pimentos
1 No. 2 can asparagus
1 env. unflavored gelatin
1/2 c. cold water
1/2 tsp. salt
2 tbsp. sugar
1/4 c. lemon juice
1/2 c. chopped celery
1/2 c. chopped green pepper

Drain pimentos; cut into strips. Drain asparagus; reserve 1 cup liquid. Bring reserved liquid to a boil. Soften gelatin in cold water. Add hot liquid; stir until dissolved. Add salt, sugar and lemon juice; stir until dissolved. Chill until thickened. Fold in celery, green pepper and pimento. Arrange asparagus in ring mold; pour gelatin mixture over asparagus. Chill until firm. Yield: 8 servings.

Annette Braswell
Monroe, Georgia

BASIC POTATO SALAD

4 cooked potatoes, peeled and diced
2 hard-cooked eggs, coarsely chopped
1/2 c. diced celery
1 1/2 tbsp. minced onion
1 tsp. salt
1/8 tsp. pepper
2 to 3 tbsp. salad dressing

Place potatoes in mixing bowl; add remaining ingredients. Mix thoroughly; chill. Serve on salad greens. Yield: 4 servings.

Sister Mary Annunciata
Hartford, Connecticut

COLESLAW WITH BACON DRESSING

4 slices bacon, cut into 1/2-in. pieces
1 sm. onion, finely chopped
1 tsp. salt
1 tsp. sugar
1 tsp. celery seed
2 tbsp. vinegar
1/4 c. mayonnaise
1 sm. head cabbage, shredded

1/4 c. chopped pimento
1 green pepper, finely chopped

Cook bacon with onion in heavy skillet until onion is tender. Add salt, sugar, celery seed, vinegar and mayonnaise; stir well. Combine cabbage, pimento and green pepper in bowl; add bacon mixture. Mix lightly; serve at once. May be chilled before serving, if desired. Yield: 4 servings.

Carolyn Wayman
Mooreland, Oklahoma

PATIO POTATO SALAD

1/3 c. Italian-style dressing
1 tsp. salt
Dash of pepper
3 med. potatoes, cooked and cubed
1 1/2 c. cottage cheese
3/4 c. chopped celery
1 hard-cooked egg, chopped
2 tsp. grated onion

1/2 tsp. dried chopped chives
Tomato wedges

Combine dressing, salt and pepper. Add to potatoes; toss lightly. Cover; store in refrigerator for several hours. Add cottage cheese, celery, egg, onion and chives; toss lightly to combine. Garnish with tomato wedges. Yield: 6-8 servings.

Photograph for this recipe above.

BETTY'S TUNA SALAD

1 6-oz. can light tuna, drained
2 hard-cooked eggs, finely chopped
1/4 c. chopped green olives
1/4 c. chopped pickles
1/2 c. mayonnaise

Flake tuna. Add eggs, olives, pickles and mayonnaise; blend well. Serve on lettuce.

Mrs. Betty Jones
Cedarville, Michigan

Meat Favorites

Meats have always been a basic part of the American diet. Few other foods can both arouse and satisfy the appetite the way meat can. Today, the American cook can choose a different cut or kind of meat for every day of the year, and an average American consumes nearly 180 pounds of meat every year, excluding poultry and wild game. Tender, wholesome meat is plentiful, and is an important source of protein in a balanced diet, as well as being full of flavor.

For the pilgrims, the meat in their diet was supplied by an abundance of wild game, birds and salt or fresh-water fish in the nearby forests and waters. Their beasts of burden, when too old or too weak to continue working, supplied what beef they ate. This is the reason for the now famous boiled dinners and pot roasts as this method of cooking tenderized the tough, stringy meat. Pigs were usually allowed to roam free and fatten naturally in the woods. This practice made pork tender and plentiful, so it is actually our oldest and most traditional meat, and probably the most versatile.

Of course, as the settlers spread throughout the nation, the supply of domestic farm animals grew. The South was first to begin to market farm animals, then Texas, which supplied the nation and the world with over 10 million Longhorns in the three decades after the Civil War. Cattle, pigs and sheep became "crops," to be raised just for sale and eating. Beef became even more popular when Shorthorn, Angus and Hereford cows were imported from Britain — and the result was, beef that was more flavorful and tender than it had ever been. Today, because the government and the meat industries work together to develop nearly perfect, standardized cattle, American meat, especially beef, is probably the tenderest, leanest and relatively the cheapest to be found anywhere.

Beef is the most popularly eaten meat in America, and for many reasons. It can serve as the basis for inexpensive as well as elegant meals, and all of those in between. Beef can be cooked to any desired doneness, from very rare to very well done, without losing its tenderness and flavor. It is available all year long, and shoppers can always be sure of quality meat.

Pork, as was stated before, is our most traditional meat, a part of American diets since the time when earliest settlers brought pigs with them from the Old World. Although second in popularity to beef, pork is certainly more versatile, and easier to preserve. Not only can it be salted and smoked, it can be made into sausage — and in enough kinds and flavors of sausage to keep the appetite interested for a long time!

Most familiar are the delicious sausages of Old World origin, such as liverwurst, knackwurst, bratwurst and bologna. Less familiar, but certainly as delicious, are sausages of purely American origin. Creole *andouilles* and *chaurice* (chorizo) are prime examples, as is the ubiquitous hot dog! Smithfield, Virginia, world famous for its highly esteemed, smoked hams, at

one time was sending six hams per week to Queen Victoria, upon her request. In 1926, the Virginia Legislature passed a law defining an authentic Smithfield Ham in order to protect the long-standing tradition and its industry from imitation.

In the past, pork has been thought of as ordinary, tasteless and even dangerous. People have cooked pork until it was dry and tough because they were afraid of the hazard of trichinosis. And the danger was very real, because in the past pigs were fattened on unsterile food, typically scraps and garbage. But, today, any pork stamped with government approval has almost certainly been fattened on sterile feed, greatly lessening the chances for the presence of any parasites dangerous to health. It has been scientifically proven that pork can be cooked to retain its naturally tender and juicy qualities and also to destroy trichinosis parasites (if they are even present) at the internal roasting temperature of 137°F (for pork loin, 170°F). This is quite a happy discovery for those who have not enjoyed their favorite pork cut in a long time!

Lamb and veal, although they deserve to be better known and more widely eaten, do not enjoy the popularity that beef and pork do.

Because they are not in as great demand as beef and pork, lamb and mutton are especially good for entertaining. Not only are they both extraordinary taste treats with a velvety smooth texture and distinctive flavor, but they also add a very special and elegant touch to the table when thoughtfully prepared.

Veal, the meat from young beef or calves, is delicate, tender and succulent with a flavor and texture very similar to chicken. A perfect compliment to many foods, its mild and delicate flavor combines well with herbs and seasonings. When mixed with fresh, crisp vegetables, it makes an excellent salad entree.

Veal, which has little natural fat, also tends to pick up the flavor of foods and liquids it is cooked with, so it is delicious when bathed in sour cream and mushroom or celery cream soups. Avoid mixing it with strong-flavored vegetables that will overpower rather than enhance its flavor. Veal is generally available all year long and because it is as adaptable as other meats, it is always a good buy.

Wild game is probably the one meat that most intimidates the modern cook. It has a reputation for being dry, tough and too strongly flavored. But for a long time, before the advent of the nationwide beef and hog markets and because domestic animals were too precious to slaughter, our forefathers ate and enjoyed wild game regularly. It is true that meat from small and large game is less tender than the meat from domestic animals, but that is because it *is* wild and contains much less fat. When a few basic rules are followed, rules that have been proven over the decades, wild game can be made tender and delicious.

First of all, after the animal has been dressed, the meat should be properly aged or stored ("hung" is the hunter's term). This aging period can last from several days to a few weeks, depending on the meat. Then, before cooking, it is often a good idea to marinate the game; again, how long to soak the meat and what kind of marinade to use depends on the kind of meat. Another important step in preparing game for cooking is to lard it well, using mildly flavored strips of fat or bacon strips for small game and heavier fats for large game. Larding simply means inserting small strips of fat into the meat by using a larding needle. These can be purchased in cookware shops. This is probably the most important step because unlarded game will be tough, dry and sinewy. Used sparingly, herbs and spices also enhance the flavor of game — especially marjoram, thyme, oregano, rosemary, basil and parsley.

The most commonly eaten large game animals are bear (except black bear), which is esteemed for its delectability, and venison (elk, deer, moose and caribou), which is like very finely textured beef and veal. Favorite small game animals include grey squirrel (red squirrels are too gamy), which is considered an essential ingredient in authentic Brunswick Stew; rabbit, which is very much like chicken with a milky-flavored finely grained meat and oppossum, which has tender, light, finely grained meat and is a favorite in the South.

Because most any variety of meat is tasty and nutritious, it is an essential part of day to day menus and should be used as often as desired or as often as your budget allows.

BEEF STOCK LENTIL SOUP

1 1/2 c. lentils
6 c. beef stock
2 lg. tomatoes, chopped
1 lg. onion, chopped
1 clove of garlic, pressed
1 tsp. caraway seed
1 onion, thinly sliced
2 tbsp. margarine
1 tbsp. lemon juice
Salt to taste
Allspice to taste
Lemon slices

Rinse lentils in cold water until water is clear. Place lentils in saucepan; add beef stock, tomatoes, chopped onion, garlic and caraway seed. Bring to a boil; reduce heat. Simmer for about 1hour. Fry sliced onion in margarine until light brown; drain on absorbent paper. Mash soup through strainer; pour back into saucepan. Heat through. Season with lemon juice, salt and allspice; serve with lemon slices and fried onion.

Photograph for this recipe on page 33.

BRAISED BEEF BRISKET

1   3-lb. boneless beef brisket
1 1/2 tsp. salt
1/4 tsp. coarsely ground pepper
3 med. onions, cut in halves
1 bay leaf
6 carrots, cut in halves
6 sm. potatoes
1/2 c. all-purpose flour
1 1/2 c. milk
1/4 c. prepared horseradish

Trim excess fat from brisket; place fat in Dutch oven. Render fat to measure 2 tablespoons; remove trimmings. Sear brisket in hot fat until brown on all sides. Place brisket on rack in Dutch oven. Season with 1/2 teaspoon salt and pepper. Add 1 cup water, onions and bay leaf; cover. Simmer for 2 hours and 30 minutes. Arrange carrots and potatoes around brisket. Cover; simmer for 45 minutes longer or until brisket is tender. Remove brisket and vegetables to heated plat-

ter. Pour dripping into 2 cup measuring cup; add enough water to measure 1 1/2 cups. Place flour and remaining 1 teaspoon salt in Dutch oven. Stir in drippings gradually until smooth. Stir in milk and horseradish. Place over low heat; cook, stirring constantly, until gravy is smooth and thick. Garnish brisket with chopped green onions. Serve with gravy. Yield: 6 servings.

Photograph for this recipe on page 48.

CONNECTICUT CORNED BEEF AND CABBAGE

1   3-lb. corned beef brisket
4 sm. potatoes
1   2-lb. head cabbage
1/2 c. (packed) dark brown sugar
Prepared mustard
2 tbsp. sugar
1 tbsp. vinegar
3 tbsp. dry mustard
1/2 c. mayonnaise

Wash corned beef in cold water. Place in large kettle; cover with water. Simmer for about 3 hours or until tender. Remove corned beef from broth. Dice potatoes; shred cabbage. Add potatoes and cabbage to broth; cook for about 15 minutes or until tender. Combine brown sugar, 3 tablespoons prepared mustard and enough broth to make a thick paste. Place corned beef in baking dish; spread mustard mixture over top. Bake at 400 degrees for about 15 minutes or until bubbly. Combine sugar, vinegar, dry mustard, 1/4 cup prepared mustard and mayonnaise; mix until smooth. Serve with corned beef and cabbage. Yield: 5 servings.

Mrs. Betty Sykes
Pottsville, Pennsylvania

PEPPER STEAK WITH MUSHROOMS

1 lb. round steak, cubed
2 tbsp. shortening
1 tbsp. flour
1/2 c. catsup

1/2 c. water
3 tbsp. soy sauce
1/8 tsp. pepper
1 beef bouillon cube
1 clove of garlic, minced
1/2 c. finely chopped onion
1 box fresh mushrooms, chopped
2 lg. peppers, cut into rings
2 med. onions, cut into rings

Brown beef cubes in shortening; remove from pan. Blend in flour to make a smooth paste. Add catsup, water, soy sauce, pepper, bouillon cube, garlic and onion; bring to a boil. Reduce heat; simmer for 20 minutes. Add beef to sauce; cook until tender. Add mushrooms and pepper and onion rings; cook for about 10 minutes or until crisp-tender. Do not add salt or Accent. Serve immediately with hot fluffy rice.

Estelle Delgado
Banning, California

ROUND STEAK BAKE

1 pkg. dry onion soup mix
2 lb. boneless round steak

Spread soup mix over half the round steak. Fold over; wrap securely in foil. Bake at 350 degrees for 2 hours. Yield: 4 servings.

Mrs. Evangeline Cox
La Puente, California

GRANDMOTHER'S CORNED BEEF HASH

1   12-oz. can corned beef, ground
2 med. onions, ground
8 med. potatoes, ground
1/4 c. shortening
1 tsp. salt
Pepper to taste
1 c. water

Combine corned beef, onions and potatoes. Melt shortening in skillet; add corned beef mixture. Season with salt and pepper; add water. Cook, covered, for 45 minutes or until onions and potatoes are tender, stirring

frequently. Remove cover; cook until lightly browned. Yield: 6 servings.

Mrs. Carolyn Fillmore Fredrick
Brighton, Michigan

BEEF ON SKEWERS

1/2 c. olive oil
3/4 tsp. salt
1/2 tsp. pepper
1/2 tsp. dried oregano or rosemary
1 lb. lean beef, cut in 1 1/2-in. cubes
8 pitted ripe olives
2 onions, cut in wedges
2 tomatoes, cut in wedges

Mix olive oil, salt, pepper and oregano. Drizzle over beef; let stand in cool place for at least 1 hour. Place beef, olives, onions and tomatoes alternately on 4 skewers, using 1/4 of each for each kabob. Place kabobs in broiler pan. Broil until beef is well browned and of desired doneness, turning skewers to brown beef evenly. Loosen and push from skewers directly onto serving plates. Yield: 4 servings.

Georgamy K. Campbell
Las Vegas, Nevada

ELEGANT BEEF STROGANOFF

1 lb. sirloin steak, cut into sm.
    pieces
1 sm. onion, sliced (opt.)
Butter
1 can sliced mushrooms
1 can beef bouillon
Salt and pepper to taste
1 c. sour cream
4 tbsp. cooking sherry

Brown beef and onion in small amount of butter. Add mushrooms and bouillon; simmer until tender. Season with salt and pepper. Add sour cream and sherry; heat thoroughly. Serve over hot fluffy rice. Two tablespoons flour may be added, if a thicker sauce is desired. Yield: 4 servings.

Tina Butler
Brantley, Alabama

ROUND STEAK WITH ONIONS AND SOUR CREAM

1/4 c. butter
1/2 c. minced onion
1 1/2 lb. round steak, diced
1/2 c. minced sauteed mushrooms
1 c. sour cream
2 tbsp. flour
3/4 tsp. salt
1/4 tsp. pepper

Melt butter in skillet. Add onion; saute until light brown. Add beef; sear on all sides. Cover; simmer for 20 minutes. Stir in mushrooms. Combine sour cream and flour; stir into beef mixture. Simmer for 5 minutes, stirring frequently. Add seasonings; mix well.

Mrs. Eloise M. Speed
Aliceville, Alabama

SOUTHERN-STYLE BROWN STEW

2 lb. boneless beef chuck, cut in
    1 1/2-in. cubes
Flour
2 tbsp. fat
4 c. boiling water
1 tsp. lemon juice
1 tsp. Worcestershire sauce
2 sm. bay leaves
2 tsp. salt
1/2 tsp. pepper
1 clove of garlic, minced
6 carrots, quartered
8 sm. onions
3 potatoes, quartered

Dredge beef with flour; brown well on all sides in hot fat. Add remaining ingredients, except carrots, onions and potatoes; simmer for 2 hours, stirring frequently. Add vegetables; cook for 30 minutes longer or until vegetables are tender. Thicken stew with flour, if desired.

Mrs. Frydis M. Hansbrough
Magee, Mississippi

POT ROAST PROVENCAL

1 5-lb. eye round of beef, tied
12 to 14 whole pimento-stuffed olives
3 or 4 lg. cloves of garlic, slivered
1 med. onion, sliced
1 stalk celery, cut into chunks
1 lg. bay leaf
4 whole cloves
1 tbsp. sugar
1 tsp. monosodium glutamate
1/4 tsp. summer savory
1/4 tsp. peppercorns
1/4 tsp. salt
1/2 c. sliced pimento-stuffed olives
1 1/2 c. dry red wine
2 tbsp. olive or salad oil
1 1/2 lb. pared new potatoes
4 carrots, cut into 2-in. sticks
1 c. diced tomatoes
1 tbsp. flour

Place beef on flat surface, fat side up. Make small but deep incisions over top of beef; insert 1 olive and 1 or 2 slices garlic in each cut. Place beef in large bowl; add onion, celery, bay leaf, cloves, sugar, monosodium glutamate, summer savory, peppercorns, salt, any remaining garlic and sliced olives. Pour wine over all; marinate overnight, turning occasionally. Remove beef; reserve marinade. Brown beef in oil in Dutch oven over low heat; pour off any excess fat. Add reserved marinade to beef; cover tightly. Simmer for 2 hours and 30 minutes to 3 hours. Add potatoes, carrots and tomatoes; cover. Simmer for about 30 minutes or until beef and vegetables are tender. Remove beef to serving platter. Remove vegetables and olives with slotted spoon; place around beef. Strain gravy, measure. Add enough water to gravy to make 2 cups liquid. Return to Dutch oven; bring to a boil. Blend flour with 2 tablespoons water; stir into boiling gravy quickly. Boil for 1 minute, stirring constantly; serve with beef. Yield: 6-8 servings.

Photograph for this recipe on page 104.

FLAVORFUL BEEF ROAST

1 4 to 4 1/2-lb. chuck or English cut roast

3 tbsp. steak sauce
1 pkg. onion soup mix
Salt and pepper to taste
1 can mushroom soup

Place roast on large sheet of aluminum foil. Spread steak sauce over roast; sprinkle with soup mix, salt and pepper. Pour mushroom soup over top; fold foil to seal tightly. Bake in 325-degree oven for 3 hours and 30 minutes. Yield: 6 servings.

Carole Pinover
Vanlue, Ohio

BEEF POT ROAST WITH VEGETABLES

1/4 c. salad oil
1   3-lb. beef pot roast
1/2 tsp. pepper
4 tsp. salt
3 1/2 c. hot water
6 med. onions, peeled
6 med. carrots, scraped and cut into
    halves lengthwise
6 med. potatoes, peeled and halved
1/4 c. flour

Heat salad oil in large skillet or Dutch oven. Wipe roast with damp cloth; sprinkle with pepper and 2 teaspoons salt. Brown slowly in hot fat. Reduce heat; add 1/2 cup water. Cover; simmer for 1 hour and 30 minutes, adding water in small amounts, as needed. Add onions; cook, covered, for about 30 minutes longer. Add carrots and potatoes; sprinkle with remaining salt. Cover; simmer for 30 minutes longer or until roast and vegetables are tender, turning occasionally. Remove to serving platter; keep hot. Make a paste of flour and remaining water; stir into pan juices. Heat to boiling point, stirring to keep smooth. Serve gravy with roast and vegetables.

Mrs. Robert C. Powell
Atkinson, Illinois

HERBED ROAST BEEF

1 tsp. salt
1/4 tsp. dried marjoram leaves
1/4 tsp. dried basil leaves
1/4 tsp. rubbed savory
Pepper
1   8 to 9-lb. rib roast
1 tsp. liquid gravy seasoning
1 c. Burgundy
1/4 c. flour
2 cans beef bouillon

Combine 1/2 teaspoon salt, herbs and 1/8 teaspoon pepper. Stand roast, fat side up, in shallow baking pan; rub herb mixture into roast on all sides. Mix gravy seasoning with 1/2 cup Burgundy; spoon part of the mixture over roast. Bake, uncovered, at 325 degrees for 3 to 4 hours or to desired doneness, basting occasionally with Burgundy sauce. Remove roast from pan; drain off all but 6 tablespoons of the drippings. Stir in flour, remaining salt and pepper to taste until smooth. Add bouillon and remaining Burgundy gradually, stirring until smooth. Bring to a boil. Reduce heat; simmer for 5 minutes. Serve gravy with roast. Yield: 10-12 servings.

Mrs. Betty Addison
Lipan, Texas

STUFFED BEEF TENDERLOIN

1   3-lb. beef tenderloin
1/2 sm. onion, chopped
1   4-oz. can mushrooms
1/4 c. butter or margarine
1 1/2 c. soft bread crumbs
1/2 c. diced celery
Salt and pepper to taste
4 slices bacon

Have butcher split and flatten tenderloin. Brown onion and mushrooms in butter. Add bread crumbs, celery and enough hot water to moisten; season with salt and pepper. Spread over half the tenderloin; fold over and secure edges. Season with salt and pepper; place bacon slices over top. Bake, uncovered, in 350-degree oven for 1 hour or to desired doneness. Yield: 6-8 servings.

Faye Ruble
Milwaukie, Oregon

COUNTRY-STYLE POT ROAST

1   3 to 4-lb. beef round or blade
      roast
All-purpose flour
1/4 c. butter
Salt
1/8 tsp. pepper
1 beef bouillon cube
6 to 8 med. onions, peeled
1 lb. carrots, peeled and quartered
3 to 4 lg. potatoes, peeled and
      quartered
1 c. sour cream, at room temperature

Coat both sides of roast with flour. Melt butter in Dutch oven; cook roast slowly on both sides until brown. Sprinkle with 1 teaspoon salt and pepper. Dissolve bouillon cube in 1/2 cup hot water; pour over roast. Cover. Bake in preheated 350-degree oven for 1 hour and 15 minutes. Add onions and carrots; cook for 15 minutes longer. Add potatoes; sprinkle with salt to taste. Bake for 30 to 40 minutes longer or until vegetables are tender. Remove roast and vegetables to warmed platter; keep warm. Pour 1 1/3 cups drippings into saucepan. Blend 3 tablespoons flour and 1/4 cup water together. Bring drippings to a boil. Stir in flour mixture gradually; cook, stirring constantly, until thickened. Reduce heat to low; stir in sour cream gradually. Heat to serving temperature.

Photograph for this recipe on page 56.

SUNDAY ROUND ROAST

1   4-lb. beef round roast, 2 to 3 in.
      thick
Salt
Pepper
1 c. flour
1/2 c. fat
2 c. hot water
2 med. onions, cut up
1 c. cut-up tomatoes

Season roast with salt and pepper to taste. Mix 1 teaspoon salt and 1/2 teaspoon pepper with flour; dredge roast on all sides. Melt fat in roaster or iron skillet. Sear roast to a medium brown. Reduce heat; add water. Add onions; cook, covered, for 1 hour. Add tomatoes and salt to taste; simmer for 1 hour longer or until tender. Slice and serve. Yield: 12 servings.

Ivy Cliff Weldon
Sylacauga, Alabama

BARBECUED SHORT RIBS

3 lb. short ribs, cut into serving
      pieces
1 onion, chopped
2 tbsp. fat
1/4 c. vinegar
2 tbsp. sugar
2 tsp. salt
1 c. catsup
1/2 c. water
3 tbsp. Worcestershire sauce
1 tsp. prepared mustard
1/2 c. sliced celery

Saute short ribs and onion in hot fat until browned. Combine remaining ingredients; pour over ribs. Cover; cook slowly for 1 hour and 30 minutes to 2 hours or until tender. Yield: 4-5 servings.

Mrs. Della O. Lindsay
Broadman, Oregon

BROILED SIRLOIN STEAK
WITH GARLIC SAUCE

3 tbsp. butter
1 tsp. garlic powder
3 tbsp. Worcestershire sauce
1/2 c. A-1 sauce
2 1/2 lb. choice sirloin steak

Melt butter in saucepan over low heat. Add garlic powder, Worcestershire sauce and A-1 sauce; stir until well mixed. Bring to boiling point; remove from heat. Place steak on broiler pan. Brush top of steak with sauce, covering well. Place 3 inches from source of heat. Broil for 5 minutes. Turn; brush generously with sauce. Broil 5 minutes longer or to desired doneness. Yield: 4 servings.

Edna S. Denby
Fayetteville, North Carolina

BROILED CHUCK STEAK

2 tsp. Worcestershire sauce
2 tbsp. catsup
1/4 c. olive oil
1 tsp. soy sauce
2 cloves of garlic, crushed
1/4 tsp. dry mustard
1/2 tsp. sage
1/4 c. sauterne or pineapple juice
2 tbsp. wine vinegar
3 lb. chuck steak, 1 in. thick

Combine Worcestershire sauce, catsup, olive oil, soy sauce, garlic, mustard and sage in small pan. Bring to a simmer; cook for 5 minutes. Remove from heat; stir in sauterne and vinegar. Pour sauce over steak; cover. Let stand in refrigerator for 24 hours, turning occasionally. Broil for 10 to 12 minutes on each side or to desired doneness, basting frequently with marinade. Yield: 4 servings.

Mrs. LaVera Kraig
Aberdeen, South Dakota

LEMON-BAKED BEEFSTEAK

3 lb. chuck steak
2 tbsp. soft butter
2 tsp. salt
1/4 tsp. pepper
1 lg. lemon, sliced
2 med. onions, sliced
1 1/2 c. catsup
2 tsp. Worcestershire sauce

Rub steak with softened butter; place in large baking dish. Season with salt and pepper; cover with lemon and onion slices. Combine catsup, Worcestershire sauce and 1/4 cup water; pour over steak. Cover tightly. Bake in 350-degree oven for 2 hours or until tender. Yield: 6 servings.

Mrs. Jo-Ann Dawson
Lonaconing, Maryland

POUNDED ROUND STEAK

6 slices round steak, 1/2 in. thick
2 tbsp. Angostura aromatic bitters
1/3 c. flour
1 1/2 tsp. salt
1/2 tsp. pepper
1/4 c. oil
1/4 c. butter or margarine
1/2 c. red wine
1/2 c. beef broth
1 onion, sliced
2 tsp. cornstarch
2 tbsp. water

Remove excess fat from steaks; brush steaks with Angostura bitters on both sides. Mix flour, salt and pepper. Sprinkle over steaks; pound into steaks until well coated. Heat oil and butter in frypan until mixture sizzles. Add steaks; cook over medium-high heat for about 5 minutes on each side. Place steaks on platter; keep warm. Add wine, broth and onion to pan drippings; simmer until onion is crisp-tender, stirring to loosen all particles. Mix cornstarch and water; stir into gravy. Cook, stirring, until thickened; spoon over steaks. Serve with French-fried onion rings; garnish with tomato wedges. Yield: 6 servings.

Photograph for this recipe on page 101.

FAMILY FAVORITE SWISS STEAK

1 2-lb. round steak
Salt and pepper to taste
1 c. flour
6 tbsp. fat
1/2 c. chopped onion
1/2 c. chopped celery
1/4 c. chopped green pepper
1 No. 2 can tomatoes

Season steak with salt and pepper; dredge with flour. Saute in hot fat in heavy skillet until browned. Remove from skillet. Stir remaining flour into hot fat; cook until browned. Return steak to skillet. Add onion, celery, green pepper, tomatoes and 1 cup water; cover. Simmer for 2 hours or until steak is tender, adding water, if needed.

Syble R. Taylor, Supvr.
Montgomery Bd. of Ed.
Montgomery, Alabama

CHICKEN-FRIED ROUND STEAK

1 1/2 lb. round steak, 1/2 in. thick
1 c. milk
1 c. flour
Seasoned salt to taste
Paprika to taste
Pepper to taste

Cut steak into serving pieces. Pound steak well; dip into milk. Combine remaining ingredients; dredge steak in flour mixture. Fry quickly in hot fat. Drain off excess fat; add a small amount of water. Cover; cook over low heat for 15 minutes or until steak is tender. Yield: 4 servings.

Mrs. Louella R. Pence
Macon, Illinois

ROUND STEAK SMOTHERED IN ONIONS

1 2-lb. round steak
1/3 c. flour
Salt and pepper to taste
2 lg. onions, sliced
1 sm. can tomato paste
Brown sugar to taste (opt.)
Chili powder to taste (opt.)

Slash fat edge of steak every 3/4 inch to prevent curling. Combine flour, salt and pepper; pound into steak. Saute steak in hot fat until browned; place in baking dish. Saute onions until browned; place over steak. Thicken pan juices with additional flour; stir in tomato paste and a small amount of water for gravy consistency. Stir in brown sugar, chili powder and salt and pepper; pour over steak. Bake, covered, at 350 degrees for 45 minutes or until steak is tender.

Margaret Nowatzki
Hazen, North Dakota

CREOLE STEAK

1 2-lb. round steak, 1 in. thick
1/4 c. flour
1 lg. onion, chopped
1 green pepper, chopped
1/2 c. chopped celery
1 can tomato sauce
1 tbsp. Kitchen Bouquet
1 1/2 tbsp. Worcestershire sauce
Salt and pepper to taste
3 tbsp. chopped green onion tops
3 tbsp. chopped parsley

Sear steak on both sides in small amount of fat in skillet. Add 2 cups boiling water. Reduce heat to simmer. Melt 3 tablespoons fat in another skillet; stir in flour. Cook, stirring constantly, until golden brown. Add chopped onion; cook until wilted. Add green pepper, celery, tomato sauce, Kitchen Bouquet and Worcestershire sauce; season with salt and pepper. Heat thoroughly; pour over steak. Cover; simmer until steak is tender. Add green onion tops and parsley; simmer for 15 minutes longer. Serve with rice or mashed potatoes.

Mrs. Odessa N. Smith, State Supvr. of Home Ec.
Home Ec. Ed., Louisiana Dept. of Ed.
Baton Rouge, Louisiana

STUFFED CUBED STEAKS

1/2 tsp. salt
Dash of pepper
2 tbsp. flour
4 cubed steaks
1 c. soft bread crumbs
1/4 tsp. poultry seasoning
1 tsp. minced onion
2 tbsp. margarine, melted
1/3 c. rice, cooked
2 1/2 c. canned tomatoes
2 tbsp. butter

Mix 1/4 teaspoon salt, pepper and flour together. Wipe steaks with a damp cloth; dredge with flour mixture. Combine bread crumbs, poultry seasoning, onion, margarine and 2 tablespoons water for stuffing. Spread each steak with 1/4 of the stuffing. Fold over; fasten with skewers or toothpicks. Place in greased shallow baking dish; place rice around steaks. Add tomatoes, remaining 1/4 teaspoon salt and butter; cover. Bake in 350-degree oven for 1 hour or until steaks are tender.

Elizabeth H. Davis
Waterford, Pennsylvania

STUFFED FLANK STEAK

2 tbsp. butter or margarine
1 med. onion, chopped
3 c. soft bread crumbs
1/2 tsp. poultry seasoning
1/2 tsp. salt
Dash of pepper
1 egg, well beaten
1   2-lb. flank steak

Melt butter in 10-inch skillet. Add onion; cook until golden brown. Add bread crumbs, poultry seasoning, 2 tablespoons fat, salt, pepper, 3 tablespoons hot water and egg; mix well. Spread on steak. Roll as for jelly roll; tie securely with string. Heat fat in the skillet. Brown steak roll on all sides. Sprinkle with additional salt and pepper; add 1/2 cup boiling water. Cover. Bake in preheated 325-degree oven for 1 hour and 30 minutes or until steak is tender. Yield: 4 servings.

Mrs. Mary Kay S. Bisignani
Greensburg, Pennsylvania

BREAST OF LAMB WITH APRICOT STUFFING

1   2-lb. breast of lamb with pocket
Salt and pepper
Lemon juice or garlic
1 1/3 c. dried apricots, cut in sm. pieces
1/2 c. minced onions
1 c. chopped celery
1/3 c. melted butter
1/4 tsp. thyme or poultry seasoning
6 c. soft bread cubes

Have butcher crack bones of breast for easier carving. Have a pocket made in breast by cutting through flesh, close to the ribs. Rub inside of pocket and outside with salt and pepper to taste and lemon juice. Place apricots in a saucepan; cover with water. Cover pan; bring to a boil. Remove from heat; let stand for about 5 minutes or until apricots are softened. Drain off liquid. Cook onions and celery in melted butter over low heat until tender but not browned. Combine onion mixture, 3/4 teaspoon salt, 1/4 teaspoon pepper, thyme and bread cubes; mix well.

Add apricots. Fill lamb pocket with apricot stuffing; fasten opening with skewers and string. Place, rib side down, in a shallow baking dish. Bake in preheated 325-degree oven for 1 hour and 45 minutes. Carve between ribs to serve.

Mrs. Dorothy Tyler
Dalton, Nebraska

LAMB CHOPS IN WINE

6 lamb chops
1 lg. clove of garlic
Salt and pepper to taste
4 tbsp. butter
2 tbsp. olive oil
8 scallions, chopped
1 tbsp. chopped parsley
2 tbsp. flour
1 1/2 c. dry white wine

Rub chops with garlic; season with salt and pepper. Heat 2 tablespoons butter and olive oil in large skillet; add chops. Brown on both sides; remove to baking dish. Add remaining 2 tablespoons butter to skillet; saute scallions and parsley until scallions are soft. Stir in flour, blending well; add wine gradually. Cook, stirring constantly, until mixture begins to thicken. Pour over lamb chops; cover. Bake in preheated 350-degree oven for 20 to 25 minutes. Remove cover; continue baking for 10 minutes longer. Yield: 3 servings.

Mrs. Estelle G. Albert
Basking Ridge, New Jersey

GOURMET LAMB SHANKS

2 tbsp. salad oil
4   1-lb. lamb shanks
1 tsp. paprika
1 lg. onion, sliced
1 c. sliced fresh mushrooms
1 c. water
1 tbsp. prepared horseradish
3/4 tsp. rosemary
1 tsp. salt
1/4 tsp. pepper
1 c. sour cream

Heat oil in skillet; add lamb. Sprinkle with paprika; add onion and mushrooms. Cook until lamb is lightly browned on all sides. Mix water, horseradish, rosemary, salt and pepper; add to skillet. Cover; cook over low heat until lamb is tender. Remove shanks; add sour cream to mixture in skillet. Heat to serving temperature over low heat, stirring constantly. Serve cream mixture over lamb shanks. Yield: 4 servings.

Louetta Greeno
Ft. Thomas, Kentucky

GREEK-STYLE LAMB SPARERIBS

3 lb. lamb spareribs
1 tsp. curry powder
1 tsp. salt
1/4 tsp. pepper
1/3 c. finely chopped celery
1/4 c. chopped parsley
1 tsp. grated lemon rind
1 c. orange juice
1 med. orange, sliced
1 med. lemon, sliced
1 med. pineapple, pared, cored and
   sliced

Place spareribs on rack in shallow roasting pan. Bake in preheated 325-degree oven for 1 hour and 30 minutes. Drain off drippings. Combine curry powder, salt, pepper, celery, parsley, lemon rind and orange juice; mix well. Pour over spareribs. Top with orange, lemon and pineapple slices. Bake for 45 minutes longer, basting lamb frequently with pan juices. Four slices drained, canned pineapple may be substituted for fresh pineapple. Yield: 4 servings.

Mrs. Hazel C. Tassis
Imperial, California

ROAST LEG OF LAMB WITH MARINADE

3 c. pineapple-grapefruit juice
1 tsp. crushed rosemary
1/2 tsp. oregano
1 bay leaf
1/4 c. chopped parsley
1/2 c. wine vinegar
1/4 c. chopped green onion
1 clove of garlic, quartered
1 tsp. salt
1 6-lb. leg of lamb
2 tbsp. butter or margarine
2 tbsp. flour
1 beef bouillon cube

Mix juice, herbs, parsley, vinegar, onion and seasonings. Place lamb in deep container; pour juice mixture over lamb. Refrigerate for 6 to 8 hours or overnight, turning lamb twice. Remove lamb from marinade; place in shallow pan. Bake in preheated 325-degree oven for 3 hours or until done. Remove lamb from roasting pan; place on platter. Melt butter in pan; stir in flour. Heat 2 cups marinade in saucepan. Add bouillon cube; stir until dissolved. Add to flour mixture slowly; bring to a boil, stirring constantly. Slice lamb; serve with hot sauce. Yield: 8-10 servings.

Mrs. Florence B. Fisackerly
Inverness, Mississippi

LAMB AND CELERY WITH LEMON SAUCE

2 lb. boneless lamb shoulder, cubed
1 med. onion, finely chopped
2 tbsp. butter
Salt and pepper to taste
1/4 tsp. dillweed
1 lg. bunch celery
2 eggs, lightly beaten
3 tbsp. lemon juice
1 c. boiling broth or stock

Saute lamb and onion in butter in heavy skillet until browned. Season with salt, pepper and dillweed. Add 1 cup water; cook for several minutes, scraping up brown bits. Cover; simmer for 1 hour and 30 minutes or until lamb is almost tender. Peel strings from celery stalks, using vegetable peeler. Cut each stalk lengthwise, then crosswise into 2-inch pieces. Add celery to lamb; simmer for 15 minutes or until tender. Add dash of salt to eggs; beat in lemon juice. Add to broth gradually, beating constantly. Add sauce to lamb; heat slowly, stirring constantly, until thickened. Do not boil. Yield: 6 servings.

Mrs. Hal J. Puett
Acworth, Georgia

ROAST LAMB SHOULDER

1/2 tsp. salt
1/4 tsp. pepper
1 tbsp. dry mustard
3 tbsp. flour
1/2 c. cold water
1 5-lb. lamb shoulder, boned and rolled
1 c. currant jelly

Combine salt, pepper, mustard and flour; blend in water. Spread over lamb. Place in roasting pan. Roast in preheated 300-degree oven for 2 hours and 30 minutes. Spread with jelly. Roast for 1 hour longer, basting every 15 minutes with pan juices.

Mrs. Mary G. Meyer
Griggsville, Illinois

BAKED PORK CHOPS IN GRAVY

4 pork chops
2 onions, sliced
2 tomatoes, sliced
2 tbsp. chopped green pepper
2 tbsp. flour
1 tsp. salt
1 c. hot water

Brown chops on both sides in skillet; place in large, shallow casserole. Arrange onion and tomato slices on each chop; sprinkle with green pepper. Drain off all but 2 table-spoons fat from skillet. Blend flour and salt into fat in skillet; cook until brown. Stir in water gradually; cook, stirring constantly, until thick and smooth. Pour over chops; cover. Bake in preheated 350-degree oven for 1 hour and 15 minutes or until tender. Yield: 4 servings.

Mrs. Joanne G. Thomas
Greencastle, Pennsylvania

BREADED PORK CHOPS

2 egg yolks
2 tsp. salt
1/4 c. cold water
6 pork chops, 3/4 to 1 in. thick
1 1/2 c. cracker crumbs

6 slices onion
1/2 c. hot water

Place egg yolks, salt and cold water in bowl; beat well. Heat 1/4 cup fat in frying pan. Dip pork chops into egg mixture, then into cracker crumbs. Place in hot fat; brown well on both sides. Place onion slices on chops; add hot water. Cover. Bake in preheated 350-degree oven for 45 minutes.

Effie Lois Greene
Paden, Mississippi

PORK CHOPS AND APPLES

6 pork chops
3 or 4 unpeeled apples, cored and sliced
1/4 c. (packed) brown sugar
1/2 tsp. cinnamon
2 tbsp. butter

Cook chops in hot fat on both sides until brown. Place apple slices in greased 1 1/2-quart baking dish; sprinkle with brown sugar and cinnamon. Dot with butter; top with chops. Cover. Bake in preheated 400-degree oven for 1 hour and 30 minutes. Yield: 6 servings.

Mrs. Helen Stone Gardner
Benton, Kentucky

LEMON-BAKED PORK CHOPS

1/2 tsp. salt
1/8 tsp. pepper
1 c. flour
4 thick lean loin chops
1/2 tbsp. shortening
4 slices lemon
1/2 c. catsup
1/2 c. water
1 1/2 tbsp. brown sugar

Mix salt, pepper and flour. Dredge chops with seasoned flour. Cook in shortening in skillet until brown on both sides. Arrange chops in baking dish. Place 1 slice lemon on each chop. Mix catsup, water and brown sugar; pour over chops. Bake in preheated

350-degree oven for 45 minutes to 1 hour or until done, adding small amount of water, if needed. Yield: 4 servings.

Barbara Waybourn
Afton, Texas

SPICED PEACHY PORK CHOP AND YAM SUPPER

1   18-oz. jar spiced crab apples
1   17-oz. can peach slices or halves
6 rib or loin pork chops, cut 1 in. thick
1 c. water
2 tbsp. lemon juice
1 1/2 tsp. salt
1/4 tsp. ground nutmeg
Dash of allspice
1 chicken bouillon cube
6 med. Louisiana yams, cooked, peeled and quartered
1 tbsp. cornstarch

Drain spiced apples, reserving 1/2 cup liquid; set aside. Drain peaches, reserving 2/3 cup syrup; set aside. Trim a piece of fat from edge of 1 pork chop. Place large skillet over medium-high heat. Rub fat over bottom of skillet to grease well. Discard fat. Add chops; cook for about 10 minutes or until well browned on both sides. Add water, reserved liquids, lemon juice, salt, nutmeg, allspice and bouillon cube to skillet. Bring to a boil, stirring to dissolve bouillon cube. Reduce heat to low; cover and simmer for about 35 minutes or until chops are tender. Remove chops to large serving platter; keep warm. Add yams, spiced apples and peaches to skillet; heat through. Arrange yams and fruit around pork chops; keep warm. Combine 2 tablespoons hot liquid from skillet and cornstarch in small dish; stir until smooth. Return to skillet. Cook over medium-high heat for about 2 minutes or until thickened, stirring constantly. Serve as sauce with pork chops, yams and fruit. One 1-pound can drained Louisiana yams may be used, if desired.

Photograph for this recipe above.

PORK CHOPS WITH FRESH TOMATOES

8 pork chops
Salt and pepper to taste
1 lg. white onion, thinly sliced
2 green sweet peppers, sliced into rings
2 lg. fresh tomatoes, sliced

Place 2 tablespoons fat in large electric skillet; cook pork chops in hot fat until brown on both sides. Add salt and pepper. Place onion slice, pepper ring and tomato slice on each chop; season with salt and pepper. Cover skillet tightly. Cook at 275 degrees for 20 minutes, adding 1/4 cup water, if needed. Yield: 8 servings.

Mrs. J. J. Durham
Hereford, Texas

STUFFED PORK CHOPS

6 loin pork chops, 1 1/2 in. thick
Apple-Raisin Dressing
1/2 tsp. salt
1/8 tsp. pepper
2 c. chicken broth
1/4 c. flour

Cut pocket through center of each chop to bone. Fill each pocket with dressing; secure with skewer or toothpick. Season chops with salt and pepper; place in baking pan. Add 1 cup broth; cover. Bake in preheated 350-degree oven for 1 hour. Uncover; bake for 30 minutes longer. Remove chops to hot platter; keep warm. Pour off excess fat from baking pan. Add flour to fat in baking pan; mix well. Add remaining chicken broth and 1 cup water; cook, stirring, for 5 minutes. May be seasoned with additional salt and pepper, if needed. Serve gravy with pork chops.

Apple-Raisin Dressing

3 c. finely diced tart apples
3/4 c. diced celery
2 tbsp. sugar
1/3 c. butter
1/3 c. water
6 c. cubed raisin bread
1 1/2 tsp. salt

1 tsp. poultry seasoning
1/4 tsp. marjoram
Rubbed sage to taste (opt.)
1/2 c. chicken broth
1 egg, beaten

Combine apples, celery, sugar, butter and water in saucepan; bring to a boil. Cover; cook for 5 minutes. Combine bread and seasonings. Combine chicken broth and egg; stir into bread mixture. Add hot apple mixture; toss with fork to mix. After pork chops are stuffed, turn remaining dressing into buttered 1 1/2-quart loaf pan or casserole. Bake in preheated 350-degree oven for 35 to 45 minutes or until brown.

Blanche Maxwell
Spring Valley, Wisconsin

DELIGHTFUL HAM LOAF

1 lb. ground smoked ham
1 1/2 lb. ground fresh ham
1 c. cracker crumbs
2 eggs
1 tbsp. prepared horseradish
2 tbsp. chopped onion
2 tbsp. chopped green pepper
1 1/2 c. milk
1 tbsp. lemon juice
1/2 c. chili sauce
1/2 c. (packed) brown sugar

Combine all ingredients except chili sauce and brown sugar; mix well. Shape into loaf; place in baking pan. Bake in preheated 300-degree oven for 1 hour and 30 minutes. Combine chili sauce and brown sugar; spread over ham loaf. Bake for 30 minutes longer. Yield: 10-12 servings.

Mrs. Doris Patterson
Shelbyville, Indiana

HAM BALLS WITH SOUR CREAM GRAVY

2 c. ground ham
1/2 tsp. dry mustard
3/4 c. fine dry bread crumbs
2/3 c. milk

1 egg
2 tbsp. butter
1 tbsp. shortening
1/4 c. water

Blend ham, mustard, crumbs, milk and egg; form into balls 1 1/2 inches in diameter. Cook balls in butter and shortening in skillet until brown. Add water; cover. Cook over low heat for 15 to 25 minutes or until done. Yield: 6 servings.

Sour Cream Gravy

2 tbsp. flour
2 tbsp. ham drippings
1 c. sour cream
1 tbsp. sugar
1/4 tsp. marjoram
1 tsp. dillseed
1/2 tsp. salt

Blend flour into ham drippings in skillet; add sour cream and sugar. Cook, stirring, until thoroughly heated and slightly thickened. Add seasonings; serve over ham balls.

Mrs. Clarice Hubbard
Mitchell, South Dakota

HONEY-GLAZED HAM

1 6-lb. smoked ham
1/3 c. honey
1/3 c. (packed) brown sugar
1/4 c. orange juice concentrate

Score ham. Place, fat side up, on rack in shallow baking pan. Bake in preheated 325-degree oven for about 2 hours and 30 minutes. Mix honey, brown sugar and orange juice concentrate. Bake ham for 30 minutes longer, basting frequently with honey mixture. Yield: 12 servings.

Mrs. Jeanette H. Stabler
St. Matthews, South Carolina

MISSOURI-BAKED HAM

1 10 to 12-lb. ham
Cinnamon to taste

Whole cloves
1/2 lb. brown sugar
1 tbsp. prepared mustard
1 1/2 c. boiling water
1 1/2 c. vinegar

Cook ham in simmering water for 1 hour; drain. Remove skin from ham; place ham in baking pan, fat side up. Score fat. Sprinkle ham with cinnamon; stud with cloves. Cover with brown sugar. Mix mustard, boiling water and vinegar; pour into bottom of pan. Cover pan with tight lid. Bake in preheated 300 to 350-degree oven for 3 hours.

Jane Parnell
Fort Sumner, New Mexico

PLANTATION-STYLE HAM SLICE

1 c. (packed) brown sugar
1 tsp. dry mustard
1 center slice ham, cut 2 in. thick
1 1/4 c. pineapple juice

Mix 3/4 cup brown sugar with mustard; rub entire mixture into ham on both sides. Place ham in roasting pan or heavy skillet; sprinkle with remaining brown sugar. Add pineapple juice to pan. Bake in preheated 350-degree oven for 2 hours or until tender, basting occasionally. Serve hot. Yield: 6 servings.

Mrs. Sanders McWhorter
Roxboro, North Carolina

SOUTHERN-FRIED HAM WITH RED-EYE GRAVY

2 tbsp. shortening or lard
1 lb. sliced country-cured ham

Place shortening and ham in cold skillet; cover. Cook over medium heat for 25 minutes, turning frequently. Remove cover; cook for 5 minutes longer. Remove ham; drain. Add 1/2 cup cold water to drippings in skillet; bring to a boil. Serve immediately with ham. Yield: 4 servings.

Hilda Harman
Smithville, Mississippi

ROAST LOIN OF PORK WITH ORANGE SAUCE

1   4 to 5-lb. loin of pork
Salt and freshly ground pepper to taste
1 sm. orange
1 sm. onion, sliced
1/4 c. chopped celery
Oregano to taste
1 c. orange juice
2 tbsp. wine vinegar

Sprinkle pork with salt and pepper; place in roasting pan, fat side up. Peel orange; remove segments with knife. Add onion, orange segments, celery, oregano, orange juice and wine vinegar to roasting pan. Bake in preheated 350-degree oven for 25 to 30 minutes per pound, basting frequently with pan juices. Place roast on heated serving platter. Remove excess fat from pan; strain pan juices into sauceboat. Sauce may be thickened with cornstarch or arrowroot mixed with cold water, if desired. Yield: 5-6 servings.

Ellen T. Rakestraw
Deshler, Ohio

SAUSAGE-APPLE STACKS

1/2 c. chopped apple
1 1/2 tbsp. chopped onion
1/4 c. bread crumbs
1 lb. bulk sausage

Combine apple, onion and crumbs. Shape sausage into 8 patties. Place 4 patties in shallow pan. Cover with apple mixture; top with remaining patties. Seal edges. Bake in preheated 350-degree oven for 45 minutes. Yield: 4 servings.

June Houchins
Massillon, Ohio

SAUSAGE ROLL-UPS

1 lb. bulk sausage
1 tsp. sausage seasoning
1 recipe biscuit dough

Mix sausage and seasoning; cook in skillet until brown. Drain sausage, reserving drip-

pings. Roll out dough on floured surface to 1/4-inch thick rectangle. Spread sausage over dough; roll up as for jelly roll. Cut into 1/2-inch slices; place in greased baking pan, cut side up. Bake in preheated 450-degree oven for 10 to 15 minutes. Serve with gravy made from reserved drippings. Yield: 6 servings.

Norma L. Brown
Beecher City, Illinois

SAUSAGE SKILLET LUNCHEON

2 lb. bulk pork sausage
1 c. diced onions
1 c. diced green peppers
1   1-lb. can tomatoes
2 c. uncooked elbow macaroni
2 tbsp. sugar
1 tbsp. chili powder
1 tsp. salt
1 c. sour cream

Cook sausage, onions and green peppers in skillet until brown. Pour off drippings; add tomatoes, macaroni, sugar, chili powder, salt and sour cream. Cover. Cook over low heat for 10 minutes. Uncover; simmer for 15 to 20 minutes longer. Serve immediately. Yield: 6 servings.

Lou Wigley
New Market, Alabama

BAKED BARBECUED SPARERIBS

4 lb. spareribs, cut in serving pieces
2 tbsp. salad oil
2 tbsp. butter
1 med. onion, finely chopped
2 tbsp. vinegar
1/8 tsp. cayenne pepper
1/4 c. lemon juice
2 tbsp. brown sugar
1 c. catsup
3 tbsp. Worcestershire sauce
1 1/2 tsp. dry mustard
1 c. water
1/2 c. finely chopped celery

Cook ribs in oil in large skillet until brown; transfer to baking pan. Melt butter in small saucepan. Add onion; cook, stirring, until brown. Add remaining ingredients; bring to a boil. Pour over ribs. Bake in preheated 350-degree oven for about 2 hours. Yield: 4-5 servings.

Mrs. F. E. Dey
Litchfield, Illinois

LANAI SPARERIBS

2 to 3 lb. spareribs
Salt and pepper to taste
1/4 c. chopped onion
1/4 c. chopped celery
1/4 c. chopped green pepper
2 tbsp. butter or margarine
1 tbsp. cornstarch
1 1-lb. 4-oz. can crushed pineapple
1/4 c. vinegar
1 tbsp. soy sauce

Season spareribs on both sides with salt and pepper; place, meat side down, on rack in roasting pan. Bake in preheated 350-degree oven for 1 hour. Cook onion, celery and green pepper in butter in saucepan for about 5 minutes. Stir in cornstarch; add pineapple. Cook until thickened, stirring constantly; stir in vinegar and soy sauce. Turn ribs; spread pineapple mixture over ribs. Bake for 45 minutes longer or until meat is tender. Yield: 4 servings.

Patricia Anderle
Lemont, Illinois

BAKED VEAL CHOPS

4 veal chops
Salt and pepper to taste
1 egg, beaten
2 slices bread, crumbled fine
1 med. onion, sliced
1 10 1/2-oz. can tomato soup
1/2 soup can water
1 tsp. oregano

Sprinkle chops with salt and pepper. Dip each chop in egg, then in bread crumbs, coating well. Brown slowly on both sides in small amount of fat in skillet. Place chops in baking dish; cover with onion slices. Mix tomato soup with water in saucepan; heat, stirring until blended. Add oregano, salt and pepper. Pour sauce over chops. Bake in preheated 350-degree oven for 30 minutes. Yield: 4 servings.

Mrs. Betty Barnes
River View, Alabama

BREADED VEAL CUTLETS

3 tbsp. butter
1 egg, slightly beaten
2 tbsp. milk
1 tsp. salt
4 or 5 veal cutlets, 1/2 in. thick
1 c. fine cracker crumbs

Preheat electric skillet to 380 degrees; add butter. Combine egg, milk and salt. Dip cutlets into egg mixture, then into crumbs. Brown in skillet for 10 minutes on each side; reduce temperature to 320 degrees. Cook until tender.

Wilma Quapp
Picture Butte, Alberta, Canada

VEAL AND MUSHROOMS

2 4 1/2-oz. cans mushroom caps
1/2 c. cooking oil
3 lb. veal, cut in 1-in. cubes
2 cans cream of mushroom soup
1 c. chicken bouillon or white wine
1/2 c. chopped onion
1 tsp. oregano
1 c. sour cream

Drain mushrooms; measure liquid, then add enough water to make 1 cup. Heat oil in skillet. Add veal; saute until browned. Stir in mushroom liquid, soup, 1/2 cup bouillon, onion and oregano. Bring to a boil; cover and reduce heat. Simmer for about 1 hour and 15 minutes or until veal is tender, stirring occasionally. Stir in mushrooms, sour cream and remaining bouillon just before serving. Serve over hot rice.

Terri Reasor
Milton, West Virginia

VEAL SCALLOPINI

1 1/2 lb. veal steak, cut 1/2 in. thick
1 tsp. salt
1 tsp. paprika
1/2 c. salad oil
1/4 c. lemon juice
1 clove of garlic
1 tsp. prepared mustard
1/4 tsp. nutmeg
1/2 tsp. sugar
1/4 c. flour
1/4 c. shortening
1 med. onion, sliced thin
1 green pepper, cut into 1/4-in. strips
1   10-oz. can chicken bouillon
1/4 lb. mushrooms, sliced
1 tbsp. butter or margarine
6 pimento-stuffed olives, sliced

Cut veal into serving pieces. Combine salt, paprika, oil, lemon juice, garlic, mustard, nutmeg and sugar. Beat well or shake in bottle to combine thoroughly. Lay veal flat in baking pan. Pour sauce over veal. Turn pieces of veal to coat with sauce. Let stand for 15 minutes. Remove garlic. Lift veal from sauce. Dip into flour. Brown well in heated shortening in skillet. Add onion and green pepper. Combine chicken bouillon with any remaining sauce; pour over veal. Cover and simmer for 40 minutes to 1 hour or until veal is tender. Brown mushrooms lightly in butter. Add mushrooms and olives to veal. Stir and dip sauce over veal. Cook for about 5 minutes longer. Serve veal with hot sauce. Yield: 6 servings.

Mary McLarnan
Ashland, Oregon

BRAISED STUFFED HEART

1   3-lb. beef heart
Buttermilk or sour milk
1 tsp. salt
2 c. soft bread crumbs
1/2 tsp. poultry seasoning (opt.)
Pepper to taste
1 egg, beaten
3/4 c. milk
1/4 c. chopped celery

1 tsp. chopped onion
2 tbsp. melted butter

Split heart open halfway down on one side. Cut away arteries and veins at top and stringy fibers and dividing membranes on inside. Wash thoroughly. Soak in buttermilk for 3 to 4 hours to tenderize. Drain; sprinkle inside with half the salt. Combine bread crumbs with remaining 1/2 teaspoon salt, poultry seasoning and pepper. Add remaining ingredients; mix well. Stuff into heart. Tie or secure heart with skewers. Place in buttered casserole or Dutch oven; add 1/2 cup water. Cover. Bake in preheated 350-degree oven for 3 hours to 3 hours and 30 minutes or until tender. Add more water if necessary. Thicken liquid for gravy, if desired. Yield: 6 servings.

Mrs. Gladyce Davis
Poteau, Oklahoma

CREAMED BRAINS IN POTATO CASES

2 pairs calves' brains
Salt
2 c. medium white sauce
1 tsp. celery salt
1 tsp. paprika
Dash of Worcestershire sauce
3 c. hot mashed potatoes

Rinse brains; remove skins and veins. Soak in cold salted water for 20 minutes; drain. Cover with boiling water; simmer for 20 minutes. Drain; cool. Cut into cubes. Mix with white sauce; add celery salt, paprika, Worcestershire sauce and 1 teaspoon salt. Heat thoroughly. Make nests of mashed potatoes on large buttered platter; fill with brains mixture. Garnish with parsley. Serve at once. Yield: 6 servings.

Mrs. Flora May Miller
Elkhart, Texas

BARBECUED FRANKFURTERS

1 onion, chopped
1 tbsp. sugar
1 tsp. dry mustard
1 tsp. salt

1/2 tsp. pepper
1 tsp. paprika
1/2 c. catsup
1/2 c. water
1/4 c. vinegar
1 tbsp. Worcestershire sauce
1/4 tsp. Tabasco sauce
12 frankfurters

Brown onion lightly in 3 tablespoons fat. Combine all remaining ingredients except frankfurters; add to onion. Simmer for 15 minutes. Split frankfurters lengthwise; place in an 8 1/2 x 11-inch baking dish. Pour sauce over frankfurters. Bake in preheated 350-degree oven for 30 minutes, basting frequently with sauce. Yield: 6 servings.

Mary Kay Pearson
Waupaca, Wisconsin

CAROLINA CORN DOGS

3/4 c. self-rising flour
1/4 c. self-rising cornmeal
1 tbsp. sugar
1 tsp. dry mustard
2 tbsp. minced onion
1 egg, beaten
1/2 c. milk
1 lb. frankfurters

Combine flour, cornmeal, sugar, mustard and onion. Combine egg and milk; mix into dry ingredients. Dip frankfurters into dough mixture, covering completely. Fry in hot deep fat until golden brown.

Mrs. Elizabeth M. Culbreth
Inman, South Carolina

BAKED BEEF LIVER AND BACON

1 egg, lightly beaten
1/4 c. milk
4 slices liver
Flour
Bread crumbs
Salt and pepper to taste
8 bacon strips

Mix egg and milk. Dip liver in flour, then in egg mixture, then in bread crumbs. Place in generously greased shallow pan. Sprinkle with salt and pepper. Cover with bacon. Bake in preheated 350-degree oven for about 20 minutes or until bacon is crisp. Yield: 4 servings.

Mrs. Carolyn Fredrick
Pinckney, Michigan

PICKLED TONGUE

1 beef tongue
2 c. vinegar
1/4 c. sugar
1 tsp. salt
1 tbsp. pickling spice

Cover tongue with cold water; simmer for 1 hour or until tender. Drain and reserve 2 cups broth. Cool tongue until able to handle, then peel off thick covering. Combine reserved broth with remaining ingredients. Place tongue in bowl or jar. Cover with vinegar mixture. Cover; chill for 48 hours. Remove from vinegar mixture; slice to serve.

Mrs. Bettie Brown
Shelton, Nebraska

SWEETBREADS A LA KING

1/2 lb. sweetbreads
1 c. chopped celery
1/2 c. chopped green sweet pepper
1/2 c. chopped red sweet pepper
1/4 c. butter or margarine
1/4 c. flour
2 c. milk
4 hard-cooked eggs, sliced
Salt and pepper to taste

Boil sweetbreads slowly in salted water until tender. Cool; remove fibers. Chop into small pieces. Cook celery and green and red peppers in small amount of boiling salted water until tender; drain. Melt butter in saucepan; blend in flour. Add milk gradually, stirring until thick. Add sweetbreads, celery, peppers and eggs. Season with salt and pepper. Serve hot on toast or in patty shells, if desired.

Kathryn Davis
Pinckneyville, Illinois

VINTNER'S-STYLE SAUTEED KIDNEY

3 tbsp. vinegar
1 qt. water
1 beef kidney
Flour
3 tbsp. butter or margarine
1 med. onion, chopped
1/4 lb. mushrooms, sliced
1 bouillon cube
1 1/2 c. boiling water
1/2 tsp. salt
1/8 tsp. pepper
1/2 tbsp. Worcestershire sauce
2 tbsp. chopped pimento
1/4 c. red cooking wine
2 tbsp. chopped parsley

Combine vinegar and water; add kidney and soak for 2 hours. Rinse; remove fat and tubes with sharp knife. Cut in small pieces; coat thoroughly with flour. Melt butter in skillet; saute onion and mushrooms. Remove onion mixture with slotted spoon; set aside. Add kidney to remaining fat in skillet; brown quickly on all sides. Add bouillon cube to boiling water; pour over kidney. Add salt, pepper, Worcestershire sauce, pimento and wine; stir in onion mixture. Cover skillet; reduce heat. Simmer for 10 minutes. Sprinkle with parsley just before serving.

Mrs. Mari Hurley
El Centro, California

RIVERBOAT RABBIT

1 dressed rabbit, disjointed
Seasoned flour
Cooking oil
2 slices bacon

Coat rabbit pieces well with seasoned flour. Brown in hot oil in skillet. Pour off excess fat. Add small amount of hot water. Arrange bacon slices over rabbit. Cover skillet; cook over low heat until rabbit is tender, adding water if needed.

Mrs. Lula S. Patrick
Monticello, Kentucky

RABBIT SMOTHERED WITH ONIONS

3 lg. onions, sliced
3 tbsp. shortening
1 3-lb. rabbit, disjointed
Flour
1 c. sour cream
Salt and pepper to taste

Fry onions in shortening in a skillet; remove onions with slotted spoon. Dredge rabbit in flour. Saute rabbit in remaining shortening in skillet until brown on both sides. Cover with onions; pour sour cream over top. Cover; cook over low heat for 1 hour or until tender. Season with salt and pepper.

Mrs. Walter Wigger
Anamosa, Iowa

VENISON CHILI

1/2 c. beef suet
2 lb. ground venison
2 cloves of garlic, minced
1 tsp. paprika
2 tbsp. chili powder
1 tbsp. salt
1 tbsp. white pepper
2 tbsp. diced chili pods

Fry suet in heavy kettle. Add venison; cook, stirring, until browned. Stir in remaining ingredients. Add enough water to cover. Cook slowly for 4 to 5 hours, stirring occasionally, adding water as needed for desired consistency. Serve with pinto beans. Freezes well.

Mrs. Fern S. Zimmerman
Cayton, New Mexico

VENISON ROAST

1 5-lb. venison roast
Salt and pepper to taste
6 1/4-in. thick slices salt pork
Juice of 1 lemon
2 tbsp. Worcestershire sauce
1 med. onion, chopped
1 lemon, sliced

Remove all fat from venison roast; season with salt and pepper. Wash salt pork to remove excess salt; line roasting pan with salt pork. Place venison roast in pan. Add lemon juice, Worcestershire sauce, onion and lemon slices; cover. Bake in preheated 325-degree oven for 2 to 3 hours or until tender, adding hot water as needed. Yield: 10 servings.

Lillian Y. Wynn
Sicily Island, Louisiana

SQUIRREL JAMBALAYA

1 med. squirrel
Salt
Red pepper
3 tbsp. cooking oil
2 lg. onions, chopped
3 stalks celery, chopped
1 clove of garlic, chopped
1/4 green pepper, chopped
4 tbsp. parsley, chopped
1 c. rice

Cut squirrel into serving pieces; season well with salt and red pepper to taste. Fry squirrel in oil in skillet until browned on all sides. Remove squirrel from skillet. Saute onions, celery, garlic, green pepper and parsley in pan drippings until wilted. Return squirrel to skillet; cover. Cook over low heat for about 30 minutes or until squirrel is tender. Add rice and 2 1/2 cups water. Cook, stirring, for 2 to 3 minutes. Add 1 teaspoon salt; cover. Simmer for about 30 minutes or until rice is cooked, adding more water, if needed. Yield: 6 servings.

Mrs. Annie R. Gonzales
Baton Rouge, Louisiana

BAKED SCALLOPS ON THE SHELL

1 lb. scallops
1/2 c. heavy cream
Salt and pepper to taste
4 tbsp. bread crumbs
4 tbsp. butter

Arrange scallops in 4 buttered scallop shells. Pour 2 tablespoons cream into each shell;

season with salt and pepper. Sprinkle 1 tablespoon bread crumbs over each shell, then add 1 tablespoon butter to each shell. Place on cookie sheet. Bake in preheated 450-degree oven for 20 minutes. Yield: 4 servings.

Ann C. Lowe
Saint John, New Brunswick, Canada

BOILED SHRIMP

2 qt. water
3 c. diced celery
1 c. chopped onions
2 lemons, quartered
2 cloves of garlic, minced
6 bay leaves
3 tbsp. salt
1 tbsp. whole allspice
2 tbsp. cayenne pepper
3 lb. headless shrimp

Bring water to a boil in large kettle; add remaining ingredients except shrimp; simmer for 15 minutes. Add shrimp; bring to a boil. Cook until shells turn pink. Remove from heat. Let stand for 20 minutes; drain. Peel off shells; remove black veins. Serve on platter of cracked ice with cocktail sauce, if desired.

Mrs. Thelma Valbracht
Oneida, Illinois

FRIED SOFT-SHELL CRABS

12 fresh soft-shell crabs, dressed
2 eggs, beaten
1/4 c. milk
2 tsp. salt
3/4 c. flour
3/4 c. dry bread crumbs

Rinse crabs in cold water; drain. Combine eggs, milk and salt. Combine flour and crumbs. Dip crabs into egg mixture; roll in crumb mixture. Fry crabs in 1/8 inch hot fat in heavy skillet, browning on both sides. Drain on absorbent paper.

Margaret W. Cyrus
Herndon, Virginia

SAUCY BAKED FISH

1   1-lb. perch or trout
1/4 c. butter
1/2 c. chopped onion
1/4 c. chopped green pepper
1   8-oz. can tomato sauce
1   2-oz. can sliced mushrooms,
     drained or 1 c. sliced fresh
     mushrooms
2 tbsp. lemon juice
1 tbsp. vinegar
1 tsp. sugar
1/2 tsp. thyme leaves
1/8 tsp. pepper

Pat fish dry with absorbent paper. Melt butter in 2-quart saucepan; saute onion and green pepper until tender. Add tomato sauce, mushrooms, lemon juice, vinegar, sugar, thyme and pepper; heat to simmering. Place fish in 2-quart buttered shallow baking dish; pour sauce over fish. Bake in preheated 350-degree oven for 20 to 30 minutes or until fish flakes easily with fork.

Photograph for this recipe above.

BAKED STUFFED FISH

1   3-lb. red snapper
Salt
2 c. crumbled corn bread
2 slices bread, crumbled
1 egg
1 onion, chopped
1/2 tsp. poultry seasoning
1/4 c. butter or margarine
2 slices bacon

Have butcher split fish down one side of backbone. Rub cavity with salt. Combine corn bread, bread, egg, 1 teaspoon salt, onion and poultry seasoning. Add enough hot water to hold mixture together. Place stuffing inside cavity of fish. Fasten with toothpicks. Pour melted butter over top of fish. Place bacon on top. Bake in preheated

325-degree oven for 1 hour and 30 minutes or until fish flakes easily.

Ruth D. Jordan
Alexander City, Alabama

OYSTERS BIENVILLE

Ice cream salt
1 doz. oysters on the half shell
1 bunch shallots, chopped
1 tbsp. butter
1 tbsp. flour
1/2 c. chicken broth
1/2 c. cooked minced shrimp
1/3 c. minced mushrooms
1 egg yolk
1/3 c. white wine
Salt and pepper to taste
Tabasco sauce to taste (opt.)
3 tbsp. bread crumbs
3 tbsp. grated cheese
Paprika to taste

Line shallow pan with foil, then pour in enough ice cream salt to hold oyster shells securely. Place oysters on half shell on salt. Bake in preheated 350-degree oven for about 6 to 8 minutes or just until oysters are partially done. Saute shallots in butter until lightly browned. Stir in flour; cook, stirring, until browned. Add chicken broth, shrimp and mushrooms. Beat egg yolk with wine; add to sauce slowly, beating vigorously. Season with salt, pepper and Tabasco sauce. Simmer for 10 to 15 minutes or until thick, stirring constantly. Spoon sauce over each oyster. Combine crumbs, cheese and paprika; sprinkle over each oyster. Return to oven for about 12 minutes or until bubbly and heated through. Yield: 2 servings.

Virginia L. Langston, Area Supvr.
Home Economics Ed.
Louisiana Dept. of Ed.
Baton Rouge, Louisiana

STUFFED LOBSTER TAILS

4 6-oz. frozen lobster tails
1/4 c. butter
2 onions, chopped
1 sm. clove of garlic, minced
1 sm. can mushrooms, drained
1 tbsp. flour
3/4 c. sherry or chicken bouillon
1 tsp. paprika
1 tsp. salt
1/4 tsp. pepper
1/2 c. grated Parmesan cheese

Cook lobster tails according to package directions; cool. Remove meat from shells, reserving shells. Cut meat into cubes. Melt 2 tablespoons butter in a heavy skillet; add onions, garlic and mushrooms. Cook over low heat for 5 minutes. Sprinkle with flour. Add sherry gradually; cook for 5 minutes longer, stirring constantly. Add lobster meat, paprika, salt and pepper. Cover; cook over low heat for 10 minutes. Place lobster shells in shallow baking pan; spoon lobster mixture into shells. Sprinkle with cheese and remaining 2 tablespoons melted butter. Bake in preheated 400-degree oven for 10 minutes. Yield: 4 servings.

Joan Farley
Waldron, Michigan

DEVILED CRAB IN SHELLS

1 can crab meat
2 hard-cooked eggs
3 tbsp. melted butter
2 eggs, separated
1/4 tsp. salt
1/8 tsp. prepared mustard
2 tbsp. vinegar
Cayenne pepper to taste
Fine bread crumbs

Drain crab; remove any cartilage. Chop hard-cooked egg whites; mash egg yolks. Combine mashed yolks with butter; add slightly beaten egg yolks, 1/4 cup boiling water, salt, mustard, vinegar and cayenne pepper. Mix well. Stir in crab and chopped egg whites. Beat egg whites until soft peaks form; fold into crab mixture. Place in greased shells or ramekins; cover with bread crumbs. Bake in preheated 350-degree oven until firm and crumbs are brown.

Frances Bailey
State Dept. of Education
Little Rock, Arkansas

Ground Beef Favorites

Ground beef, one of the most popular meats in America, just began gaining its fame this century. Americans have always loved beef ever since the first cattle were brought to this country. Breeding for high quality beef originated with Cortez, the great Spanish explorer, who developed the breed known as Texas Longhorn. Since that time, there has been an influx of many different breeds from England and Scotland, each one producing a higher quality of beef than the one before. Cattle farming has steadily grown into big business as the American demand for beef continues to grow year after year.

Even in the early days of our ancestors, man realized the need for tender, juicy cuts of meat. Trying to perfect a breed that would yield just that, they experimented with different types of feed and climate and began cross-breeding. The results — the high quality beef of today, guaranteed to please the most discriminating tastes. The invention of grinding beef, however, is relatively new. In the states bordering the Baltic Sea of northern Europe, people ground the beef and then ate it raw, hence the dish called *Beef Tartar*. The first to actually cook ground beef were the people of Hamburg who shaped the meat into patties and ate it with bread. This was the beginning of the hamburger as we know it today. Americans were introduced to the hamburger at the St. Louis World's Fair in 1904. Since then, many variations of the hamburger have been developed in different regions of the country, and ground beef, prepared in hundreds of ways, has become a staple in the diet of every family in this country.

What makes ground beef so acceptable on tables all across America? Many things — it's versatile, economical, nutritious and satisfying. There's no limit to the number of dishes that can be prepared using ground beef. Casseroles, meat loaves, meatballs, pies, sandwiches, soups and stews — the list goes on and on. The taste of ground beef can be altered in so many ways simply by adding vegetables, cheeses, pastas, sauces or spices. Because it does mix and match so well, cooking with ground beef can really be fun as you create combinations galore.

Relatively inexpensive, compared pound per pound to the cost of other meats, ground beef is just what the budget-conscious homemaker of today is looking for. Chances are, if you go to any supermarket any day of the week, you will find at least one package of ground beef in every shopper's basket. One reason it is such a reasonably priced meat is its characteristic of being easily stretched. A single pound of hamburger meat can feed between four and ten persons, depending on how it is prepared. Finding something that the whole family likes is often difficult. But, ground beef seems to please people of all ages. Whether you are serving a dinner or a snack, ground beef can be made just right for the occasion, thus satisfying each and every need from a party to an evening meal.

In addition it is one of the most nutritious foods you can eat, supplying protein and vitamins your body needs to remain healthy. Thanks to our forefathers, who never knew what ground beef had to offer, we can enjoy a meat that they helped to perfect.

Ground beef is also one of the easiest meats to prepare. The busy homemaker of today, always on the go, continuously searches for foods that are delicious to eat yet require a minimum amount of effort to fix. For example, the many packaged skillet dinners recently placed on the market were instant successes. They require only a pound of ground beef and they can be left cooking unattended on the stove. Mastering the art of preparing ground beef is not difficult. It's learning the differences in grades of beef, the types that yield the results desired and when to buy them.

The quality of beef is quite important. Although beef is divided into eight different grades, only six are ever stocked by grocery stores. These are U.S. Prime, Choice, Good, Standard, Commercial and Utility. As you may guess, prime is the best quality of beef, and choice, having less fat, is next. Although lower in price, good can be as flavorful as either prime or choice when cooked correctly. Standard tastes mild and contains even less fat than the others. The lower grades, commercial and utility, are not very flavorful or tender at all.

Types of ground beef depend upon the percentage of fat that each contains. While the amount of fat that can be sold in ground beef is limited under federal regulation, between 15 and 30 percent fat is needed for the meat to be as tender and juicy as it should be. Hamburger, consisting of the maximum amount of fat allowed by law, rates as the lowest type of ground beef. Regular ground beef is better than hamburger for it has approximately 20 to 25 percent fat and less shrinkage. Probably the best type for all purposes is ground chuck. Although it costs more than the other two, it is made from a better cut of beef and contains just 15 to 25 percent fat. Ground round is made up of even less fat, only 11 percent, and it is a leaner, tastier type. The highest priced and, likewise, most delicious of all ground beef is ground sirloin. Both it and ground round may require a little fat to be added as it is being ground. Occasionally, meat loaf mixes of ground beef, pork and veal are featured in grocery stores, bringing a completely new taste sensation to your table.

The most important thing to look for when buying ground beef is freshness. A bluish-red color is one of the best guarantees that the meat is not old. Since ground beef should not be kept in either the refrigerator or the freezer for an extended period of time, freshness at the time of purchase is essential.

Even though the history of ground beef is short compared to the history of our country, it holds an important place in the annals of American cuisine. That's why the Home Economics teachers wanted to share their favorite ground beef recipes with you. As we celebrate the 200th birthday of this glorious nation, let's make 1976 the best year ever! And, serve only the very best of meals to your family, using ground beef often.

BEEF-TOMATO-CABBAGE SCALLOP

1 lb. ground beef
2 tbsp. shortening
1/4 c. chopped onion
1 c. chopped celery
2 1/2 c. chopped fresh or canned tomatoes
2 tsp. salt
1 tsp. pepper
4 c. chopped cabbage
1 c. soft bread crumbs

Cook beef in shortening until brown. Add onion and celery; cook for 5 minutes. Add tomatoes, salt and pepper; bring to boiling point. Alternate layers of cabbage and beef mixture in buttered 2-quart baking dish; top with bread crumbs. Bake in preheated 375-degree oven for 40 to 45 minutes or until done. Yield: 6 servings.

Mrs. Virginia Collie
Dry Fork, Virginia

CHILI-CHIP CASSEROLE

1 lb. ground beef
1 c. chopped onion
1 pkg. chili seasoning mix
1 6-oz. can tomato paste
4 c. corn chips
1 1-lb. can pinto beans
1 c. sliced ripe olives
2 c. grated Cheddar cheese

Cook beef in skillet until brown. Stir in onion, chili seasoning mix, tomato paste and 3/4 cup water; simmer for 10 minutes. Place 2 cups corn chips in 2-quart casserole; spoon 1/2 of the beef mixture over chips. Place 1/2 cup pinto beans over beef mixture; add 1/2 of the olives. Sprinkle with 1 cup cheese. Add remaining beef mixture. Add remaining beans, then add remaining olives. Place remaining corn chips over top; sprinkle with remaining cheese. Cover. Bake in preheated 350-degree oven for 30 minutes. Uncover; bake for 10 minutes longer. Yield: 4 servings.

Mrs. Nell Fenoglio
West Covine, California

ENCHILADA CASSEROLE

1 med. onion, diced
2 tbsp. salad oil
2 lb. ground beef
1 12-oz. can corn with green and red peppers
1/4 tsp. rosemary
1/4 tsp. oregano
1/4 tsp. marjoram
2 tsp. salt
1/2 tsp. pepper
2 8-oz. cans tomato sauce
1 10-oz. can enchilada sauce
12 tortillas
2 c. grated sharp cheese

Saute onion in salad oil until tender. Add ground beef; cook, stirring, until brown. Add corn, rosemary, oregano, marjoram, salt and pepper. Combine tomato sauce and enchilada sauce. Pour half the sauce mixture over beef mixture; simmer for 5 minutes. Arrange 6 tortillas in large casserole. Pour beef mixture over tortillas; cover beef mixture with 1 cup cheese. Cover with remaining tortillas; sprinkle remaining cheese over tortillas. Pour remaining sauce over top. Bake in preheated 350-degree oven until heated through and cheese is melted. Yield: 6-8 servings.

Edith B. Carroll
Salt Lake City, Utah

HAMBURGER-TATER TOT CASSEROLE

1 1/2 lb. ground round
1/4 c. chopped onion
1 pkg. frozen Tater Tots
1 can cream of mushroom soup

Press ground round into 8 x 8 x 2-inch pan. Sprinkle with onion; add Tater Tots. Pour soup over top. Bake in preheated 325-degree oven for 1 hour and 30 minutes. Yield: 4-6 servings.

Mrs. Eugene Freier
Lake View, Iowa

HARVEST SPECIAL

1 med. onion, chopped
2 green peppers, sliced
1/4 c. margarine
1 lb. ground beef
1 1/2 tsp. salt
1/4 tsp. pepper
1/2 tsp. thyme
2 c. fresh-cut corn
4 tomatoes, sliced
1/2 c. soft bread crumbs

Cook onion and green peppers in margarine until soft. Add beef, breaking into small particles with fork; cook until beef loses red color. Season with salt, pepper and thyme. Arrange layers of half the corn, beef mixture and tomatoes in 2-quart casserole. Repeat layers; cover with crumbs. Bake in preheated 350-degree oven for 35 minutes. Drained canned corn and tomatoes may be substituted for fresh corn and tomatoes. Yield: 4 servings.

Mrs. Inez F. Klein
Malverne, New York

SPANISH DELIGHT

8 oz. egg bow macaroni
6 c. boiling water
1 1/2 tsp. salt
1 lg. onion, chopped
1 lg. green pepper, chopped
3 tbsp. oil
1 lb. ground chuck, crumbled
1   1-lb. can cream-style corn
1 can tomato soup
1   3-oz. can mushroom stems and pieces
1 tsp. Worcestershire sauce
1 tsp. seasoned salt
1 tsp. chili powder
1/8 tsp. pepper
1 c. grated Cheddar cheese

Cook macaroni in boiling water with salt until tender; drain. Cook onion and green pepper in oil for 3 minutes. Add ground chuck; cook until beef loses pink color. Stir in corn, tomato soup, mushrooms, Worcestershire sauce, seasonings, macaroni and 1/2 cup cheese. Pour into 9 x 13 x 10-inch baking dish; sprinkle with remaining cheese. Cover. Bake in preheated 350-degree oven for 30 to 40 minutes. Uncover; bake for 10 to 15 minutes longer. Yield: 6-8 servings.

Mrs. Marguerite Woods
Modesto, California

LUNCHEON CASSEROLE

1 1/2 lb. ground beef
1 c. chopped onion
1 c. chopped celery
1   4-oz. can mushrooms
1 can cream of mushroom soup
1 can chicken-noodle soup
1 can chicken with rice soup
1   8-oz. can peas
1/2 c. rice
3 tbsp. soy sauce
Pinch of salt
1 pkg. chow mein noodles

Cook first 3 ingredients in skillet until brown. Mix mushrooms and soups in saucepan; heat through. Add undrained peas, rice, soy sauce and salt; stir in beef mixture. Place in casserole. Bake in preheated 325-degree oven for 1 hour and 30 minutes. Sprinkle noodles over top; bake until noodles are heated through.

Mrs. Carol Ludtke
Morton, Minnesota

MOCK CHICKEN CASSEROLE

2 lb. hamburger
1 tsp. salt
1/2 tsp. pepper
2 cans chicken soup
1 can cream of celery soup
3 soup cans milk
1   8-oz. package stuffing mix

Cook hamburger in skillet until brown; add salt and pepper. Stir in remaining ingredients; blend thoroughly. Place in casserole. Bake in preheated 350-degree oven for 30 minutes. Yield: 12-14 servings.

Mrs. Shirley Deyo
London, Ohio

MOCK RAVIOLI

1 1/2 lb. ground beef
3 lg. onions, finely chopped
1 lg. garlic clove, minced
Salt and pepper to taste
1 lb. shell or egg bow macaroni
1 No. 2 can spinach
1 tsp. oregano
1 tsp. sage
1 tsp. rosemary
1/2 c. chopped parsley
1 can sliced mushrooms
2 cans tomato sauce
1 c. grated cheese

Cook beef, onions, garlic, salt and pepper in skillet until beef is brown. Cook macaroni in boiling, salted water until tender; drain. Combine spinach, herbs, parsley, mushrooms and tomato sauce in saucepan; cook for 1 hour. Place alternate layers of beef mixture, macaroni and spinach mixture in greased casserole; top with cheese. Bake in preheated 350-degree oven for 20 minutes. One package frozen chopped spinach may be substituted for canned spinach. Yield: 6-8 servings.

Mrs. Marlene Figone
Manteca, California

NEAPOLITAN BEEF PIE

1 lb. lean ground beef
1 8-oz. can tomato sauce
1/4 c. chopped fresh parsley
1/2 tsp. salt
1/4 tsp. pepper
2 8-oz. packages refrigerator crescent
   rolls
3 eggs
1 2 1/2-oz. box grated Parmesan cheese
1 med. onion, sliced
6 slices mild cheese
1 tbsp. water

Cook beef in skillet until brown; pour off fat. Remove from heat; stir in tomato sauce, parsley, salt and pepper. Line 9-inch pie plate with 1 package rolls. Combine 2 eggs, 1 egg white and Parmesan cheese; spread half the mixture over dough in pan. Spread beef mixture evenly over egg mixture; arrange onion and cheese slices over beef mixture. Spread remaining egg mixture over cheese. Mix remaining egg yolk with water; brush on pastry edge. Press remaining crescent rolls into a ball. Roll out on floured surface to 12-inch circle; arrange over filling. Trim, seal and flute edge; cut steam vents in top. Brush pastry with remaining egg yolk mixture. Bake in preheated 350-degree oven for about 1 hour or until done. Pastry may be covered with foil if browning too quickly. Let pie stand for 10 minutes before cutting. Yield: 6 servings.

Mrs. Ethel Reagan
Ludlow, Massachusetts

CLASSIC LASAGNE

1 med. onion, chopped
2 cloves of garlic, crushed
4 tbsp. olive oil
1 1-lb. 12-oz. can tomatoes
2 6-oz. cans tomato paste
Salt
1/2 tsp. basil leaves
1/2 tsp. oregano leaves
1/8 tsp. crushed red pepper
1 lb. ground chuck
1/2 lb. ground lean pork
1/4 c. chopped parsley
2 eggs
1/2 c. fine dry bread crumbs
Freshly grated Parmesan cheese
1/8 tsp. pepper
1 lb. curly edge lasagne
1 lb. ricotta cheese or creamed
   cottage cheese
1/2 lb. mozzarella cheese, sliced

Saute onion and garlic in saucepan in 2 tablespoons oil until lightly browned. Add tomatoes, tomato paste, 1/2 cup water, 1/2 teaspoon salt, herbs and red pepper. Simmer, covered, for 1 hour. Combine beef, pork, parsley, eggs, bread crumbs, 2 tablespoons Parmesan cheese, pepper and 1/2 teaspoon salt. Shape into 1/2-inch meatballs. Saute in remaining oil until browned; add to sauce. Simmer for 15 minutes. Add 2 tablespoons

salt to 6 quarts rapidly boiling water in large saucepan. Add lasagne gradually so water continues to boil. Cook, stirring occasionally, until tender. Drain in colander. Arrange layers of lasagne, meatball mixture, ricotta cheese and Parmesan cheese to taste in large greased casserole. Repeat layers until all ingredients are used. Top with mozzarella cheese. Bake at 375 degrees for about 25 minutes.

Photograph for this recipe above.

BACON MEAT LOAF WITH OLIVE STUFFING

1 lb. ground beef
1/2 lb. ground veal
1/2 lb. ground pork
2 1/2 tsp. salt
1/4 tsp. pepper
2 tbsp. butter
1 tbsp. chopped onion
1 1/2 c. coarse dry bread crumbs
8 stuffed olives, sliced
1 egg, slightly beaten
1/2 c. boiling water
1/2 lb. sliced bacon

Combine beef, veal, pork, 2 teaspoons salt and pepper; mix well. Place waxed paper on cutting board; place meat mixture on waxed paper. Press into 8 x 11-inch rectangle. Melt butter in saucepan. Add onion; cook until onion is tender. Mix with bread crumbs, remaining 1/2 teaspoon salt, olives and egg. Add boiling water; mix well. Shape into roll; place at 1 end of meat rectangle. Roll as for jelly roll, starting at dressing mixture end; pinch edges together. Place, seam side down, in oiled baking pan; place bacon over top of roll. Bake in preheated 325-degree oven for 1 hour; garnish with parsley and stuffed olives. Yield: 12 servings.

Catherine Dicks
Advisory Ed., Bd of Ed
University Park, New Mexico

HAMBURGER PINWHEEL

1 1/2 lb. ground beef
1 egg
1/4 c. finely chopped onion
1/2 tsp. salt
1/4 tsp. pepper
1/3 c. dry bread crumbs
2 8-oz. cans tomato sauce with
mushrooms
Filling

Mix beef with egg, onion, salt, pepper, bread crumbs and 1/2 can tomato sauce. Pat out on sheet of foil to 9 x 10-inch rectangle. Spread Filling over beef mixture. Roll as for jelly roll; place on foil, seam side down. Place in shallow baking pan. Bake in preheated 350-degree oven for 40 minutes. Pour off excess fat; pour remaining tomato sauce over loaf. Bake for 30 minutes longer. Yield: 6 servings.

Filling

1/4 c. chopped celery
1/4 c. chopped green pepper
2 c. cooked rice
1/4 tsp. poultry seasoning
1/2 tsp. salt
1/8 tsp. pepper

Combine all ingredients; mix well.

Mrs. Ann Hoit
Arlington, Texas

BEST-EVER PARTY MEAT LOAF

2 eggs
1   8-oz. can tomato sauce or tomato juice
1 tbsp. prepared mustard
1 tbsp. unsulphured molasses
1 tbsp. vinegar
1/4 tsp. Tabasco sauce
3 c. soft bread crumbs
1 med. onion, finely chopped
1/4 c. finely chopped parsley
2 tsp. Accent
2 tsp. salt
1/2 tsp. thyme
3 lb. ground beef

Beat eggs slightly in large bowl. Add tomato sauce, mustard, molasses, vinegar and Tabasco sauce; blend well. Mix in bread crumbs, onion, parsley, Accent, salt and thyme. Add ground beef; mix well. Pack into 9 x 5 x 3-inch loaf pan. Bake in preheated 350-degree oven for 1 hour and 30 minutes. Turn out onto platter. Serve with whole baby carrots and new potatoes. Yield: 12 servings.

Photograph for this recipe above.

BUTTERMILK MEAT LOAF

1 lb. ground beef
1 egg, slightly beaten
1/2 c. buttermilk
1/2 c. catsup
3/4 tsp. salt
Pepper to taste
1/4 c. chopped onion
1/2 c. dry bread crumbs
1 tsp. prepared mustard
1/2 tsp. poultry seasoning
Flour

Mix ground beef with egg. Add remaining ingredients except flour in order listed; mix well. Form into loaf; place in baking pan. Rub small amount of flour on top of loaf. Bake in preheated 350-degree oven for about 45 minutes or until done. Yield: 6 servings.

Frances E. Cummins
Astoria, Oregon

FROSTED MEAT LOAF

1 lb. ground beef
1 tsp. salt

1/2 tsp. pepper
1 tbsp. chopped green pepper (opt.)
2 tbsp. minced onion
Dash of oregano
1 egg
1/2 c. rolled oats or bread crumbs
1/4 c. milk
1/2 c. sour cream
1/2 can cream of mushroom soup

Mix all ingredients except sour cream and soup. Shape into loaf; place in baking pan. Bake in preheated 350-degree oven for 45 to 50 minutes. Mix sour cream with soup; pour over meat loaf. Bake for 10 minutes longer. Sour cream and soup may be heated in saucepan and poured over meat loaf on serving platter, if desired. Yield: 4 servings.

Elaine Gutzmer
Anita, Iowa

CRUNCHY ORIENTAL MEATBALLS

1   6-oz. can water chestnuts
2 eggs
1/4 c. milk
1 lb. ground beef
1/2 c. chopped onion
2 tbsp. chili sauce
2 tbsp. soy sauce
1 tsp. salt
1/4 tsp. pepper
1   3-oz. can chow mein noodles, crushed

Drain water chestnuts; chop. Beat 1 egg and milk in bowl. Add ground beef, onion, sauces, salt, pepper and water chestnuts; mix well. Form into balls. Beat remaining egg with 2 tablespoons water. Dip meatballs in egg mixture; roll in noodles. Fry in deep, hot fat until golden brown.

Mrs. Bonnie Bess C. Alexander
Pensacola, Florida

LITTLE PORCUPINES

1/2 c. rice
1 lb. hamburger
1 tbsp. finely chopped onion
2 tbsp. chopped green pepper
1 tsp. salt

1/2 tsp. celery salt
1 clove of garlic, finely chopped
2 c. tomato juice
4 whole cloves
1/2 tsp. oregano or dry horseradish
2 tbsp. Worcestershire sauce

Combine rice, hamburger, onion, green pepper, salt, celery salt and garlic; form into balls about 1 1/2 inches in diameter. Heat tomato juice, cloves, oregano and Worcestershire sauce in skillet; add meatballs. Cover tightly; simmer for 50 minutes. Yield: 5-6 servings.

Mrs. Leota Condray
El Paso, Texas

MEATBALLS SPECTACULAR

1 c. soft bread crumbs
2/3 c. milk
1 lb. ground beef
1 egg, well beaten
1 1/2 tsp. minced onion
1/4 tsp. mace
1/8 tsp. allspice
2 1/2 tsp. salt
1/4 tsp. pepper
2 tbsp. butter
2 tbsp. flour
1 can cream of celery soup
1 c. white wine
1/2 c. evaporated milk
2 tsp. chopped parsley

Soak bread crumbs in milk in bowl for 5 to 10 minutes. Add beef, egg, onion, mace, allspice, 1 1/2 teaspoons salt and 1/8 teaspoon pepper; mix thoroughly. Moisten hands; shape beef mixture into walnut-sized balls. Heat butter in large, heavy skillet. Add meatballs; brown well on all sides. Remove meatballs from skillet. Add flour to drippings; stir until well blended. Add soup, wine and evaporated milk; cook, stirring constantly, until thickened and smooth. Add parsley and remaining salt and pepper. Return meatballs to gravy; cover skillet. Simmer for 20 minutes. Serve over buttered noodles, if desired. Yield: 6 servings.

Mrs. Robert C. Powell
Atkinson, Illinois

LEMON-OLIVE MEATBALLS

1 lb. ground beef
3 tbsp. lemon juice
1 tsp. salt
1 c. grated sharp cheese
12 olives, finely chopped
1/4 green pepper, finely chopped
1 c. soft bread crumbs
1/2 c. milk
1 egg, beaten
12 slices bacon, partially cooked

Mix all ingredients except bacon; shape into 12 balls. Wrap bacon slice around each ball; fasten with a toothpick. Arrange in baking dish. Bake in preheated 350-degree oven for about 40 minutes.

LaVelle McCain
Mount Hope, Alabama

SWEET AND SOUR BEEF BALLS

1 lb. ground beef
1 egg
4 tbsp. cornstarch
1 tsp. salt
2 tbsp. chopped onion
Dash of pepper
1 c. pineapple juice
1 tbsp. cooking oil
1 tbsp. soy sauce
3 tbsp. vinegar
6 tbsp. water
1/2 c. sugar
4 slices pineapple, cut in pieces
3 lg. green peppers, cut in lengthwise
   strips

Mix ground beef, egg, 1 tablespoon cornstarch, salt, onion and pepper; form into balls. Cook in small amount of fat in skillet until brown; drain. Add pineapple juice to oil in saucepan; bring to a boil over low heat. Mix remaining cornstarch, soy sauce, vinegar, water and sugar; stir into juice. Cook until thickened, stirring constantly. Add meatballs, pineapple and green peppers; heat thoroughly. Serve hot. Yield: 6-8 servings.

Mrs. Jewell Vermilyea
Bondurant, Iowa

CHICKEN-FRIED PATTIES

1 lb. ground beef
1 tsp. salt
1/2 tsp. pepper
Flour
1 egg, beaten
1/2 c. evaporated milk
1 c. cracker crumbs

Shape ground beef into 6 patties. Sprinkle each side with salt and pepper; dredge patties with flour. Mix egg and milk in bowl. Dip patties in egg mixture; coat with crumbs. Cook in small amount of fat in skillet until golden brown on both sides. Yield: 6 servings.

Mrs. Earline Baier Alsobrook
Brenham, Texas

GROUND BEEF PATTIES WITH MUSHROOM GRAVY

1 1/2 lb. ground beef
2 tbsp. minced onion
1 tsp. salt
1/2 c. rolled oats
Dash of pepper
2 eggs
1 c. evaporated milk
1 can cream of mushroom soup

Mix all ingredients except soup; shape into patties. Cook in lightly oiled skillet until brown on both sides. Place mushroom soup on each patty; pour enough water into skillet to reach tops of patties. Cover; simmer for 20 minutes. Remove patties; serve soup mixture with patties.

Mrs. Marilyn Orban
Flint, Michigan

SALISBURY STEAKS

1/2 c. minced green pepper
1/3 c. chopped celery
1/2 c. minced onion
1/4 c. butter or bacon fat
2 lb. ground beef
1 clove of garlic, minced
1 tbsp. minced parsley

1/2 tsp. dry mustard
1/4 tsp. paprika
1 tsp. salt
1/2 tsp. pepper
Dash of thyme and marjoram

Saute green pepper, celery and onion in 2 tablespoons butter until soft. Combine remaining ingredients. Add celery mixture; mix well. Shape into 6 patties about 1 inch thick. Cook in remaining butter in frypan until brown on both sides. Yield: 6 servings.

Mrs. Rose Bryan
Leechburg, Pennsylvania

CHEESEBURGER PIE

1 lb. ground beef
1/2 tsp. oregano
1 1/2 tsp. salt
1/4 tsp. pepper
1/4 c. chopped onion
1/4 c. chopped green pepper (opt.)
1/2 c. fine bread crumbs
1 8-oz. can tomato sauce
1 9-in. unbaked pie shell
2 c. grated mild cheese
1 egg, beaten
1/4 c. milk
1/2 tsp. dry mustard
1 tsp. Worcestershire sauce
1/2 c. chili sauce

Cook beef in small amount of hot fat in skillet until brown; stir in oregano, 1 teaspoon salt, pepper, onion, green pepper, bread crumbs and 1/2 cup tomato sauce. Press mixture in pie shell. Blend cheese, egg, milk, remaining 1/2 teaspoon salt, mustard and Worcestershire sauce; pour over beef mixture. Bake in preheated 425-degree oven for about 30 minutes; cut into wedges. Mix remaining tomato sauce and chili sauce; heat through. Serve with pie wedges. Yield: 8 servings.

Mrs. Helen J. Watson
Winter Garden, Florida

GROUND BEEF HARVEST PIE

1 med. onion, chopped
1/4 c. cooking oil

1 lb. ground beef
Salt and pepper to taste
1 8-oz. can English peas, drained
1 8-oz. can sliced carrots, drained
1 can tomato soup
5 med. potatoes, cooked
1/2 c. warm milk
1 egg, beaten
Dash of celery salt

Cook onion in hot oil until golden; stir in ground beef, salt and pepper. Place in bottom and around side of 10-inch pie pan. Add peas, carrots and tomato soup. Mash potatoes; stir in milk and egg. Stir in celery salt, salt and pepper; spoon over pie. Bake in preheated 350-degree oven for 30 minutes. Two tablespoons butter may be substituted for oil; cream of mushroom or celery soup may be used instead of tomato soup. Yield: 6 servings.

Mrs. Benton Williamson
Five Points, Alabama

UPSIDE-DOWN HAMBURGER PIE

1/2 lb. ground beef
3/4 c. chopped onion
3/4 c. chopped celery
1/4 c. chopped green pepper
1/2 can tomato soup
1 tsp. barbecue sauce
1/2 tsp. salt
Dash of pepper
2 c. biscuit mix
2/3 c. milk
1 tbsp. chopped parsley
1/2 tsp. celery seed

Cook beef in 1 tablespoon hot fat until brown. Add onion, celery and green pepper; cook until onion is golden. Stir in soup, barbecue sauce, salt and pepper; turn into 8-inch round 1 1/2-inch deep pan. Mix biscuit mix and milk; stir in parsley and celery seed. Roll out on floured surface into circle to fit pan; arrange over beef mixture. Bake in preheated 450-degree oven for 15 minutes. Invert onto platter to serve. Yield: 6 servings.

Eloise Guerrant
Robert Lee, Texas

BARBECUEBURGERS

2 slices bread
2 lb. ground beef chuck
1 lg. onion, chopped
1/2 c. chopped green pepper
1 egg
1/2 c. chili sauce
2 tsp. salt
1/4 tsp. pepper
1 tbsp. Worcestershire sauce
Garlic Buns

Soak bread in water; squeeze dry. Add remaining ingredients except Garlic Buns; blend well. Shape into 8 patties. Broil in broiler or over gray charcoal coals 6 inches from heat for 5 to 8 minutes on each side. Place on Garlic Buns; add desired accompaniments.

Garlic Buns

1/4 c. melted butter or margarine
1/4 tsp. garlic powder
8 hamburger buns, split

Blend butter and garlic powder; spread on buns. Place on baking sheet, buttered-side up. Broil until toasted.

Lorraine R. Fiedler
Carleton, Michigan

TACOS

3 1/2 c. flour
1/2 c. cornmeal
2 tsp. salt
1/2 c. shortening
1 c. lukewarm water
1 1/2 lb. ground beef
Dash of Tabasco sauce
1 tbsp. Worcestershire sauce
1 tsp. chili powder
1   8-oz. can tomato sauce
Diced onions
Grated cheese
Shredded lettuce
Chopped tomatoes

Sift flour, cornmeal and salt together into mixing bowl; cut in shortening until well blended. Pour in water; blend until mixed. Turn out onto lightly floured board; knead about 50 times. Divide dough into 12 equal pieces; shape each piece into ball. Cover with cloth; let stand for 15 minutes. Roll out each ball into 8-inch round taco. Cook in moderately hot oil until brown on both sides; drain on paper toweling. Cook beef in skillet until brown; stir in Tabasco sauce, Worcestershire sauce, chili powder and tomato sauce. Cover each taco with beef mixture; sprinkle with desired amounts of onions, cheese, lettuce and tomatoes. Yield: 12 servings.

Janelle L. Jones
Howard, South Dakota

SPICY MEAT TACOS

1   9-oz. package frozen tortillas
Oil
2 tbsp. butter
2 med. onions, chopped
2 sm. green peppers, chopped
1 clove of garlic, chopped
2 lb. lean ground beef
2 tsp. Angostura aromatic bitters
1   8-oz. can tomato sauce
1   4-oz. can sweet green chilies, chopped
Salt and cayenne pepper to taste
2 med. tomatoes, thinly sliced and halved
1/2 head Iceberg lettuce, shredded

Thaw tortillas as directed on package; separate. Fry tortillas in shallow oil. Fold in half when soft; hold and fry until crisp. Drain on absorbent paper. Melt butter; saute onions, green peppers and garlic until golden and tender. Add beef; cook until brown. Drain off excess fat and juices. Add Angostura bitters, tomato sauce, chilies, salt and cayenne pepper. Simmer until very hot. Fill fried tortillas; top each taco with tomato slices and shredded lettuce. Yield: 12 tacos.

Photograph for this recipe on page 87.

CHEESE ENCHILADAS

2 tsp. butter
1 c. all-purpose flour
1/2 c. yellow cornmeal
1/2 tsp. salt
1 2/3 c. milk
1 egg
Meat Mixture
2 c. shredded Cheddar cheese
1 c. chopped Spanish onions
Tomato Sauce
Black olives
Parsley sprigs

Melt butter in an 8-inch skillet. Combine flour, cornmeal and salt in mixing bowl. Add milk, egg and melted butter from skillet; set skillet aside. Beat cornmeal mixture until smooth. Place the skillet over medium heat. Pour 3 tablespoons batter into skillet for each tortilla; rotate skillet immediately. Cook until light brown. Turn; brown other side. This makes 12 tortillas. Divide Meat Mixture evenly between tortillas; sprinkle with 1 cup cheese. Sprinkle onions over cheese; roll up each tortilla. Place in buttered 13 x 9 x 2-inch baking dish; pour Tomato Sauce over top. Bake in preheated 350-degree oven for 15 minutes or until heated through. Sprinkle with remaining 1 cup cheese; bake for 5 minutes longer or until cheese is melted. Garnish with olives and parsley.

Meat Mixture

2 tbsp. butter
1/2 c. chopped onion
1 clove of garlic, minced
1 lb. ground chuck
2 c. water
1 tsp. oregano
1/2 tsp. salt
1/8 tsp. cumin

Melt butter in skillet; saute onion and garlic in butter until tender. Add chuck; cook until brown. Drain off excess fat. Add water, oregano, salt and cumin; simmer for about 45 minutes or until liquid is almost evaporated.

Tomato Sauce

2 tbsp. butter
1/2 c. chopped onion
1 1-lb. 12-oz. can tomatoes
1 can tomato soup
1 8-oz. can tomato sauce
2 tbsp. chili powder
1 cinnamon stick
2 whole cloves
1 tsp. salt
1 tsp. sugar
1/4 c. butter

Melt butter in skillet; saute onion in butter until tender. Add tomatoes, tomato soup, tomato sauce, chili powder, cinnamon, cloves and salt. Simmer, stirring occasionally, for about 45 minutes or until reduced by one-third; strain. Add sugar and butter; heat, stirring, until butter melts.

Photograph for this recipe on page 36.

CHILI WITH BEANS

2 1-lb. cans kidney beans
2 lb. ground beef
2 c. chopped onions
2 1-lb. 13-oz. cans tomatoes
1 8-oz. can tomato sauce
1 tbsp. sugar
1 1/2 to 2 tbsp. chili powder
2 tsp. salt

Drain beans; reserve liquid. Cook beef and onions in large kettle until brown; stir in tomatoes, tomato sauce, reserved kidney bean liquid and seasonings. Simmer for 45 minutes, stirring occasionally. Stir in beans; simmer for 15 minutes or to desired consistency. May be frozen. Yield: 6-8 servings.

Mrs. Nancy Kores
Scottsdale, Arizona

MACARONI CHILI

2 lb. ground round
3 tbsp. olive or salad oil
1 28-oz. can tomatoes
1 qt. tomato juice
2 c. chopped onions
3 cloves of garlic, minced

Salt
2 tbsp. chili powder
1/2 tsp. ground cumin seed
1/2 tsp. oregano leaves
1/2 tsp. pepper
1 bay leaf
1 15-oz. can red kidney beans,
    drained
1 c. sweet mixed pickles, chopped
2 c. elbow macaroni

Brown beef in oil in Dutch oven, stirring frequently. Add tomatoes, tomato juice, onions, garlic, 4 teaspoons salt and remaining seasonings. Simmer, covered, for 1 hour; stir in kidney beans and pickles. Cook for 30 minutes longer. Remove bay leaf. Add 1 tablespoon salt to 3 quarts rapidly boiling water. Add macaroni gradually so water continues to boil. Cook, uncovered, stirring occasionally, until tender. Drain in colander. Combine with chili. Serve in bowls. Yield: 10 servings.

Photograph for this recipe on page 74.

MEAL-IN-A-SKILLET

1 lb. ground beef
4 lg. potatoes, thinly sliced
2 1-lb. cans tomatoes
1 1-lb. can whole kernel corn
1 onion, thinly sliced
Salt and pepper to taste

Cook beef in skillet until brown. Add potatoes, tomatoes, corn and onion in layers; sprinkle with salt and pepper. Cover skillet; reduce temperature. Simmer for 1 hour.

Sandra McDonald
Crandall, Texas

GROUND BEEF SOUP DELUXE

1 med. onion, diced
3 tbsp. cooking oil
1 lb. ground beef
1 tsp. salt
1/2 tsp. pepper
Dash of celery salt and onion salt
Dash of garlic salt and dried parsley leaves
2 tbsp. Worcestershire sauce
1/2 c. rice

2 med. Irish potatoes, diced
3 carrots, diced
2 celery stalks, chopped
1 1-lb. can tomatoes
1 c. cooked elbow spaghetti
1 can tomato sauce

Saute onion in cooking oil until tender. Add ground beef and seasonings; cook over medium heat, stirring, until beef is brown. Add rice, potatoes, carrots, celery and tomatoes; add enough water to cover all ingredients. Mix well. Simmer until vegetables are tender. Add spaghetti, tomato sauce and enough water to make medium consistency; heat through. Yield: 6-8 servings.

Mrs. Mary A. Campbell
Fort Necessity, Louisiana

IRENE'S SKILLET BEEF-ARONI

1/4 c. butter
1 lb. ground beef
1 7-oz. package elbow macaroni
1 med. onion, chopped
1 clove of garlic, minced
1/2 c. chopped green pepper
1 tsp. salt
1 1/2 tsp. seasoned salt
1/4 tsp. pepper
1 tsp. oregano
2 c. water
1 tbsp. flour
1 lg. can evaporated milk
2 tbsp. chopped pimento
1/3 c. grated Parmesan cheese

Melt butter in large frypan. Stir in ground beef, uncooked macaroni, onion, garlic, green pepper, salt, seasoned salt, pepper and oregano. Cook over medium heat, stirring occasionally, until beef is brown and onion is transparent. Stir in water; bring to a boil. Cover; reduce heat. Simmer for 20 minutes or until macaroni is tender. Sprinkle flour evenly over beef mixture; blend in until smooth. Stir in milk, pimento and cheese; simmer for 5 minutes longer, stirring occasionally. Garnish with pimento strips and parsley, if desired. Yield: 6 servings.

Mrs. Irene Kathy Lee
El Dorado, Arkansas

Poultry Favorites

Poultry has been a familiar sight on the American table since the earliest settlers landed at Jamestown. It was recorded that Plymouth Succotash, quite distinguished from common succotash by the inclusion of chicken and other meats, was served in many Plymouth homes each year on December 21, to celebrate the date of the Pilgrims' landing.

One of several birds belonging to the poultry family, chicken has withstood the test of time and emerged as the third most popular main course in America. Chicken, one of the homemaker's best buys today, has not always been as cheap or as plentiful as it is now. Only on the most special occasions was chicken ever served in grandma's day, for the birds were usually kept until they could no longer produce eggs. Yet, even then, people realized the nutritional value of chicken, which is high in iron, protein and niacin. And, its delicious, mild flavor is one which people seem to never get enough of. Whether it is broiled, baked, fried or roasted, the same satisfying taste is there.

Typically, the methods of preparation vary according to a particular region of the country. While the South is famous for its crispy fried chicken, the Southwest is known for barbecuing chicken over hot coals, and so on. In fact, there are so many different ways to cook chicken, entire cookbooks have been written on this subject alone. And, in 1949, a National Chicken Cooking Contest was initiated which has since evolved into an annual festival. There's no end to the hundreds of savory chicken dishes combining richly seasoned sauces, farm-fresh vegetables or breads that can be created. Even chicken dishes made with leftovers can become some of the most delicious meals you have ever eaten. Suitable for almost every occasion, chicken can be served at a picnic, luncheon or dinner party and win compliments from everyone there.

The most elite in the chicken family, the Cornish Hen, is also the most expensive. The smallest, youngest and juiciest of all chickens, it is considered to be a true delicacy. Even though they can usually be found in most any supermarket, Cornish hens bring a taste of the "rare and exotic" to any meal.

When we think of Thanksgiving, one of our most special holidays, the tantalizing aroma of turkey roasting in the oven until golden brown instantly comes to mind. The more the Pilgrims explored this bountiful land, the more their amazement grew at the abundance of wild turkey and other game birds.

Although turkey was served at that first thanksgiving feast at Plymouth Colony, the tradition of setting aside a certain day every year to give thanks for our many blessings did not actually begin until the mid 1800's. Once thirty states celebrated the occasion on the same date in 1859, it was considered a national event. Because of the efforts of one woman who petitioned for the need of such a day,

President Lincoln established a uniform day of thanks in 1863. Turkey, both then and now, has always been considered the symbol of an authentic Thanksgiving dinner.

Perfecting the preparation of a tender, juicy turkey is one cooking art that the New World introduced to the world as a whole. The turkey we enjoy now is not the big, tough-meated bird that it was in the past. Gradually, it has been bred down to its smaller size of today, the best size for price and taste being between 16 to 24 pounds. Because the threat of extinction was very real at the beginning of this century, steps were taken to preserve the treasured bird. Due to conservation and controlled breeding, there are over a million fine specimens inhabiting the country today. However, the wild turkey, which makes its home throughout eastern America, offers a much more flavorful meat than the domesticated bird readily available in stores.

Because our woodlands and waters are so well stocked with game birds of every description, hunting as a sport has continued to grow in popularity. Rising early to reach their stands by dawn, hunters are willing to spend hours waiting for a chance to shoot even one bird. What a change from the days of our forefathers when hunting was a necessity! Then, the men set out, not for fun, but to bring home meat for their families.

For many years, cooks have experimented with wild game, looking for ways to elicit its best flavor. While most game birds are at their best when roasted, this does not apply to the quail. Its tender, white meat can be cooked in the same manner as any domestic bird.

The most popular game bird is the duck. Both those who have experienced the thrill of capturing one of these crafty creatures and those who have enjoyed the succulent meal they provide can understand why. Although ducks are quite plentiful all across the nation, the best wild ducks can be found in the region surrounded by the Chesapeake Bay. Ducklings, on the other hand, are thought of as an American delicacy. Young ducks, known as Long Island Ducklings, were brought to this country on a clipper ship from Peking. Since that ship docked in New York in 1873, this variety has multiplied so that there is quite an availability today.

During bird hunting season, hunters comb the fields in search of dove and quail. Small in size, these birds can be made into a meal that is truly big in flavor. The real gourmet's delight is the pheasant. Highly regarded as a delicacy, it is a game bird sought by those who appreciate the finer things in life. Abundant in the northern states of America, pheasant is usually served on very rare occasions, when nothing but the most savory poultry dish will suffice.

Poultry refers to such a great variety of meats; yet, each and every one can be prepared in a way that makes it unique. Our ancestors began developing these recipes many years ago. Thus, there are hundreds from which to choose today. So that you can be assured of serving only the most delectable poultry dishes, the Home Economics teachers chose this bicentennial year to pass along their favorites to you.

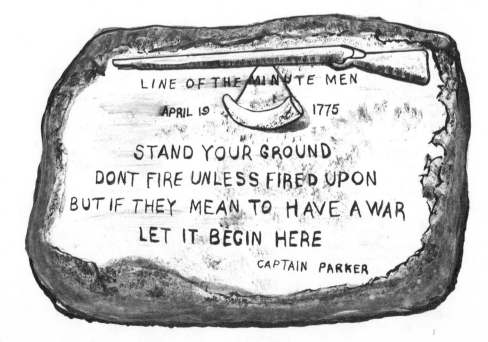

LINE OF THE MINUTE MEN
APRIL 19   1775

STAND YOUR GROUND
DONT FIRE UNLESS FIRED UPON
BUT IF THEY MEAN TO HAVE A WAR
LET IT BEGIN HERE

CAPTAIN PARKER

BRUNSWICK STEW

1 5-lb. stewing chicken
4 slices bacon, chopped
2 c. diced potatoes
1 10-oz. package frozen lima beans
1 1-lb. can tomatoes
1 med. onion, chopped
2 tsp. salt
1/4 tsp. pepper
1 1/2 tsp. Worcestershire sauce
1 10-oz. package frozen whole kernel
   corn

Cook chicken in large kettle in water to cover until tender; cool. Remove skin and bones, then cut into small pieces. Fry bacon until crisp; reserve drippings. Measure chicken broth; add enough water to make 1 quart, if needed. Combine reserved drippings and all ingredients except corn in large kettle. Simmer for 1 hour. Add corn; simmer for 30 minutes longer. Yield: 8 servings.

Mrs. Helen Godwin
Greensboro, North Carolina

CHICKEN-CORN SOUP

1 5 to 6-lb. stewing chicken
1 or 2 med. onions, chopped
Salt
1/4 tsp. pepper
8 to 10 ears of corn, cut from cob
1 c. flour
1 egg, beaten
4 hard-cooked eggs, chopped
3 tbsp. chopped parsley
Celery salt to taste
Onion salt to taste

Cut chicken into serving pieces. Place in large stewing pan; add 3 to 4 quarts water. Add onions, 1 tablespoon salt and pepper. Cover; cook over low heat until chicken is tender. Remove chicken from broth; remove and discard skin and bones. Cut chicken in 1 to 1 1/2-inch pieces. Return chicken to broth; add corn. Cook over low heat for 15 to 20 minutes, stirring frequently. Combine flour, 1/8 teaspoon salt and beaten egg in a bowl; mix to form crumbs. Bring soup to a boil; add crumbs gradually. Cook for 15 minutes. Drop in hard-cooked eggs and parsley; simmer for several seconds. Add seasonings. Soup may be made ahead and frozen for future use.

I. Eugenia Spangler
Newville, Pennsylvania

CHICKEN BREASTS IN WHITE WINE SAUCE

8 chicken breasts
Butter
1/2 c. white wine
Seasonings to taste
3 c. rich medium-thick white sauce
1 c. button mushrooms
1/2 c. slivered toasted almonds

Saute chicken breasts in butter until light brown. Arrange in baking dish. Add wine and seasonings to white sauce; stir in mushrooms. Pour over chicken. Bake in preheated 350-degree oven for 1 hour. Sprinkle with almonds. Bake for 10 minutes longer. Two cans mushroom soup may be used for white sauce, if desired.

Evelyn Cotney
Home Economics Education
Montevallo, Alabama

CHICKEN ROYALE

3 c. chopped cooked chicken
2 c. soft bread crumbs
1 1/2 c. cooked rice
2 eggs, beaten
1 c. chicken broth or bouillon
1 c. milk
1/4 c. chopped pimento
1/2 tsp. salt
1/2 tsp. paprika
1/4 tsp. pepper
Cream of Mushroom Sauce
Carrot and Green Bean Combo

Combine chicken, bread crumbs, rice, eggs, broth, milk, pimento, salt, paprika and pepper in large bowl. Turn into 1 1/2-quart buttered loaf dish; place in pan of hot water. Bake in preheated 350-degree oven for 1 hour. Let stand for 10 minutes; invert onto serving platter. Serve with Cream of Mushroom Sauce and Carrot and Green Bean Combo. Yield: 8 servings.

Cream of Mushroom Sauce

1 chicken bouillon cube
1/2 c. milk
1 can cream of mushroom soup
1/2 c. sour cream
2 tbsp. chopped parsley

Dissolve bouillon cube in milk in saucepan over low heat; stir in soup, then sour cream. Heat to serving temperature; do not boil. Add parsley; mix well.

Carrot and Green Bean Combo

1/2 c. butter
1/2 tsp. nutmeg
1 lb. carrots, peeled and cooked
2 9-oz. packages frozen French-cut
    green beans, cooked

Melt butter in small saucepan; stir in nutmeg. Arrange carrots and green beans around Chicken Royale; pour butter mixture over vegetables.

Photograph for this recipe on page 90.

BAKED CHICKEN DIVAN

2 pkg. frozen broccoli spears
2 cans cream of chicken soup
1 tsp. nutmeg
2 tsp. Worcestershire sauce
1 c. grated Parmesan cheese
4 lg. cooked boned chicken breasts
3/4 c. heavy cream, whipped
1/3 c. mayonnaise

Cook broccoli in boiling salted water until tender; drain. Place broccoli in oblong shallow baking dish. Combine soup, nutmeg and Worcestershire sauce; pour half the mixture over broccoli. Sprinkle with 1/3 cup cheese. Slice chicken; place over broccoli. Pour remaining soup mixture over chicken; sprinkle with 1/3 cup cheese. Bake at 400 degrees for 25 minutes. Fold whipped cream into mayonnaise; spread over chicken mixture. Sprinkle with remaining cheese. Broil for 2 to 3 minutes or until golden brown.

Mrs. Elizabeth L. Prew
Agawam, Massachusetts

DELICIOUS CHICKEN KIEV

9 med. chicken breast halves
Salt
White pepper
1/2 c. butter, chilled
1 lg. egg
1 tbsp. milk
1 c. fine dry bread crumbs
1/4 tsp. pepper
1/2 tsp. celery salt
1 tsp. paprika
Flour
3 lb. vegetable shortening

Remove skin and bones from each chicken breast. Place 1 breast, boned side up, between pieces of waxed paper; pound to 1/4-inch thickness with a wooden mallet. Remove waxed paper; sprinkle with salt and white pepper. Cut butter into 9 pieces. Place 1 piece near end of cutlet; roll as for jelly roll, tucking in sides. Secure with a toothpick. Repeat with remaining breasts. Chill for at least 1 hour. Beat egg and milk together with fork. Combine bread crumbs, 2 teaspoons salt, pepper, celery salt and paprika. Remove toothpicks; dust each stuffed breast with flour. Dip into egg mixture; roll in seasoned bread crumbs until well coated. Place on rack to dry for 20 minutes. Heat shortening in heavy 4-quart saucepan to 340 degrees. Fry 3 breasts at a time for 8 minutes. Remove with tongs; drain on absorbent paper. Yield: 9 servings.

Junia Marie Schlinkert
Willow Lake, South Dakota

OVEN-BAKED CHICKEN BREASTS

1 tsp. salt
1/2 c. melted margarine
8 chicken breasts
2 c. crushed potato chips

Add salt to margarine. Dip chicken into margarine; coat with potato chips. Place, skin side up, in baking pan. Bake in preheated 350-degree oven for 1 hour to 1 hour and 15 minutes or until chicken is tender.

Mrs. Elwanda M. Brewer
Charleston, Mississippi

CHICKEN WITH ORANGE RICE

1/3 c. flour
Salt and pepper to taste
Paprika to taste
Onion salt to taste
4 chicken breasts, halved
Butter
2 cans cream of chicken soup
1 c. sour cream
1   4-oz. can mushrooms
Orange Rice

Combine flour, salt, pepper, paprika and onion salt; dredge chicken with seasoned flour. Melt butter in skillet; brown chicken on both sides. Remove chicken to casserole. Combine soup and sour cream; spoon over chicken. Cover. Bake in preheated 350-degree oven for 1 hour or until tender. Remove chicken from casserole. Add mushrooms to pan drippings for gravy. Serve gravy with Orange Rice and chicken.

Orange Rice

Chopped onion to taste
1 c. chopped celery
2 tbsp. butter
1 c. rice
Grated rind of 1 orange
Juice of 2 oranges
1/2 tsp. salt
1/8 tsp. thyme

Saute onion and celery in butter in skillet until limp; stir in rice and orange rind. Add enough water to orange juice to equal 2 1/2 cups liquid. Add orange liquid, salt and thyme to rice mixture; spoon into casserole. Bake in preheated 350-degree oven for 30 minutes or until liquid is absorbed.

Borghild Strom
Lansing, Michigan

CHICKEN LOAF WITH MUSHROOM SAUCE

1   3 1/2 to 4-lb. chicken
3 eggs
1 1/2 c. soft bread crumbs
1 c. cooked rice

1/2 c. light cream
3/4 c. milk
1 sm. can pimentos, chopped
Salt to taste
Hot sauce to taste
Grated cheese
Crumbled saltines
Paprika to taste
Butter
Mushroom Sauce

Cook chicken in boiling salted water in large pot until tender. Remove bones; dice chicken. Reserve stock. Place eggs in large bowl; beat well. Add bread crumbs, rice, chicken, cream, milk, 3/4 cup reserved chicken stock, pimentos, salt and hot sauce; mix thoroughly. Pour into buttered loaf pan; sprinkle with cheese, saltines and paprika. Dot with butter. Bake in preheated 350-degree oven for about 1 hour or until done. Turn out of loaf pan; serve with Mushroom Sauce.

Mushroom Sauce

1/4 c. butter
1/4 c. flour
1 c. chicken stock
1 c. milk
1 c. light cream
1/2 lb. fresh or canned mushrooms
1/2 tsp. chopped parsley
1/4 tsp. paprika
Salt and pepper to taste
Onion salt to taste

Melt butter in saucepan; blend in flour. Combine stock and milk; add to flour mixture gradually, stirring constantly. Cook and stir until thickened. Add cream; bring to a boil. Chop mushrooms. Add mushrooms, parsley, paprika, salt, pepper and onion salt to white sauce; mix well.

Mrs. Virginia O. Savedge
Eastville, Virginia

CHICKEN STUFFED WITH RICE

1 can cream of mushroom soup
1 c. chicken broth

1 c. instant rice
1 tsp. salt or to taste
1/4 c. butter or margarine
2   3-lb. broiler-fryers
2 tbsp. thinly slivered orange peel
1/4 c. orange juice
1/2 c. light corn syrup
1/4 tsp. ginger
1/2 tsp. monosodium glutamate

Combine mushroom soup, broth, rice, salt and butter in covered saucepan; cook according to package directions for rice. Let stand for 15 minutes or until rice is fluffy. Fill cavities of fryers with rice mixture; place fryers, breast side up, in an 8 x 11-inch baking dish or pan. Place remaining rice mixture around fryers. Bake in preheated 375-degree oven for 1 hour and 30 minutes. Combine remaining ingredients; brush chickens with glaze. Bake for 15 minutes longer. Let set for several minutes before carving.

Mrs. Alice Hansberger
Canton, Illinois

DILLED CHICKEN-RICE CASSEROLE

2   10-oz. packages frozen broccoli
   spears
1/3 c. butter or margarine

1/2 lb. fresh mushrooms, sliced
3/4 c. chopped onions
1 med. garlic clove, crushed
2 cans chicken gravy
3 c. cooked rice
2 c. cubed cooked chicken
2 c. sliced celery
2 tbsp. dry sherry
3/4 tsp. Spice Islands dillweed,
   crushed
1/4 tsp. salt
1/4 tsp. Spice Islands ground white
   pepper

Thaw and drain broccoli. Trim broccoli flowerets; reserve for garnish. Coarsely chop stalks; set aside. Melt butter in large saucepan. Add mushrooms, onions and garlic; saute over medium heat, stirring occasionally, for about 5 minutes or until onions are tender. Stir in undiluted chicken gravy, rice, chicken, celery, chopped broccoli, sherry, dillweed, salt and white pepper. Cook over low heat, stirring constantly, for about 5 minutes. Pour into ungreased 3-quart casserole; cover. Bake in preheated 400-degree oven for 30 minutes. Uncover; garnish top with flowerets. Bake, uncovered, for about 10 minutes or until center is bubbly. Yield: 6 servings.

Photograph for this recipe above.

OVEN-BAKED CHICKEN

2   2 1/2 to 3-lb. fryers, quartered
2 cans cream of chicken soup
1/2 c. grated Parmesan cheese
Chicken-Milk Gravy

Place chicken in single layer in jelly roll pan, skin side up. Blend soup and cheese in bowl; spread evenly over chicken. Bake in preheated 350-degree oven for 1 hour and 15 minutes to 1 hour and 30 minutes or until chicken is tender and brown. Remove chicken to warm platter; spoon sauce over chicken or use as drippings for Chicken-Milk Gravy. Yield: 6-8 servings.

Chicken-Milk Gravy

1 1/2 c. drippings
2 c. milk
1/3 to 1/2 c. all-purpose flour

Combine drippings with 1 1/2 cups milk in saucepan; place over medium heat until hot. Add remaining 1/2 cup milk gradually to flour in small bowl, stirring until smooth; add flour mixture to hot milk gradually. Cook, stirring constantly, until thickened; cook for 2 minutes longer. Serve over chicken.

Photograph for this recipe above.

ROAST CHICKEN AND CORN BREAD DRESSING

1   4-lb. dressed hen and giblets
Salt
4 c. corn bread crumbs
1 c. finely chopped celery
3 hard-boiled eggs, chopped
1 tsp. sage
5 biscuits, crumbled
4 tbsp. minced onion
1/2 tsp. freshly ground pepper
2 eggs, beaten
1/4 c. butter
1/4 c. flour

Cover hen and giblets with water; add 1 1/2 tablespoons salt. Bring to a boil; simmer until almost tender. Remove hen and giblets from broth; chop giblets. Place hen in baking pan. Bake in preheated 375-degree oven for 40 minutes or until well browned and tender. Bring chicken broth to a boil. Place corn bread crumbs in mixing bowl; add 3 cups chicken broth. Cover; let stand for 5 minutes. Add celery, 2 hard-boiled eggs, sage, biscuits, onion, pepper and beaten eggs; mix well. Add more broth, if needed for desired consistency. Pour into greased baking dish. Bake at 375 degrees for 1 hour. Melt butter. Add flour and 1/2 teaspoon salt; blend well. Add 2 cups chicken broth, giblets and remaining hard-boiled eggs; cook until thick, stirring constantly. Serve with chicken and dressing.

Hilda Harman
Smithville, Mississippi

PRIZEWINNING HOT CHICKEN SALAD

1/8 tsp. ginger
1/2 tsp. nutmeg
1/4 tsp. garlic powder
Pepper to taste
1/3 c. white cooking wine
3 tbsp. lemon juice
4 whole chicken breasts
9 hard-cooked eggs, chopped
1/2 c. chopped onion
1/4 tsp. basil
1/4 tsp. rosemary
3/4 c. slivered almonds
2 cans cream of celery soup
1 can cream of chicken soup
1 1/2 c. mayonnaise
1 1/3 c. finely crushed potato chips

Combine ginger, 1/4 teaspoon nutmeg, garlic powder, pepper, wine and lemon juice. Place chicken breasts in baking pan; pour wine mixture over top. Bake, covered, in preheated 325-degree oven until tender. Let chicken cool in pan juices. Remove chicken from bones; chop coarsely. Add eggs, onion, remaining nutmeg, basil, rosemary, almonds, soups, mayonnaise and 2/3 cup potato chips; place in baking dish. Sprinkle remaining potato chips on top. Bake in preheated 350-

degree oven for 30 to 35 minutes. May be served as hot dip by heating after mixing and omitting 2/3 cup potato chip crumbs.

Mrs. Linda Bailey
Powhatan, Virginia

BUTTERMILK-PECAN CHICKEN

1/2 c. margarine
1 c. buttermilk
1 egg, lightly beaten
1 c. flour
1 c. ground pecans
1 tbsp. paprika
1 tbsp. salt
Pepper to taste
1/4 c. sesame seed
2 broiler-fryer chickens, disjointed
1/4 c. pecan halves

Melt margarine in 13 x 9 x 2-inch baking dish. Blend buttermilk and egg in shallow dish. Combine flour, ground pecans, paprika, salt, pepper and sesame seed in separate dish. Dip chicken in buttermilk mixture; roll in flour mixture. Place chicken, skin side down, in melted margarine in baking dish, turning each piece to coat well. Place several pecan halves on each piece. Bake in preheated 350-degree oven for 1 hour and 15 minutes or until tender. Yield: 8 servings.

Mrs. Patsy Lenz
Windsor, Illinois

ROASTERS WITH PARSLEY RICE

1 box long grain wild rice
1/4 c. fresh chopped parsley
2 roaster chickens
Salt and pepper to taste

Cook rice according to package directions; stir in parsley. Stuff chickens lightly with rice; place in greased baking pan with small amount of water. Sprinkle with salt and pepper. Bake, covered, in preheated 350-degree oven for 1 hour. Uncover; bake for 30 minutes longer or until tender.

Photograph for this recipe on page 102.

CHICKEN BOMBAY

1/3 c. flour
1 tsp. paprika
1 tsp. salt
8 chicken pieces
1/4 c. butter
1 med. onion, sliced
4 chicken bouillon cubes
1 1/2 c. packaged precooked rice
1/2 c. white raisins
1/2 c. flaked coconut
1 sm. can mandarin oranges
1 tsp. curry powder
1/2 c. sliced almonds

Combine flour, paprika and 1/2 teaspoon salt; coat chicken well with flour mixture. Brown chicken in butter in large skillet over medium heat; remove chicken. Saute onion in remaining butter in skillet. Dissolve bouillon cubes in 1 1/2 cups boiling water. Stir rice, bouillon, raisins, coconut, oranges and curry powder into onion; blend well. Spoon mixture into 13 x 9 x 2-inch baking dish; arrange chicken over top. Bake in preheated 350-degree oven for 1 hour; sprinkle with almonds. Bake for 15 minutes longer.

Barsha Elzey
San Rafael, California

CHICKEN COUNTRY CAPTAIN

1   4-lb. chicken, disjointed
Seasoned flour
Shortening
2 med. onions, finely chopped
2 green peppers, finely chopped
1 clove of garlic, minced
1 tsp. salt
2 tsp. curry powder
2 No. 2 cans tomatoes
1 tsp. sugar
1 tsp. finely cut parsley
1/2 tsp. thyme
2 c. cooked rice
3 tbsp. currants or white raisins
1/2 lb. chopped toasted almonds

Dredge chicken with seasoned flour. Place enough shortening in frying pan to measure 1/2 inch deep. Fry chicken until golden brown. Remove from pan; place in Dutch oven. Drain all but 3 or 4 tablespoons fat from skillet; add onions, green peppers and garlic to skillet. Cook for about 5 minutes over low heat, stirring constantly. Add salt, curry powder, tomatoes, sugar, parsley and thyme. Pour over chicken. Add enough hot water to cover. Cover tightly. Bake in preheated 350-degree oven for about 45 minutes until chicken is tender. Place rice on large platter. Sprinkle with currants and almonds. Arrange chicken around edge of platter. Serve sauce with each serving.

Inez Wallace
Home Economics Education
Atlanta, Georgia

CHICKEN AND SPINACH ROLL

2   10-oz. packages frozen spinach
4 c. biscuit mix
1 c. grated sharp Cheddar cheese
2 eggs
1 c. milk
2 c. finely diced cooked chicken or ham
1 tbsp. Angostura aromatic bitters
4 slices bread, crumbled
1 egg, well beaten
1 tbsp. instant minced onion
Salt and pepper to taste

Cook spinach according to package directions. Drain; squeeze dry. Combine biscuit mix, cheese, eggs and milk; mix well. Knead several times on heavily floured board; shape into smooth ball. Roll out to 10 x 12-inch rectangle. Combine spinach and remaining ingredients; spread over dough. Roll as for jelly roll, starting at 10-inch side. Turn under ends; place in well-greased 9 x 5 x 3-inch loaf pan. Bake in preheated 375-degree oven for 1 hour or until well browned. Cover with foil during last part of baking time if top becomes too brown. Remove from pan; cut into 1-inch thick slices. Serve with tomato sauce or mushroom sauce, if desired.

Photograph for this recipe on page 101.

Recipes on pages 58, 100 and 131.
Recipes on pages 99, 106 and 108.

BEAN POT CHICKEN

4 chicken legs and thighs
2 whole chicken breasts
2 tbsp. minced onion
6 tbsp. butter or margarine
Juice of 1/2 lemon
1/2 can mushroom soup

Place chicken, onion, butter and lemon juice in electric bean pot or crock pot; cover. Cook on low heat for several hours or until tender. Strain liquid; combine with mushroom soup. Pour over chicken. Heat in pot and serve.

Grace F. Harrison
Connecticut Dept. of Education
Hartford, Connecticut

CHICKEN PROVENCALE

2   2-lb. broilers, disjointed
Salt and pepper to taste
1/3 c. olive oil
3/4 c. sauterne or dry white wine
1 clove of garlic, finely chopped
2 lg. onions, chopped
1/2 lb. sliced mushrooms
3 lg. tomatoes, peeled, seeded and diced
2 tbsp. chopped parsley

Season chicken on both sides with salt and pepper. Brown well in oil. Reduce heat; add 1/4 cup sauterne. Cover; cook for 12 minutes. Add garlic and onions. Brown lightly; add mushrooms and tomatoes. Turn chicken; distribute vegetables evenly. Cook, covered, until chicken is tender. Remove chicken to hot platter. Add remaining 1/2 cup sauterne to sauce in pan; blend well. Season with salt and pepper; add parsley. Pour over chicken. Serve with buttered rice, if desired. Yield: 4 servings.

Corinne Lipchitz
Dracut, Massachusetts

CHICKEN AND DUMPLINGS

1 c. flour
Salt
1/2 tsp. baking powder
1/8 tsp. soda
2 tbsp. shortening
1 egg, beaten
1/4 c. buttermilk
1   3-lb. chicken, disjointed
1 bay leaf
1 sm. carrot
1 stalk celery
Pepper to taste

Sift flour, 1/2 teaspoon salt, baking powder and soda together. Cut in shortening; add egg and buttermilk. Mix until well blended. Turn out on well-floured board; knead until smooth, adding more flour as needed. Roll out thin. Let stand for 2 to 3 hours to dry. Place chicken, bay leaf, carrot and celery in kettle; add water to cover. Season with salt and pepper. Cook, covered, for about 45 minutes or until chicken is tender. Remove chicken to platter; keep warm. Strain broth; return to kettle. Bring to a boil. Cut dough into strips about 1 inch wide and 3 to 4 inches long. Add strips to gently boiling broth, pushing down dumplings as strips are added. Cover; simmer for 20 minutes. May add 1/2 cup milk mixed with flour to thicken, if desired.

Alma Keys, Director
Home Economics Education
Little Rock, Arkansas

MABEL'S FRIED CHICKEN

1   4-lb. chicken
1/2 c. cornmeal
1/2 c. flour
1/2 tsp. salt
1/4 tsp. pepper
1/2 tsp. seasoned salt
2 eggs, well beaten

Cut chicken into serving pieces. Combine cornmeal, flour, salt, pepper and seasoned salt in shallow bowl; mix well. Dip chicken into eggs; coat with cornmeal mixture. Fry chicken in hot fat in skillet over medium heat until tender and golden brown.

Maria Campo
Glenrock, Wyoming

Recipes on page 185.

Recipe on page 54.

CHICKENBURGERS

2 c. minced cooked chicken
1/4 c. chopped almonds
1/2 tsp. grated onion
1/4 c. dry bread crumbs
2 tsp. chopped parsley
1 tsp. lemon juice
1/4 c. milk
Salt and pepper to taste
2 to 4 tbsp. melted butter
8 hamburger bun halves, toasted

Combine all ingredients except butter and buns; mix well. Shape into 8 patties. Place on broiler tray; brush with melted butter. Broil on both sides until browned. Serve on toasted buns. Yield: 8 servings.

Mrs. Raymond Brown
Pensacola, Florida

POOR RICHARD'S RAREBIT SANDWICH

2 tbsp. butter
2 tbsp. flour
1 c. milk
2 c. shredded American cheese
1/2 tsp. mustard
1 tsp. Worcestershire sauce
Salt to taste
6 slices crisp toast
Sliced cooked chicken
Paprika

Melt butter in saucepan over low heat; blend in flour. Add milk, stirring constantly. Cook, stirring, until sauce is smooth and thickened. Add cheese, mustard, Worcestershire sauce and salt. Stir over low heat only until cheese is melted. Arrange toast in shallow baking pan; top with chicken slices. Cover with cheese sauce; sprinkle lightly with paprika. Broil until lightly browned. Yield: 6 servings.

Mrs. Susan Haigler
Fort Deposit, Alabama

APRICOT-STUFFED CORNISH HENS

4 Cornish hens with giblets
Flour

Salt and pepper to taste
1/2 c. butter
1 c. rice
14 dried apricot halves, chopped
4 tsp. minced onion
4 tsp. minced parsley

Simmer giblets in 4 cups water until tender. Combine 1/2 cup flour with salt and pepper; coat hens with flour mixture. Brown hens on all sides in butter in Dutch oven. Remove from skillet; cool slightly. Combine rice, apricots, onion and parsley; mix well. Stuff hens with rice mixture; truss securely. Return hens to Dutch oven; add giblet broth. Season with 1 teaspoon salt and additional pepper to taste. Cook, covered, over medium heat for 1 hour. Remove hens to warm platter. Thicken pan juices for gravy, if desired.

Kathryn Frazior
Port Neches, Texas

CORNISH HENS WITH ORANGE-RICE STUFFING

1 lg. can mandarin oranges
1 c. rice
1 tsp. curry powder
1 tbsp. chopped parsley
1 c. melted butter
4 Cornish hens
1/2 c. white wine

Drain oranges; reserve juice. Cook rice according to package directions, using reserved juice as part of the water. Stir in curry powder, parsley, 1/2 cup butter and oranges. Stuff hens lightly with rice mixture; secure openings with skewers. Place hens on broiler pan. Combine remaining butter and wine; brush hens generously with butter mixture. Bake in preheated 350-degree oven for 1 hour to 1 hour and 15 minutes, basting frequently with butter mixture.

Photograph for this recipe on page 102.

BURGUNDY ROCK CORNISH HENS

1 stalk celery, chopped
1/4 green pepper, chopped
1/4 onion, chopped

6 tbsp. butter
1 c. cooked rice
1/4 tsp. salt
1/4 tsp. pepper
1/2 tsp. poultry seasoning
2 Rock Cornish hens
1/4 c. Burgundy

Saute celery, green pepper and onion in 2 tablespoons butter. Stir in rice and seasonings. Stuff hens with mixture. Place hens in baking pan. Combine Burgundy and remaining 4 tablespoons butter. Bake in preheated 350-degree oven for 1 hour and 30 minutes, basting with Burgundy mixture every 30 minutes during baking time. Yield: 4 servings.

Helena T. Martines
Los Angeles, California

CORNISH HENS IN ORANGE AND HONEY SAUCE

1 pkg. wild rice
2 Cornish hens
Salt to taste
Butter or margarine
4 slices bacon, halved
1/2 c. honey
1/2 c. concentrated orange juice
1 tbsp. lemon juice

Cook rice according to package directions. Sprinkle hens inside and out with salt. Stuff hens with rice; truss securely. Rub hens with butter. Place bacon in glass baking dish; arrange hens over bacon. Bake in preheated 350-degree oven for 1 hour. Combine honey, orange juice and lemon juice. Baste hens with half the orange sauce; bake for 5 minutes longer. Turn hens; baste again. Bake for 15 minutes longer; add remaining sauce. Bake for 15 minutes longer. Remove hens and bacon; arrange on warm platter. Drain off excess fat from sauce; serve over hens.

Beverly Schneider
Kew Gardens, New York

RICE-STUFFED CORNISH HENS

1/2 c. butter
1 lb. fresh mushrooms, sliced

1/2 c. chopped onions
1/2 c. minced parsley
1 c. chopped celery
3 c. cooked brown rice
Salt and pepper
4 Cornish hens

Melt butter in heavy skillet; add mushrooms. Cook mushrooms for 5 minutes; remove from skillet with slotted spoon. Stir onions, parsley and celery into remaining butter in skillet. Cook, stirring frequently, until onions are golden. Stir in rice, mushrooms, 1 teaspoon salt and 1/8 teaspoon pepper. Mix thoroughly; remove from heat. Stuff hens with rice mixture; truss. Rub outside of hens with additional salt and pepper. Arrange hens in shallow roasting pan. Bake in preheated 325-degree oven for 1 hour and 30 minutes or until tender, basting occasionally with pan drippings.

Mrs. Marlene Figone
Manteca, California

LONG ISLAND DUCKLING WITH CHERRIES

2 young Long Island ducklings
Salt
1/4 c. kirsch
1 1/2 c. brown sauce
1 c. sour cherries
Pepper

Rub ducks inside and out with salt; place on rack in shallow pan. Bake in preheated 350-degree oven for 12 to 13 minutes per pound. Duck is done when leg joints move easily. Temperature may be increased to 500 degrees last 15 minutes of baking for crisper duck, if desired. Remove ducks to hot platter. Skim off all excess fat from pan. Add kirsch to pan; scrape up particles in bottom. Add to brown sauce in small saucepan; bring to a boil. Reduce heat; simmer for 2 to 3 minutes. Add cherries; bring to boiling point. Add salt and pepper to taste, if needed; pour around duck. Canned brown gravy may be substituted for brown sauce. Yield: 4-6 servings.

Mrs. Mary V. Watson
Kingsport, Tennessee

STUFFED DUCK WITH ORANGE SAUCE

1 duckling
Salt
Pepper
Paprika
1/4 lb. wild rice
2/3 c. brown rice
1 c. diced celery
1/3 c. sliced green onions
5 tbsp. butter
3 tbsp. parsley flakes
1 c. sugar
2 tbsp. cornstarch
1 tbsp. flour
1 1/4 c. orange juice
1/4 c. lemon juice
1 tsp. grated orange and lemon rind

Rinse duckling in water; rub inside and out with salt, pepper and paprika. Score skin at 1-inch intervals with sharp knife. Cook rices according to package directions; mix. Saute celery and onions in 4 tablespoons butter until tender; add to rice. Add parsley, 1/8 teaspoon paprika and 1/4 teaspoon salt; toss lightly. Place in cavity of duckling; place duckling in 9 x 13-inch shallow pan. Bake, uncovered, in preheated 325-degree oven for 3 hours to 3 hours and 30 minutes or until brown and crisp. Mix sugar, 1/4 teaspoon salt, cornstarch and flour in saucepan; stir in orange juice, lemon juice and 1/2 cup water. Boil for 3 minutes. Add remaining 1 tablespoon butter and grated rinds; mix well. Serve with duck. Yield: 4 servings.

Mrs. Jean Mason
Seibert, Colorado

GOOSE STUFFED WITH SAUERKRAUT

1 goose
1/2 lb. bacon, diced
2 lg. cans sauerkraut
3 apples, grated
Salt and pepper to taste

Place goose in baking pan. Bake in preheated 400-degree oven for 20 minutes. Reduce oven temperature to 300 degrees. Fry bacon in skillet until crisp. Remove bacon; drain. Pour off all drippings except 1/4 cup; add sauerkraut and apples to skillet. Cook for 10 minutes. Add bacon; toss. Season goose with salt and pepper; stuff cavity with half the sauerkraut mixture. Cover. Bake until goose is tender and legs move easily. Place goose on platter. Reheat remaining sauerkraut mixture; arrange around goose.

Photograph for this recipe on page 102.

BAKING A TURKEY

1 12 to 16-lb. frozen turkey
Salt
Monosodium glutamate
Soft shortening

Leave turkey in original wrap. Place on tray; place in refrigerator until thawed. Remove wrap; rinse turkey with cold water. Drain; pat dry. Rub skin and cavity lightly with salt and monosodium glutamate. Fold wings akimbo; bring wing tips onto back. Push drumsticks under band of skin at tail or tie with soft string. Line shallow roasting pan with foil; place turkey on rack in foil-lined pan. Brush entire turkey with shortening. Tear off sheet of heavy-duty foil 5 to 10 inches longer than turkey; crease lengthwise through center. Place over turkey; press foil gently at drumsticks to anchor. Bake turkey in preheated 350-degree oven for 4 hours to 4 hours and 45 minutes or until tender. Giblet gravy may be prepared and served with turkey.

Mrs. Dorothy Sue T. Hill
Oberlin, Louisiana

OVEN-SMOKED TURKEY

1 10 to 12-lb. turkey
1/4 c. salad oil
1/2 c. salt
2 tbsp. liquid smoke
1 c. vinegar
1/4 c. pepper
2 tsp. finely chopped parsley

Rinse turkey; pat dry with paper towels. Make a paste of salad oil and salt; rub 1/4 cup of the mixture on inside and neck cavity of turkey. Truss turkey; brush with additional oil. Place on rack in roaster, breast side up. Bake in preheated 350-degree oven for 1 hour. Combine remaining salt paste, liquid smoke, vinegar, pepper and parsley; baste turkey with vinegar mixture. Bake for 3 hours and 30 minutes longer or until turkey is tender, basting with vinegar mixture every 30 minutes. Let turkey stand for at least 15 minutes before carving.

Mrs. Ruth H. Burch
Tulsa, Oklahoma

SOUTHERN TURKEY AND DRESSING

12 slices day-old bread, toasted
1 recipe baked corn bread
3 c. chopped celery
3 c. chopped onions
1 c. turkey fat or butter
1/2 tsp. sage
Salt and pepper to taste
1 can mushroom soup
2 c. turkey broth
1 doz. hard-boiled eggs, chopped
1   14 to 16-lb. turkey, baked

Break toast into small pieces; crumble corn bread. Cook celery and onions in turkey fat until transparent. Add toast and corn bread; stir in sage, salt, pepper, mushroom soup, turkey broth and eggs; mix thoroughly. Place in baking pan. Bake in preheated 350-degree oven for about 30 minutes or until brown. Serve with sliced turkey and gravy. Yield: 20-25 servings.

Alma Keys
Director, Home Economics Education
Little Rock, Arkansas

SWEET AND SOUR TURKEY

1   1-lb. 4-oz. can pineapple chunks
1 chicken bouillon cube
1/4 c. vinegar
1/4 tsp. prepared mustard
1 tbsp. soy sauce
1/2 tsp. salt
1/4 c. (packed) brown sugar
2 tbsp. cornstarch

2 to 3 c. diced cooked turkey, heated
Chow mein noodles
3/4 c. green pepper strips
1/4 c. thinly sliced onion

Drain pineapple; reserve syrup. Combine bouillon cube, vinegar, mustard, soy sauce and salt in saucepan; cook until bouillon cube is dissolved. Combine brown sugar, cornstarch and 1/2 cup reserved pineapple syrup; stir into hot liquid. Cook, stirring constantly, until thick and clear; pour over hot turkey. Serve over chow mein noodles; top with pineapple chunks, green pepper strips and onion slices. May serve over rice, if desired.

Jill R. Olsen
Arlington Heights, Illinois

TURKEY STRATA SUPREME

5 slices buttered bread
2 1/2 c. diced cooked turkey
1 c. grated Cheddar cheese
3 eggs
2 c. milk
1/2 tsp. salt
1/4 tsp. pepper
1 can cream of chicken soup
1/2 can cream of mushroom soup
1/2 c. water
1/2 tsp. curry powder
1 c. canned mushroom stems and pieces

Remove crusts from bread; cut bread into 1-inch squares. Place layer in 8 x 8 x 2-inch oiled casserole or baking dish. Add layer of turkey, then layer of cheese. Repeat layers 3 times. Beat eggs slightly. Add milk, salt and pepper; blend well. Pour over cheese layer. Cover; let stand in refrigerator overnight. Remove from refrigerator; bring to room temperature. Bake in preheated 325-degree oven for 1 hour. Combine soups in saucepan; add water gradually. Add curry powder; stir until smooth. Stir in mushrooms; cook over low heat, stirring frequently, until heated through. Serve over strata. Cooked chicken, pheasant or capon may be substituted for turkey.

Mrs. EulaLee Coumbe
Minneapolis, Minnesota

TURKEY SUPREME

1 1-lb. 13-oz. can pineapple chunks
3 c. light cream
1 c. shredded coconut
1/2 c. butter
1/2 c. flour
2 tsp. salt
1/4 tsp. pepper
1/2 c. chopped cashew nuts
3 c. diced cooked turkey
2 tbsp. brandy
1 recipe hollandaise sauce

Drain pineapple; reserve 1 1/2 cups juice. Combine reserved juice, cream and coconut in saucepan. Heat to scalding. Melt butter in large skillet. Stir in flour, salt and pepper; cook for 1 minute. Add scalded cream mixture gradually; cook, stirring, until thickened. Add cashew nuts, turkey, pineapple and brandy. Spoon into 9 x 15-inch casserole; pour hollandaise sauce over top. Broil until brown; serve at once. Yield: 8-10 servings.

Mrs. Donna N. Ray
Vancouver, Washington

PECAN-STUFFED PHEASANT

1/2 c. butter
1 1/3 c. dry bread crumbs
2/3 c. broken pecans
2 pheasant
2 tbsp. flour
3/4 tsp. salt
1/4 tsp. pepper
1/3 c. sherry

Melt half the butter; pour over bread crumbs. Add pecans; toss lightly. Stuff pheasant and truss. Combine flour, salt and pepper; sprinkle lightly over pheasant. Melt remaining butter in a heavy skillet. Brown pheasant; transfer to roasting pan. Add 1 1/2 cups hot water and sherry to browned butter, scraping up brown bits; pour over pheasant. Bake, covered, in preheated 350-degree oven for 1 hour, basting every 15 minutes with pan juices. Remove cover; bake for 20 minutes longer or until crisp. Thicken pan

drippings for gravy, if desired. Yield: 6 servings.

Mrs. Gertrude Collins
Sycamore, Illinois

PHEASANT MUSCATEL

3 1 1/2-lb. pheasant, halved
1/2 lemon
Salt and pepper to taste
1/3 c. butter
3 oranges
1 c. white raisins
1 tsp. grated lemon peel
1/3 c. muscatel
1 c. chicken broth

Rinse pheasant with warm water; drain well. Rub surfaces with lemon; season with salt and pepper. Place in baking dish, breast side up; spread with butter. Squeeze juice from oranges and reserve shells. Add orange juice, raisins, lemon peel, muscatel and chicken broth to baking dish. Bake in preheated 350-degree oven for 45 minutes, basting every 10 minutes. Chicken may be substituted for pheasant. Yield: 6 servings.

Nutted Rice In Fluted Orange Cups

2 c. chicken broth
1 c. rice
2 tbsp. butter
2/3 c. chopped pecans
2 tbsp. minced parsley
Salt to taste

Combine chicken broth and rice in saucepan; bring to a boil. Stir and cook, covered, over low heat for 14 minutes. Remove from heat. Stir in butter, pecans and parsley; season with salt. Flute reserved orange shells; spoon rice into shells. Serve with Pheasant Muscatel.

Margaret Bruce
Larkspur, California

SPIT-ROASTED PHEASANT

2 2-lb. pheasant
Salt and pepper to taste

Cashew Stuffing
8 slices bacon

Rinse pheasant; drain and pat dry. Sprinkle cavity with salt and pepper. Stuff pheasant with Cashew Stuffing; close opening with skewers or with needle and cord. Wrap bacon around each pheasant in 3 places, over wings, over upper leg and thigh and over lower leg. Place one strip of bacon lengthwise over breast bone of each pheasant. Tie each strip of bacon in place with cord. Thread one spit prong or fork onto spit so that points are away from handle. Insert spit in one pheasant just below breast and bring out above tail. Repeat with second pheasant; center pheasant on spit. Thread second prong onto spit. Push prongs into pheasant; fasten securely. Arrange coals in back half of barbecue. Place a drip pan, about 4 inches longer than pheasant, in front half of barbecue. Shape pan from foil, if desired. Attach spit to motor when coals have reached medium temperature. Grill pheasant for about 1 hour and 15 minutes or until pheasant are browned and leg meat seems tender when pressed with fingers. Remove pheasant from spit; serve immediately.

Cashew Stuffing

1 c. coarsely chopped cashew nuts
1 c. chicken broth
4 slices bacon, diced
1 tsp. butter
1/4 tsp. salt
Dash of pepper
1/4 tsp. sage
1/4 tsp. poultry seasoning

Simmer cashews in chicken broth, uncovered, until cashews are tender and all the liquid is absorbed. Fry bacon until crisp. Add bacon and remaining ingredients to cashews; mix well.

Photograph for this recipe on page 302.

TEXAS PANHANDLE QUAIL

1 c. flour
Salt

1/2 tsp. garlic powder
1 tsp. lemon pepper
1 tsp. paprika
2 quail per person
1/2 c. butter
1 c. dry white wine
1 tbsp. minced parsley
1 tbsp. fines herbes
1 tsp. dillweed
1/4 tsp. curry powder
Pepper to taste
2 tbsp. cognac
1 c. sour cream

Combine flour, 2 teaspoons salt, garlic powder, lemon pepper and paprika; coat quail with flour mixture. Brown in butter in skillet. Combine wine, parsley, fines herbes, dillweed, curry, salt and pepper to taste. Pour over browned quail. Cover; simmer for 20 to 25 minutes, spooning sauce over quail occasionally. Do not overcook. Remove quail; keep warm. Stir cognac and sour cream into pan drippings; blend and heat through. More wine may be added if sauce cooks down too much. Pour part of sauce over quail and serve remaining in gravy boat.

Rebecca F. Hutchison
Snyder, Texas

SHERRIED DOVE

14 to 16 dove
Salt and pepper to taste
Flour
1/2 c. salad oil
1/2 c. chopped green onions
1 1/2 c. water
1 c. sherry
1/4 c. chopped parsley

Season dove with salt and pepper. Dredge with flour. Place in oil in heavy roaster. Bake in preheated 400-degree oven until brown. Add onions, water and sherry; cover. Bake until tender, basting occasionally with pan juices. Add parsley to gravy just before serving. Yield: 6-8 servings.

Mrs. Ouida Hicks
Montgomery, Alabama

Vegetable Favorites

Known throughout the world as "the land of plenty," America has never been surpassed in its production of food. Vegetables, which grew abundantly in the New World, are one of the best examples of the bounty that is characteristic of this great nation.

In 1607 when the first colonists began exploring the unfamiliar countryside, they were amazed at the richness of the soil. One of the first settlers wrote that the new land was "nature's nurse to all vegetables," for both plants from the Caribbean and seeds planted in English gardens flourished here. Primarily, the Pilgrims' three vegetable crops were corn, beans and squash. Because they knew little about planting and harvesting, they depended upon the limited skills of an Indian called Squanto, and others from around the New England village. Even though the Indians' methods of planting corn, beans, pumpkins and squash, so that the vines and stalks came up together, was primitive, it worked. While the crops that were English in origin, such as wheat and peas, failed, the Indian plants thrived and produced an abundance of vegetables. Thankful for the many blessings of that first harvest season, the Pilgrims declared a holiday which has evolved into the Thanksgiving we celebrate today.

Working together, the Pilgrims and Indians gradually devised different ways to prepare the vegetables they grew. Although all were relatively simple methods, the variety of boiled, roasted and dried foods kept meals as interesting as possible. One of the most well-known dishes resulting from this period in history was succotash, a mixture of corn, beans and other foods, often including meat and potatoes. Plymouth Succotash is still the favorite dish on December 21, the day the Mayflower landed! Boston Baked Beans was another dish that immediately became popular. It was this dish, a culinary delight, that played such an important role in the religious observance of Puritan Sabbath. Believing strictly that the Sabbath was to be a day of rest, the Puritans would absolutely not allow any work to be done from sundown Saturday to sundown Sunday. In order to keep their families fed during this time, the women prepared large kettles of enough baked beans to last three meals. Although this practice ended in the 1800's, the popularity as well as variety of baked beans has continued to rise.

Squash was as much an important part of our forefathers' diets as corn and beans. Although it is not clear whether the first settlers had seen squash before reaching this great land, we do know that the Indians had been enjoying a variety of squash known as acorn squash long before the Pilgrims arrived. Not satisfied with the Indians' boiled squash, the New Englanders began baking this vegetable. This produced quite an excellent flavor which is still enjoyed today.

As times have changed, so have the methods of farming. Due to mechanization and experimentation, thousands of acres of the largest, highest grade and above all, tastiest vegetables ever known to man are grown throughout the country. However, even today, different regions of the country are noted for particular vegetables that are suited more to their climate than any other. For example, Alaska is known for its cabbage, Washington for mushrooms and Louisiana for its sweet potatoes. A good way to tell what the people in a certain area enjoy is by stopping at a roadside vegetable stand. Usually the favorites are stocked in quantities and can be purchased at a lower price than some of the others on hand. Whereas greens, okra and black-eyed peas can be found in the South, green beans and onions are abundant in the Northwest.

Yet, of all the vegetables grown in the United States, including asparagus, carrots, cauliflower, potatoes, spinach, tomatoes and cucumbers, corn remains the most important in our cuisine. One reason must be its versatility. In 1862 the Nebraska Farmer gave 33 methods of cooking fresh and dried corn. Since that time, the list of ways to prepare it and other uses for corn has become even longer.

While agriculture has become big business, today's farmer still knows and feels the pride that our ancestors felt as they looked at their fields of thriving vegetables. In fact, people all across this nation are beginning to understand just how rewarding the life of a farmer really is. Recently, small backyard vegetable gardens have become quite a familiar sight in neighborhoods everywhere. People want the freshest vegetables they can get at the lowest possible cost. Thus, this renewed interest in family gardening has resulted.

Long ago people realized that the fresher vegetables are, the better they are. For this reason, one of the first morning tasks was picking the vegetables to be cooked that same day. More and more people have come to realize the goodness of ripe, juicy vegetables cooked and served straight from the garden. A man who really appreciated fresh vegetables was Thomas Jefferson. According to history, he had 30 different varieties of garden peas plus numerous other types of vegetables growing behind his Monticello home in Virginia.

For those who enjoy the taste of garden-fresh vegetables but are unable to plant a garden, canned and frozen vegetables are the answer. Most of these can be boiled, baked, steamed and fried in many of the same, flavorful ways as fresh vegetables.

Whether they are cooked with meats, in casseroles or alone, vegetables of all kinds bring something special to a meal. Bright in color, rich in vitamins and minerals and low in cost and calories, they are foods which add needed texture to our diets. And, contrary to early beliefs, vegetables take only a minimum amount of cooking time. These are just a few of the reasons why Home Economics Teachers want to share their favorite vegetable recipes with you. Make mealtime special this bicentennial year by surprising your family with tasty, new vegetable dishes they'll surely love.

GARDEN PATCH DINNER DISH

1 10-oz. package frozen whole okra pods
1 10-oz. package frozen yellow or crookneck squash
1 c. frozen cut green beans
1 lg. onion, coarsely chopped
1 green pepper, coarsely chopped
2 tbsp. butter or margarine
1 lg. ripe tomato, chopped
1/2 c. heavy cream
Salt and pepper to taste
Dash of Tabasco sauce
Noodle Ring

Cook frozen vegetables according to package directions or until tender but crisp. Drain well. Saute onion and green pepper in hot butter until clear but not brown. Stir in tomato, cooked vegetables and cream; season with salt, pepper and Tabasco sauce. Simmer over low heat for several minutes or until heated through. Spoon vegetables into prepared Noodle Ring.

Noodle Ring

1 8-oz. package noodles
2 tbsp. butter or margarine
Salt and paprika to taste
1 c. creamy cottage cheese

Cook noodles according to package directions; drain well. Return to saucepan; toss with butter, salt and paprika. Add cottage cheese; toss until well mixed. Spoon mixture into oiled 6-cup ring mold. Place mold in shallow pan; add hot water to pan to come about halfway up side of mold. Bake in preheated 350-degree oven for 25 minutes. Unmold on platter for serving.

Photograph for this recipe on page 112.

HOW TO COOK ARTICHOKES

4 lg. artichokes
1/4 c. salad oil or olive oil
2 tbsp. lemon juice
2 sm. bay leaves
1 clove of garlic, split
1 tsp. salt
Dash of pepper

Trim stalks from artichokes; cut a 1-inch slice from tops. Remove discolored leaves; snip off spike ends of leaves. Wash artichokes in cold water; drain well. Tie each artichoke with twine to hold leaves in place. Combine 6 quarts water, salad oil, lemon juice, bay leaves, garlic, salt and pepper; bring to a boil. Place artichokes in boiling water; reduce heat. Simmer, covered, for 30 minutes or until tender. Drain well; remove twine. Serve with mayonnaise, tartar sauce or lemon butter. Yield: 4 servings.

Mrs. Helen Penny Hill
Turnersville, Texas

ASPARAGUS BEARNAISE

2 pkg. frozen asparagus
1 1/2 tsp. monosodium glutamate
3 egg yolks
2 tbsp. lemon juice
1/4 tsp. minced onion
1/4 tsp. minced parsley
1/2 tsp. dried tarragon
Dash of cayenne pepper
1/2 c. butter

Prepare asparagus according to package directions; season with monosodium glutamate. Combine egg yolks, lemon juice, onion, parsley, tarragon and cayenne pepper. Melt butter; blend into egg yolk mixture, stirring constantly. Pour over hot asparagus; serve immediately. Yield: 8 servings.

Mrs. Ruth B. Marsh
Millersville, Pennsylvania

MATTIE'S ASPARAGUS CASSEROLE

3 c. cooked asparagus
2 tbsp. flour
1/4 c. melted fat
2 c. milk
1/2 c. grated American cheese
1/4 tsp. salt
1/2 tsp. pepper
3/4 c. dry bread crumbs
2 tbsp. butter
1/3 c. chopped blanched almonds

Place asparagus in casserole. Blend flour into fat; add milk, gradually. Cook, stirring constantly, until thickened. Add cheese, salt and pepper; pour over asparagus. Sprinkle with bread crumbs; dot with butter. Top with almonds. Bake at 350 degrees for 30 minutes. Yield: 8 servings.

Mattie Mary Green
McLain, Mississippi

GREEN BEANS WITH MIXED HERB BUTTER

1 lb. green beans
1/4 c. butter or margarine
3/4 c. minced onions
1 clove of garlic, minced
1/4 c. minced celery
2 tbsp. sesame seed
1/4 tsp. rosemary
1/4 tsp. dried basil
3/4 tsp. salt
1/4 c. snipped parsley

Wash and trim beans; cut diagonally. Cook, covered, in 1/2 inch boiling, salted water for 15 minutes or until tender; drain. Melt butter in saucepan; add onions, garlic, celery and sesame seed. Saute for 5 minutes. Add remaining ingredients; simmer, covered, for 10 minutes. Toss with beans to serve. Yield: 4 servings.

Jo Anna Littrel
Columbus Junction, Iowa

HOT MARINATED BEANS

1 No. 303 can French-cut green beans
1 No. 303 can bean sprouts
1/2 c. cooking oil
1 clove of garlic
1/2 c. sugar
1/2 c. vinegar

Drain beans and bean sprouts; add oil, garlic, sugar and vinegar. Let stand for 3 hours. Heat through but do not boil. Remove garlic when ready to serve. Yield: 6 servings.

Kemper R. Russell
Logansport, Louisiana

GREEN BEANS WITH GOLDEN MUSHROOM SAUCE

1/4 c. sliced green onion
2 tbsp. butter or margarine
1 can Campbell's golden mushroom soup
1/4 c. water
1/2 c. chopped canned tomatoes
1 tsp. Worcestershire sauce
2 9-oz. packages frozen green beans, cooked and drained

Cook onion in butter in saucepan until tender. Add remaining ingredients; heat thoroughly, stirring occasionally. Yield: 6 servings.

Photograph for this recipe below.

GREEN BEANS WITH BACON

2 slices bacon, chopped
1/3 c. chopped onion
2 1/2 tbsp. chopped green pepper
1 1/3 c. cooked or canned green beans
1/3 c. bean stock
1/4 tsp. salt

Brown bacon lightly. Add onion and green pepper; cook for 1 to 2 minutes or until onion is golden. Remove from heat. Add beans, bean stock and salt; simmer until most of the liquid has evaporated. Serve hot. Yield: 4 servings.

Mrs. Mamie Tays
Hazlehurst, Mississippi

CREAMY GREEN LIMA BEANS

2 c. green lima beans
3/4 c. water
1 tsp. salt
1 tbsp. butter
1/2 tsp. sugar (opt.)
1/3 c. heavy cream

Combine all ingredients except cream in saucepan. Cook until beans are tender and only a small amount of liquid remains. Add cream; simmer for 5 minutes. Serve hot. Yield: 6-8 servings.

Mrs. Sarah Perry
North Webster, Indiana

BEETS WITH ORANGE SAUCE

1/3 c. sugar
2 tbsp. cornstarch
1/8 tsp. salt
1 c. orange juice
1 tbsp. butter
3 c. cooked diced beets

Combine dry ingredients in top of double boiler. Add orange juice and butter; cook, stirring constantly, for 5 minutes. Add beets; let stand for several hours. Heat through before serving. Yield: 6-8 servings.

Mrs. Shirley Kimmich
Ontario, California

HARVARD BEETS

2 tbsp. cornstarch
1 tbsp. sugar
1/4 tsp. salt
1/4 tsp. cloves (opt.)
1/2 c. mild vinegar
1/2 c. beet juice
2 c. cubed cooked beets

Combine cornstarch, sugar, salt and cloves in saucepan. Mix vinegar with beet juice; add to dry ingredients slowly, stirring constantly to prevent lumping. Cook until thickened, stirring constantly. Add beets; heat through. Yield: 4-6 servings.

Zada V. Lines
Eloy, Arizona

BROCCOLI WITH HERB BUTTER

3 lb. broccoli, cooked
1/2 c. butter
1/4 c. lemon juice
1 clove of garlic, minced
1/4 tsp. oregano
1/4 tsp. salt
Pepper to taste

Drain hot broccoli. Heat remaining ingredients; pour over broccoli. Serve immediately. Yield: 6 servings.

Mrs. Reba Rehberg
Panama City, Florida

BROCCOLI WITH ALMONDS

2 10-oz. packages frozen broccoli, cooked
1/2 c. mayonnaise
1 tbsp. lemon juice
1/2 c. sharp Cheddar cheese
1 c. cream of mushroom soup
1 c. crushed cheese crackers
1 sm. can pimento, chopped
1/4 c. slivered almonds

Place broccoli in buttered casserole. Combine mayonnaise, lemon juice, cheese and soup; pour over broccoli. Top with cracker crumbs, pimento and almonds. Bake in pre-heated 350-degree oven for 20 minutes or until heated through and bubbly. Yield: 4-6 servings.

Mrs. Mary K. Adams
New Troy, Michigan

BRUSSELS SPROUTS IN CELERY SAUCE

2 qt. Brussels sprouts
1 1/8 tsp. salt
2 1/4 c. boiling water
1 1/2 c. diced celery
6 tbsp. butter
6 tbsp. flour
Milk
Dash of pepper

Cook Brussels sprouts until tender; drain well. Add salt to water; stir in celery. Cook for 15 minutes; drain well, reserving celery liquid. Melt butter; blend in flour. Combine celery liquid with enough milk to measure 3 cups liquid; stir into flour mixture. Cook until smooth and thick, stirring constantly. Add celery and pepper; pour over Brussels sprouts. Yield: 8 servings.

Mrs. Margaret Cepelka
Berryville, Virginia

SCALLOPED BROCCOLI

1 lg. bunch broccoli, trimmed
1/4 c. minced onion
1/4 c. melted butter
1/4 c. flour
1 tsp. salt
2 c. milk
1 1/2 c. grated Cheddar cheese
1/2 c. buttered bread crumbs

Cook broccoli until almost tender; drain. Saute onion in butter until tender; blend in flour and salt. Add milk; cook until thickened, stirring constantly. Remove from heat; stir in cheese until melted. Place alternate layers of broccoli and cheese sauce in greased 1-quart casserole; top with crumbs. Bake in preheated 350-degree oven for 20

minutes or until heated through and bubbly. Yield: 6 servings.

Kathleen Burchett
Jonesville, Virginia

COMPANY CABBAGE

5 c. finely shredded cabbage
1 c. finely shredded carrots
1/2 c. chopped green onions and tops
1/2 tsp. salt
1/8 tsp. pepper
1 beef bouillon cube
1/4 c. hot water
1/4 c. butter
1 tsp. prepared mustard
1/3 c. chopped pecans
1/4 tsp. paprika

Combine cabbage, carrots, green onions, salt and pepper in large heavy saucepan. Dissolve bouillon cube in hot water; add to vegetables in saucepan. Toss with fork to blend thoroughly. Cover tightly; cook over low heat for 5 minutes, stirring and turning once during cooking. Drain; turn into warm dish. Melt butter in small saucepan over low heat; stir in mustard and pecans. Heat thoroughly. Pour over vegetables; sprinkle with paprika. Serve immediately. Yield: 6 servings.

Mrs. Jean C. Vandergrift
Roanoke, Virginia

CAULIFLOWER A LA ROMAGNOLA

1 cauliflower, cooked and cooled
2/3 c. fine dry bread crumbs
1 tsp. grated Parmesan cheese
1/2 tsp. salt
1/4 tsp. pepper
2 eggs, beaten
1/4 c. milk

Separate cauliflower into flowerets. Combine bread crumbs, cheese, salt and pepper. Mix eggs and milk together. Dip flowerets into egg mixture; roll in crumb mixture. Fry in deep fat at 365 degrees for 2 to 4 minutes or until golden brown, turning occasionally. Drain on absorbent paper. Yield: 4 servings.

Mrs. Catherine R. Trotter
Independence, Louisiana

CHEESE-FROSTED CAULIFLOWER

1 med. cauliflower
Salt to taste
1/2 c. mayonnaise
2 tsp. prepared mustard
3/4 c. shredded process sharp cheese

Remove leaves and trim base from cauliflower. Cook whole cauliflower in boiling, salted water for 12 to 15 minutes; drain. Place cauliflower in shallow baking pan; sprinkle with salt. Combine mayonnaise and mustard; spread over cauliflower. Top with cheese. Bake in preheated 375-degree oven for 10 minutes or until cheese is melted and bubbly. Yield: 4-5 servings.

Mrs. Janice Feil
Gibbon, Minnesota

CARROT CIRCLES AND PINEAPPLE

1/2 c. pineapple juice
1/2 c. carrot stock
1 tbsp. cornstarch
1/2 tsp. salt
1/8 tsp. pepper
1 tbsp. butter
2 c. sliced cooked carrots
1/2 c. drained pineapple chunks

Combine first 3 ingredients in saucepan; bring to a boil. Cook until thickened, stirring constantly. Add remaining ingredients; heat through. Yield: 4-6 servings.

Mrs. Gloria Melby
St. Cloud, Minnesota

GLAZED WHOLE CARROTS

8 sm. carrots
3 tbsp. butter or margarine
1/4 c. sugar
1 tbsp. chopped parsley

Cook carrots in boiling salted water until tender; drain. Melt butter in frying pan; stir in sugar. Add carrots; cook over moderate heat, turning several times, until well glazed. Garnish with parsley. Yield: 4 servings.

Mrs. Wanda Newlin
Atwood, Illinois

DELICIOUS CELERY BAKE

4 c. chopped celery
1/4 c. chopped pimento
1 can water chestnuts, sliced
1 can cream of chicken soup
1/4 c. slivered almonds
Buttered bread crumbs

Cook celery in salted water for 8 minutes; drain well. Combine celery and remaining ingredients except bread crumbs; place into casserole. Sprinkle with buttered bread crumbs. Bake in preheated 375-degree oven for 35 minutes or until bubbly. Yield: 6 servings.

Mrs. Ken Arnsdorf
Springfield, Minnesota

FESTIVE CORN BAKE

1 No. 2 can cream-style corn
2 eggs, beaten
3/4 c. cracker crumbs
1/2 c. milk
1/4 c. thinly sliced water chestnuts
1/4 c. chopped green pepper
1/4 c. sliced mushrooms
1/4 c. finely diced onion
2 tbsp. chopped pimento
1 tsp. salt
1/2 tsp. pepper
2 tbsp. melted butter

Combine all ingredients; mix thoroughly. Turn into greased casserole. Bake in preheated 350-degree oven for 45 minutes or until done. Yield: 6 servings.

Joan F. Klingbeil
Cumberland, Wisconsin

MOCK OYSTERS

3 eggs, separated
2 c. cooked fresh corn, drained

2 tbsp. milk
1 tsp. melted butter
2 tbsp. flour
1 tsp. salt
1/2 tsp. pepper

Beat egg yolks; add corn, milk, butter, flour and seasonings. Fold in stiffly beaten egg whites. Drop from teaspoon onto hot greased griddle or frying pan. Cook until done, turning to brown on all sides. Yield: 6 servings.

Mrs. J. M. Clyburn
Bethune, South Carolina

OLD-FASHIONED CORN PUDDING

2 tbsp. honey
1 c. milk
1 1/2 tbsp. flour
3 eggs, beaten
1 1-lb. can cream-style corn
2 tbsp. melted butter or margarine
1/2 tsp. salt
Dash of allspice

Combine honey and milk; add gradually to flour, stirring until smooth. Add eggs, corn, butter and salt; mix well. Turn into greased 1-quart baking dish. Sprinkle with allspice. Place baking dish in pan of hot water. Bake in preheated 300-degree oven for 1 hour and 45 minutes or until custard is set. Yield: 4-6 servings.

Mrs. Mary F. Dunn
Byers, Texas

SQUAW CORN

4 strips bacon
1 lg. onion, coarsely chopped
1 sm. green pepper, coarsely chopped
1 1-lb. can whole kernel corn, drained
2 tbsp. chopped pimento
12 pitted ripe olives, chopped
1/2 tsp. monosodium glutamate
Dash of salt and pepper
3/4 c. crushed Chip-O's

Fry bacon until crisp; set aside. Reserve 2 tablespoons drippings. Add onion and green pepper to reserved drippings; fry gently until tender, but not soft. Add corn, pimento, olives, monosodium glutamate, salt and pepper. Break bacon into bite-sized pieces; add to corn mixture. Pour mixture into buttered shallow baking dish; sprinkle top with Chip-O's. Bake in preheated 350-degree oven until heated through. Do not overcook. Yield: 4 servings.

Mrs. Robbie White
Sumner, Texas

FRIED CUCUMBERS

2 lg. cucumbers
1 egg, beaten
2 tbsp. cream
1 tsp. thyme
Cracker meal
Dash of salt and pepper
Butter or margarine

Cut cucumbers into 8 pieces. Combine egg, cream and thyme; mix well. Dip cucumber slices in egg mixture; roll in cracker meal. Season with salt and pepper. Fry in butter until golden. May dot with butter and broil, if desired. Yield: 4-6 servings.

Mary Ida Farmer
Midvale, Ohio

HOT CUCUMBER STICKS

3 cucumbers
1 1/2 tsp. salt
1/8 tsp. mace

Wash cucumbers; dry thoroughly. Do not remove skins. Cut in halves lengthwise; cut each half into long strips. Place in saucepan with salt and mace. Cover; cook gently over low heat for about 15 minutes, allowing cucumbers to cook in own juice. Drain and serve hot as a vegetable or as a garnish. Yield: 3-4 servings.

Barbara MacRitchie
Northville, New York

EGGPLANT-TOMATO CASSEROLE

1 med. eggplant, peeled
2 med. onions, sliced
1 med. green pepper, sliced
4 tomatoes, sliced
Salt and pepper to taste
1/2 c. Parmesan cheese
Butter

Cut eggplant into 1/2-inch thick slices; soak in salted water for 15 to 20 minutes. Pat dry. Place half the eggplant slices in greased 2-quart casserole; add half the onion. Place half the green pepper slices on onion; add half the tomato slices. Season with salt and pepper; add half the cheese. Repeat layers; dot with butter. Cover casserole. Bake in preheated 375-degree oven for 45 minutes. Yield: 6 servings.

Barbara Ann West
Portsmouth, Virginia

FRENCH-FRIED EGGPLANT

1 med. eggplant, peeled and sliced 1 in.
   thick
2 tsp. salt
2 egg, beaten
1/2 to 3/4 c. flour

Sprinkle eggplant slices with salt; let stand for 5 to 10 minutes. Blend eggs and flour into a heavy batter; stir in 1 teaspoon salt. Cut eggplant slices into 1-inch strips; coat thoroughly with batter. Brown in deep fat; drain well. May be frozen and reheated in oven. Yield: 6 servings.

Mrs. Virginia B. Firth
Smyrna, Delaware

STUFFED GREEN PEPPER BOATS

4 lg. green peppers, halved lengthwise
2 1/4 c. cooked rice
3/4 lb. American cheese, cubed
1 can cream of tomato soup

Remove seeds from peppers; parboil for 5 minutes. Drain well. Combine rice, cheese

and soup; stuff peppers with mixture. Place each pepper half in aluminum foil cup; place in baking pan. Bake in preheated 350-degree oven for 30 minutes or until heated through. Yield: 6-8 servings.

Mrs. Lee Sandager
Forest Lake, Minnesota

MUSHROOMS A LA KING

3 stalks celery, finely chopped
1 lb. mushrooms
3 tbsp. butter
2 tbsp. flour
2 c. milk
Salt and pepper to taste
Paprika to taste
3 hard-cooked eggs, thinly sliced
1/4 c. sliced ripe olives
2 tbsp. sherry

Cook celery in small amount of water until tender; drain. Slice mushrooms; saute in butter. Stir in flour and milk; cook until thickened, stirring constantly. Season with salt, pepper and paprika. Add celery, eggs and olives; heat thoroughly. Add sherry just before serving. Serve over toast, if desired. Yield: 4 servings.

Mrs. Eugenia Holderith
Franklin, New Jersey

STUFFED MUSHROOM CAPS

18 to 24 fresh mushrooms, 1 1/2 to 2 in.
   in diameter
1   4 1/2-oz. can deviled ham
1 tbsp. chopped onion
1 tbsp. chopped celery
1 tbsp. chopped green pepper
1/2 c. cracker crumbs
1/2 tsp. salt
1/2 tsp. Worcestershire sauce
1/4 c. evaporated milk
1/4 c. melted butter

Wash mushrooms thoroughly. Remove stems; chop fine. Combine chopped stems and remaining ingredients except butter; fill mushroom caps. Place on baking sheet, cavity side up; brush with butter. Broil for 5 to 7 minutes or until heated through. Serve hot. Yield: 6 servings.

Mrs. Henrietta Mook
Mercer, Pennsylvania

STEWED OKRA AND TOMATOES

2 slices bacon, cut up
1 lg. onion, chopped
1 med. green pepper, chopped
1 to 2 lb. okra, cut up
1 to 2 lb. tomatoes, peeled and chopped
1 tsp. salt
1/2 tsp. pepper

Fry bacon in heavy skillet until brown; remove from skillet. Saute onion and pepper in bacon fat; add bacon and remaining ingredients. Cover; cook for 30 to 40 minutes. May remove cover during last few minutes of cooking, if desired. Yield: 6 servings.

Mrs. Ina C. Hooper
Elizabeth, Louisiana

CRUSTY CREAMED ONIONS

2 lb. tiny whole onions, cooked and
   drained
Butter
2 tbsp. flour
1/4 tsp. salt
1/8 tsp. pepper
1 c. milk
1 1/2 c. bread cubes

Place onions in buttered 1-quart baking dish. Melt 2 tablespoons butter in heavy saucepan over low heat. Blend in flour, salt and pepper; cook, stirring, until mixture is smooth. Remove from heat; stir in milk. Bring to a boil, stirring constantly; boil for 1 minute. Pour sauce over onions. Melt 1/4 cup butter; mix with bread cubes. Sprinkle buttered cubes over onion mixture. Bake in preheated 375-degree oven until topping is a crisp golden brown. Yield: 4 servings.

Kathleen Wood
Britton, Michigan

FRIED ONION RING DIP

2/3 c. evaporated milk
1 egg, slightly beaten
1 tbsp. cooking oil
1 c. self-rising flour
Onion rings
Fat

Combine milk, egg and oil; stir in flour. Dip onion rings in batter; drain for 5 minutes. Drop into hot fat. Fry until golden. This dip can also be used for eggplant, chicken and shrimp. Yield: 4-6 servings.

Virginia S. McEwen
Rockford, Alabama

ONION-CHEESE PIE

1 1/2 c. finely crushed soda crackers
1/2 c. melted butter
2 1/2 c. sliced onions
1 1/2 c. milk
3 eggs, slightly beaten
1 tsp. salt
1/4 tsp. pepper
1/2 lb. cheese, finely grated

Combine crackers and butter; press into 9-inch pie pan. Fry onions in additional butter until light brown and tender; spread over pie crust in layers. Scald milk; add to eggs, stirring constantly. Stir in salt, pepper and cheese; pour over onions. Bake in preheated 350-degree oven for 40 to 45 minutes. Garnish center with parsley. Yield: 6-8 servings.

Mrs. Ann Edwards
Corsicana, Texas

HONEY-BUTTER PEAS

1 pkg. frozen peas
1/4 c. honey
1/4 c. butter

Prepare peas according to package directions; drain well. Combine honey and butter; whip until fluffy. Serve over hot peas. Yield: 4 servings.

Mrs. Barbara Jeanne Rice
Eugene, Oregon

DEVILED BLACK-EYED PEAS AND RICE WITH SAUTEED TOMATOES

1 10-oz. package frozen black-eyed peas
Salt
1 sm. garlic clove, chopped
1 sm. onion, chopped
1/2 sm. green pepper, chopped
1/2 c. finely chopped celery
1 chicken or beef bouillon cube
2 c. boiling water
1 4 1/2-oz. can deviled ham
2 c. cooked rice
1 tbsp. butter
Pepper to taste
4 med. firm ripe tomatoes
1/4 c. grated Parmesan cheese
1/2 c. packaged seasoned crumbs
Tabasco sauce to taste
Oil

Combine peas, 1/2 teaspoon salt, garlic, onion, green pepper, celery and bouillon cube in saucepan. Add boiling water; cover. Cook over moderate heat for 20 to 25 minutes or until peas are tender, stirring frequently to prevent sticking; drain. Stir in deviled ham. Add rice, butter, salt to taste and pepper; toss until mixed. Keep hot. Cut each tomato into three slices; mix cheese and crumbs. Dip tomato slices into cheese mixture; dash with Tabasco sauce. Saute slices in small amount of hot oil until heated through. Arrange tomato slices in overlapping ring around edge of serving platter; heap peas mixture in center. Garnish with parsley; serve hot. Yield: 6 servings.

Photograph for this recipe on page 124.

FRENCH PEAS

1 1/2 tbsp. butter or margarine, melted
2 tbsp. water
1/2 c. thinly sliced mushrooms
1 1/2 c. fresh peas
1 sm. onion, thinly sliced
1/2 tsp. salt

Combine all ingredients in saucepan. Cook over medium heat for 12 to 16 minutes or until peas are tender, shaking pan occasionally. One 10-ounce package frozen peas, cooked for 5 to 15 minutes, may be used. Yield: 4 servings.

Ruth W. Wingo
Kaufman, Texas

HOPPING JOHN

1 ham hock, halved
1 8-oz. package dried black-eyed peas
1 sm. onion, chopped
1 tsp. salt
1 tsp. cayenne pepper
1 c. rice

Place ham hock in large saucepan; cover with water. Cook for 30 minutes. Add peas, onion, salt, pepper and enough water to cover. Cook, covered, for 45 minutes, adding water as needed. Stir in rice; cover. Cook for 30 minutes longer or until rice and peas are tender. May add 1 can tomatoes, if desired. Yield: 6 servings.

Photograph for this recipe on page 271.

STUFFED BAKED POTATOES

8 baking potatoes
1/2 c. hot milk
3/4 tsp. salt
1/4 tsp. pepper
1 tsp. grated onion
4 tbsp. melted butter
Grated cheese

Scrub potatoes thoroughly; dry well. Rub with fat. Place on baking sheet. Bake in preheated 450-degree oven for 45 to 50 minutes or until done. Cut a slice from top of each potato; scoop potato from shells into bowl. Add milk; beat until fluffy. Season with salt, pepper and onion. Add part of the butter; pile lightly into potato shells. Brush with remaining melted butter; sprinkle with grated cheese. Broil until cheese melts. Yield: 8 servings.

Mary Ella Ingram
Wagram, North Carolina

DUCHESS POTATOES

3 c. hot mashed potatoes
Butter
6 tbsp. milk
1 1/2 tsp. salt
1/8 tsp. pepper
3 eggs, separated

Combine potatoes, 3 tablespoons butter, milk, salt, pepper and egg yolks; mix well. Fold in stiffly beaten egg whites. Place mixture in pastry bag with tube. Form rosettes on greased baking sheet or shape border around meat or fish. Brush with butter. Bake in preheated 425-degree oven for 5 minutes or until brown. Yield: 6-8 servings.

Mrs. Charlene Strickland
Danielsville, Georgia

POTATO FRITTERS

2 c. grated raw potatoes
1/4 c. grated onion
1 egg, beaten
1/4 tsp. salt
Dash of pepper
1 1/4 tsp. chopped parsley
1/2 tsp. baking powder
1/4 c. flour

Drain potatoes well. Combine potatoes, onion, egg, salt, pepper, parsley, baking powder and flour; mix well. Drop by spoonfuls into deep fat at 375 degrees. Fry for 6 minutes or until done; drain. Yield: 4-6 servings.

Lucinda Beverage
Monterey, Virginia

POTATOES ROMANOFF

5 c. cooked diced potatoes
2 tsp. salt
2 c. creamed cottage cheese
1 c. sour cream
1/4 c. finely minced green onions
1 sm. clove of garlic, crushed
1/2 c. shredded American cheese
Paprika

Sprinkle potatoes with 1 teaspoon salt. Combine cottage cheese, sour cream, onions and garlic with remaining salt; fold in potato cubes. Pour into buttered 2 1/2-quart casserole; top with American cheese and paprika. Bake in preheated 350-degree oven for 40 to 45 minutes or until heated through and bubbly. Yield: 10-12 servings.

Mrs. Ray A. Waters
Texarkana, Arkansas

DELICIOUS SCALLOPED POTATOES

2 tbsp. butter
2 tbsp. flour
2 c. milk
1 1/2 tsp. salt
1/8 tsp. pepper
1/4 c. chopped onion
3 1/2 c. sliced potatoes

Melt butter; blend in flour. Add milk slowly; cook over low heat until thickened, stirring constantly. Add salt, pepper and onion. Place layers of potatoes and sauce in greased 10 x 6 x 1 1/2-inch casserole. Bake, covered, in preheated 350-degree oven for 30 minutes. Uncover; bake for 30 minutes longer or until done. Yield: 6-8 servings.

Mrs. Sara Carnahan
Wamego, Kansas

SPINACH PIE

1/2 c. shortening
2 1/2 c. flour
1/2 c. (or more) water
4 c. chopped fresh spinach
4 eggs
4 c. milk
1 1/4 tsp. salt
1/2 c. chopped bacon

Cut shortening into flour; add just enough water to hold ingredients together. Roll out on floured board; place pastry in baking pan. Place spinach in pastry. Combine eggs, milk and salt; mix well. Pour custard over spinach; top with bacon. Bake in preheated 450-degree oven for 10 minutes. Reduce oven temperature to 350 degrees; bake until custard is set. A beaten egg white may be brushed over pastry shell to prevent sogginess, if desired. Yield: 6 servings.

Janice Bendshadler
Turner, Oregon

SPRINGTIME SPINACH

1 c. sour cream
2 tsp. flour
1/8 tsp. mace
Dash of salt
1/4 tsp. lemon juice
2 c. cooked fresh or frozen spinach

Combine sour cream, flour, mace, salt and lemon juice in saucepan; cook over very low heat until thoroughly heated, stirring occasionally. Spoon over cooked spinach. Yield: 4-6 servings.

Mrs. Elizabeth Isbell Vaught
Olden, Texas

SQUASH FRITTERS

1/2 c. flour
1/2 tsp. baking powder
2 c. cold cooked mashed squash
2 eggs
1 tsp. salt

Sift flour and baking powder together; stir in remaining ingredients. Shape into cakes. Fry cakes on hot oiled griddle until done. Add milk if needed to moisten. Yield: 4 servings.

Mrs. Janice Sawyer
St. Johnsbury, Vermont

SQUASH RING

1 1/2 qt. yellow squash, cut into 1/2-in.
   pieces
1 med. onion, diced
1/2 med. green pepper, diced
1 clove of garlic, diced
1 tsp. salt
2 tbsp. sugar
1/4 c. butter

1 tbsp. Worcestershire sauce
1/2 tsp. pepper
1/2 tsp. Tabasco sauce
1 c. bread crumbs
3 eggs, well beaten
1/2 c. milk

Cook squash, onion, green pepper and garlic in water until tender; drain well. Add remaining ingredients; mix well. Place in greased 1 1/2-quart ring mold. Bake over water in preheated 350-degree oven for 40 minutes. Keep warm until ready to serve. Unmold; fill center of ring with buttered green lima beans or English peas, if desired. Garnish with tiny whole pickled beets. Yield: 12 servings.

Mrs. Ernestine E. Hodson
Grand Prairie, Texas

ZESTY STUFFED ZUCCHINI

4 sm. zucchini
6 c. water
1/4 lb. ground beef
1/2 c. chopped onion
1 tbsp. olive oil
1 c. canned tomatoes
2 tsp. chopped parsley
1/2 tsp. salt
Dash of pepper
1/2 c. fine dry bread crumbs
3 tbsp. melted butter
1 tbsp. grated Parmesan cheese

Cook whole zucchini in boiling salted water for 10 minutes or until tender. Cut into halves lengthwise; remove pulp carefully, reserving shells. Brown ground beef and onion in oil. Combine zucchini pulp, tomatoes, parsley, salt and pepper; mix well. Stir into beef mixture; bring to boiling point. Fill zucchini shells with beef mixture, allowing about 1/4 cup mixture for each shell. Combine remaining ingredients; sprinkle over tops of zucchini. Place in greased 13 x 9 x 2-inch pan. Bake in preheated 350-degree oven for 15 minutes or until heated through. Yield: 8 servings.

Virginia T. Bond
Madison, West Virginia

WAGON WHEELS

1/4 c. cornmeal
1/2 tsp. salt
Several dashes of pepper
1 firm long yellow or green squash,
   thinly sliced
2 tbsp. cooking oil

Combine cornmeal, salt and pepper; dredge squash slices with cornmeal mixture. Saute squash in hot oil until a delicate brown, turning once and adding more oil if necessary. Yield: 4-6 servings.

Irene G. Carlson
Mountain View, Alaska

CANDIED SWEET POTATOES WITH HONEY

4 lg. sweet potatoes, cooked
1/4 c. melted butter
3/4 c. honey
3/4 c. orange juice
1/4 tsp. salt
1 tbsp. cornstarch

Peel potatoes; cut into halves. Place in greased 8 x 8 x 2-inch pan. Combine butter, honey, orange juice, salt and cornstarch in saucepan; cook until slightly thickened, stirring constantly. Pour over potatoes. Bake in preheated 450-degree oven for 10 minutes or until done. Yield: 6-8 servings.

Jeanne Yoxall
Stafford, Kansas

CREAMY SWEET POTATOES

5 med. sweet potatoes, cooked
3 tbsp. flour
1 tsp. salt
1 c. (packed) brown sugar
2 tbsp. butter
8 marshmallows
1/2 c. chopped almonds
1 c. light cream

Peel potatoes; cut in half lengthwise. Arrange in greased 1 1/2-quart casserole. Combine flour, salt and brown sugar; pour over potatoes. Dot with butter; add marshmallows and almonds. Cover with cream. Bake in preheated 350-degree oven for 40 to 45 minutes or until done. Yield: 6-8 servings.

Mrs. Verna Wertz
Trenton, Nebraska

SCALLOPED YAMS AND APPLES WITH ROAST PORK

1 3 1/2-lb. loin pork roast
Cider Sauce
6 med. Louisiana yams, cooked,
   peeled and sliced or 3 16-oz. cans
   Louisiana yams, drained
3 med. apples, pared and sliced
1/2 c. chopped pecans

Place pork on rack in shallow pan. Bake in preheated 325-degree oven for 2 hours or to 170 degrees on meat thermometer, basting frequently with 1 1/2 cups Cider Sauce during last 30 minutes of baking time. Arrange yams and apple slices in buttered 3-quart casserole; sprinkle pecans on top. Pour remaining 1 1/2 cups Cider Sauce over top; place in same oven with pork 30 minutes before pork is done. Bake for 30 minutes or until heated through, basting frequently. Yield: 6 servings.

Cider Sauce

1 1/2 c. apple cider or apple cider
2 c. (firmly packed) light brown sugar
1/4 c. butter or margarine
3 tbsp. lemon juice
2 tsp. ground allspice

Combine apple cider, brown sugar and butter in saucepan; bring to a boil. Boil over low heat for 5 minutes, stirring frequently. Remove from heat; stir in lemon juice and allspice. Yield: 3 cups sauce.

Photograph for this recipe on page 129.

BROILED CHEESE TOMATOES

4 tomatoes
1 tsp. salt
1/8 tsp. pepper
1/4 c. crumbs
1/4 c. grated cheese
Butter

Wash and core tomatoes; cut into halves crosswise. Sprinkle halves with salt, pepper, crumbs and cheese; dot with butter. Place on baking sheet. Broil for 10 minutes or until heated through and cheese is melted. Yield: 4 servings.

Mrs. Grace E. Kukuk
Negaunee, Michigan

FRIED GREEN TOMATOES

4 or 5 med. green tomatoes
1/3 c. flour
3/4 tsp. salt
Dash of pepper (opt.)
1/4 c. shortening

Wash tomatoes; remove stem ends. Cut crosswise into 1/2-inch slices. Combine flour, salt and pepper; dredge tomato slices with flour mixture. Brown quickly in shortening on one side; turn. Reduce heat; cook until slices are soft in center. Remove to hot platter; serve hot. Yield: 4-5 servings.

Mrs. Patricia D. Chappell
Griffin, Georgia

STEWED TOMATOES

4 med. tomatoes, halved
1 tsp. minced onion
1/2 tbsp. sugar
1/8 tsp. pepper
2 tbsp. butter
1/2 c. soft bread cubes
1 bay leaf or 1/2 tsp. oregano

Combine all ingredients in 2-quart saucepan; simmer for 15 minutes or until tomatoes are tender. Remove bay leaf; serve hot. Yield: 4 servings.

Eugenie Eaves
Littleton, Massachusetts

TURNIP GREENS WITH CORNMEAL DUMPLINGS

Turnip greens
1/2 c. sifted flour
1 tsp. baking powder
1/2 tsp. garlic salt
1/2 c. yellow cornmeal
1/8 tsp. pepper
1 egg
1/4 c. milk
1 tbsp. melted butter

Cook greens in kettle until done; remove greens. Sift dry ingredients into mixing bowl. Add egg, milk and butter; stir until batter is well mixed. Drop batter by teaspoonfuls into simmering broth. Cover tightly; simmer for 15 minutes. Do not lift cover while dumplings cook. Chicken broth may be substituted for turnip broth. Yield: 4 servings.

Mrs. Thelma L. Fowler
Counce, Tennessee

TURNIP STICKS

2 c. thinly sliced white turnips
1 tbsp. salt
2 tbsp. vinegar

Combine turnips and salt in bowl; let stand for 15 minutes. Drain off liquid. Add 1/4 cup water and vinegar; let stand for about 1 hour. Drain; press out any excess liquid. Serve with sweet-sour spareribs, if desired.

Christine Boneta
Brookwood, Alabama

BUTTERED RUTABAGAS

1 1/2 to 2 lb. rutabagas
1 1/2 tsp. Worcestershire sauce

1/4 tsp. onion powder
1/4 c. sugar
1 tsp. salt
3 or 4 drops of Tabasco sauce
Butter to taste

Peel rutabagas; cut into small pieces. Place in saucepan; add Worcestershire sauce, onion powder, sugar, salt and Tabasco sauce. Cover with water; bring to a boil. Cook until tender. Add butter; mash with a fork.

Mrs. Anne Sutphen Welch
Knoxville, Tennessee

BAKED PARSNIPS

1 lb. parsnips
4 tbsp. butter
1/4 c. hot water

Scrape or pare parsnips; cut in lengthwise slices, removing hard core, if necessary. Place parsnips in baking dish. Add butter and hot water; cover. Bake in preheated 375-degree oven for 30 to 40 minutes or until tender, removing cover during last few minutes of baking. Yield: 4-6 servings.

Mrs. Jeanette Bogne
Clara City, Minnesota

LETTUCE SOUP

6 slices bacon, chopped
1 onion, chopped
2 c. sliced celery
1 can beef broth
1 can cream of chicken soup
1 can cream of mushroom soup
3 c. water
1 head Boston lettuce
1 tbsp. Angostura aromatic bitters
1 lb. ground round
1 tsp. salt
1/4 tsp. pepper
Grated Parmesan cheese

Fry bacon in Dutch oven or deep 4-quart kettle until crisp; remove bacon pieces. Add onion and celery to Dutch oven; saute until golden. Add broth, soups and water; bring to boiling point. Core lettuce; separate lettuce into leaves. Add lettuce to soup; cook, stirring, until wilted. Add Angostura bitters. Mix ground round, salt and pepper; shape into small balls. Drop into soup; simmer for about 15 minutes or until meatballs are done. Serve with Parmesan cheese and bacon pieces. Yield: 8 servings.

Photograph for this recipe on page 101.

SKILLET CABBAGE

1/4 c. butter
1 tender cabbage, finely shredded
1 tsp. salt
1/2 tsp. pepper
Dash of garlic powder (opt.)
1/3 c. thin cream or milk

Melt butter in skillet; add cabbage, seasonings and cream. Cover tightly; simmer for 10 minutes. Yield: 6-8 servings.

Helen Pangborn
Tacoma, Washington

SWEET-SOUR RED CABBAGE

1 2-lb. head red cabbage, shredded
1 c. chopped cooking apples
1/2 c. water
1/4 c. (firmly packed) light brown
    sugar
1/2 tsp. salt
1/4 tsp. allspice
1/2 c. white vinegar
1/4 c. softened butter

Combine cabbage, apples, water, brown sugar, salt and allspice in 3-quart saucepan; cover. Bring to a boil; reduce heat. Simmer for 8 to 10 minutes or until cabbage and apples are tender; remove from heat. Add vinegar and butter; toss lightly to mix. Yield: 6-8 servings.

Photograph for this recipe on page 98.

Casserole Favorites

Casseroles, though they seem like a modern dish, go further back
into history than most people realize. Long ago, the hunter's catch
was added to a big pot with wild vegetables, roots and berries to
simmer over the fire until tender and tasty. Even today, some southwestern American Indians cook "one pot" meals in waterproof
baskets that they invented hundreds of years ago. The modern
casserole (meaning "little pot") is probably most closely linked with
the French "pot au-feu," a mixture of leftovers . . . meat and
vegetable scraps with a sauce that simmers constantly on the back of
the stove.

Certainly the pioneer cooks knew the value of the leftover vegetable
or meat scraps, and how they could serve as the basis for a complete
and nutritious meal when cooked and served together in one dish.
Even today in our land of plenty, the one-dish meal is valuable, tasty
and nutritious. The modern casserole has certainly become more
sophisticated, as its ingredients are only as limited as the cook's
imagination and budget. And, the casserole is no longer in the
"hurried, last-minute meal" category either. Although this is one of
its virtues, there are also casseroles that take time and planning. As
proof of its versatility, the casserole can grace the simplest of tables
or the most elegant and still be as easy or as complicated as
the cook desires.

Basically, the ingredients for casseroles are meats, poultry, seafood, vegetables, pastas and cereals, eggs and dairy products. But, the inherent magic of casseroles lies in the imaginative combining of any of these ingredients. The ingredients do not have to be expensive, but they can be. It is most important that, whether economical or expensive, the foods that go into casseroles should be of good quality, especially when they are leftovers.

In combining foods for a casserole, pleasing blends and contrasts of flavors and textures are basic characteristics to work toward. Hearty meats, tender vegetables and smooth sauces are a starting point. While pasta and cereals are perfect extenders, spices add interest, and cheese or crumb toppings add color and zest to the flavor. Or it can be the other way around, using cheese and pasta or cereals as the starting point, with small bits of meat added for delicate flavor, or vegetables may be used as a topping or garnish.

In any combination of ingredients, it is important not to let any one flavor dominate all the others, or the magic is lost. Of course there can be a focal flavor — the meat, the vegetable or the cheese — but the other foods should complement and enhance the main flavor. The whole range of seasonings and spices adds a delightful, piquant touch to casseroles when used with a thoughtful hand. Used carelessly, the result can be disastrous.

Experimentation is part of the fun of casseroles, and ease is part of the joy. Once the ingredients are mixed, sea-soned and topped (the whole procedure often accomplished with one mixing bowl), the dish is ready for the freezer, to be kept for a few hours, or for the oven. This ease of preparation benefits both the busy homemaker and the hostess who prefers to spend time with her party guests rather than in the kitchen.

It is conveniently wise, when mixing up a casserole for a family meal, to save time and energy by making two — one to cook and one to freeze. A few hints for freezing casseroles can make this trick even more worthwhile. If a freezerproof dish is unavailable, or if the ones available need to be in circulation, there are other ways to freeze a casserole. Place the mixture into a foil-lined casserole dish, being sure that the edges of the foil overlap well on all sides of the dish. Place the dish in the freezer, and after the mixture is frozen solid, remove it carefully from the dish, wrap thoroughly in freezer paper, tape, label and return to the freezer. Plastic containers and aluminum foil are also good for short-term freezing.

Keep in mind the following tips when freezing various foods:

— Salad greens, raw vegetables and fried foods do not freeze very well.

— Add diced potatoes before reheating casseroles as they become mushy when frozen.

— Fats, which become rancid after 2 months, should be used sparingly in frozen dishes.

— Seasonings, except onions, become stronger after freezing, so use sparingly. Onions tend to lose flavor strength when frozen.

— Toppings for casseroles should be added just before reheating, as should MSG (to bring out the flavor of meats and vegetables).

— Undercook the casseroles that will be frozen, or the ingredients will be overcooked or mushy when reheated.

Casserole is not only the name of the combinations of foods cooked together for a one-dish meal, but is also the name of the dish in which these recipes are prepared. These dishes are available in a great variety of sizes, shapes, colors, materials and designs.

The most versatile, of course, are the heatproof glass casseroles that can move directly from the freezer to the oven, and from the oven to the table. They have their own lids, are pretty enough for the table, and clean easily. Souffle dishes, ramekins and the shallow, rectangular ovenproof glass pans are equally as useful. Chafing dishes, fondue pots and double boilers are also very good for casseroles.

Easy, economical, elegant, elaborate — all of these words only begin to describe casseroles. They are also tasty, hearty and nutritious. Here, Home Economics Teachers have gathered together their best ideas for casseroles, hoping to make the cooking and eating of all kinds and combinations of favorite foods a happy experience for a long time to come!

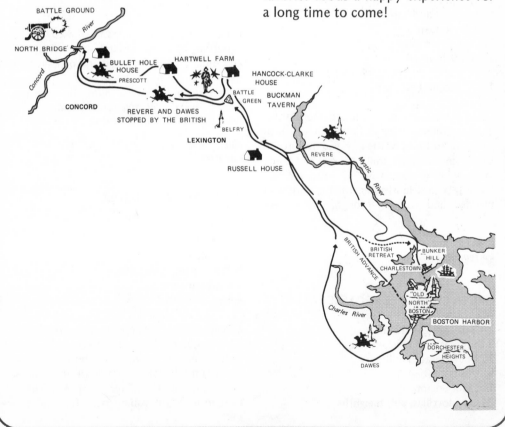

CHEESE-PECAN ROAST

3/4 c. chopped onions
2 c. chopped celery
3 tbsp. minced parsley
1/2 c. butter
2 c. cottage cheese
4 c. ground pecans
2 c. bread crumbs
3 tsp. salt
10 eggs, beaten
1 qt. milk

Saute onions, celery and parsley in butter until onions are tender. Add remaining ingredients; mix well. Pour into 9 x 13 x 2-inch casserole. Bake in preheated 350-degree oven for 45 minutes to 1 hour.

Mushroom Sauce

4 lg. cans mushrooms
1/2 c. butter
1/2 c. sifted flour
1 1/2 tsp. salt
Milk or half and half
Paprika to taste
1/2 tsp. garlic salt
1/2 tsp. onion salt
Spice Islands seasoning salt to taste
1 env. spaghetti sauce mix

Drain mushrooms; reserve liquid. Melt butter in large saucepan; stir in flour and salt until smooth. Add part of the reserved mushroom liquid and enough milk to make a thick sauce, stirring constantly. Stir in seasonings, sauce mix and mushrooms; cook until well blended and heated through. Serve over roast.

Gloria Taylor
Gaston, Oregon

GREEN CHILI-CHEESE CASSEROLE

1 7-oz. can green chilies
3 cans cream of chicken soup
1 can evaporated milk
Salt to taste
1 c. sour cream
24 corn tortillas, cut in eighths

1 med. onion, finely chopped
4 c. shredded Cheddar cheese

Drain chilies; chop. Combine soup, milk, salt, sour cream and chilies in large saucepan; heat to simmering point. Place alternate layers of soup mixture, tortillas, onion and cheese in well-greased 4-quart casserole. Bake in preheated 350-degree oven for about 45 minutes or until hot and bubbly. Yield: 12 servings.

Mrs. Carolyn K. Simpson
Burbank, California

EGGS AND CHIPS

2 c. crushed potato chips
6 hard-cooked eggs, sliced
1 can cream of mushroom soup
1/2 c. milk
2 tbsp. chopped onion
1/2 tsp. salt
1/4 tsp. pepper
1/2 c. grated cheese

Place 1 cup potato chips in greased 1-quart casserole; add eggs. Blend soup with milk and onion; season with salt and pepper. Pour over eggs; sprinkle cheese over top. Cover with remaining potato chips. Bake in preheated 400-degree oven for 25 minutes or until bubbly. Yield: 6 servings.

Mrs. B. Fred German
Copperhill, Tennessee

PUFFY EGG CASSEROLE

2 tbsp. butter
4 slices bread
1 c. milk
Salt and pepper to taste
1 c. grated cheese
4 eggs, separated

Spread butter on bread; cut bread into 1-inch squares. Combine bread, milk, salt, pepper and cheese in mixing bowl. Beat egg yolks until lemon colored; stir into cheese mixture. Fold in stiffly beaten egg whites; turn into 9-inch square pan. Bake in preheated 325-degree oven for 30 to 35 minutes.

Opal Pruitt
Buda, Illinois

HOMINY CASSEROLE

2 c. canned hominy
1 c. canned mushroom soup
1 tsp. Worcestershire sauce
1/2 tsp. salt
1 sm. can chopped mushrooms
1/2 c. corn flake crumbs
1 tbsp. butter

Mix hominy, mushroom soup, Worcestershire sauce, salt and mushrooms; pour into buttered casserole. Sprinkle with corn flake crumbs; dot with butter. Bake in preheated 300-degree oven until brown. Yield: 4 servings.

Mary E. Jones
Port Arthur, Texas

SPAGHETTI WITH CHEESE-HAM SAUCE

1 tbsp. butter or margarine
1/2 c. finely chopped onion
1 med. clove of garlic, crushed
1/2 lb. cooked ham, cut into
    julienne strips
1 can Cheddar cheese soup
1 c. milk
1/2 c. dark seedless raisins
1/2 tsp. chili powder
1 tbsp. salt
3 qt. boiling water
1 8-oz. package spaghetti

Melt butter in large saucepan. Add onion and garlic; saute over medium heat, stirring constantly, for about 3 minutes or until onion is tender. Stir in ham, undiluted soup, milk, raisins and chili powder. Cook over low heat until hot, stirring occasionally; do not boil. Keep warm over low heat until spaghetti is cooked; stir frequently. Add salt to rapidly boiling water; add spaghetti gradually so that water continues to boil. Cook, stirring occasionally, until tender; drain in colander. Place spaghetti on serving plate; serve sauce with spaghetti. Yield: 4-6 servings.

Photograph for this recipe on page 132.

MACARONI AND CHEESE CASSEROLE

1 4-oz. box macaroni
Salt
2 1/2 c. grated sharp cheese
1 1/2 c. milk
2 eggs
1/4 c. margarine

Cook macaroni in 8 cups water and 1 tablespoon salt for about 12 minutes or until tender; drain. Arrange alternate layers of macaroni and cheese in buttered baking dish. Combine milk, 1/4 teaspoon salt and eggs in bowl; beat well. Pour over macaroni mixture; dot with margarine. Bake in preheated 375-degree oven for 25 minutes. Yield: 6-8 servings.

Mrs. Elaine L. Gregory
Shelby, North Carolina

MACARONI-MUSHROOM CASSEROLE

1 pkg. macaroni
1/2 c. chopped green pepper
1/2 c. chopped onion
1 can cream of mushroom soup
1/2 c. sliced mushrooms (opt.)
1 c. mayonnaise
4 c. grated cheese
1/2 c. chopped pimento
Crushed crackers

Cook macaroni in boiling, salted water until tender; drain. Cook green pepper and onion in small amount of fat in skillet until tender. Combine all ingredients except cracker crumbs in large mixing bowl; place in 2 buttered medium casseroles or 1 large casserole. Cover with cracker crumbs. Bake in preheated 350-degree oven for 30 minutes or until cheese melts and cracker crumbs are brown. Yield: 12 servings.

Mildred H. Morris
Notasulga, Alabama

CORNED BEEF-MACARONI CASSEROLE

1 6-oz. package macaroni
1 12-oz. can corned beef
1 can cream of chicken soup
1 c. milk
1 c. cubed American cheese
1/2 c. chopped onion
3/4 c. crumbled potato chips

Cook macaroni according to package directions. Break corned beef into small pieces. Combine macaroni, corned beef and remaining ingredients except potato chips; place in greased casserole. Top with potato chips. Bake in preheated 375-degree oven for 1 hour. Yield: 4-6 servings.

Mrs. Ellen Goolsbey
Appleton, Wisconsin

DRIED BEEF-NOODLE-BROCCOLI CASSEROLE

1/2 c. margarine or butter
6 tbsp. flour
4 c. milk
2 lb. fresh broccoli, cooked and drained
1 tsp. salt
1/2 tsp. pepper
1/2 lb. dried beef, chopped
1 tsp. Worcestershire sauce
1 8-oz. package noodles
1 c. bread crumbs

Melt 1/4 cup margarine in saucepan; stir in flour. Add milk gradually; cook until thickened, stirring constantly. Cut broccoli into bite-sized pieces; add to sauce. Add salt, pepper, dried beef and Worcestershire sauce. Cook noodles according to package directions; place in greased 3-quart casserole. Spoon sauce over noodles; toss lightly. Melt remaining margarine in saucepan. Add bread crumbs; stir until mixed. Sprinkle over casserole. Bake in preheated 375-degree oven for 20 minutes. Two 10-ounce packages frozen broccoli, cooked and drained, may be used instead of fresh broccoli. Yield: 6-8 servings.

Jaci Courte
New Lebanon, Ohio

PEPPERED TENDERLOIN CASSEROLE

2 lb. boneless beef tenderloin or
   sirloin
4 tbsp. butter or margarine
2 tbsp. olive oil
1 tsp. salt
1/2 tsp. coarsely ground pepper
Dash of ground sage
Dash of ground cumin
1 lb. mushrooms
2 cloves of garlic, finely chopped
1 med. onion, cut into wedges
2 med. green peppers, cut into 1-in.
   squares
2 med. tomatoes, cut into wedges
1/2 c. soy sauce
2 tbsp. cider vinegar
2 tbsp. tomato paste

Cut beef into 1/4-inch wide strips. Cook, small amount at a time, in 2 tablespoons butter and 1 tablespoon olive oil in large frying pan until brown. Place in 3-quart baking dish; sprinkle with salt, pepper, sage and cumin. Toss lightly to mix. Trim mushrooms; cut into quarters. Saute mushrooms in remaining butter and olive oil in same frying pan for 2 minutes; add to beef mixture. Stir garlic, onion and green peppers into drippings in frying pan; saute for 2 minutes. Add to beef mixture; add tomatoes. Combine soy sauce, vinegar and tomato paste in frying pan; bring to a boil, stirring constantly. Pour over beef mixture; toss lightly to mix. Cover. Bake in 350-degree oven for 30 minutes. Yield: 6 servings.

Audrey Swanson
Tinley Park, Illinois

SURPRISE CASSEROLE

1 2-lb. sirloin tip or round steak, cut
   into cubes
2 tbsp. minced onion
1/2 c. butter or margarine
1 3-oz. can whole mushrooms
1 bay leaf
1 tsp. Worcestershire sauce
2 c. cooked wide noodles
1/2 c. evaporated milk

1/2 c. water
1 tsp. salt
1/4 c. grated Cheddar cheese
1 c. croutons
2 tbsp. pimento strips

Saute steak and onion in 2 tablespoons butter in skillet until lightly browned. Drain mushrooms; add mushroom liquid to skillet. Add bay leaf and Worcestershire sauce; cover. Simmer for 30 minutes or until beef is tender; remove bay leaf. Combine beef with pan juices, mushrooms, noodles, remaining butter, milk, water and salt in greased 1 1/2-quart casserole; sprinkle with cheese and croutons. Bake in preheated 325-degree oven for 1 hour; garnish with pimento strips. Yield: 4-6 servings.

Dorothy G. Scothorn
Kennedy, Minnesota

GROUND BEEF-MACARONI BAKE

1 lb. ground beef
1 sm. onion, diced
1   7-oz. package macaroni, cooked
1 1/2 c. tomato juice
1/2 c. tomato paste
1/2 c. cottage cheese
1/2 c. sour cream
1 1/2 tsp. salt
Dash of pepper
1 c. grated cheese

Cook ground beef and onion in skillet until brown; drain off excess fat. Mix all ingredients, reserving 1/2 cup grated cheese. Place in casserole; top with reserved cheese. Bake in preheated 350-degree oven for 45 minutes or until cheese is melted and beef mixture is bubbly. Yield: 6-8 servings.

Joyce Be Miller
Indianapolis, Indiana

IRMA'S TAGLIARINI

1 med. onion, chopped
1/2 green pepper, chopped
3 tbsp. butter
1 lb. ground beef
1 c. tomato sauce

2 c. water
2 c. uncooked noodles
Salt to taste
1 can whole kernel corn
1/2 c. chopped ripe olives
1 c. grated cheese

Cook onion and green pepper in butter until tender. Stir in ground beef; cook until brown. Add tomato sauce, water and noodles; cook until noodles are tender. Add salt, corn and olives; pour into large buttered casserole. Sprinkle with cheese. Bake in preheated 350-degree oven for 45 minutes. Turn off heat; leave casserole in oven for 15 minutes longer. Yield: 6 servings.

Mrs. Irma B. Morley
Allegan, Michigan

SPAGHETTI-ALMOND CASSEROLE

1 1/2 lb. lean ground beef
2 tbsp. olive oil
2 lg. onions, sliced
1 green pepper, diced
1 clove of garlic, minced
2 8-oz. cans tomato sauce
1 4-oz. can mushrooms, drained
Salt and pepper to taste
2 bay leaves
1 tbsp. Worcestershire sauce
1 7-oz. package spaghetti
2 c. grated sharp cheese
2 c. slivered almonds

Cook ground beef in olive oil in skillet until brown. Add onions, green pepper and garlic; cook until onions are soft. Stir in tomato sauce, mushrooms, salt, pepper, bay leaves and Worcestershire sauce. Reduce heat; cook for 30 minutes, stirring frequently and adding water if mixture becomes too thick. Remove bay leaves. Break spaghetti into 2-inch pieces; cook according to package directions. Drain. Toss with beef mixture; spoon into two 1 1/2-quart casseroles. Sprinkle with cheese, then almonds. Bake in preheated 350-degree oven for 30 minutes. One casserole may be frozen; bake frozen casserole for 1 hour. Yield: 8-10 servings.

Mrs. Kay Ryan
Pontiac, Michigan

ARMENIAN-STYLE LAMB

6 carrots, peeled
8 med. potatoes, peeled and halved
1 eggplant, cut in chunks
2 onions, peeled and sliced
1 lb. squash, cut in 1/2-in. slices
4 fresh tomatoes, halved
Several sprigs of parsley, chopped
1 bay leaf
1 clove of garlic, minced
2 tsp. salt
1/2 tsp. pepper
6 lamb chops
1/4 c. all-purpose flour

Arrange carrots, potatoes, eggplant, onions and squash in deep baking dish or Dutch oven. Top with tomatoes. Combine parsley, bay leaf, half the garlic, 1 1/2 teaspoons salt and 1/4 teaspoon pepper; sprinkle over vegetables. Rub lamb chops with remaining garlic, salt and pepper; arrange over vegetables. Bake, covered, in preheated 375-degree oven for 1 hour. Remove from oven. Mix flour with 1/2 cup water until smooth. Lift chops in several places; stir flour mixture into pan juices. Bake, uncovered, for 20 minutes longer or until gravy is thickened. One 28-ounce can tomatoes may be substituted for fresh tomatoes. Drain tomatoes; reserve 1/2 cup liquid to mix with flour. Yield: 6 servings.

Mrs. Marie Heltzel
Lake Butler, Florida

PORK CHOP AND POTATO CASSEROLE

6 pork chops
8 med. potatoes, pared and sliced
1/4 c. minced onion
1 c. diced mild cheese
1 can cream of mushroom soup
1 c. milk
2 tsp. salt
Dash of pepper

Fry pork chops in skillet until brown; trim off fat. Place alternate layers of potatoes, onion and cheese in greased casserole. Combine mushroom soup, milk and seasonings in bowl; blend well. Pour soup mixture over cheese. Top with pork chops; cover. Bake in preheated 350-degree oven for 1 hour and 15 minutes or until potatoes are done. Yield: 6 servings.

Mrs. Paula Calhoun
Fisher, Illinois

TAMALE PIE

1 onion, chopped
1 clove of garlic, minced
3 tbsp. oil
2 lb. lean ground pork
Cumin seed to taste
Salt to taste
1/2 tsp. chili powder
1 tbsp. sugar
2 c. tomato sauce
2/3 c. flour
3/4 c. sliced olives
1 can white hominy, drained
1 can yellow hominy, drained
2 tbsp. melted shortening

Saute onion and garlic in oil until tender. Add pork; cook, stirring, until brown. Cover with water; cook for about 1 hour or until pork is tender. Stir in seasonings. Combine tomato sauce and 1/3 cup flour until smooth; stir into pork mixture. Add olives; mix well. Grind hominy. Mix hominy with remaining 1/3 cup flour and shortening. Reserve small amount of the hominy mixture; line casserole with remaining hominy mixture. Pour pork mixture into casserole; top with reserved hominy mixture. Bake in preheated 350-degree oven for 40 minutes.

Audrey E. Macedo
Milpitas, California

BEAN AND WATER CHESTNUT CASSEROLE

1 10-oz. package French-style green beans
1 tbsp. butter
1 tbsp. flour
3/4 c. milk
2 tbsp. soy sauce
1 5-oz. can water chestnuts

1 c. sour cream
2 c. cubed cooked ham
1 c. buttered soft bread crumbs
Paprika

Cover beans with boiling water; let stand until separated. Drain well. Melt butter in saucepan; blend in flour. Stir in milk and soy sauce; cook over medium heat, stirring, until thickened. Drain water chestnuts; cut in thin slices. Add sour cream, ham, beans and water chestnuts to sauce; mix well. Pour into greased 10 x 6 x 1 1/2-inch baking dish. Sprinkle crumbs over ham mixture; sprinkle with paprika. Bake in preheated 350-degree oven for 30 minutes or until heated through. Yield: 6 servings.

Mrs. Dorothy M. Scanlon
West Mifflin, Pennsylvania

OLIVE SOUFFLE CASSEROLE

1/2 lb. Spanish or sweet Italian
   sausage

1 c. sliced onions
4 tbsp. olive or salad oil
4 med. cooked potatoes, peeled
   and diced
1/2 c. sliced pimento-stuffed olives
1 1-lb. can stewed tomatoes
6 eggs, separated

Parboil sausage; slice. Saute sausage and onions in 1 tablespoon oil in large skillet until lightly browned; remove to shallow 2 1/2-quart casserole. Heat remaining oil in skillet. Add potatoes; saute for 3 minutes. Add olives and tomatoes; pour over sausage mixture. Bake in preheated 400-degree oven for 15 minutes. Beat egg whites until soft peaks form. Beat egg yolks in separate bowl until light and fluffy; fold into egg whites. Stir potato mixture; pour eggs over top. Bake for 17 minutes longer or until eggs test done when wooden pick is inserted in center. Garnish with parsley and whole olives. Yield: 4-6 servings.

Photograph for this recipe below.

EUNIE'S SAUSAGE AND RICE

2 env. dry noodle soup mix
2 lb. bulk sausage
1 stalk celery, chopped
1 green pepper, chopped
1 onion, chopped
3/4 c. packaged precooked rice
1 c. slivered almonds

Prepare soup mix according to package directions. Remove from heat; set aside. Fry sausage in skillet, stirring to break up, until brown; drain off grease. Add celery, pepper and onion; cook until onion is tender. Add soup mixture, rice and almonds; place in greased casserole. Bake in preheated 350-degree oven for 45 minutes. Yield: 8 servings.

Marilee Joyce
Washburn, Illinois

SAUSAGE-POTATO SUPPER CASSEROLE

1 1/2 lb. bulk sausage
5 or 6 slices dry bread, cut into cubes
2 c. milk
1 1/2 tsp. salt
1 med. onion, chopped
1 tsp. thyme
4 med. potatoes, diced

Fry sausage in skillet until brown; drain. Combine bread and milk in bowl; let soak for several minutes. Add sausage, salt, onion, thyme and potatoes; mix lightly. Turn into greased casserole; cover. Bake in preheated 325-degree oven for 1 hour and 30 minutes.

Lois J. Smeltzer
Myerstown, Pennsylvania

LIVER AND RICE CREOLE

2 lb. sliced liver
1 c. flour
1 c. chopped onions
1 tbsp. salt
6 c. pureed tomatoes
1/2 c. chopped green pepper

4 c. cooked rice
2 c. Rice Krispies
2 tbsp. margarine

Cut liver into 1/2-inch cubes; dredge with flour. Cook in 1/4 cup hot fat in skillet until brown. Add onions; cook until onions are tender. Add salt, tomatoes and green pepper; simmer for 5 minutes. Spread alternate layers of rice and tomato mixture into 10 x 16-inch baking pan. Mix Rice Krispies with margarine; sprinkle over tomato mixture. Bake in preheated 325-degree oven for about 30 minutes. Yield: 12 servings.

Mrs. LeNora Hudson
Sulphur, Oklahoma

WIENER QUICKIE

3 med. tomatoes
Flour
6 wieners
1 med. green pepper, sliced
1 can whole kernel corn
1 lg. onion, thinly sliced
1/2 tsp. salt
1/4 tsp. pepper
1 clove of garlic, minced

Cut tomatoes in 1-inch thick slices; dredge slices with flour. Cut wieners in 1/2-inch pieces. Arrange tomato slices, wieners, green pepper slices, corn and onion slices in alternate layers in greased 1 1/2-quart casserole, sprinkling each layer with salt, pepper and garlic. Cover. Bake in preheated 350-degree oven for 30 minutes. Yield: 4-6 servings.

Lynnell Holland
Chiloquin, Oregon

CHICKEN-CRAB MEAT ROSEMARY

2 tbsp. chopped onion
1/2 c. butter
7 tbsp. flour
3/4 tsp. salt
3/4 tsp. paprika
1 tsp. crushed rosemary
2 c. chicken broth
2 c. sour cream

3 c. chopped cooked chicken
2 6 1/2-oz. cans crab meat, flaked
1 1/2 c. avocado chunks with lemon juice
1 c. buttered coarse toast crumbs

Saute onion in butter in saucepan until golden. Blend in flour, salt, paprika and rosemary; heat until bubbly. Remove from heat; add chicken broth gradually. Bring to a boil; cook, stirring constantly, for 2 minutes. Remove from heat; blend in sour cream, small amount at a time. Add chicken and crab meat. Add avocado; mix well. Pour into 2-quart baking dish; cover with crumbs. Bake in preheated 350-degree oven for 30 minutes. Remove from oven; garnish with parsley or watercress. Serve immediately. Yield: 8 servings.

Laura Lynn Porter
Boron, California

FAMILY SUCCESS CASSEROLE

1 lb. ground beef
1 lb. ground pork
1 med. onion, chopped
1 lg. green pepper, chopped
1 1-lb. package egg noodles, cooked
Salt and pepper to taste
1 3-oz. package cream cheese
3 tbsp. Worcestershire sauce
2 cans tomato soup
2 soup cans water

Cook ground beef, ground pork, onion and green pepper in small amount of bacon fat until light brown. Drain off excess fat. Add noodles and remaining ingredients to beef mixture; mix well. Place in casserole. Bake in preheated 325-degree oven for about 1 hour and 15 minutes. Yield: 12 servings.

Mrs. A. W. Cummings
Kingsford, Michigan

MAGIC MEAT AND RICE

3/4 c. rice
2 c. boiling water
1 tsp. salt
1 lb. beef, cubed
1 lb. lean pork, cubed

2 tbsp. shortening
1 c. diced celery
1/4 c. chopped green pepper
1/2 c. chopped onion
1 can cream of mushroom soup
1 can chicken-noodle soup
2 tbsp. soy sauce

Place rice in greased 2-quart casserole; add water and salt. Set aside. Cook meats in shortening in skillet over low heat until brown. Place meats, celery, green pepper and onion over rice; stir in soups and soy sauce. Cover. Bake in preheated 325-degree oven for 2 hours. Yield: 6-8 servings.

Mrs. Dorothy Smith
Virginia, Illinois

CURRIED SHRIMP AND HAM CASSEROLE

1 4-oz. can sliced mushrooms
2 5-oz. cans shrimp
Milk
1/4 c. butter
1/4 c. chopped onion
1/4 c. chopped celery
1/4 c. flour
1 tsp. curry powder
1/2 tsp. salt
1/8 tsp. pepper
1/2 tsp. monosodium glutamate
2 c. chopped ham
3 c. cooked rice or noodles

Drain liquids from mushrooms and shrimp; pour liquids into 2-cup measure. Add enough milk to make 2 cups liquid. Melt butter in saucepan over low heat. Add onion and celery; cook until onion is transparent. Blend in flour and seasonings; heat until mixture is bubbly, stirring constantly. Remove from heat; add milk mixture gradually. Return to heat; bring to a boil. Cook, stirring, until thickened; stir in mushrooms, shrimp and ham. Place in casserole. Bake in preheated 325-degree oven for 20 to 30 minutes. Serve over rice. One can Spam, chopped, may be substituted for ham. Yield: 6 servings.

Mrs. Delores Linaman Ginsbach
Sisseton, South Dakota

SWISS TURKEY-HAM BAKE

1/2 c. chopped onion
5 tbsp. melted butter or margarine
3 tbsp. all-purpose flour
1/2 tsp. salt
1/4 tsp. pepper
1 3-oz. can sliced mushrooms
1 c. light cream
2 tbsp. dry sherry
2 c. cubed cooked turkey
1 c. cubed cooked ham
1 5-oz. can water chestnuts
1/2 c. shredded Swiss process cheese
1 1/3 c. soft bread crumbs

Cook onion in 2 tablespoons butter until tender but not brown; blend in flour, salt and pepper. Add mushrooms, cream and sherry; cook, stirring, until thickened. Add turkey and ham. Drain water chestnuts; slice. Add to turkey mixture; mix well. Pour into 1 1/2-quart casserole; top with cheese. Mix crumbs and remaining 3 tablespoons butter; sprinkle around edge of casserole. Bake in preheated 400-degree oven for 25 minutes or until lightly browned. Chicken may be substituted for turkey. Yield: 6 servings.

Mrs. Patricia Langston
Alamosa, Colorado

HAM-CHICKEN BAKE

1/2 c. chopped onion
1/2 c. chopped celery
1/4 c. butter or margarine
1/4 c. flour
1 1/2 c. chicken broth
1 1/2 c. light cream
2 c. diced cooked ham
2 c. diced cooked chicken
1 3-oz. can sliced mushrooms
1 tsp. poultry seasoning
3/4 tsp. salt
Dash of pepper
1/2 tsp. monosodium glutamate
1 c. mashed cooked yams
1/3 c. melted butter
1 egg, beaten

1 c. sifted flour
2 tsp. baking powder

Saute onion and celery in butter until tender; blend in flour. Stir in broth and cream; cook, stirring, until mixture comes to a boil. Add ham, chicken, mushrooms, poultry seasoning, 1/4 teaspoon salt, pepper and monosodium glutamate; heat through. Pour into ungreased baking dish. Combine yams, melted butter and egg in bowl. Sift flour, baking powder and remaining salt together; blend into yam mixture. Drop by spoonfuls around edge of baking dish. Bake in preheated 350-degree oven for 30 to 35 minutes.

Mrs. Guy Mitchell
Chataignier, Louisiana

CHICKEN AND DRESSING COMPANY CASSEROLE

3 sm. fryers
1 whole onion
1 whole carrot
2 tsp. salt
1/2 c. butter
1/2 c. minced onion
1 c. minced celery
1 1/2 loaves bread
2 tsp. poultry seasoning
2 cans cream of chicken soup
1 lg. can evaporated milk
Bread crumbs

Place fryers, whole onion, carrot and salt in large kettle. Pour in 2 quarts water; cook until fryers are tender. Remove fryers from broth; cool. Reserve broth. Remove skins and bones from chicken; cut chicken into bite-sized pieces. Melt butter in frypan. Add minced onion and celery; saute until transparent. Break bread into small pieces; add sauteed vegetables and poultry seasoning. Add enough reserved broth to moisten. Mix soup and milk until smooth. Place bread mixture in greased casserole; pour in half the soup mixture. Arrange chicken over soup mixture; add remaining soup mixture. Cover with bread crumbs. Bake in preheated 375-degree oven for 30 minutes. One stew-

ing chicken may be substituted for fryers. Yield: 12-15 servings.

Bonnie Muirbrook
Roy, Utah

NOODLE-CHICKEN AND GARDEN VEGETABLE CASSEROLE

Salt
1 8-oz. package med. egg noodles
2 ears of corn
3 tbsp. butter or margarine
1 3-lb. fryer, disjointed
1 c. chopped onions
3 med. carrots, cut into
    1 1/2-in. strips
1 med. zucchini, sliced
1 med. green pepper, cut into 1-in.
    pieces
1 lg. clove of garlic, crushed
3/4 tsp. crushed thyme
1/8 tsp. pepper
2 chicken bouillon cubes
3 med. tomatoes, cut into wedges (opt.)

Add 1 tablespoon salt to 3 quarts rapidly boiling water; add noodles gradually so that water continues to boil. Cook, stirring occasionally, until tender; drain in colander. Set aside. Place corn on cutting board; cut corn kernels from cob with sharp knife. Set aside. Melt butter in large skillet. Add chicken; cook for about 15 minutes or until brown. Remove chicken from skillet. Add onions, carrots, zucchini, green pepper, garlic and corn to skillet drippings; saute over medium-high heat for 2 minutes, stirring constantly. Stir in thyme, pepper and 1 1/2 teaspoons salt. Combine noodles and corn mixture; pour into ungreased 13 x 9-inch baking dish. Top with chicken pieces. Dissolve bouillon cubes in 3/4 cup boiling water; pour over chicken and noodle mixture. Cover dish with foil. Bake in preheated 350-degree oven for 45 minutes. Remove dish from oven; remove foil. Line edges of baking dish with tomato wedges. Increase heat to broiler setting. Place dish under broiler; broil until tomatoes are hot. One 10-ounce package frozen corn, thawed, may be substituted for fresh corn. Yield: 6 servings.

Photograph for this recipe above.

CRUSTY CHICKEN AND BROCCOLI CASSEROLE

2   10-oz. packages frozen broccoli
4 c. diced cooked chicken
2 cans cream of chicken soup
1 c. mayonnaise
1 tsp. curry powder
2 tbsp. lemon juice
1 c. bread crumbs
1/2 c. melted butter

Cook broccoli according to package directions until just tender; drain. Arrange in greased 11 x 7-inch baking pan. Arrange chicken on broccoli. Combine soup, mayonnaise, curry powder and lemon juice; spread over chicken. Combine crumbs and butter; sprinkle over soup mixture. Bake in preheated 350-degree oven for 50 minutes.

Mrs. Marlys Folkers
Cedar Falls, Iowa

MAKE-AHEAD TURKEY CASSEROLE

6 slices bread
2 c. diced cooked turkey
1/2 c. chopped onion
1/2 c. chopped celery
1/4 c. chopped green pepper
1/2 c. mayonnaise
3/4 tsp. salt
Dash of pepper
2 eggs, beaten
1 1/2 c. milk
1 can cream of mushroom soup
1/2 c. shredded Cheddar cheese

Trim crusts from 4 slices of bread; set bread aside. Crumble bread crusts. Cut remaining 2 slices bread into cubes; combine with crust crumbs. Place in 8-inch square baking dish. Combine turkey, onion, celery, green pepper, mayonnaise, salt and pepper; spoon over bread in baking dish. Arrange the 4 slices of bread over turkey mixture. Combine eggs and milk; pour over bread slices. Cover; chill for 1 hour or overnight. Stir mushroom soup until smooth; spread over bread. Bake in preheated 350-degree oven for 55 minutes.

Sprinkle cheese on top; bake for 5 minutes longer.

Mrs. Deborah Wheeler
Cabot, Vermont

BAKED FLOUNDER FILLET SUPREME

1   4-oz. can mushrooms
2 lb. flounder fillets
Seasoned salt to taste
1 lg. tomato
6 slices Swiss cheese
2 sm. onions, sliced
2 tbsp. butter
1 1/2 tbsp. flour
1/4 c. parsley flakes
Salt to taste
6 tbsp. sherry
1 c. light cream
2 c. rice, cooked

Drain mushrooms; reserve liquid. Sprinkle flounder fillets with seasoned salt; roll as for jelly roll. Secure with toothpicks. Cut tomato into 6 slices; cut cheese slices in half. Arrange half the flounder rolls in casserole; top with half the tomato slices. Place half the cheese slices over tomato slices; repeat layers. Saute mushrooms and onions in butter in saucepan until onion is tender; stir in flour, parsley flakes and salt. Add enough reserved mushroom liquid to sherry to measure 1/2 cup liquid. Add sherry mixture and cream to mushroom mixture; mix well. Bring to a boil, stirring constantly; pour over cheese slices. Bake in preheated 400-degree oven for 20 minutes; serve with rice. Yield: 6 servings.

Mrs. Bill Dobrinski
St. Charles, Missouri

SALMON-ALMOND CASSEROLE DELUXE

1   7 3/4-oz. can salmon
Milk
1/2 c. chopped onion
2 tbsp. diced green pepper
2 tbsp. butter or margarine
1 c. cooked rice
1 can mushroom soup
1 tbsp. lemon juice

1 tsp. Worcestershire sauce
1 3/4 c. crushed potato chips
1/4 c. blanched slivered almonds

Drain salmon; reserve liquid. Remove bones; flake salmon. Combine reserved liquid with enough milk to measure 2/3 cup liquid. Cook onion and green pepper in butter until tender; stir in salmon and rice. Combine soup, milk mixture, lemon juice and Worcestershire sauce. Place half the potato chips in greased 1 1/2-quart casserole; spread salmon mixture over potato chips. Pour soup mixture over salmon mixture; cover with remaining potato chips. Sprinkle with almonds; cover. Bake in preheated 350-degree oven for 20 to 30 minutes.

Mrs. Hilda B. Lye
Halifax, Nova Scotia, Canada

NEW ENGLAND TUNA CASSEROLE

1   6 1/2-oz. can tuna
3 hard-cooked eggs, sliced
1 c. cooked green peas
2 tbsp. chopped onion
2 tbsp. chopped parsley
2 tbsp. butter
2 tbsp. flour
2 c. milk
1 tsp. salt
1/2 tsp. pepper
1 1/2 c. mashed potatoes
1/2 c. grated American or Cheddar cheese

Drain and flake tuna; place in 2 1/2-quart buttered casserole. Arrange eggs over tuna; add peas. Cook onion and parsley in butter until onion is transparent; blend in flour. Add milk gradually; cook over low heat, stirring constantly, until thickened. Add salt and pepper; pour over peas. Arrange mashed potatoes around edge of casserole; sprinkle with cheese. Bake in preheated 350-degree oven for 25 to 30 minutes. Yield: 6 servings.

Susan Carothers
Murrysville, Pennsylvania

ROCK LOBSTER AND POTATOES NORMANDE

3   6-oz. frozen South African rock
    lobster tails

3 c. sliced cooked potatoes
2 tbsp. butter or margarine
2 tbsp. flour
2 c. milk
1 tsp. salt
1/2 tsp. pepper
1/4 c. drained capers
1/2 lb. Cheddar cheese, grated

Drop lobster tails into boiling, salted water. Bring to a boil; boil for 5 minutes. Drain immediately; drench with cold water. Cut away underside membrane with kitchen shears. Insert fingers between shell and lobster meat at heavy end of tail; work lobster meat loose from shell. Slice. Combine potatoes and lobster meat in greased 2-quart casserole. Melt butter in saucepan; stir in flour. Add milk gradually; cook over low heat, stirring constantly, until smooth and thickened. Add salt, pepper and capers. Stir in cheese; cook, stirring, until cheese is melted. Pour sauce over lobster mixture in casserole. Bake in preheated 375-degree oven for 20 minutes. Yield: 6 servings.

Photograph for this recipe on page 35.

OVERNIGHT CRAB SOUFFLE

8 to 10 slices bread, crusts removed
1 c. crab meat
1/2 c. mayonnaise
1 sm. onion, chopped
1 c. chopped celery
4 eggs, beaten
2 1/2 c. milk
1 can cream of mushroom soup
1 c. grated cheese

Crumble bread; place half the bread in buttered casserole. Combine crab meat, mayonnaise, onion and celery; place over bread. Add remaining bread. Combine eggs and milk in bowl; pour over bread. Cover; refrigerate overnight. Bake, uncovered, in preheated 325-degree oven for 1 hour. Stir soup until smooth; pour over casserole. Top with cheese. Bake for 15 minutes longer. Yield: 4 servings.

Marilyn Mills Anderson
Spokane, Washington

DEVILED CRAB CASSEROLE

1/2 c. chopped onion
1/4 c. chopped green pepper
3 tbsp. butter or margarine
3 tbsp. flour
1 1/2 c. half and half
2 egg yolks, slightly beaten
Dash of cayenne pepper
1/2 tsp. salt
2 tsp. Worcestershire sauce
1 tbsp. prepared mustard
1 tbsp. finely chopped chives
2 7 3/4-oz. cans crab meat or tuna
1 c. soft bread crumbs
2 tbsp. melted butter

Saute onion and green pepper in butter in saucepan until tender. Add flour; mix until smooth. Stir in half and half gradually; cook over medium heat, stirring constantly, until thickened. Stir small amount of hot sauce into egg yolks; add to remaining sauce in pan. Cook, stirring constantly, for 2 minutes; remove from heat. Add cayenne pepper, salt, Worcestershire sauce, mustard and chives, mix well. Stir in crab meat. Spoon into buttered 1-quart casserole. Combine bread crumbs and melted butter; sprinkle over crab mixture. Bake in preheated 375-degree oven for 20 to 25 minutes.

Susan J. Thomas
New Ipswich, New Hampshire

LOBSTER-CRAB MEAT AU GRATIN

2 or 3 boxes frozen lobster tails
2 tbsp. butter
2 tbsp. flour
1/2 c. milk
1/2 c. cream
1 egg yolk, beaten
1/4 tsp. pepper
1 c. grated Parmesan cheese
1 sm. onion, chopped fine
1 7-oz. package frozen King crab, thawed
Bread crumbs
Paprika

Cook lobster tails according to package directions; remove shells. Cut lobster into pieces. Melt butter in heavy saucepan; stir in flour until smooth. Add milk and cream gradually; cook, stirring constantly, until smooth and thick. Stir small amount of hot sauce into egg yolk; stir egg yolk mixture into hot sauce. Add pepper and cheese; cook until cheese is melted. Saute onion in small amount of fat until clear. Stir lobster, crab meat and onion into cheese sauce; pour into casserole. Cover with bread crumbs; sprinkle with paprika. Bake in preheated 400-degree oven until bubbly and brown; serve with rice.

Joan Joslin
Rome, New York

SCALLOPS AU GRATIN

2 tbsp. butter
1/4 c. all-purpose flour
1 c. milk
1 12-oz. package frozen scallops, thawed and drained
1 4-oz. can sliced mushrooms
1/4 c. chopped green onions
1 tsp. grated lemon peel
1/8 tsp. garlic powder
1/8 tsp. nutmeg
1 c. shredded Cheddar cheese
2 tbsp. fine dry bread crumbs
Paprika
English muffin halves, buttered and toasted
Tomato slices

Melt butter in large skillet; blend in flour. Cook over low heat, stirring, until smooth. Remove from heat; stir in milk. Add scallops, mushrooms with liquid, onions, lemon peel, garlic powder and nutmeg. Cook over medium heat, stirring, for about 5 minutes or until thickened. Turn into 1-quart buttered baking dish. Combine cheese and bread crumbs. Sprinkle over scallop mixture; sprinkle with paprika. Bake in preheated 325-degree oven for 20 minutes or until bubbly. Top each English muffin half with 1 slice tomato; spoon scallop mixture over tomato. Yield: 4 servings.

Photograph for this recipe on page 149.

SCALLOPED OYSTERS

1 qt. oysters
1 egg, beaten
1 c. milk
2/3 c. butter
4 c. toasted bread crumbs
1 tsp. salt
1/4 tsp. paprika
1/4 c. finely chopped celery
4 drops of Tabasco sauce

Drain oysters; reserve liquid. Combine reserved liquid, egg and milk. Melt butter in saucepan; stir in crumbs, salt, paprika, celery and Tabasco sauce. Place half the crumb mixture in 2 1/2-quart baking dish; cover with half the oysters. Add half the milk mixture. Add remaining crumb mixture; cover with remaining oysters. Pour remaining milk mixture over top. Bake in preheated 350-degree oven for 30 to 45 minutes or until done. Cracker crumbs may be substituted for bread crumbs. Yield: 8 servings.

Evelyn B. Willey
Gatesville, North Carolina

FAVORITE SHRIMP CASSEROLE

8 hard-cooked eggs
1/2 tsp. prepared mustard
2 drops of Tabasco sauce
1/2 c. mayonnaise
1/4 tsp. sugar
Salt and pepper to taste
1/2 c. butter
1/2 c. flour
1 qt. milk
1 tbsp. dry mustard
1 tbsp. seasoned salt
1 tbsp. Worcestershire sauce
1/2 c. shredded sharp Cheddar cheese
1 tsp. garlic salt
1 tbsp. catsup
1/4 c. dry sherry or vermouth
2 tbsp. parsley flakes
2 lb. cooked cleaned shrimp
Buttered cracker crumbs

Cut eggs into halves lengthwise; remove yolks. Mash yolks in bowl. Add prepared mustard, Tabasco sauce, mayonnaise, sugar, salt and pepper; mix well. Fill egg whites with yolk mixture; set aside. Melt butter in saucepan; stir in flour until smooth. Add milk gradually; cook, stirring constantly, until thickened. Add remaining ingredients except crumbs; mix well. Place half the egg halves in baking dish; cover with half the shrimp sauce. Repeat layers. Cover with buttered cracker crumbs. Bake in preheated 350-degree oven for 25 to 30 minutes or until bubbly and brown. One clove of garlic, pressed, may be used instead of garlic salt.

Mrs. Lois W. Gerald
Whiteville, North Carolina

MRS. DUHON'S SHRIMP CASSEROLE

1/2 c. butter or margarine
1/2 c. chopped bell pepper
1/2 c. chopped onion
1/2 c. sliced celery
1/2 clove of garlic, minced
2 c. cleaned fresh shrimp, chopped
2 tbsp. chopped green onion
2 tbsp. chopped parsley
1 tsp. salt
1/2 tsp. pepper
1/2 tsp. paprika
1 sm. jar pimentos
1 can cream of mushroom soup
2 c. cooked rice
1/2 c. dry bread crumbs

Melt butter in skillet. Add bell pepper, onion, celery and garlic; cook until tender. Add shrimp, green onion, parsley, salt, pepper and paprika; cook until shrimp turn pink. Drain pimentos; chop. Add to shrimp mixture. Stir in soup and rice; pour into casserole. Top with crumbs; cover. Bake in preheated 375-degree oven for 45 minutes. Yield: 6 servings.

Mrs. Ann McDonald
Houston, Texas

CABBAGE AU GRATIN

3 c. shredded cabbage
1 tsp. salt
1 tsp. sugar
1/3 c. water
2 tbsp. butter

2 tbsp. sifted flour
1 c. milk
1/2 c. shredded Cheddar process cheese
Buttered bread crumbs

Place cabbage in saucepan; add 1/2 teaspoon salt, sugar and water. Cover; cook for 8 to 10 minutes. Melt butter in 1-quart saucepan over low heat; add flour. Mix until smooth. Add remaining 1/2 teaspoon salt and milk; cook over medium heat, stirring, until smooth and thickened. Add cheese; reduce heat to low. Stir until cheese melts. Place half the cabbage in casserole; pour half the sauce over cabbage. Repeat layers; cover with bread crumbs. Bake in preheated 350-degree oven for 20 minutes or until brown and bubbly. Yield: 6 servings.

Mildred Tate
Lebanon, Virginia

PEPPERY CORN CASSEROLE

1 sm. can pimentos
1 green pepper, chopped
1 med. onion, chopped
1/2 c. margarine
1/4 c. flour
2 c. whole kernel corn
1 can mushroom soup
2 hard-cooked eggs, finely chopped
1 tsp. Worcestershire sauce
1 1/2 tsp. salt
Pepper to taste
2 c. cooked rice
1/2 tsp. Tabasco sauce
Grated cheese or crushed potato chips

Drain pimentos; chop. Cook green pepper and onion in margarine until tender. Add flour; stir until blended. Add pimentos and remaining ingredients except cheese; mix well. Pour into greased casserole; cover with cheese. Bake in preheated 325 to 350-degree oven until brown. Yield: 8 servings.

Ovelle Benefield
Sylvania, Alabama

EGGPLANT PARMIGIANA

1 lg. eggplant, peeled
Salt

4 tbsp. butter
1 lb. ground beef
2 tbsp. chopped parsley
1/2 c. chopped onion
1/4 tsp. pepper
4 med. tomatoes, peeled and sliced
1/4 c. grated Parmesan cheese
3 slices mozzarella cheese

Cut eggplant into 12 slices; sprinkle with salt to taste. Let stand for 5 minutes; pat dry. Saute in butter until golden brown; drain on paper toweling. Brown beef; stir in parsley, onion, pepper, 1 teaspoon salt and tomatoes. Cook for about 10 minutes. Place 6 eggplant slices in shallow casserole; add meat sauce. Top with remaining eggplant; cover with Parmesan cheese and mozzarella cheese. Bake in preheated 350-degree oven for 30 minutes or until done. Yield: 6 servings.

Linda Louise Givens
Richmond, Virginia

POTATO-OLIVE BAKE

3 tbsp. butter or margarine
3 tbsp. flour
1 tsp. salt
1/8 tsp. pepper
1 1/2 c. milk
1 onion, grated
1/2 c. sliced ripe olives
1 c. shredded sharp cheese
3 c. diced cooked potatoes
1 c. soft bread crumbs
2 tbsp. melted butter

Melt butter in saucepan over low heat. Stir in flour, salt and pepper until blended. Add milk, stirring constantly; cook until thick, stirring frequently. Remove from heat. Add onion, olives and cheese; stir until cheese is melted. Add potatoes; pour into greased casserole. Mix bread crumbs and melted butter; sprinkle over potato mixture. Bake in preheated 350-degree oven for 35 to 40 minutes. Yield: 6 servings.

Mrs. J. W. Poole
Wytheville, Virginia

Quick and Easy Favorites

In this modern age of fast food restaurants and TV dinners, the emphasis on cooking seems to be the quicker the better. While quality meals are still demanded, the time it takes to prepare them does not seem as important as it once was. In fact, more compliments are won by dishes that appear and taste as if they were difficult to prepare than those dishes which really do require a lot of effort to make.

Concerned housewives and mothers striving to provide well-balanced meals for their families often find it hard when there is little time to spend in the kitchen. Because so many of us were raised hearing grandma's tales of the old days when her mother cooked from morning to night, we often feel neglectful when we don't spend hours cooking a meal. In those days, work began at sunup and ended at sundown. Men, women and children had their chores to keep them busy throughout most of the day. To keep up the strength needed for such strenuous labor, large meals were a must. Gradually, as technology has continued to develop, jobs have changed and, in turn, our need for large quantities of food is not as great. However, nutrition is still as important now as it was then. And, homemakers are beginning to realize that they can easily provide their families with nutritious foods with a minimum amount of effort.

Have you ever caught yourself wishing dinner would instantly appear on the table? On those tiring days when the shopping has to be done, the house needs cleaning and the children have to be picked up from school, why not let the Home Economics Teachers come to your aid? Their ideas and recipes for Quick and Easy Favorites are suited to the busy life of today's wife, mother and career woman and will surely be a big help to you.

Planning ahead is one of the most beneficial things you can do. Be ready when guests drop in unexpectedly or when you are late getting home from the office. Keep your kitchen stocked with a variety of quick foods including soups, meats, fish, fruits, vegetables, starches, bread mixes, desserts and miscellaneous items such as pickles, nuts, powdered milk and mayonnaise. Canned and packaged foods can bring just the rescue you need in an emergency while providing many of the nutrients that we require. Usually, people don't like to think of eating "out of a can" but, many delicious meals have been prepared exactly this way. Tuna casseroles, ham sandwiches, pear salads, mashed potatoes, blueberry muffins and a chocolate cake can all be made in no time at all with the help of convenience foods such as these.

Another innovation which has proven to be quite a time-saver for the homemaker is frozen food. A freezer well stocked with prepackaged seafood, vegetables and breads can often be the answer to breakfast, lunch or dinner. Although canned, packaged and frozen foods are sometimes more expensive than fresh foods, time is often very valuable, making them worth a little extra expense. On the other hand, freezing homemade foods is something you can do yourself. On those days when you can enjoy being in the kitchen, double your recipes. Dishes such as meat loaf, spaghetti and casseroles freeze very well and can practically serve as complete meals in themselves.

Times have certainly changed since pioneer women cooked their meals for hours in heavy iron pots hanging in the fireplace. While the actual cooking was long, hot work, so was the planting, cultivating and harvesting that had to be done each and every year. Without a doubt, those hard workers would be more than amazed if they could see today's grocery store shelves lined with canned corn, beans and peas.

Once you have stocked your shelves with these foods, the trick is to know how to use them. Be familiar with your recipes so you can easily plan meals in a hurry. Know what foods can be combined to make both a well-balanced and delectable meal.

Make sure that the recipes you turn to are reliable ones. Part of a Home Economics Teacher's duty is to keep up-to-date on nutrition and new foods. Consequently, this collection of tested recipes is one of the best you'll find anywhere. Because they are the Home Economics Teachers' favorites, they are ones you can depend on too. In fact, some of these recipes have been developed especially for the busy homemaker. All of them will take the guesswork out of mixing something together quickly and easily.

Typically, every cook has her own way of doing things in the kitchen. And, everyone has developed certain tricks-of-the-trade to facilitate the cooking process. Throughout the years, these tips have been passed down from generation to generation — closely guarded shortcut secrets that yield excellent results every time. Those days spent watching mother and grandmother prepare a meal were ideal times to learn the simplest ways to cook.

Quick and easy food preparation also requires an organized kitchen. Keeping such things as pots, pans, utensils, spices and hot pads close at hand is a must, for knowing exactly where to locate them will save you both time and effort.

Finally, be sure you are making the most of your electrical appliances. Probably the latest time-saving devices on the market are the slow cooker or crock pot and the microwave oven. Ideal for the working wife or housewife on the run, a crock pot can be turned on early in the morning before leaving the house, cook at a low tem-perature all day, and have supper ready and waiting to be served when you arrive home that evening. Today many women are enjoying this convenience. Also the microwave oven cooks an enormous variety of foods in a fraction of the time it normally takes. Two other major appliances that are tops for quick and easy cooking are the pressure cooker and the blender. Both cut time and work to a minimum in that the pressure cooker produces a hot meal in minutes and the blender reduces chopping, grating and mincing time.

Methods of cooking have certainly changed since the days of our forefathers. But, the same nutritious, taste-tempting dishes that were enjoyed then are still loved today. The only difference is the amount of time spent preparing them. The Home Economics Teachers want you to be just as proud of the meals you prepare as the pioneer women were hundreds of years ago. As we take time to look back at our country's great past, we can also save time by trying the quick and easy recipes gathered here.

HOT CHOCOLATE MIX

1 c. cocoa
1/2 c. confectioners' sugar
1/4 tsp. salt
1/2 c. non-dairy coffee creamer
4 c. instant nonfat dry milk

Combine all ingredients; store in covered container. Stir 6 tablespoons hot chocolate mix into 3/4 cup hot water to serve.

Mrs. Mary Jo Clapp
Sidell, Illinois

RUSSIAN TEA

1/2 c. instant tea
2 1/2 c. sugar
2 c. Tang
2 sm. packages lemonade mix
1 tsp. cloves
2 tsp. ground cinnamon

Mix all ingredients together; store in covered jar. Dissolve 2 teaspoons tea mixture in 1 cup hot water to serve.

Mrs. Evelyn Wagner
Eidson, Tennessee

EASY CALIFORNIA FRUIT SALAD

1 c. mandarin oranges, drained
1 c. pineapple chunks, drained
1/2 c. maraschino cherries, drained
1 c. flaked coconut
1 c. miniature marshmallows
1 c. sour cream

Mix all ingredients in bowl; chill for several hours. Yield: 8 servings.

Mrs. Sharon Doke
Weed, California

PEACH HALVES DELIGHT

1 3-oz. package cream cheese
2 to 3 tbsp. salad dressing
1/4 c. chopped pecans
4 lg. peach halves
4 lettuce leaves

Mash cream cheese with a fork. Add salad dressing gradually; mix until smooth and creamy. Stir in pecans. Fill each peach half with cheese mixture; serve on a lettuce leaf. Yield: 4 servings.

Mrs. Quincy Rollins
McKinney, Texas

SLICED FROZEN FRUIT SALAD

1 1-lb. can fruit cocktail
4 lettuce leaves
Whipped cream or salad dressing

Freeze can of fruit cocktail. Open both ends of can; push fruit cocktail out. Cut into 4 slices. Serve on lettuce; garnish with whipped cream. Serve immediately. Yield: 4 servings.

Catherine Thomas
Dyer, Tennessee

CHEESE AND BACON PINWHEEL

8 slices bacon
6 slices American cheese, quartered
4 eggs
1/2 c. milk
1/4 c. chopped pimento
1/4 tsp. salt

Place bacon in shallow baking pan. Bake in preheated 350-degree oven for 15 minutes. Arrange cheese in lightly greased 9-inch pie pan. Beat eggs; stir in milk, pimento and salt. Pour over cheese; arrange bacon strips in pinwheel fashion on top. Bake in preheated 350-degree oven for 25 minutes or until knife inserted in center comes out clean. Yield: 3-4 servings.

Mrs. Jean Hall
Frackville, Pennsylvania

CHEESE RAREBIT

1 can Cheddar cheese soup
1/4 tsp. prepared mustard
1/4 c. milk
4 slices tomato
4 slices toast

Blend soup, mustard and milk in saucepan; heat through, stirring frequently. Place tomato slices on toast; pour sauce over tomatoes. Yield: 4 servings.

Dorothy E. Brevoort
Beach Haven, New Jersey

CHEESE SURPRISE

1 10-oz. package frozen chopped broccoli
12 slices bread
3/4 lb. sliced sharp process cheese
2 c. diced ham
6 eggs, slightly beaten
3 1/2 c. milk
1/4 tsp. salt
1 tsp. dried onion flakes
1/2 tsp. dry mustard

Cook broccoli according to package directions; drain well. Place half the bread slices in 13 x 9 x 2-inch pan. Cover with layers of cheese, broccoli and ham; top with remaining bread. Mix eggs, milk, salt, onion and mustard; pour over bread. Place in refrigerator overnight. Bake in preheated 325-degree oven for 55 minutes or until done. Yield: 6 servings.

Mrs. Lois Brown
Blue River, Wisconsin

CREAMED EGGS WITH PEAS

1 10-oz. package frozen peas
1/2 c. milk
1 can cream of celery soup
6 hard-cooked eggs, sliced
1 6-oz. can fried noodles

Cook peas according to package directions; drain. Combine milk and soup in saucepan. Add eggs and peas; heat through. Serve over noodles. Yield: 6 servings.

Mrs. Mary A. E. Gregory
Ephrata, Pennsylvania

RANCH RICE

1 c. uncooked rice
1 can consomme

1 can onion soup
1 2 1/2-oz. can mushroom stems and pieces
1/2 c. melted margarine

Combine all ingredients in 1 1/2-quart casserole; cover. Bake in preheated 350-degree oven for 45 minutes to 1 hour, stirring once while baking. Yield: 4-6 servings.

Mrs. Elaine Buston Booker
Ft. Myers, Florida

CHILI TWIST

2 c. egg noodles
3 qt. boiling water
1 tbsp. salt
2 15 1/2-oz. cans chili con carne
1 tbsp. parsley flakes
1/2 tsp. sweet basil leaves, crushed
1/4 tsp. powdered oregano
2 8-oz. cans tomato sauce

Cook noodles in boiling water with salt until tender; drain. Place in saucepan. Add remaining ingredients; mix well. Heat through. Yield: 4-6 servings.

Mrs. Darlene La Borde
Richland, Washington

TOMATO-CHEESE MACARONI

2 c. macaroni
1 can tomato soup
1/2 c. milk
2 c. shredded Cheddar cheese
1/4 c. chopped parsley
2 tbsp. buttered bread crumbs

Cook macaroni according to package directions. Mix soup, milk and 1 1/2 cups cheese in saucepan; place over low heat until cheese melts. Stir in parsley and macaroni; pour into greased 2-quart casserole. Top with remaining cheese, then bread crumbs. Bake in preheated 400-degree oven for 20 minutes or until heated through. Yield: 6 servings.

Mrs. C. William Franks
Ravenna, Ohio

FLANK STEAK SUPREME

1 flank steak
Onion salt to taste
1 can mushroom steak sauce

Place steak on 12 x 24-inch piece of aluminum foil; season with onion salt. Spread mushroom steak sauce over steak; roll steak as for jelly roll. Wrap with the foil; seal. Place in baking pan. Bake in preheated 350-degree oven for 1 hour and 30 minutes. May be cooked in pressure cooker for 45 minutes. Yield: 4 servings.

Mrs. Joyce Ferrce
McLean, Illinois

GROUND BEEF CHOW MEIN

2 lb. ground beef
1 c. chopped celery
1/2 c. chopped onion
1 can cream of mushroom soup
1 can cream of chicken soup
1 5-oz. can chow mein noodles

Cook ground beef, celery and onion until beef is brown. Add soups and noodles; mix well. Place in large casserole. Bake in preheated 350-degree oven for 40 to 50 minutes. May be made ahead and stored in refrigerator before baking. Yield: 8 servings.

Dorothy Deare Stutz
Bellevue, Washington

SPANISH BEEF WITH NOODLES

1 lb. ground beef
1 med. onion, chopped
2 tbsp. shortening
2 tsp. salt
1 tsp. chili powder
Dash of Tabasco sauce
1 can tomato soup
1 soup can water
1 c. whole kernel corn with peppers
1 6-oz. package noodles

Cook beef and onion in large frying pan in shortening until brown. Add salt, chili powder and Tabasco sauce; cook for 2 minutes.

Mix soup with water; add to beef mixture. Stir in corn and noodles; simmer until noodles are tender. Yield: 6 servings.

Dora Nicholson Greene
Lucedale, Mississippi

PORK CHOPS SUPREME

4 pork chops, 1 in. thick
Salt and pepper to taste
4 slices onion
4 slices tomato

Place pork chops in shallow pan; sprinkle with salt and pepper. Place onion slice on top of each chop; sprinkle with salt and pepper. Place tomato slice on top of each onion slice; season with salt and pepper. Add enough water to cover bottom of pan. Bake in preheated 350-degree oven for 1 hour, adding water, if needed. Yield: 4 servings.

Eunice F. Lewis
Chesapeake, Virginia

HAM AND OKRA CUSTARD CASSEROLE

2 tbsp. butter or margarine, softened
5 tbsp. flour
1 tbsp. minced onion
Dash of Tabasco sauce
1 tsp. Worcestershire sauce
1 qt. milk, scalded
5 eggs, separated
1 10-oz. package frozen cut okra,
    cooked according to package directions
1 c. finely chopped cooked ham
1/2 tsp. salt

Blend butter and flour to smooth paste in large mixing bowl. Stir in onion, Tabasco sauce and Worcestershire sauce. Add milk gradually, stirring until smooth and blended. Beat in egg yolks, one at a time. Stir in okra and ham. Combine egg whites and salt; beat until stiff peaks form. Fold into milk mixture. Turn into lightly greased 3-quart souffle dish or straight-sided casserole. Bake in preheated 350-degree oven for 35 to 40 minutes. Serve at once. Yield: 6 servings.

Photograph for this recipe on page 159.

CHINESE PORK AND RICE

2/3 c. rice
2 tbsp. salad oil
1 tsp. salt
1 1/2 c. boiling water
1 bouillon cube
2 tsp. soy sauce
1 med. onion, chopped
2 stalks celery, chopped
1 green pepper, chopped
1 1/2 c. diced cooked pork

Cook rice in hot oil in saucepan until golden brown. Stir in salt, water, bouillon cube and soy sauce; cover. Cook for 20 minutes. Add remaining ingredients; cover. Cook for 10 minutes longer, adding small amount of water, if needed. Yield: 4-6 servings.

Mrs. La Vera Kraig
Aberdeen, South Dakota

QUICKIE MEAT PIE

Sliced leftover pork or beef roast
1 can cream of chicken soup
1/2 soup can water
1/4 tsp. Accent
1/2 tsp. dried onion flakes
Dash of celery salt
Dash of dill salt
Dash of Lawry's seasoning
1 can refrigerator biscuits

Arrange desired amount of pork roast slices in casserole. Pour chicken soup over pork; add water. Add seasonings; arrange biscuits over top. Bake in preheated 425-degree oven until biscuits are brown.

Ruth C. Peabody
Sunnyside, Washington

HAM HASH

1 tbsp. oil
2 c. diced ham
2 tbsp. minced onion
1 sm. package frozen mixed vegetables
1 c. frozen hashed brown potatoes

Heat oil in heavy skillet. Add ham and onion; cook until brown. Add 1/2 cup boiling water and vegetables; bring to a boil. Reduce heat; simmer for 6 to 10 minutes or until vegetables are just tender. Yield: 4 servings.

Mrs. M. E. Friels
Duncan, Oklahoma

SOUP KETTLE SUPPER

8 slices bacon, diced
1 c. diced cooked ham
1 1/3 c. beef broth
2 c. water
1 1/3 c. whole kernel corn
1 2/3 c. cut green beans
2 c. canned tomatoes
2 tsp. salt
1/8 tsp. pepper
1 4 1/2-oz. package instant rice
1 tbsp. minced parsley

Fry bacon in large, heavy saucepan until nearly crisp; pour off all except 2 tablespoons drippings. Cook ham in drippings until lightly browned. Add remaining ingredients except rice and parsley; bring to a boil. Add rice; cover. Let stand for 10 minutes. Add parsley; serve immediately. Yield: 8-10 servings.

Mrs. Ina Hooper
Elizabeth, Louisiana

KRAUT AND LINKS PAN-DANGO

1 16-oz. can whole tomatoes
1 lb. pork sausage links
1 med. onion, chopped
1 garlic clove, minced
3 1/2 c. drained sauerkraut
1 med. green pepper, diced
2 tbsp. (packed) dark brown sugar
1 1/2 tsp. salt
1 tsp. basil, crushed

Drain tomatoes, reserving liquid. Quarter each tomato; set aside. Cook sausage according to package directions in large skillet; drain on paper toweling. Reserve about 2 tablespoons drippings. Add onion and garlic to reserved drippings in skillet. Saute over medium heat, stirring occasionally, for about 5 minutes or until onion is tender. Stir in reserved tomato liquid, quartered tomatoes and remaining ingredients. Cook, uncovered, for about 5 minutes, stirring frequently. Top kraut mixture with cooked sausages. Cook for about 5 minutes or until sausages are heated through. Yield: 4 servings.

Photograph for this recipe on page 152.

QUICK SAUSAGE PIE

1 lb. sausage
2 lg. onions, chopped
1 green pepper, chopped
1 lb. ground beef
1 recipe corn bread batter

Combine sausage, onions and green pepper in skillet; fry until sausage is partially cooked. Crumble ground beef; stir into sausage mixture. Cook until ground beef is brown. Spread in 11 x 13-inch baking pan; pour corn bread batter over top. Bake in preheated 375-degree oven for 20 minutes or until corn bread is done. Yield: 12 servings.

Mrs. Dorothy Bent
Bethel, Vermont

ASPARAGUS POULTRY DELIGHT

2 c. diced cooked chicken or turkey
1 1/2 c. cooked cut asparagus
1/2 c. sliced water chestnuts
1 1/2 c. chicken consomme or stock
1 1/2 tbsp. flour
1/2 tsp. salt
1/2 tsp. pepper

Combine chicken, asparagus and water chestnuts in greased casserole. Heat consomme; blend in flour and seasonings. Pour over chicken mixture. Bake in preheated 325-degree oven for 20 minutes or until heated through and bubbly. Yield: 4-6 servings.

Mrs. Mary Pinkston Whaley
Northport, Alabama

CHICKEN-NOODLE CASSEROLE

1/2 lb. noodles
1 can cream of mushroom soup
6 chicken legs and thighs
Salt, pepper and paprika to taste

Cook noodles in boiling water until just tender; drain well. Mix with soup. Place in 3-quart casserole; arrange chicken on top of noodles. Sprinkle with salt, pepper and paprika. Bake, covered, in preheated 350-degree oven for 1 hour or until chicken is tender. Yield: 6 servings.

Mrs. Doris Atkinson
Erie, Pennsylvania

CHICKEN SPAGHETTI

1 1/2 c. cooked chicken
2 c. consomme or broth
1/2 c. tomato soup
3/4 clove of garlic, chopped
3 tbsp. chopped onion
2 whole cloves
3 tbsp. mushrooms
3/4 tsp. salt
3/4 c. broken spaghetti

Cut chicken into 1-inch pieces. Combine chicken, consomme, soup, garlic, onion and cloves in saucepan. Add mushrooms; cook over moderate heat for 10 minutes. Season with salt. Add spaghetti; boil gently for 10 minutes or until spaghetti is tender. Serve hot. Yield: 6 servings.

Mary Jo Baty
Shelbyville, Texas

CHICKEN SOPA

1 doz. corn tortillas
1 5-oz. can boned chicken
1 sm. can chopped green chilies
1 lb. grated Velveeta cheese
1 can chicken soup

Place 1/3 of the tortillas in greased casserole; cover with 1/3 of the chicken, chilies and cheese. Repeat layers 2 times; spread soup over top layer. Bake, covered, in preheated 350-degree oven for 20 minutes or until heated through. May be prepared a day ahead and refrigerated until ready to bake. Yield: 8 servings.

Billye Slaton
Marfa, Texas

EASY CHICKEN AND RICE

1/2 to 1 c. rice
1 can onion soup
1 fryer, disjointed
Salt and pepper to taste
1 can cream of celery or chicken soup

Sprinkle rice into baking pan; pour onion soup over rice. Add 1 cup water. Sprinkle chicken with salt and pepper; place over onion soup. Spread cream of celery soup over chicken. Bake, uncovered, in preheated 325 to 350-degree oven for 1 hour to 1 hour and 30 minutes. Add water, as necessary, to keep moist. Curry powder may be added, if desired. Yield: 4 servings.

Mrs. Larry D. Schmidt
Velva, North Dakota

WORKING GIRL'S CHICKEN

4 whole chicken legs
4 whole chicken breasts
1 tsp. salt
1/2 tsp. pepper
1/8 tsp. garlic powder
1 can cream of mushroom soup
1 soup can milk

Season chicken with salt, pepper and garlic powder. Dilute soup with milk. Place chicken in buttered casserole; cover with soup. Bake in preheated 400-degree oven for 1 hour or until tender.

Mrs. Mercer Clementson
Chattanooga, Tennessee

IN A JIFFY TURKEY

1 1/2 c. chopped celery
1 sm. onion, chopped
Melted margarine
4 c. cooked cubed turkey
2 tbsp. minced parsley
1 1/2 c. mayonnaise
2 cans water chestnuts, drained and
    sliced
1 can cream of mushroom soup
2 c. corn bread stuffing mix
3/4 c. hot water

Saute celery and onion in 2 tablespoons melted margarine until onion is tender. Combine onion mixture, turkey, parsley, mayonnaise, water chestnuts and soup; spoon into 9 x 13-inch baking pan. Mix stuffing mix and water; sprinkle over turkey mixture. Drizzle with 1/3 cup melted margarine. Bake in preheated 350-degree oven for 30 minutes or until brown.

Mrs. Patricia A. Gannon
Kenmore, New York

QUICK TURKEY LOAF

4 eggs, beaten
2/3 c. milk or broth
1 tsp. salt
1 c. soft bread crumbs
2 tbsp. chopped green pepper
2 tbsp. chopped pimento
1/2 tbsp. parsley flakes
2 tbsp. melted butter
3 c. chopped cooked turkey

Combine eggs, milk, salt, bread crumbs, green pepper, pimento, parsley, butter and turkey; mix well. Spoon into greased 7 x 4 x 4-inch loaf pan. Bake in preheated 325-degree oven for 45 to 50 minutes.

Lucille S. Brown
Narrows, Virginia

BAKED SOLE

1 lg. onion
4 fillets of sole
Salt and pepper to taste
1 tbsp. dried parsley
1 No. 303 can tomatoes

Slice onion; place half the slices in lightly greased casserole. Place sole on top; sprinkle with salt, pepper and parsley. Arrange remaining onion slices over sole; pour tomatoes over top. Bake in preheated 350-degree oven for 35 minutes or until sole is tender. Yield: 4 servings.

Mrs. Forrest Schaad
Fair Oaks, California

EASY SEAFOOD CASSEROLE

1 can mushroom soup
1/3 c. salad dressing
1/3 c. milk
6 oz. crab, tuna or shrimp
1 can water chestnuts, drained
1 c. diced celery
Pinch of coarsely ground pepper
Small amount of onion (opt.)
2 c. cooked macaroni
2 tbsp. paprika

Combine all ingredients except paprika; mix well. Place in baking dish; sprinkle with paprika. Bake in preheated 350-degree oven for 30 to 40 minutes or until heated through and bubbly. Yield: 6 servings.

Mrs. Joan Murphy
Chinook, Montana

MIXED SEAFOOD CASSEROLE

1 can white crab meat, drained
2 cans shrimp, drained
1/2 c. chopped green pepper
3/4 c. chopped celery
3/4 c. mayonnaise
1 c. grated cheese
2 tsp. Worcestershire sauce
1/2 tsp. salt
Cracker crumbs

Combine all ingredients except crumbs; toss lightly. Place in buttered casserole; sprinkle crumbs on top. Bake in preheated 350-degree oven for 30 minutes or until heated through and bubbly. Freezes well. Yield: 6 servings.

Mrs. Rachel Nicholson
Union, Mississippi

QUICK CHINESE SUPPER

1 3-oz. can chow mein noodles
1 15-oz. can peas, drained
1 can mushroom soup
2 7-oz. cans tuna
1/2 soup can milk
2 tbsp. chopped celery
1 tsp. chopped onion (opt.)

1/2 c. cashew nuts (opt.)
1/2 c. drained mandarin oranges (opt.)

Reserve 1/2 cup noodles. Combine remaining noodles and all ingredients except mandarin oranges; pour into buttered 1 1/2-quart casserole. Top with reserved noodles. Bake in preheated 350-degree oven for 25 to 30 minutes or until heated through. Garnish with additional mandarin oranges.

Mrs. Norma Booshey
Sumner, Washington

TUNA CHOW MEIN CASSEROLE

1 can cream of mushroom soup
1 1-lb. can peas and liquid
1 4-oz. can pimento, diced
2 tbsp. chopped onion
1 tbsp. lemon juice
1 3-oz. can chow mein noodles
2 7-oz. cans tuna in oil, drained

Combine soup, peas, pimento, onion and lemon juice in 1 1/2-quart casserole. Reserve 1 cup noodles; fold remaining noodles and tuna into soup mixture. Arrange reserved noodles around edge of casserole. Bake in preheated 375-degree oven for 25 minutes or until heated through. Yield: 6 servings.

Mrs. Minta Skaggs
Hazard, Kentucky

TUNA-NOODLE CASSEROLE

2 6 1/2-oz. cans tuna
1 can cream of mushroom soup
10 stuffed olives, chopped
6 oz. egg noodles, cooked and drained
1/2 c. grated Cheddar cheese

Combine tuna, soup and olives. Place half the noodles in casserole; cover with half the tuna mixture. Repeat layers using remaining noodles and tuna. Sprinkle grated cheese over top. Bake, covered, in preheated 400-degree oven for 20 minutes. Uncover; bake for 10 minutes longer or until top is lightly browned. Yield: 6 servings.

Anita Dugger
Phoenix, Arizona

SHRIMP SCAMPI

1/4 c. butter or margarine
2 lb. large shrimp, shelled and deveined
2 garlic cloves, minced
2   16-oz. cans apricot halves, drained
1/3 c. chopped parsley
2 tbsp. lemon juice
3/4 tsp. salt
1/4 tsp. pepper

Melt butter in large skillet; add shrimp and garlic. Saute, stirring constantly, for about 3 to 5 minutes or until shrimp turns pink. Stir in apricots and remaining ingredients. Cook, stirring gently, for about 2 to 3 minutes or until apricots are heated through. Serve immediately. Two pounds frozen shrimp, thawed and drained, may be used, if desired.

Photograph for this recipe above.

FISH FILLETS WITH RICE

1/4 c. chopped onion
5 tbsp. butter
2 c. cooked rice
2 tbsp. lemon juice
1 egg, lightly beaten
Salt and pepper to taste
1 lb. frozen fish fillets, partially
   thawed
Paprika to taste

Cook onion in 2 tablespoons butter until slightly tender; stir into rice. Mix in lemon juice, egg and a dash of salt. Place half the fillets in buttered 10 x 6 x 1 1/2-inch baking dish; season with salt and pepper. Top with rice mixture; arrange remaining fillets over rice. Brush with remaining melted butter; sprinkle with salt, pepper and paprika. Bake in preheated 375-degree oven for 35 minutes or until fish is tender, brushing occasionally with additional melted butter, if needed. Yield: 4 servings.

Velva Johnson
Adams, Minnesota

BAKED TOMATO-ZUCCHINI CASSEROLE

4 med. zucchini
6 med. tomatoes
1 sm. onion, minced

1 tsp. salt
1/2 c. bread crumbs
1/4 c. grated cheese

Cut ends off unpeeled zucchini; cut zucchini into 1/4-inch slices. Peel tomatoes; chop. Combine tomatoes, zucchini, onion and salt; place in casserole. Sprinkle with bread crumbs, then grated cheese. Bake in preheated 350-degree oven for 45 minutes.

Maxine J. Rader
Boone Grove, Indiana

ENGLISH PEAS SUPREME

1 1-lb. can English peas with onions
1 can cream of celery or mushroom soup
1/2 c. evaporated milk
1 can water chestnuts, drained and sliced
8 saltine crackers, crushed
Margarine

Mix English peas with onions and soup, milk and water chestnuts in large bowl. Place in greased casserole; top with crushed crackers. Dot with margarine. Bake in preheated 325-degree oven for 20 to 25 minutes or until golden brown. Frozen English peas with onions, cooked, may be substituted for canned peas. Yield: 6 servings.

Mrs. Joyce M. Graham
Tracy City, Tennessee

PEAS AND ASPARAGUS CASSEROLE

1 1-lb. 4-oz. can asparagus, drained
1 1-lb. 4-oz. can English peas, drained
1 can cream of mushroom soup
1 c. milk
1 1/2 c. grated cheese
1/2 c. bread crumbs

Place asparagus, then peas in buttered baking dish. Mix mushroom soup, milk and cheese in saucepan; place over low heat until cheese is melted. Pour over peas; sprinkle with bread crumbs. Bake in preheated 350-degree oven for 25 minutes. Yield: 8 servings.

Mrs. Grady Nunnery, Jr.
Richburg, South Carolina

GARLIC BREADSTICKS

1 11-in. unsliced loaf sandwich bread
1/2 c. melted butter
2 cloves of garlic, pressed
1/4 c. toasted sesame seed

Trim crusts from bread. Cut loaf in half crosswise, then in half lengthwise. Cut each piece crosswise into 4 sticks. Combine butter and garlic; brush on all sides of breadsticks. Sprinkle with sesame seed; arrange 1 inch apart on baking sheet. Toast until brown on all sides. Yield: 16 sticks.

Janet McGhee
Winkelman, Arizona

ONION BREAD

1 loaf French bread
5 scallions
1/2 c. softened butter or margarine

Cut loaf in half lengthwise. Chop scallions; mix with butter. Spread on bottom half of the loaf; add top half of bread. Wrap in aluminum foil; place on baking sheet. Bake in preheated 400-degree oven for 20 minutes. One envelope onion soup mix may be used instead of scallions. Yield: 4-6 servings.

LaVonne Geisler
Carlisle, Iowa

PINEAPPLE UPSIDE-DOWN BREAKFAST ROLLS

1/2 c. (packed) brown sugar
1/2 c. butter
3/4 c. drained crushed pineapple
1 tsp. cinnamon
1 can refrigerator biscuits

Melt brown sugar and butter in 8-inch square cake pan. Add pineapple and cinnamon; mix well. Place biscuits on top. Bake in preheated 425-degree oven for 10 minutes. Invert pan onto serving plate. Yield: 10 rolls.

Mrs. Carolyn Saxe
Albion, Illinois

COTTAGE CHEESE-CHIVE MUFFINS

2 c. all-purpose flour
3 tsp. baking powder
2 tbsp. sugar
2 tbsp. chopped chives
2 eggs, beaten
3/4 c. milk
3 tbsp. melted butter
1 c. creamed small curd cottage cheese

Sift flour, baking powder and sugar together into bowl; stir in chives. Blend eggs with milk and butter; stir in cottage cheese. Add to flour mixture; stir until mixed. Spoon into greased muffin cups to fill 1/2 full. Bake in preheated 425-degree oven for 15 to 20 minutes. Cool for several minutes; remove from muffin pans. Yield: 1 1/2 dozen.

Jessie K. Lannan
Sherrard, West Virginia

SAGE CHEESE BREAD

1   13 3/4-oz. package hot roll mix
1 egg
1/2 c. grated Cheddar cheese
1 1/2 tsp. ground sage

Pour 3/4 cup warm water into medium mixing bowl. Sprinkle yeast from the hot roll mix over water; stir until dissolved. Stir in egg, cheese and sage. Add flour mixture from package; blend well. Cover; let rise in warm place for 30 to 45 minutes or until doubled in bulk. Shape dough into loaf; place in greased 8 1/2 x 4 1/2 x 2 1/2-inch loaf pan. Let rise again until doubled in bulk. Bake in preheated 350-degree oven for 30 to 40 minutes or until browned. Cool and slice. Yield: 1 loaf.

Photograph for this recipe below.

CHEESY DROP BISCUITS

2 c. all-purpose buttermilk biscuit
   mix
1 tsp. instant minced onion
1/3 c. water
1/3 c. sour cream
2 to 3 tbsp. grated Parmesan cheese

Combine biscuit mix and onion in bowl; stir in water and sour cream just until dry ingredients are moistened. Drop by heaping table-

spoonfuls onto greased baking sheet. Sprinkle with Parmesan cheese. Bake in preheated 450-degree oven for 10 minutes or until lightly browned.

Photograph for this recipe on page 48.

APPLE BETTY

1 can pie apples
1/4 c. margarine, cut in sm. pieces
1 3/4 c. graham cracker crumbs

Combine all ingredients in casserole. Bake in preheated 400-degree oven for 25 minutes. Serve topped with whipped cream, if desired. Yield: 4 servings.

Mrs. Jean Head
Attalla, Alabama

APRICOT PIE

1 can sweetened condensed milk
1/4 c. lemon juice
1 No. 303 can peeled apricot halves,
    drained and crushed
1/2 pt. whipped cream
Wafers

Combine milk, lemon juice, apricots and 3 to 4 tablespoons whipped cream. Line 9-inch pie pan with wafers; add apricot filling. Top with remaining whipped cream; chill until ready to serve. Yield: 6 servings.

Willie Dean Flowers
Walnut Grove, Mississippi

APRICOT UPSIDE-DOWN CAKE

1 1-lb. 6-oz. can apricot pie filling
1 sm. package white cake mix
1 egg
1/2 c. flaked coconut
1/2 c. chopped pecans
1/2 c. butter, melted

Spread pie filling in 9 x 9 x 2-inch baking dish. Combine cake mix, 1/3 cup water and egg. Beat for 4 minutes, using electric mixer at medium speed. Pour over pie filling; sprinkle with coconut and pecans. Drizzle melted butter over top. Bake in preheated 350 degree oven for 40 minutes. Serve warm. Yield: 9 servings.

Lois B. Jenkins
Franklin, Pennsylvania

HELLO DOLLIES

1 c. butter or margarine
1 c. graham cracker crumbs
1 c. shredded coconut
1 c. chocolate chips
1 c. chopped walnuts
1 c. sweetened condensed milk

Melt butter; pour into 13 x 9 x 2-inch cake pan. Sprinkle graham cracker crumbs over melted butter. Sprinkle with coconut, chocolate chips and walnuts. Pour milk over top. Bake in preheated 350-degree oven for 25 minutes or until top begins to brown lightly. Let cool thoroughly; cut into squares to serve.

Susan Kerr
Panama, New York

APRICOT SAUCE

2 jars strained baby apricots
1 tbsp. lemon juice
1 tsp. grated orange rind
1 tsp. grated lemon rind

Combine all ingredients; mix well. May serve over ice cream, angel food cake or pound cake and garnish with low-calorie topping.

Mrs. Doris W. Larke
Peoria, Illinois

HOT FUDGE SAUCE

1 can sweetened condensed milk
1 can chocolate syrup

Combine ingredients in saucepan; cook over low heat, stirring constantly, until bubbly. Remove from heat; serve immediately as topping.

Mrs. Martha Zimmerman
Taylorville, Illinois

Money-Saving Favorites

The Pilgrim and pioneer women who helped to settle this country instinctively knew how to make the most out of what food provisions they had on hand, in plenty and in want. Not only was their cookery simple and nourishing, it was well planned so that there was no waste. Most of these women brought remarkable food skills with them from their homelands, and put them to good use as productive farm communities sprang up all across the new nation.

The self-sustaining farm was one strong economic base that this country was founded upon; each individual farm produced everything that it needed and purchased very little. The people that lived on these farms were industrious, skilled and renowned for their thrift. They typically did so well that they could market the surplus farm produce in the cities. These "farmers' markets" are characteristic sights in all regions of America, even now.

Today, the dynamics of our economy are totally different. The farmer produces not only enough for himself, but enough for at least 40 other people as well. The country has become more and more urbanized and city dwellers very much depend on the farmer for food. We find now that we must budget our money first, and only then can we work to make the most of the food available to us for the most reasonable amount of money possible. In this section, Home Economics Teachers have combined their expertise to offer their advice on ways to get the most economical use from your food dollar.

The average family in this country spends well over one-third of its income on meals, and becoming an expert meal and money manager can be very rewarding. The goal of food management is to provide nutritious, well-balanced meals at the lowest possible cost. Planning ahead is the first step to achieving this goal. Start by reading the food ads, which appear in the newspaper on Wednesday or Thursday of each week. Choose the best values and plan the entire week's menu around these specials if possible. Before shopping, make a detailed list of what is needed to follow this menu, as well as those things that are running low in the cabinets and refrigerator. And, don't grocery shop when you are hungry or, as studies have proved, a six or seven dollar increase in the food bill will be the result.

Although comparison shopping in five or six different stores is inconvenient, it definitely saves food dollars. But, whether comparison shopping in various stores or shopping in only one store, always compare the cost *per serving* between fresh, frozen and canned foods. Compare also the cost *per serving* of various cuts of meats. Remember too, that store brands are of comparable quality at cheaper prices than nationally advertised brands.

When in the store, follow your shopping list exactly! Impulse buying adds costly items to a well-planned list. Understand that advertised specials, which are mostly to attract customers to the store, are not the only specials. Handwritten signs often signal unadvertised specials, especially when marked "Reduced for Quick Sale."

Taking a sincere interest in meal planning shows, not only in an improved budget, but to your family and to the people you shop with. The store manager, the cashier and the stock and bag boys will probably show interest in return to a regular, knowledgeable customer.

What is a nutritious, well-balanced diet? Experts agree that well-planned meals not only supply the nutrients necessary for growth and health, but also provide harmony in color, flavor and texture that pleases the palate as well as the eye. Prepare foods that family members enjoy, and that suit your skills, energy and schedule.

Saving money with salads is easy. Since salad greens are in season all year, they will never appear as a luxury item in the budget. All salad vegetables are loaded with vitamins and should be served once a day, particularly the leafy, green vegetables. When buying salad ingredients, consider local sources such as curb markets and local stores. National chain stores may not have the freshest produce because they buy from large suppliers, and as they often prepackage their produce, it is sometimes hard to examine it for freshness.

Soups and stews are probably the money saver's most economical dishes. Frequently made from meat and vegetable leftovers, soups conserve both the flavors and the nutrients of these foods in a delicious and economical way. Cheaper cuts of meats and older vegetables may also be used. But, whatever the combination of ingredients, if cooked and seasoned artfully, soups and stews always make mouthwatering, money-saving entrees.

Although meats are usually the most expensive item in the budget, they are also the best source of protein in the diet. Make the most of the place for meats in the diet by first purchasing only as much as is needed, and then know not only the cost per pound, but more importantly the cost of each serving. For example, a boneless, canned ham may seem expensive but it serves 5 people per pound, while a picnic ham serves only 2 per pound. Look for nothing short of quality when buying meats. Meats stamped and graded by the US Department of Agriculture assure consumers of high quality.

The 200 varieties of fish and seafood, when bought in season, are probably a better buy than meats. When buying fresh fish, smell for a mild odor and look for bright, clear eyes, red gills, irridescent skin and firm flesh. Avoid buying frozen fish that has not been stamped and graded by the US Department of the Interior. Canned fish, such as tuna and salmon, are a good buy, while frozen, breaded fish sticks are a poor buy. Fresh shellfish are often quite economical in coastal areas as are frozen shellfish in inland areas.

Vegetables, when bought and cooked correctly, add most of the variety in flavor, color and texture to meals. They are most economical and at their best then bought fresh, in season. Out of season, frozen vegetables are typically the best buy for the best flavor. As a rule, canned vegetables are also reasonably priced, especially the private or "in-house" labels. These are packed by the national canners, but sold at prices below the national brands. Specially cut vegetables, such as French and julienne styles, are good for special occasions, but of course are more expensive per serving than other cuts.

Desserts don't have to be expensive additions to meal planning. Fruits, especially when purchased in season, make one of the most wholesome and money-wise desserts available. Canned fruits provide flavorful nutrition, often for only pennies a serving. Left-over bread makes perfect bread pudding, especially when its ingredients include fruits, nuts or sugar. Watch for grocery store specials on frozen cream pies and out-of-season fruit pies. These are always welcome desserts, besides saving time and money. When preparing pancakes, make extra or save leftovers and freeze them tightly in foil. Later, thaw them and heat lightly in butter. They can then be rolled and filled with jam, fruit or chocolate for an excellent, inexpensive dessert.

Saving money on the food budget is not as impossible as it may seem. Thoughtful menu planning, careful shopping and preparation that uses various foods to their fullest degree — Home Economics Teachers agree that these three things will help you get the most food, enjoyment and nutrition for your money.

ECONOMICAL FRUIT PUNCH

4 oz. citric acid
5 lb. sugar
1   12-oz. can frozen orange juice
1   6-oz. can frozen lemon juice
1   36-oz. can pineapple juice
1 lg. bag crushed ice

Combine citric acid and 1 pint water in jar; cover tightly. Let stand for several hours or overnight. Dissolve sugar in citric acid solution, adding several quarts water. Add fruit juices, crushed ice and more water, if desired. Red and green cherries, crushed pineapple or orange and lemon slices may be added for garnish.

Mrs. Jean T. Sutherland
Brownwood, Texas

FRUIT PUNCH FOR A CROWD

4 c. sugar
1/8 tsp. salt
1 qt. strong tea
1 lg. can orange juice
1   1-pt. bottle lemon juice
4 qt. ice water
1 lg. can pineapple juice
1 qt. ginger ale

Combine sugar, salt and 1 quart water in saucepan; heat, stirring, until sugar dissolves. Boil for 5 minutes. Let cool. Add tea, orange juice, lemon juice, ice water and pineapple juice; chill thoroughly. Pour into punch bowl; add ginger ale and ice ring just before serving. Other fruit juices may be used for different color schemes or holidays.

Mrs. Clara Schmalzle
Eldred, New York

BURR'S FISH CHOWDER

2 lb. sea bass
1 qt. diced potatoes
1/4 lb. salt pork, diced
2 med. onions, chopped
1/4 c. flour
1 c. strained tomatoes
Salt and pepper to taste
Cayenne pepper to taste
Dash of hot sauce
Chopped parsley

Cut bass into 2-inch pieces; place in saucepan. Add 1 quart water. Cook until tender; drain, reserving liquid. Cook potatoes in 1 quart water; drain, reserving liquid. Fry salt pork and onions until lightly browned; cover. Cook for 10 minutes. Blend in flour; add reserved liquids slowly. Bring to a boil, stirring constantly; add tomatoes, bass and potatoes. Mix lightly. Season with salt, pepper, cayenne pepper and hot sauce; sprinkle with parsley. Yield: 8 servings.

Mrs. Doris Burr
Hayward, California

CHILI MAC

1/2 lb. ground beef
1 sm. onion, chopped
1/2 med. green pepper, chopped
Cooking oil
1 c. macaroni
1   8-oz. can kidney beans
1   8-oz. can tomato sauce
1/2 c. water
1/2 tsp. chili powder
1/2 tsp. salt
1/2 c. shredded Cheddar cheese

Brown ground beef, onion and green pepper in small amount of oil in large heavy skillet. Drain off fat; add macaroni, kidney beans, tomato sauce, water, chili powder and salt to skillet. Cover; simmer for 15 minutes, stirring occasionally. Top with cheese; heat until cheese is melted. Yield: 2-3 servings.

Mrs. Nancy S. Claibourne
Batavia, Ohio

GOLDEN NUGGET BUDGET SOUP

3 med. potatoes, diced
2 carrots, diced
1 med. onion, diced
1 c. whole kernel corn
2 tbsp. margarine
Salt and pepper to taste

1 can cream of chicken soup
2 c. milk

Combine vegetables and margarine in soup kettle; add water to cover. Bring to a boil. Reduce heat; simmer until vegetables are tender. Stir in seasonings, soup and milk; heat through gently. Yield: 4 servings.

Lorna Hinson
Hickory Grove, South Carolina

SAVORY STEW

1   5-lb. chicken
3 No. 2 cans tomatoes
1   8-oz. can tomato paste
2 No. 2 cans okra
2 No. 2 cans corn
3 lg. onions, diced
Salt to taste
Crushed red pepper to taste
3 lb. potatoes
1/2 c. margarine

Place chicken in large kettle; add about 3 quarts water. Cook until chicken is tender. Strip chicken from bones; return to broth. Add tomatoes, tomato paste, okra, corn, onions and seasonings; mix well. Simmer, stirring frequently, for about 2 hours. Peel potatoes; cut in small pieces. Place potatoes in saucepan; add water to cover. Cook until potatoes are tender. Mash potatoes; do not drain. Stir in margarine; stir into stew, adding water, if needed. Cook for 15 minutes longer, stirring constantly.

Mrs. E. C. Henry
Canton, Mississippi

WHITE BEAN SOUP

2 c. navy beans
1 meaty hambone
1/2 c. mashed potatoes
3 onions, finely chopped
1 stalk celery, chopped
1 clove of garlic, minced
1/4 c. minced parsley

Soak beans overnight in 3 quarts water. Add hambone; bring to a boil. Reduce heat; sim-

mer for 1 hour. Add potatoes, onions, celery, garlic and parsley; mix well. Simmer for 1 hour. Remove hambone; cut ham from bone. Return ham to soup; heat through.

Mrs. Lillian Herman
Bay City, Texas

BAKED TUNA SANDWICH

1 loaf French bread
Butter
1 can tuna
1/4 c. mayonnaise
1 onion, sliced
1 tomato, sliced
Sliced cheese

Cut bread into 3 lengthwise slices. Spread cut surfaces with butter. Combine tuna and mayonnaise; mix well. Spread tuna mixture on bottom slice of bread; top with onion. Place middle slice of bread over onion; cover with layer of tomato and cheese. Place top slice of bread over cheese. Wrap in foil; place on baking sheet. Bake in preheated 350-degree oven for about 35 minutes or until heated through.

Karen I. Perreten
Mitchell, Nebraska

CORNED BEEF CHEESEBURGER

1   12-oz. can corned beef, chopped
3 tbsp. finely chopped onion
1 tbsp. prepared mustard
3 tbsp. mayonnaise
1 1/2 tsp. horseradish
3 tbsp. butter or margarine
9 hamburger buns
Butter
9 slices American cheese

Combine first 6 ingredients; mix well. Spread buns with butter. Spoon corned beef mixture on bottom halves of buns; top with slices of cheese. Toast under broiler until cheese melts. Toast bun tops; place over cheese slices. Serve immediately. Yield: 9 servings.

Mrs. William H. Buxton
Cowden, Illinois

THRIFTY BURGERS

1 med. onion, chopped
1/4 c. chopped green pepper
1/2 c. chopped celery
1 lb. ground beef
1 1/2 tsp. salt
1 tsp. pepper
1 can chicken gumbo soup
2 tbsp. catsup
1 tsp. Worcestershire sauce
8 hamburger buns, heated

Heat 1 tablespoon fat in skillet; add onion, green pepper and celery. Cook for 6 to 8 minutes, stirring frequently. Stir in beef, salt and pepper; cook until beef loses pink color. Add soup, catsup and Worcestershire sauce; simmer for 30 minutes. Serve on buns. Yield: 8 servings.

Mrs. Rachel Nicholson
Union, Mississippi

THRIFTY WIENER LOAF

1/2 loaf French bread
1 tbsp. prepared mustard
2 tbsp. soft butter
2 c. pork and beans
1/4 c. chopped onion
2 tbsp. brown sugar
1/2 c. shredded sharp American cheese
5 frankfurters
5 sm. sweet pickles, cut in fans
Catsup

Cut bread lengthwise. Combine mustard and butter; spread on bread. Mix beans, onion and brown sugar together; spoon on buttered bread. Sprinkle with cheese. Broil 7 inches from heat for 5 minutes. Split frankfurters lengthwise without cutting through. Place, split side up, on beans; broil for 5 minutes longer. Garnish with pickles; drizzle catsup down center of franks. Cut loaf into 5 slices so each serving has a frankfurter and a pickle fan. Yield: 5 servings.

Mrs. Garth Waller
Littlefork, Minnesota

ALWAYS READY FROZEN FRUIT SALAD

1   3-oz. package cream cheese
2 tbsp. cream
2 tbsp. lemon juice
1/8 tsp. salt
1 c. diced pineapple, drained
1/2 c. miniature marshmallows
1 c. quartered maraschino cherries
1 banana, mashed
2 c. whipped cream
3/4 c. mayonnaise

Combine cream cheese, cream, lemon juice and salt; mix until smooth. Add pineapple, marshmallows, cherries and banana. Combine whipped cream and mayonnaise. Fold into fruit mixture. Pour into ice trays; freeze. Serve on lettuce. Yield: 16 servings.

Rachael A. Dix
Montpelier, Vermont

PICNIC COLESLAW

1 tbsp. flour
1 tbsp. sugar
1 tsp. salt
1/2 tsp. celery seed
Dash of pepper
1/3 c. cider vinegar
1/4 c. water
1 tsp. prepared mustard
1 tbsp. grated onion
3 egg yolks, slightly beaten
1/4 c. butter
1 c. sour cream
2 qt. shredded cabbage
1/2 c. grated carrot

Combine flour, sugar, salt, celery seed and pepper in saucepan; stir in vinegar gradually. Add water, mustard and onion; cook over medium heat, stirring constantly, until mixture thickens and loses starchy taste. Stir small amount of hot mixture into egg yolks; stir egg yolks into hot mixture. Cook, stirring constantly, for 1 minute longer. Add butter; stir until melted. Chill thoroughly. Fold in sour cream. Combine cabbage and carrot. Pour on sour cream dressing; toss lightly to blend. Yield: 6-8 servings.

Photograph for this recipe on page 175.

APPLE-CARROT SALAD

3 med. apples, diced
2 carrots, grated
1/2 c. chopped pecans
3 tbsp. sugar
1/2 c. mayonnaise
1/3 c. raisins

Combine apples, carrots and pecans. Mix in sugar and mayonnaise. Add raisins; blend well. Refrigerate until ready to serve. Yield: 6-8 servings.

Mrs. Mildred Bullard
Wilson, North Carolina

CHEF'S SALAD

8 c. chopped mixed salad greens
1 c. diced celery
1 c. cooked ham strips
2 hard-cooked eggs, chopped
2 tbsp. chopped parsley
4 tomatoes, cut in wedges
1 c. garlic or French dressing

Chill all ingredients. Combine all ingredients except dressing; toss. Add dressing; toss again. Yield: 12 servings.

Myrtle Stevens
Gracemont, Oklahoma

PRESSED CHICKEN

2 env. unflavored gelatin
1 c. chicken stock
1 cooked hen, cut fine
1 can chopped pimentos, drained
2 c. finely cut celery
6 hard-boiled eggs, chopped
2 tbsp. pickle relish
Salt to taste
1 c. mayonnaise

Soften gelatin in 1 cup cold water; add hot chicken stock. Heat, stirring, until gelatin is dissolved. Cool. Combine chicken, pimentos, celery, eggs and pickle relish. Season with salt. Stir in gelatin, then mayonnaise. Press into shallow pan; cover. Refrigerate overnight or until firm. Cut into squares to serve.

Garnish with olives. Serve with additional mayonnaise.

Ethel F. Johnson
New Brockton, Alabama

CORN-FRANKFURTER BAKE

6 frankfurters
2 c. cream-style corn
1/2 c. toasted bread crumbs
2 tbsp. minced onion
1/4 tsp. dry mustard
1 egg, beaten
1/4 c. catsup

Cut frankfurters into 1/4-inch pieces; reserve 2 frankfurters for top. Combine corn, bread crumbs, onion, mustard, egg and frankfurters; pour into greased casserole. Arrange reserved frankfurters in circle on top of casserole; spoon catsup into center. Bake in preheated 350-degree oven for 30 minutes. Yield: 4-6 servings.

Mabel Ann Sanders
Morton, Texas

HAM AND MACARONI CASSEROLE

1/2 lb. elbow macaroni
2 tbsp. butter
1 tbsp. minced onion
1 tbsp. flour
1/4 tsp. dry mustard
1/2 tsp. salt
Dash of pepper
2 c. milk
1 1/2 c. chopped cooked ham
2 c. grated Cheddar cheese
2 tbsp. melted butter
3/4 c. fresh bread crumbs

Cook macaroni according to package directions; drain. Melt butter in top of double boiler. Add onion, flour, mustard, salt and pepper; mix well. Stir in milk gradually; cook over boiling water until smooth and thickened, stirring constantly. Add ham and 1 1/2 cups cheese; cook, stirring, until cheese is melted. Place macaroni in greased 2-quart casserole; pour ham sauce over macaroni. Toss lightly with fork until macaroni is coated. Sprinkle remaining cheese over top. Mix melted butter with bread crumbs; sprinkle over cheese. Bake in preheated 400-degree oven for 20 minutes. Yield: 4-6 servings.

Mrs. Olga Banks
Midland, Texas

SCALLOPED POTATOES WITH VIENNA SAUSAGES

3 c. sliced potatoes
8 Vienna sausages, diced
1 8-oz. can sliced mushrooms
1/4 c. flour
1 tsp. salt
1/8 tsp. pepper
3 tbsp. minced onion
1 c. milk
1 tomato, sliced
1/4 c. grated American cheese
Parsley

Arrange half the potatoes, sausages and mushrooms in greased casserole; sprinkle with half the flour, salt, pepper and onion. Repeat layers; pour milk over top. Cover. Bake in preheated 350-degree oven for 45 minutes. Top with tomato slices, then cheese. Bake, uncovered, for 30 minutes longer. Garnish with parsley. Yield: 4 servings.

Dorothy Marie Salter
Midlothian, Texas

TURKEY CASSEROLE SUPREME

3 c. chicken consomme
1/3 c. rice
2 1/2 c. diced cooked turkey
3/4 c. chopped celery
1/4 c. chopped pimento
2 eggs, beaten
Salt
Dash of poultry seasoning
2 tbsp. minced onion
3 tbsp. butter
3 tbsp. flour
1/2 c. heavy cream
1 c. sliced mushrooms
Pepper

Pour 2 cups consomme into saucepan; bring to a boil. Add rice; cover. Reduce heat; simmer for 10 minutes. Stir in turkey, celery, pimento, eggs, 3/4 teaspoon salt and poultry seasoning; mix well. Pour into greased casserole. Bake in preheated 325-degree oven for 45 minutes. Saute onion in butter until tender; blend in flour. Add remaining 1 cup consomme and cream slowly; cook over low heat until thickened, stirring constantly. Add mushrooms; season with salt and pepper to taste. Heat through; serve over turkey casserole.

Thelma S. Vogel
McAlester, Oklahoma

CORN STUFFING

1 12-oz. can whole kernel corn
1 1-lb. can cream-style corn
1 egg, beaten
1 c. soft bread crumbs
1/4 c. chopped onion
1/4 c. chopped green pepper
2 tbsp. chopped pimento
1 1/2 tsp. salt

Drain whole kernel corn. Combine all ingredients; mix well. Use for stuffing pork roast.

Evelyn B. Willey
Gatesville, North Carolina

GREEN RICE

2 c. cooked rice
2 c. chopped spinach
2 eggs, beaten
1/2 c. melted butter
1 c. milk
1 1/2 tsp. salt
1 onion, grated
1 c. grated Cheddar cheese

Combine all ingredients; mix lightly. Pour into greased casserole. Bake in preheated 300-degree oven for about 1 hour or until set. Yield: 6-8 servings.

Mrs. Marie M. Mingledorff
Douglas, Georgia

HOMEMADE NOODLES

1 c. flour
2 eggs, beaten
1 tbsp. water
Salt to taste

Mix flour, eggs, water and salt in bowl. Place on breadboard; knead in additional flour until dough is stiff. Roll out thin; let dry for 1 hour. Cut into noodles. Drop in boiling water or broth; cook until noodles are tender.

Mrs. Virginia Jones
Houston, Texas

MOCK NOODLES ROMANOFF

1 6-oz. package noodles
1 c. cottage cheese
1 c. sour cream
1 tsp. minced onion
1 sm. clove of garlic, minced
1/2 tsp. salt
1 tsp. Worcestershire sauce
1/4 c. grated cheese

Cook noodles in boiling, salted water until tender; drain. Combine cottage cheese, sour cream and noodles. Add onion, garlic, salt and Worcestershire sauce; mix well. Place in greased 2-quart casserole; sprinkle with cheese. Bake in preheated 350-degree oven for 40 minutes. Sour cream may be omitted and cottage cheese increased to 2 cups. Yield: 6 servings.

Myrtle Stevens
Ninnekah, Oklahoma

HAM LOAF AND RAISIN SAUCE

1 1/2 lb. ground smoked ham
2 lb. ground fresh pork
1 c. milk
1 c. cracker crumbs
1 c. tomato juice
2 tbsp. flour
2 tbsp. butter
1 c. apple cider or fruit juice
2 tbsp. brown sugar
1/4 c. raisins
1/8 tsp. salt

Combine ham, pork, milk, crumbs and tomato juice; shape into loaf. Place in 7 x 10-inch baking pan. Bake in preheated 325-degree oven for 1 hour and 40 minutes. Combine flour and butter; add cider gradually, stirring constantly. Add remaining ingredients; mix well. Spread over ham loaf. Bake for 20 minutes longer. Slices of pineapple may be arranged on loaf just before loaf is done, if desired. Yield: 8-10 servings.

Mrs. Theresa H. Smith
Warner Robins, Georgia

WAGON WHEEL PIE

1 1/2 pkg. frozen mixed vegetables
1/2 c. chopped onion
2 tbsp. butter
1 12-oz. can luncheon meat
1 c. evaporated milk
2 tbsp. flour
1/2 c. grated Cheddar cheese
2 eggs, beaten
1/2 tsp. salt
1/4 tsp. paprika
1 unbaked pie shell

Cook mixed vegetables according to package directions until partially done; drain. Combine onion and butter in saucepan; simmer, covered, for 10 minutes. Cut luncheon meat lengthwise into 1/4-inch slices; reserve 5 slices. Cut remaining slices into bite-sized pieces. Add small amount of milk to flour, mixing to smooth paste; combine flour mixture, remaining milk, partially cooked vegetables, onion mixture, bite-sized luncheon meat pieces, cheese, eggs, salt and paprika; mix well. Pour into pie shell. Cut reserved luncheon meat slices in half diagonally; arrange spoke fashion over top. Bake in preheated 400-degree oven for 35 to 40 minutes. Cool for 10 minutes before serving. Yield: 6 servings.

Mrs. Gretta E. Litchfield
Taunton, Massachusetts

BEEF AND BEAN BAKE

2 lb. boneless beef stew meat
1 c. dried navy beans
6 c. water
2 tbsp. flour
2 tsp. salt
2 tbsp. lard or drippings
1 8-oz. can tomato sauce
3 sm. onions, halved
2 tbsp. mustard
1 tsp. chili powder

Cut beef into 1-inch cubes. Sort and rinse beans; cover with water. Bring to a boil. Reduce heat; simmer for 2 to 3 minutes. Remove from heat; let stand for 1 hour. Combine flour and salt; dredge beef cubes with seasoned flour. Saute in lard until browned. Pour off drippings. Drain beans, reserving 2 cups liquid. Combine beef, beans, reserved liquid, tomato sauce, onions, mustard and chili powder; cover. Bake in preheated 325-degree oven for 2 hours to 2 hours and 30 minutes or until beans and beef are tender. Yield: 6-8 servings.

Photograph for this recipe below.

HAM AND CHEESE STRATA

8 slices white bread
2 c. shredded Cheddar cheese
1 1/2 c. chopped baked ham
1   2-oz. can sliced mushrooms, drained
1/4 c. chopped parsley
2 1/4 c. milk
4 eggs, slightly beaten
1 tsp. salt
1/4 tsp. dry mustard
1/8 tsp. paprika
Dash of pepper

Trim crusts from 5 slices bread; set slices aside. Place remaining 3 slices and trimmings in buttered 9-inch square baking dish; top with cheese, ham, mushrooms and parsley. Cut reserved bread slices in half diagonally; place over cheese in two rows. Combine milk, eggs, salt, mustard, paprika and pepper; pour over top. Cover; refrigerate for 3 hours or overnight. Bake in preheated 325-degree oven for 45 to 60 minutes or until knife inserted near center comes out clean. Let stand for 5 minutes before serving. Yield: 6 servings.

Photograph for this recipe on page 168.

RAINY DAY BEEF DISH

1/4 lb. bacon, diced
1 1/2 lb. ground beef
2 lg. onions, chopped
2 green peppers, chopped
1 sm. can chopped mushrooms
1 can kidney beans
2 c. noodles, cooked
1 No. 2 can tomatoes
Grated cheese

Fry bacon in large ovenproof skillet until crisp. Add ground beef; cook, stirring, until beef is browned. Add onions, green peppers, mushrooms, kidney beans, noodles and tomatoes; mix well. Simmer for 1 hour. Sprinkle with cheese. Bake at 325 degrees until cheese is melted. Yield: 8 servings.

Mrs. Sara Yowell
Hayetteville, Arkansas

T-BONE STEAKETTES

4 slices stale bread
1 lb. hamburger
3/4 c. tomato juice
1/4 c. catsup
2 tbsp. minced onion
1 tsp. salt
1/2 tsp. pepper
1 egg, beaten
Thin carrot strips

Place bread in deep bowl; cover with cold water. Let stand for 1 hour; squeeze bread dry, crumbling well. Combine hamburger, tomato juice, catsup, onion, salt, pepper, egg and bread crumbs; mix well. Shape mixture to resemble small steaks, using carrot strips for bones. Place on broiler pan. Broil for about 10 minutes on each side or to desired doneness.

Mrs. Louise H. Motes
Laurens, South Carolina

THRIFTY CHOW MEIN

1 lb. cubed pork
1/2 lb. round steak, cubed
1 1/2 c. diced onion
1 1/2 tsp. salt
1/2 tsp. pepper
1 1/2 c. sliced celery
1 1/2 c. bean sprouts
6 peeled radishes, sliced
1/4 c. cornstarch
1 tbsp. soy sauce
1 1/2 tsp. sugar

Brown meats in small amount of fat; add onion. Cook until transparent. Add salt, pepper, celery and 1 1/2 cups hot water. Cook for 10 minutes. Add bean sprouts and radishes. Pour meat mixture into casserole. Mix remaining ingredients with 1/2 cup cold water. Pour cornstarch mixture over meat mixture. Bake at 350 degrees for 10 minutes. Serve hot over chow mein noodles, if desired. Yield: 6 servings.

LeNora Hudson
Sulphur, Oklahoma

CHICKEN A LA KING

1 green pepper, chopped
8 tbsp. butter
6 tbsp. flour
3 c. milk
1 1/2 tsp. salt
1/2 tsp. paprika
1 cooked chicken, diced
1 can pimentos, chopped
1 lg. can mushrooms, drained
Nutmeg to taste

Saute green pepper in 3 tablespoons butter. Melt remaining 5 tablespoons butter in saucepan; blend in flour. Stir in milk gradually; cook, stirring constantly, until thickened. Stir in remaining ingredients; heat through. Serve on toast. Yield: 8 servings.

Antoinette Kelemen
Shelbyville, Kentucky

MEAL-STRETCHER CHICKEN TETRAZZINI

1   2 1/2-lb. chicken, quartered
Salt to taste
1 sm. can sliced mushrooms, drained
3 tbsp. butter
1/2 lb. spaghetti
2 tbsp. flour
1 c. heavy cream
3 tbsp. dry sherry
Grated Parmesan cheese

Simmer chicken in boiling salted water until tender. Cool in broth. Shred chicken. Simmer broth until reduced to 2 cups; strain and reserve. Saute mushrooms in 1 tablespoon butter over moderate heat until lightly browned. Break spaghetti into small pieces; cook in large amount of boiling salted water for 15 minutes or until tender. Drain. Melt remaining 2 tablespoons butter; stir in flour. Add reserved chicken broth gradually, stirring until smooth. Bring to a boil. Stir in cream and sherry. Add chicken to 1/2 of the sauce; add spaghetti and mushrooms to remaining sauce. Place spaghetti mixture in baking dish; pour chicken mixture into center. Sprinkle with cheese. Bake in preheated 350-degree oven for 10 minutes or until lightly browned. Yield: 6-8 servings.

Christine C. Risher
Macon, Mississippi

ORANGE-GRILLED CHICKEN

Salt and pepper to taste
Poultry seasoning to taste
1/2 tsp. monosodium glutamate
1 sm. can frozen orange juice, thawed
1/4 c. melted butter
1   2 1/2-lb. broiling chicken, halved

Combine salt, pepper, poultry seasoning and monosodium glutamate; add orange juice and butter. Grill chicken over low heat for about 1 hour, turning and basting with orange juice mixture at 10-minute intervals. Chicken is done when leg bone turns easily in socket. Yield: 4 servings.

Mrs. Kathryn Leischner
DeLand, Illinois

QUICK CHICKEN STROGANOFF

2 1/2 to 3 lb. chicken thighs and legs
2 tbsp. butter
1 clove of garlic, minced
1/4 c. minced onion
1 tsp. salt
1/8 tsp. pepper
1 c. sour cream
1 8-oz. can tomato sauce
1 4-oz. can mushrooms, drained
1 8-oz. package noodles

Brown chicken lightly in butter; push to one side. Add garlic and onion; cook until lightly browned and tender. Sprinkle with salt and pepper. Add sour cream to tomato sauce gradually, stirring to combine. Pour over chicken. Simmer, covered, for 30 minutes or until tender, turning and basting once. Add mushrooms; heat through. Prepare noodles according to package directions; place on platter. Arrange chicken and sauce over noodles. Yield: 6 servings.

Mrs. Dalpha Boley
Splendora, Texas

BAKED FISH WITH TOMATO SAUCE

2 pkg. frozen fish fillets, thawed
2 tbsp. minced onion
1 clove of garlic, minced
1 tbsp. butter
2 8-oz. cans tomato sauce
1 tsp. sugar
1/2 tsp. Worcestershire sauce
2 tbsp. lemon juice
Chopped parsley

Arrange fish in greased shallow baking dish. Saute onion and garlic in butter until onion is transparent. Add tomato sauce, sugar, Worcestershire sauce and lemon juice; mix well. Simmer for 5 minutes. Pour over fish. Bake in preheated 400-degree oven for 20 to 25 minutes or until fish flakes easily. Sprinkle with parsley. Yield: 6 servings.

Eva Jane Schwartz
Gettysburg, Pennsylvania

BATTER-FRIED CATFISH

1 can shortening
2 eggs, beaten
1 c. milk
12 lb. catfish steaks
Salt and pepper to taste
Cornmeal

Melt shortening in deep heavy skillet. Combine eggs and milk. Season catfish with salt and pepper. Dip into milk mixture; roll in cornmeal. Drop into hot shortening. Fry until brown, turning once. Drain on absorbent paper. Serve hot with hush puppies, if desired. Yield: 12 servings.

Mrs. Mary Joe Gresham
Hickory Flat, Mississippi

CREAMED TUNA

1 7-oz. can tuna
1/2 c. sliced celery
2 tbsp. chopped onion
1 tbsp. butter or margarine
1 can Cheddar cheese soup
1/2 c. milk
2 tbsp. chopped pimento

1/2 c. cooked green peas
Chopped parsley
Cooked rice

Drain and flake tuna. Cook celery and onion in butter in saucepan until tender. Blend in soup and milk. Add tuna, pimento and peas. Heat through, stirring occasionally. Garnish with parsley; serve over rice. Yield: 4 servings.

Ilona M. Wooten
Tyner, Tennessee

SALMON LOAF WITH SAUCE

2 c. flaked salmon
1 c. soft bread crumbs
2 tsp. lemon juice
1/4 tsp. salt
Dash of cayenne pepper
2 eggs, lightly beaten
3 c. thick white sauce
1/2 c. cooked green peas
2 tsp. chopped parsley
2 hard-cooked eggs, chopped

Combine salmon, bread crumbs, lemon juice and seasonings; add eggs. Mix well; blend in 2 cups white sauce. Turn mixture into greased 9-inch loaf pan. Bake in preheated 350-degree oven for 25 minutes or until firm. Combine peas, parsley, eggs and remaining 1 cup white sauce in saucepan. Heat to serving temperature. Serve sauce over salmon loaf.

Ruth W. Williams
Belmont, North Carolina

SPAGHETTI WITH SHRIMP SAUCE

2 cloves of garlic, finely chopped
1/4 c. cooking oil
1 1-lb. can tomatoes
2 1/2 tsp. salt
1/2 tsp. dried basil
1 6-oz. can tomato paste
1 tsp. dried oregano
1/2 lb. cooked shrimp, deveined
1/2 tsp. garlic salt
1 tsp. prepared horseradish

8 oz. spaghetti, cooked
Grated Parmesan cheese

Saute garlic in oil in saucepan. Add tomatoes, salt and basil; mix well. Simmer, uncovered, for 30 minutes. Stir in tomato paste and oregano; simmer for 15 minutes longer. Stir in shrimp, garlic salt and horseradish; heat through. Serve over hot spaghetti; sprinkle with cheese.

Elizabeth Miller
Fulton, Mississippi

RICE-STUFFED EGGPLANT

2/3 c. chopped green peppers
2/3 c. chopped celery
1 c. chopped onions
2 tbsp. butter
1/2 c. rice
1 lg. eggplant
1 1-lb. 13-oz. can tomatoes
1 1/2 tsp. salt
1/8 tsp. pepper
1 tsp. sweet basil
2 tsp. Worcestershire sauce
Grated cheese

Saute green peppers, celery and onions in butter; push vegetables to one side. Add rice; saute until golden brown, stirring occasionally. Cut eggplant in half; scoop out pulp, leaving 1/2-inch shell. Chop pulp; add to rice mixture. Stir in tomatoes and seasonings. Simmer, covered, for 20 minutes or until rice is tender; turn into eggplant shells. Bake in preheated 350-degree oven for 1 hour. Sprinkle with cheese; bake until cheese is melted. Yield: 5-6 servings.

Elceone Roberts
Alta Loma, Texas

CHEESE-CREAMED ONIONS

18 to 20 sm. onions
1/2 c. water
1 1/2 tsp. salt
1/4 c. melted butter
1/4 c. flour
1 1/2 c. milk
1 c. shredded cheese
1/2 c. chopped pecans

Combine onions, water and 1 teaspoon salt in 1 1/2-quart saucepan; cover. Bring to a boil over high heat; reduce heat. Simmer for 15 minutes or until tender; drain. Blend butter and flour together in saucepan; stir in milk and remaining 1/2 teaspoon salt. Cook, stirring constantly, over medium heat until thickened. Add cheese; cook, stirring, until melted. Stir in onions; heat through. Turn into serving dish; sprinkle with pecans. Yield: 4-6 servings.

Mrs. Juanita Patton
Inola, Oklahoma

ZESTY LOW-COST CARROTS

6 to 8 carrots, cut lengthwise
2 tbsp. grated onion
2 tbsp. horseradish
1/2 c. mayonnaise
1/2 tsp. salt
1/4 tsp. pepper
1/4 c. cracker crumbs
1 tbsp. melted butter
Dash of paprika

Cook carrots in water to cover until tender; drain. Place in shallow baking dish. Combine 1/4 cup water, onion, horseradish, mayonnaise, salt and pepper; pour over carrots. Combine cracker crumbs, butter and paprika; toss to mix. Sprinkle over carrot mixture. Bake in preheated 375-degree oven for 15 to 20 minutes or until top is browned. Yield: 6 servings.

Naomi Austin
Gainesville, Texas

MAYONNAISE BISCUITS

2 c. self-rising flour
1 c. milk
1/4 c. mayonnaise

Combine all ingredients, mixing well. Drop into greased muffin tins. Bake in preheated 400-degree oven for 12 to 15 minutes. Yield: 12 biscuits.

Mrs. Virginia Collie
Dry Fork, Virginia

BLUEBERRY-ORANGE TEA MUFFINS

1/4 c. shortening
2 eggs
2 c. flour
2 1/2 tsp. baking powder
2 tbsp. sugar
Grated rind of 1 orange
1/2 c. milk
1/2 c. orange juice
1 c. fresh blueberries

Cream shortening in large bowl. Add eggs; mix well. Sift flour, baking powder and sugar together; stir in orange rind. Add flour mixture, milk and orange juice alternately to shortening, stirring well after each addition. Batter will be stiff. Fold in dry blueberries carefully. Fill each well-greased muffin cup half full of batter. Bake in preheated 375-degree oven for about 20 minutes or until nicely browned. Yield: 2 dozen small muffins.

Photograph for this recipe above.

DOUBLE BLUEBERRY PANCAKES

1 c. milk
2 tbsp. light corn syrup
1 tbsp. corn oil
1 egg, lightly beaten
1 c. pancake mix
3/4 c. blueberries
1/3 c. cottage cheese
Blueberry syrup

Combine milk, corn syrup, corn oil and egg in mixing bowl. Add pancake mix; stir until dry ingredients are moistened. Batter will be lumpy. Stir in blueberries and cottage cheese carefully. Pour 1/4 cup batter onto hot griddle; cook until brown, turning once. Repeat cooking until all batter is used. Serve with blueberry syrup. Yield: 8 pancakes.

Photograph for this recipe on page 201.

FRESH POTATO-FRUIT COFFEE CAKE

1 pkg. dry yeast
1 c. scalded milk
1/2 c. shortening
1 c. fresh hot mashed potatoes
Sugar
2 tsp. salt
2 lg. eggs, lightly beaten
8 1/2 c. (about) sifted flour
6 tbsp. melted butter
1 c. diced mixed glaceed fruits
3/4 tsp. ground cinnamon
1 lg. egg white

Sprinkle yeast over 1/2 cup warm water; stir until dissolved. Mix milk, shortening, potatoes, 1/3 cup sugar and salt in large bowl; cool to lukewarm. Add yeast and eggs; blend well. Add 1 1/2 cups flour; mix well. Cover; let rise in warm place for about 1 hour or until bubbly. Stir in enough remaining flour to make stiff dough. Turn onto lightly floured board; knead until smooth and elastic. Place in lightly greased bowl; turn to grease surface. Cover; refrigerate overnight. Roll out on lightly floured board to 1-inch thickness. Cut with a 2-inch biscuit cutter. Dip each round into melted butter, then into glaceed fruits. Combine 3/4 cup sugar and cinnamon; dip rounds in cinnamon mixture. Stand rounds up in 2 greased and lightly floured 8-inch ring molds. Sprinkle with any remaining fruits. Beat egg white until foamy; brush on cakes. Let rise in warm place for about 1 hour or until doubled in bulk. Bake in preheated 350-degree oven for 35 minutes. Serve warm.

Photograph for this recipe on page 103.

FRESH POTATO ROLLS

1 pkg. dry yeast
2/3 c. scalded milk
1/2 c. shortening
1 c. fresh hot mashed potatoes
1/4 c. sugar
2 tsp. salt
3 lg. eggs, lightly beaten
8 1/2 c. (about) sifted flour
3 tbsp. melted butter

Sprinkle yeast over 1/2 cup warm water; stir until dissolved. Combine milk, shortening, potatoes, sugar and salt in large bowl; cool to lukewarm. Add yeast and eggs; blend well. Add 1 1/2 cups flour; mix well. Cover; let rise in warm place for about 1 hour or until bubbly. Stir in enough remaining flour to make stiff dough. Turn onto lightly floured board; knead until smooth and elastic. Place in lightly greased bowl, turning to grease surface. Cover; refrigerate overnight. Shape into small balls. Place 4 balls of dough in each greased and lightly floured muffin cup; brush with melted butter. Let rise in warm place for 1 hour and 15 minutes or until doubled in bulk. Bake in preheated 425-degree oven for 20 minutes. Yield: About 40 medium rolls.

Photograph for this recipe on page 103.

BUTTERED BREADSTICKS

6 tbsp. butter or margarine
2 c. biscuit mix
1 tbsp. sugar
1/2 c. milk

Place butter in 13 x 9 x 2-inch baking pan; place in preheated 400-degree oven to melt. Combine biscuit mix, sugar and milk in mixing bowl; stir with fork until soft dough is formed. Beat dough vigorously until stiff, but still sticky. Dust board lightly with additional biscuit mix; turn dough out on board. Knead gently for about 10 times. Roll to 12 x 8-inch rectangle. Cut dough in half lengthwise with floured knife; cut each half crosswise into 16 strips. Dip each strip in melted butter in pan, turning to coat both sides. Arrange in baking pan in 2 rows. Bake for about 12 minutes or until golden brown. Serve warm. Yield: 32 bread sticks.

Mrs. Floyd Craig
Nolan, Texas

BUTTERMILK HOT CAKES

2 eggs, well beaten
2 c. buttermilk
1 tsp. soda
2 1/4 c. sifted flour
2 tsp. baking powder
1 tsp. salt
2 tsp. sugar
1/4 c. shortening, melted

Combine eggs, buttermilk and soda. Sift flour, baking powder, salt and sugar together. Add flour mixture and shortening to buttermilk mixture. Drop batter by spoonfuls onto hot griddle or heavy iron skillet. Cook until brown on both sides. Serve hot. Yield: Twenty 4-inch hot cakes.

Patsy Savage Harris
Spring, Texas

POPOVERS

2 eggs, beaten
1 c. milk
1 tbsp. melted shortening
1 c. sifted all-purpose flour
1/2 tsp. salt

Combine eggs, milk and shortening. Add flour and salt; beat with hand beater until smooth. Fill hot, oiled custard cups or iron muffin pans half full. Bake in preheated 450-degree oven for 15 minutes. Reduce temperature to 350 degrees; bake for 15 to 20 minutes longer or until done. Do not open oven door for at least 25 minutes. One-fourth cup grated sharp Cheddar cheese may be added, if desired. Yield: 8-12 servings.

Mrs. Marjorie West
Lauderdale, Mississippi

CHEESE FLOWERPOT BREAD

1 cake or pkg. yeast
1/4 c. warm water
1 egg
2 tbsp. sugar
1 tsp. salt
2 tbsp. softened butter
1 c. scalded milk
3 3/4 to 4 1/4 c. all-purpose flour
1 1/2 c. shredded Cheddar cheese
Melted butter
7 clean 3 1/4 x 3 1/4-in. flowerpots
1 egg yolk

Soften yeast in water. Beat egg in mixing bowl; add sugar, salt and softened butter. Stir in milk gradually; cool until lukewarm. Add yeast and 1/2 of the flour; beat for 2 minutes with electric mixer at medium speed, scraping bowl occasionally. Add cheese and 1/2 cup flour; beat at high speed for 2 minutes, scraping bowl occasionally. Stir in enough remaining flour to make stiff dough. Knead dough on floured surface for 8 to 10 minutes or until smooth and satiny. Place in large buttered bowl; brush top with melted butter. Cover; let rise in warm place for about 1 hour or until doubled in bulk. Punch down. Turn out onto board; cover. Let rest for 10 minutes. Divide dough into 7 parts; shape each part into 4 balls. Cover hole in bottom of each seasoned flowerpot with aluminum foil. Place 1 ball in bottom of each flowerpot. Place remaining 3 balls on top; brush with melted butter. Cover; let rise in warm place for about 30 minutes or until doubled in bulk. Mix egg yolk with 1 tablespoon water; brush on dough. Bake in preheated 375-degree oven for 17 to 19 minutes. Remove from flowerpots; cool on wire racks. To season clay flowerpots, grease insides of each flowerpot thoroughly; place on baking sheet. Bake in preheated 375-degree oven for about 30 minutes; cool. Repeat 3 times. Do not wash pots once they have been seasoned.

Photograph for this recipe on page 34.

NO-FAIL WHITE BREAD

3 pkg. yeast
1/3 c. lukewarm water
3/4 c. sugar
2 1/2 tbsp. salt
1 qt. scalded milk
1 qt. boiling water

1/2 c. shortening
25 c. (about) sifted flour

Soften yeast in lukewarm water. Combine sugar, salt, milk, boiling water and shortening in large bowl; cool to lukewarm. Add yeast and half the flour; beat until smooth. Work in enough remaining flour to make easily handled dough. Knead dough on floured board until smooth. Cover; let rise until doubled in bulk. Punch dough down; shape into 8 loaves. Place in greased pans; let rise until doubled in bulk. Bake in preheated 400-degree oven for 30 minutes or until bread tests done. Wrap extra loaves securely; freeze for future use.

Mrs. Louella R. Pence
Macon, Illinois

FAMILY RICE PUDDING

1 qt. milk
1 c. sugar
1 c. rice
Pinch of salt
1 tsp. vanilla extract

Combine all ingredients in baking dish; stir lightly. Bake in preheated 325-degree oven for 1 hour or until rice is tender, stirring twice. Yield: 8 servings.

Barbara Newton
Hudson Falls, New York

LEMON MOUSSE

1 lg. can evaporated milk
1 c. sugar
1/4 c. lemon juice
1 1/2 c. graham cracker crumbs

Pour milk into stainless steel mixing bowl; freeze until icy. Whip milk until stiff, beating in sugar and lemon juice gradually. Line two 10-inch cake pans with half the crumbs; pour in lemon mixture. Top with remaining crumbs. Chill or freeze for several hours. Yield: 12 servings.

Mrs. Billy Marks
Pulaski, Tennessee

BUTTERMILK PIE

1 c. sugar
3 tbsp. flour
2 eggs, beaten
1/2 c. melted margarine
1 c. buttermilk
2 tsp. vanilla extract
1 tsp. lemon flavoring
1 unbaked pastry shell

Combine sugar and flour in bowl. Add eggs, margarine, buttermilk and flavorings; mix well. Turn into pastry shell. Bake in preheated 425-degree oven for 10 minutes. Reduce oven temperature to 350 degrees; bake for 30 minutes longer. Yield: 6-8 servings.

Mrs. Molly Bedrich
Lancaster, Texas

LUSCIOUS BANANA PUDDING

1/4 c. cornstarch
1 c. sugar
1/4 tsp. salt
2 c. milk
3 eggs, separated
2 tbsp. butter
1/2 tsp. vanilla extract
1 pkg. vanilla wafers
1 lb. bananas, sliced

Blend cornstarch with 2/3 cup sugar and salt in top of double boiler; stir in milk gradually. Cook over boiling water for about 10 minutes or until thickened, stirring constantly. Stir small amount of hot mixture into lightly beaten egg yolks gradually; stir back into remaining hot mixture. Cook for 5 minutes, stirring constantly; remove from heat. Add butter and vanilla; mix well. Cool. Arrange alternate layers of vanilla wafers, bananas and custard in baking dish. Beat egg whites until foamy. Beat in remaining 1/3 cup sugar gradually; beat until stiff peaks form. Spread over pudding. Bake in preheated 450-degree oven for about 5 minutes or until lightly browned. Yield: 6-8 servings.

Mrs. Frances J. Jacox
Halls, Tennessee

Pie and Pastry Favorites

Although pies are certainly not an American invention, the art of pie and pastry making has long been of great importance to the American cook. Long ago, New England sailors would while away the hours at sea carving intricate pie-jaggers out of bone for their wives back home. Even the colonial brick ovens were described in terms of how many pies they could hold — there were even 20-pie ovens. Because pies were eaten at almost every meal, some farm cooks were known to "mass produce" as many as 50 or 100 pies at one time. The pies were then stored either in a pie closet in an unheated room, or even frozen outside in the snow!

In some areas, pie is still served for breakfast, which sounds very extravagant in this calorie-conscious age. But, most nutritionists agree that people should start the day with a good breakfast — and what better way is there than with a delicious, fruit-filled piece of homemade pie?

Probably the most American pie is apple pie. Apples were being successfully grown and harvested in colonial New England as early as the mid-seventeenth century, and soon became the most commonly used fruit for pies. But, Americans also love cherry pie, wild blueberry pie, rhubarb pie, cranberry pie — the list is almost endless.

In the recipes for all fruit pies, the flavorings for the fillings differ in dozens of delicious ways, while the standards for pie crust have remained relatively constant over the years. And because pies are so often judged by their crusts, a delicious filling is wasted if the crust is tough and chewy. The best pie pastry is delicate, flaky and evenly browned. When cut or broken with a knife or fork, it should reveal even layers of flat flakes stacked one above the other with air spaces in between. Achieving a crust of this perfection is certainly no accident. Successful pastries are the result of following long-proven recipes and rules exactly, and using the right equipment.

The essential equipment for ease in making pies and pastries is usually inexpensive and easy to find in almost any store. The metal *pastry blender* is the best utensil for cutting the shortening into the dry ingredients and for blending in the water. The pastry blender, which has a series of metal "blades" attached to a wooden handle, creates "flakes" of shortening and flour and ensures a flaky pie crust.

Two other pieces of equipment that help to insure a flaky crust are a *cloth-covered rolling pin and board.* The cloth keeps the pastry dough from sticking to either utensil whereas if too much flour is used instead of the cloth, it may toughen the pastry. The cloth works to absorb the flour, releasing just enough to keep the pastry dough from sticking. Neither of these clothes has to be purchased. A child's white cotton sock can be cut to fit the rolling pin, and a coarse dish cloth may be used to cover the board.

Although not an essential tool, the *pastry wheel* lends a professional and artful touch to pie crusts. It cuts lattice strips with a scalloped edge, making them distinctive and attractive. A *pastry brush* may be used to glaze the crust with egg white or milk and sugar for a shiny, flavored or colorful crust. *Pie tape* is used to cover the edge of the pie crust during the baking period to prevent overbrowning. Aluminum foil can be used in place of the pie tape with equally good results. Bake the crust in a nonshiny pan for even browning.

Following proven methods and hints for mixing, handling and rolling pie pastry dough is the key to excellent results. The water should be ice cold and the shortening as well as the flour should be thoroughly chilled. Some cooks even insist on refrigerating the mixing bowl and the pastry blender as an extra measure. Instead of guessing, measure the ingredients accurately. At least 1/3 cup of shortening should be used for every cup of sifted flour. The amount of water varies with the dryness of the flour and the amount of shortening used, but two to four tablespoons of water are usually required for one cup of sifted flour.

After sifting the measured flour and salt together, lightly cut the shortening into the flour mixture until it resembles cornmeal. Then, one tablespoon at the time, sprinkle the ice cold water into the flour and shortening mixture, mixing it with a fork in a tossing motion. Enough water has been added when the pastry dough cleans the bowl.

Although the pastry dough is now ready for rolling, some cooks prefer to chill it, covered, for as long as 12 hours before rolling. This is said to make it tender, easier to handle and less likely to shrink during baking. Remove the pastry dough from your refrigerator about an hour before rolling. A light hand during rolling, just as in mixing it, is another key to flakiness. Too much pressure will melt the shortening particles, ensuring a tough crust. Immediately patch tears in the dough with fingers dipped in ice water. Never reroll pie pastry dough!

To begin rolling, softly press the pastry dough into a ball, then roll it from the center of the ball out, lifting the pin each time. Do not use a back and forth motion, as this tends to stretch and toughen pastry dough. When the pastry reaches 1/8-inch thickness, cut it to a diameter of 1 to 2 inches larger than the pie plate. Loosen the pastry dough, fold it in half and lift it into the pie pan with the fold at the center of the pan, then unfold. Or, after loosening the pastry dough from the board, roll it around the rolling pin and unroll it into the pan. This method can also be used to place top crusts. Pat the crust easily and evenly into the pan to remove air pockets, then trim off any excess neatly from around the rim. The prepared pastry may be stored in the freezer (baked or unbaked), or kept in the refrigerator for a week or so.

An easy, but versatile and delicious, pie crust can be made with various cookie crumbs. Graham cracker, zwieback cracker, ginger snap and chocolate wafer crusts all lend a delightful flavor to pies. Cookie crumb crusts do not have to be baked before filling, although baking gives the crust a nutlike flavor. This type of crust must be thoroughly chilled before filling though, or it will fall apart. Finely chopped almonds, pecans and walnuts are tasty additions to crumb crusts, as are a few delicate sprinklings of complementary spices. Bread, cake and cereal crumbs may also be used to make a pie crust.

Although pies with fruit fillings are probably the most popular, cream-filled pies are probably the easiest to make. An airy texture and a light, foamy filling characterize chiffon pies, while custard pies are rich and creamy.

Cream puffs and eclairs are delicate puff pastes filled with generous amounts of custard or whipped cream, and coated with a chocolate or fruit-flavored glaze. The term pastries is a general one, describing any number of sweet, fancy baked goods. The crusts are crisp or crumbly and are often filled, topped or mixed with fruit, preserves, jam or mincemeat. Tarts are small, open pastries with a rich crumbly crust. Tarts and tassies (miniature tarts) may be filled with fruit, jam or custard.

Home Economics Teachers know that men and children boast about home-baked pies and pastries. This superb collection will surely give the ones at your house something to talk about.

AMERICAN GLORY APPLE-CHEESE PIE

1 recipe 2-crust pie pastry
2 c. grated Cheddar cheese
6 c. peeled sliced apples
2 tsp. lemon juice
3/4 c. sugar
2 tbsp. flour
1/2 tsp. cinnamon
1/8 tsp. salt
4 or 5 crushed graham crackers
1/2 c. chopped nuts (opt.)
2 tbsp. butter

Prepare pie pastry, adding 1 cup cheese. Roll out on floured board. Line deep 10-inch pie shell with pastry. Sprinkle apples with lemon juice. Combine sugar, flour, cinnamon and salt. Add apples, tossing lightly. Sprinkle crumbs and nuts in pie shell. Place 1/3 of the apple mixture in shell. Top with 1/2 of the remaining cheese. Repeat layers of apples and cheese, ending with apples. Mound last layer of apples slightly in center. Dot with butter. Bake in preheated 450-degree oven for 10 minutes. Reduce oven temperature to 350 degrees. Bake for 40 minutes longer.

Mrs. Nancy J. Bledsoe
Fordsville, Kentucky

OPEN-FACED SOUR CREAM-APPLE PIE

2 lg. tart apples, peeled
1 c. sour cream
3/4 c. sugar
Flour
1/4 tsp. salt
1 tsp. vanilla extract
1 egg
Pastry for 1 8-in. pie shell
1/2 c. (packed) brown sugar
1/4 c. soft butter

Cut apples into 1/4-inch thick slices; cut each slice into thirds. Combine sour cream, sugar, 2 tablespoons flour, salt, vanilla extract and egg. Beat with electric mixer until

sugar is dissolved. Stir in apples. Spoon into pie shell. Bake in preheated 400-degree oven for 25 minutes. Combine brown sugar and 1/3 cup flour; cut in butter with pastry blender or fork until mixture is crumbly. Remove pie from oven. Sprinkle topping over pie. Bake for 20 minutes longer or until topping and crust are lightly browned.

Mrs. Diane Manono May
Denver, Colorado

FRENCH PECAN-APPLE PIE

1 c. sifted flour
1/2 tsp. salt
1/3 c. shortening
2 tbsp. cold water
3/4 c. sugar
1 tsp. cinnamon
6 to 7 c. pared, cored and sliced
   Washington State apples
1/4 c. pecans
1 1/2 tbsp. butter
Topping

Sift flour and salt together in mixing bowl. Cut in shortening until mixture resembles fine crumbs. Add water; toss until pastry clings together. Roll out on floured board. Fit into 9-inch pie pan; flute edge. Mix sugar and cinnamon together; mix carefully with apples and pecans. Place in pie crust; dot with butter. Sprinkle Topping over top. Bake in preheated 425-degree oven for 50 to 60 minutes or until done. Serve warm with whipped cream or ice cream, if desired. Washington golden delicious or winesap apples are suggested for this recipe.

Topping

1/2 c. butter
1/2 c. (firmly packed) brown sugar
1 c. flour
1/4 c. pecans

Combine butter, brown sugar and flour; mix well. Add pecans.

Photograph for this recipe on page 193.

CHERRY-TOASTED ALMOND PIE

Sugar
3 tbsp. cornstarch
Salt
3/4 c. cherry juice
1 1/2 tsp. lemon juice
1/4 tsp. almond extract
1/2 tsp. red food coloring
3 c. drained tart red cherries
1 c. sifted all-purpose flour
1/3 c. shortening
3 tbsp. cold water
3 egg whites
1/2 c. toasted almonds

Place 1/3 cup sugar, cornstarch and 1/4 teaspoon salt in saucepan; mix. Stir in cherry juice; cook until thick, stirring frequently. Add 2/3 cup sugar; cook until glossy. Remove from heat; stir in lemon juice, almond extract and food coloring. Add cherries; mix. Cool. Sift flour and 1/2 teaspoon salt together; cut in shortening with pastry blender until mixture is size of small peas. Sprinkle with water; mix until particles hold together. Form into smooth ball; chill. Roll out on floured surface into circle 1 inch larger than pie plate. Place in pie plate; press with fingers to fit pie plate. Fold pastry under; flute edge. Pour filling into crust; place piece of aluminum foil over edge of crust. Bake in preheated 450-degree oven for 10 to 15 minutes; remove foil. Decrease temperature to 350 degrees; bake for 25 to 30 minutes. Beat egg whites until stiff peaks form, adding 6 tablespoons sugar gradually. Spread over pie; sprinkle with almonds. Bake for 15 minutes longer.

Nancy Stewart
Trenton, Michigan

BLUEBERRY PIE WITH ORANGE-NUT CRUST

2 c. flour
1/4 tsp. salt
Sugar
3/4 c. shortening
1 tsp. grated orange rind
1/3 c. finely chopped walnuts or pecans
4 c. fresh blueberries

1/4 c. cornstarch
1/2 tsp. nutmeg
2 tbsp. butter
Confectioners' sugar

Combine flour, salt and 2 teaspoons sugar in bowl. Cut in shortening until mixture resembles coarse meal. Stir in orange rind and walnuts. Sprinkle mixture with 5 tablespoons water, 1 tablespoon at a time, blending lightly until dough forms a ball. Chill for 1 hour before using. Roll out half the pastry; line 9-inch pie pan. Combine blueberries, 1 cup sugar, cornstarch and nutmeg in large bowl; mix carefully. Pour into pastry-lined pan; dot with butter. Roll out remaining pastry; place over filling. Seal and flute edge; cut vents in top. Bake in preheated 375-degree oven for 1 hour. Remove from oven; cool on rack. Sprinkle with confectioners' sugar.

Magdalene Beehler
Crookston, Minnesota

PEACH-PECAN PIE

Flour
1/2 tsp. salt
1/2 c. vegetable shortening
1/4 c. lemon juice
1 egg yolk
1 c. sugar
2 tbsp. cornstarch
2 tbsp. orange juice
1 tsp. grated orange rind
2 tbsp. butter
2 c. sliced peaches
1/4 c. chopped pecans

Place 1 1/2 cups sifted flour and salt in bowl; cut in shortening until mixture is of coarse cornmeal consistency. Place lemon juice and egg yolk in a small bowl; beat well. Stir lemon juice mixture into flour mixture with a fork until mixture holds together. Form into ball; roll out on lightly floured surface. Fit into 9-inch pie pan; crimp edge. Set aside. Combine sugar, 2 tablespoons flour and cornstarch in saucepan; stir in orange juice, rind and butter. Cook over low heat, stirring constantly, until thick. Arrange peaches in pastry shell; sprinkle with pecans.

Pour cooked mixture over pecans. Bake in preheated 450-degree oven for 10 minutes. Reduce temperature to 325 degrees. Bake for 30 minutes longer. Serve with whipped cream, if desired.

Mrs. Jeanne Bunch
Deshler, Ohio

STRAWBERRY-PECAN PIE

1 10-oz. package pie crust mix
1/2 c. finely chopped toasted pecans
1 qt. butter pecan or vanilla ice cream,
    slightly softened
2 pt. chilled California strawberries,
    sliced
Light brown sugar

Prepare pie crust mix according to package directions, adding pecans; fit into 9-inch pie plate. Bake as directed; let cool thoroughly. Spoon ice cream into cooled crust. Mix strawberries with sugar to taste; spoon over ice cream. Serve immediately. Pie shell filled with ice cream may be frozen, if desired. Remove from freezer to refrigerator 20 minutes before serving time for easier slicing.

Photograph for this recipe on page 188.

FARM FRESH RHUBARB PIE

1 recipe 2-crust pie pastry
3 c. diced rhubarb
1 c. sugar
2 tbsp. cornstarch
1/8 tsp. salt
1/2 tsp. grated orange rind
2 tbsp. butter

Roll out half the pastry; line 9-inch pie pan. Combine rhubarb with sugar, cornstarch, salt and orange rind; mix well. Pour into pastry-lined pan; dot with butter. Roll out remaining pastry; place over filling. Seal and flute edge; cut vents in top. Bake in preheated 450-degree oven for 10 minutes. Reduce oven temperature to 350 degrees. Bake for 30 minutes longer or until crust is golden.

Mrs. J. T. Barnett
Tulia, Texas

PEACHY PEAR PIE

3 c. sliced peaches
2 1/2 c. pared sliced pears
3 tbsp. quick-cooking tapioca
1 1/2 c. sugar
1 recipe pie pastry
Butter or margarine
1/2 c. flour
3 1/2 tsp. cinnamon

Drain peaches; reserve 1/2 cup juice. Combine peaches, pears, tapioca, reserved juice and 1 cup sugar. Roll out pastry on floured surface; place in 9-inch pie pan. Place pear mixture in pastry; dot with 1 tablespoon butter. Mix flour, remaining 1/2 cup sugar and cinnamon; cut in 4 teaspoons butter. Sprinkle over pear mixture. Bake in preheated 400-degree oven for 40 to 45 minutes.

Mrs. Elisa K. Burke
Clearfield, Iowa

THREE-FRUIT PIE

1 No. 303 can sour red cherries
1 No. 2 can crushed pineapple
2 c. sugar
1/2 c. cornstarch
1 tsp. vanilla extract
1 tsp. red food coloring
1 c. chopped pecans
6 sliced bananas
2 baked 9-in. pie shells
2 c. whipped cream

Drain cherries and pineapple; reserve juices. Add enough water to reserved juices to make 2 cups liquid. Combine sugar and cornstarch in saucepan; stir in liquid. Cook, stirring constantly, until thick. Add vanilla extract and food coloring; let stand until cool. Stir in cherries, pineapple and pecans. Arrange alternate layers of cherry mixture and sliced bananas in pie shells. Top with whipped cream to serve.

Mrs. Thea Moore
San Antonio, Texas

BANANA CREAM PIE

2 c. milk
3/4 c. sugar
1/4 tsp. salt
5 tbsp. flour
2 tbsp. cornstarch
2 egg yolks
2 tbsp. butter
3/4 tsp. almond flavoring
1 baked 9-in. pie shell
2 lg. bananas, sliced
1 recipe meringue

Scald milk in double boiler. Combine sugar, salt, flour and cornstarch in saucepan; mix well. Stir milk into sugar mixture gradually. Cook over medium heat, stirring constantly, until thickened. Return to double boiler; cook for 15 minutes, stirring occasionally. Beat egg yolks slightly. Add small amount of hot mixture to egg yolks, stirring constantly until well blended. Return to hot mixture, stirring to blend. Cook for 5 minutes longer, stirring constantly. Add butter; mix well. Cool. Stir in flavoring. Spread 1/3 of the mixture in pie shell. Cover with 1/2 of the banana slices. Add half the remaining filling and remaining banana slices. Top with remaining filling. Spread meringue over filling, sealing to edge. Bake in preheated 350-degree oven until lightly browned.

Mrs. Linda Coombs
La Jara, Colorado

OLD-FASHIONED BUTTERSCOTCH CREAM PIE

3 tbsp. butter or margarine
2 c. (packed) brown sugar
2 c. milk
3 eggs, separated
1/4 c. flour
1/2 tsp. salt
1 1/4 tsp. vanilla extract
1 baked 9-in. pie shell
3 tbsp. sugar

Place butter in heavy 10-inch skillet; heat until melted. Add brown sugar and 1/2 cup milk; mix well. Bring to a boil; cook for 5 minutes, stirring constantly. Beat egg yolks;

stir in remaining milk. Combine flour and salt. Stir egg mixture into flour mixture. Add small amount hot brown sugar mixture gradually; return to sugar mixture in skillet. Cook over low heat, stirring constantly, until thickened. Cool slightly; add 1 teaspoon vanilla. Pour into pie shell. Beat egg whites until stiff peaks form, adding sugar gradually; fold in remaining vanilla. Pile on top of pie, sealing to edge. Bake in preheated 325-degree oven for about 15 minutes or until lightly browned.

Ann W. Stewart
Greenfield, Ohio

GLAZED RASPBERRY PIE

2 c. fresh whole raspberries
1 baked 9-in. pie shell
3 tbsp. cornstarch
1 1/4 c. sugar
3/4 c. mashed raspberries
Dash of lemon juice

Arrange whole raspberries in pie shell. Combine cornstarch, sugar, mashed raspberries, 1/2 cup water and lemon juice in saucepan; cook until clear, stirring constantly. Pour over whole raspberries; chill until ready to serve. Top with whipped cream, if desired.

Mrs. Alice Sheppard
Grand Forks, North Dakota

WEST VIRGINIA MOUNTAIN TOP PIE

1 c. flour
1/4 c. (packed) light brown sugar
1/2 tsp. salt
1/3 c. cold butter
1 tsp. rolled oats
1/3 c. coarsely chopped black walnuts
1 sq. unsweetened chocolate, grated
1 tsp. vanilla extract
1 tbsp. ice water
3/4 c. butter
Confectioners' sugar
3 eggs
2 sq. unsweetened chocolate, melted
2 tsp. instant coffee
1 c. heavy cream
1 1/2 tsp. cocoa

Sift flour, brown sugar and salt together into mixing bowl. Cut cold butter into small pieces. Add oats, butter, walnuts and grated chocolate to flour mixture; mix until well blended. Add vanilla and water; mix until pastry holds together. Roll out pastry between 2 sheets of waxed paper; remove top paper. Invert pastry into 9-inch pie pan; remove waxed paper. Round off edge; prick shell generously with fork. Bake in preheated 350-degree oven for about 20 minutes or until light brown; cool. Cream butter and 1 1/4 cups confectioners' sugar in mixing bowl. Add eggs, one at a time, beating well after each addition. Stir in melted chocolate and coffee; mix well. Pour into pie crust; chill for 20 minutes. Beat cream, cocoa and 1 tablespoon confectioners' sugar together until stiff peaks form; spoon over pie filling. Sprinkle with additional grated chocolate.

Katherine P. Crouch
Bluefield, West Virginia

TWO CRUST SLICE O'LEMON PIE

1 1/4 c. sugar
2 tbsp. flour
1/8 tsp. salt
1/4 c. butter, softened
3 eggs
1/2 c. water
1 tsp. grated lemon rind
1 med. lemon

Combine sugar, flour and salt in bowl; blend in butter. Reserve 1 teaspoon egg white for crust. Beat remaining eggs; add to flour mixture. Add water and lemon rind; mix well. Peel lemon; cut into thin slices. Add to sugar mixture; stir well. Set aside.

Pastry

2 c. sifted flour
1 tsp. salt
2/3 c. vegetable shortening
6 to 7 tbsp. cold water
Sugar
Cinnamon

Mix flour and salt in bowl; cut in shortening. Add enough water to moisten; form into 2 balls. Roll out half the pastry on floured surface; fit into 8-inch pie pan. Add lemon filling. Roll out remaining pastry; place over filling. Cut slits in top to allow steam to escape; brush crust with reserved egg white. Sprinkle with sugar and cinnamon. Bake in preheated 400-degree oven for 30 to 35 minutes or until done.

Meredith Whitaker
Andrews, North Carolina

LIMELIGHT PIE

3/4 c. all-purpose flour, sifted
1/2 tsp. salt
2 tbsp. sugar
1/4 c. vegetable shortening
1 tbsp. cold water
1/2 sq. chocolate, melted
1   14-oz. can sweetened condensed milk
1/4 c. lime juice
1 c. drained crushed pineapple
4 drops of green food coloring
3/4 c. heavy cream
1 tbsp. confectioners' sugar
1/2 tsp. vanilla extract
1/2 sq. chocolate, grated

Combine flour, 1/4 teaspoon salt and sugar in mixing bowl; cut in shortening until mixture resembles coarse cornmeal. Sprinkle with water; drizzle with melted chocolate. Toss with fork until mixed; form into ball. Roll out on floured surface to 10-inch circle; pastry will have marbleized appearance. Fit into 9-inch pie plate; flute edge. Prick all over with fork. Bake in preheated 400-degree oven for 10 to 12 minutes; cool. Blend sweetened condensed milk, lime juice and remaining 1/4 teaspoon salt in mixing bowl until thickened. Add pineapple and food coloring; mix well. Chill for 2 to 3 hours. Whip cream in small bowl until stiff. Fold in confectioners' sugar and vanilla; fold into lime mixture. Place in pie shell; chill. Garnish with grated chocolate just before serving.

Mrs. Virginia Olsen
West Redding, Connecticut

CHERRY-CHEESE DREAM PIE

1 1/4 c. sifted flour
Sugar
1/4 tsp. salt
1/2 c. soft butter
2 sm. egg yolks, beaten
1 tsp. vanilla extract
1 3-oz. package cream cheese
1/4 c. confectioners' sugar
1 tsp. lemon juice
1 tbsp. milk
1 env. dessert topping mix
1/4 c. chopped pecans
1 1-lb. 4-oz. can frozen sweetened
   pitted sour cherries
2 tbsp. cornstarch
1/4 tsp. almond flavoring

Sift flour, 1/4 cup sugar and salt into mixing bowl; cut in butter thoroughly. Add egg yolks and vanilla; mix thoroughly. Press pastry over bottom and side of 9-inch pie pan. Bake in preheated 350-degree oven for 25 minutes; cool. Whip cheese until soft and smooth. Combine confectioners' sugar, lemon juice and milk; stir into cream cheese. Beat until smooth and fluffy. Prepare topping mix according to package directions, omitting vanilla; add pecans. Fold whipped topping into cheese mixture; spread in bottom of pie shell. Chill until set. Drain cherries, reserving juice. Pour reserved juice into saucepan. Combine 1/3 cup sugar and cornstarch, blending well; stir into juice. Cook over medium heat, stirring constantly, until clear and thickened. Add cherries and flavoring; stir to blend. Cool. Spoon over cheese filling; chill until served. Garnish with slivered almonds, if desired.

Mrs. Vera Journey
Clarendon Hills, Illinois

CHESS PIE

1 1/2 c. all-purpose flour
1/2 tsp. salt
2/3 c. shortening
3 eggs
1 tbsp. cornmeal
1/8 tsp. mace
1 1/2 c. sugar
1/2 c. melted butter or margarine
1 tbsp. cider vinegar
1 tsp. vanilla

Combine flour and salt in mixing bowl; cut in shortening until mixture resembles small peas. Sprinkle in 3 to 4 tablespoons water to make a stiff dough, stirring with fork. Do not knead. Gather pastry into ball; turn out on floured board. Roll into circle 1 inch larger than 9-inch pie plate. Fit into pie plate; flute edge. Beat eggs slightly. Combine cornmeal, mace and sugar; stir into eggs. Stir in remaining ingredients; mix well. Pour into pie shell. Bake in preheated 325-degree oven for 1 hour or until brown and firm.

Mrs. Ethelyne Wooten
Ruleville, Mississippi

STRAWBERRY-ALMOND CREAM PIE

All-purpose flour
1 tsp. salt
1/2 c. shortening
1/2 c. blanched slivered almonds
3/4 c. sugar
4 tbsp. cornstarch
2 c. milk
1 egg, slightly beaten
1/2 c. heavy cream, whipped
1 tsp. vanilla extract
1/2 c. crushed fresh strawberries
1 1/2 c. whole fresh strawberries

Sift 1 cup flour and 1/2 teaspoon salt together into medium bowl; cut in shortening with pastry blender. Stir in 2 to 4 tablespoons cold water or enough to hold ingredients together; form into ball. Roll out on lightly floured surface until 2 inches larger than inverted 9-inch pie pan; fit into pie pan. Trim edge to 1 1/2 inches; fold under. Flute edge; prick entire surface of pastry with fork. Refrigerate for 30 minutes. Bake in preheated 450-degree oven for 8 to 10 minutes or until golden brown; cool completely. Reduce oven temperature to 300 degrees. Place almonds in shallow baking pan. Bake, stirring frequently, for about 10 minutes or until lightly browned; sprinkle on pie shell. Blend 1/2 cup sugar, 3 tablespoons cornstarch, 3 tablespoons flour and remaining 1/2 teaspoon salt in top of double boiler.

Stir in milk gradually; mix until smooth. Place over boiling water; cook for 8 to 10 minutes or until thickened, stirring constantly. Cover; cook for 10 minutes longer. Remove from heat. Stir small amount of cooked mixture into egg; stir back into cooked mixture. Return to heat; cook for 2 minutes longer, stirring constantly. Do not overcook. Pour into bowl; cover. Refrigerate for about 2 hours or until chilled and thick. Beat with electric mixer until smooth; fold in whipped cream and vanilla. Mix crushed strawberries and 1/2 cup water in small saucepan. Place over low heat; cook for 5 minutes. Strain off liquid; discard strawberries. Mix remaining 1/4 cup sugar and remaining 1 tablespoon cornstarch in same saucepan. Stir in strawberry liquid; mix until smooth. Bring to a boil over low heat, stirring constantly; mixture will be thick and translucent. Cool; refrigerate for 1 hour. Wash whole strawberries; hull. Slice strawberries in half; drain on absorbent paper. Spoon chilled filling into pie shell; arrange strawberry halves on filling, cut side down, starting at edge and working toward center. Cover with chilled glaze; refrigerate for 2 hours or until chilled.

Mrs. Shirley E. Jensen
Pleasant Valley, New York

FAVORITE CUSTARD PIE

1 c. sifted flour
Salt
1/3 c. yellow vegetable shortening
3 lg. eggs
1/3 c. sugar
1 tsp. vanilla extract
1/8 tsp. nutmeg
2 c. milk

Sift flour and 1/2 teaspoon salt together; cut in shortening. Add enough ice water slowly to hold ingredients together, mixing lightly. Roll out on lightly floured board. Line 8-inch pie plate; flute edge above rim of plate. Beat eggs slightly. Stir in sugar, 1/8 teaspoon salt, vanilla and nutmeg. Scald milk; pour into egg mixture slowly, stirring constantly. Pour into pastry shell. Sprinkle with additional nutmeg. Bake in preheated

425-degree oven for 22 minutes or until firm.

Mrs. Phebe G. Walker
Lebanon, New Hampshire

INNKEEPER'S PIE

2 c. sifted all-purpose flour
1 tsp. salt
Baking powder
1/3 c. shortening
1 1/2 sq. unsweetened chocolate
1 1/2 c. water
Sugar
1/4 c. butter or margarine
3 tsp. vanilla extract
1/4 c. soft shortening
1/2 c. milk
1 egg
1/2 c. chopped walnuts
1 c. whipping cream

Combine 1 cup flour, 1/2 teaspoon salt and 1/8 teaspoon baking powder in bowl; mix well. Cut in shortening until particles resemble peas. Add 2 tablespoons cold water, tossing with fork until moistened. Roll into circle slightly larger than deep 9-inch pie plate. Fit into pie plate, building a high rim. Set aside. Melt chocolate in water in saucepan; add 2/3 cup sugar. Bring to a boil, stirring constantly. Add butter and 1 1/2 teaspoons vanilla. Remove from heat. Combine remaining 1 cup flour, 3/4 cup sugar, 1 teaspoon baking powder and remaining 1/2 teaspoon salt in bowl; add soft shortening, milk and 1/2 teaspoon vanilla. Beat at medium speed of electric mixer for 2 minutes. Add egg; beat for 2 minutes longer. Pour into prepared pie shell. Stir chocolate mixture; pour over batter slowly. Sprinkle with walnuts. Bake in preheated 350-degree oven for 55 to 60 minutes or until toothpick inserted in center comes out clean. Cool until slightly warm. Whip cream, adding 2 tablespoons sugar, 1 tablespoon at a time. Add remaining 1 teaspoon vanilla; beat until fluffy. Pile whipped cream around edge of pie. Garnish with additional chopped walnuts. Serve immediately.

Penelope H. Merrill
Portland, Maine

BLACK BOTTOM PIE

1 2/3 c. chocolate wafer crumbs
5 tbsp. butter, melted
2 c. sugar
1 1/2 tbsp. flour
2 c. milk
4 egg yolks, slightly beaten
2 oz. unsweetened chocolate, melted
3 tsp. vanilla extract
1 env. unflavored gelatin
4 egg whites
1/4 tsp. cream of tartar
1 c. heavy cream
2 tbsp. confectioners' sugar

Combine crumbs and butter in bowl; mix well. Press into bottom and over side of 9-inch pie pan. Bake in preheated 300-degree oven for 5 minutes. Combine 1 1/2 cups sugar and flour in saucepan; add milk gradually. Blend in egg yolks; cook over low heat until custard mixture coats spoon. Combine 1 cup custard with melted chocolate and 1 teaspoon vanilla; blend well. Spread over crust. Soften gelatin in 1/4 cup water; add to remaining custard. Cool completely. Beat egg whites with cream of tartar until soft peaks form; add remaining sugar and 1 teaspoon vanilla gradually. Fold into custard mixture; spread over chocolate mixture. Whip cream; add confectioners' sugar and remaining 1 teaspoon vanilla gradually. Spread topping over pie; sprinkle with grated chocolate. Refrigerate overnight.

Patricia Allen
Smyrna, Tennessee

CRANBERRY CHIFFON PIE

Sugar
1/4 c. flour
1 env. unflavored gelatin
1/2 tsp. salt
2 c. cranberry juice cocktail
3 egg whites
1/2 c. heavy cream, whipped
1 baked 9-in. pie shell

Combine 1/2 cup sugar, flour, gelatin and salt in saucepan; stir in cranberry juice. Cook bubbly, stirring constantly. Chill until mixture is partially set. Beat egg whites until frothy; add 1/3 cup sugar gradually, beating until stiff peaks form. Fold into cranberry mixture; fold in whipped cream. Spoon into pie shell; chill for several hours or overnight. Garnish with additional whipped cream, if desired.

Mrs. Betty Otteson
Pearl City, Illinois

LEMON CHIFFON PIE

1/4 c. (firmly packed) brown sugar
1 c. flour
1/2 c. chopped pecans
1/2 c. butter
1 c. sugar
1 env. unflavored gelatin
2/3 c. water
1/3 c. lemon juice
4 eggs, separated
1 tbsp. grated lemon rind
1/2 tsp. cream of tartar

Combine brown sugar, flour and pecans in bowl. Add butter; mix until blended thoroughly. Spread in 13 x 9 1/2 x 2-inch pan. Bake in preheated 400-degree oven for 15 minutes; remove from oven. Stir with spoon. Reserve 3/4 cup for topping; press remaining crumb mixture in bottom and up side of 9-inch pie pan. Cool. Combine 1/2 cup sugar and gelatin in saucepan; add water and lemon juice, stirring to mix well. Add slightly beaten egg yolks; cook over low heat, stirring constantly, until mixture comes to a boil. Remove immediately from heat; stir in lemon rind. Place pan in cold water; cool, stirring, until mixture mounds when dropped from a spoon. Beat egg whites until frothy; add cream of tartar. Add remaining 1/2 cup sugar gradually, beating until stiff and glossy. Fold lemon mixture into meringue. Pour into prepared crust. Sprinkle reserved crumbs over top. Chill for 1 hour.

Mrs. Jessie Pritchard
Plant City, Florida

Recipe on page 185.

Recipe on page 228.

SWEET POTATO NUT PIE

Pastry for 1 9-in. pie
1/2 c. chopped pecans
3 eggs, slightly beaten
1 c. (packed) brown sugar
1 c. milk
1 tsp. cinnamon
1/2 tsp. nutmeg
1/2 tsp. ginger
1/2 tsp. salt
1/4 c. lemon juice
2 tbsp. melted butter
1 1/2 c. sieved cooked sweet potatoes
1 1/2 c. whipped cream

Line pie pan with pastry; press 1/4 cup pecans into pastry. Combine eggs, brown sugar, milk, cinnamon, nutmeg, ginger and salt in bowl; mix well. Add lemon juice and butter; beat until well blended. Blend in sweet potatoes and remaining pecans; pour into pastry shell. Bake in preheated 375-degree oven for about 50 minutes to 1 hour or until knife inserted near center of pie comes out clean. Top with whipped cream. Yield: 8 servings.

Photograph for this recipe on page 204.

ALMOND BUTTERSCOTCH PUFFS

1 c. water
1/2 c. butter
1 tsp. sugar
1/4 tsp. salt
1 c. sifted flour
4 eggs

Combine water, butter, sugar and salt in saucepan; bring to a full rolling boil. Add flour all at once. Stir vigorously over low heat for about 1 minute or until mixture forms thick smooth ball that leaves side of pan clean. Remove from heat; cool slightly. Add eggs, one at a time, beating well after each addition until paste is shiny and smooth. Drop by spoonfuls, 3 inches apart, onto ungreased baking sheet. Bake in preheated 400-degree oven for about 40 minutes or until puffed and golden. Remove to wire rack; cool. Remove tops; scoop out centers.

Recipe on page 233.

Recipe on page 205.

Butterscotch Cream Filling

1/2 c. flour
2/3 c. (firmly packed) brown sugar
2 c. milk
4 egg yolks
1 tsp. vanilla extract
2 tbsp. butter
1 c. heavy cream
1/2 c. slivered almonds, toasted

Combine flour and brown sugar in medium saucepan. Stir in milk slowly; bring to a boil, stirring constantly. Reduce heat; cook for 3 minutes, stirring constantly. Remove from heat. Beat egg yolks slightly; beat in about 1 cup of hot mixture gradually. Return to saucepan. Cook, stirring, for about 1 minute, or until thickened. Remove from heat; add vanilla extract and butter. Cool completely. Whip cream; fold cream and almonds into filling. Fill puffs. Garnish with caramel sauce, if desired.

Mrs. Karen Eiseth
Gillett, Wisconsin

MINCE CHIFFON PIE

1 1/2 c. graham cracker crumbs
Sugar
1/4 c. melted margarine
1 box mincemeat
2 env. unflavored gelatin
1/2 c. heavy cream, whipped
3 egg whites

Combine crumbs, 1/4 cup sugar and margarine; blend well. Press evenly into 9-inch pie pan. Prepare mincemeat according to package directions. Dissolve gelatin in 1/2 cup warm water; blend gelatin into mincemeat. Chill until partially set. Fold whipped cream into mincemeat. Beat egg whites until stiff but not dry; add 6 tablespoons sugar gradually, beating well after each addition. Fold egg white mixture into mincemeat, mixing well. Spoon filling into pie shell. Refrigerate until firm. Serve with whipped cream, if desired.

Mrs. Mary F. Zappe
San Antonio, Texas

CHOCO-WALNUT PEPPERMINT PIE

1 env. unflavored gelatin
1/4 c. cold water
1 1/2-oz. unsweetened chocolate, chopped
1 c. brewed coffee
2 eggs, separated
2/3 c. sugar
1 tsp. vanilla extract
2 or 3 drops of peppermint extract
1/4 tsp. salt
1 c. finely chopped California walnuts
1 baked 9-in. pie shell, cooled

Soften gelatin in cold water. Combine gelatin, chocolate and coffee in small saucepan; stir over medium-low heat until chocolate is melted and gelatin is dissolved. Remove from heat. Beat egg yolks; beat in 1/3 cup sugar, vanilla extract, peppermint extract and salt. Add to chocolate mixture; beat until well blended. Set aside to cool and thicken until mixture mounds on a spoon. Beat egg whites until soft peaks form; beat in remaining 1/3 cup sugar until stiff peaks form. Fold chocolate mixture into meringue; add 3/4 cup walnuts. Turn into pastry shell; sprinkle remaining 1/4 cup walnuts on top. Chill for several hours or until firm. Decorate pie with ruffle of sweetened whipped cream; sprinkle with crushed peppermint candy, if desired.

Photograph for this recipe above.

PUMPKIN CHIFFON PRALINE PIE

1 unbaked 9-in. pie shell
1/3 c. butter
1/3 c. (packed) brown sugar
1/3 c. chopped pecans
1 c. sugar
1 env. unflavored gelatin
1 1/2 tsp. pumpkin pie spice
1 tsp. salt
1 1-lb. can pumpkin
4 eggs, separated
3/4 c. milk

Bake pie shell in preheated 450-degree oven for 15 minutes. Combine butter, brown sugar and pecans; spread on bottom of shell.

Bake for 5 minutes longer. Cool crust. Combine 3/4 cup sugar, gelatin, spice and salt in double boiler. Stir in pumpkin, slightly beaten egg yolks and milk. Cook, stirring constantly, over hot water for 15 minutes. Chill until thickened. Beat egg whites until foamy. Beat remaining 1/4 cup sugar, 1 tablespoon at a time, into egg whites until stiff peaks form. Place meringue in bowl of ice. Beat pumpkin mixture until fluffy; fold into meringue. Turn into pie shell. Chill until firm. Serve topped with whipped cream.

Mrs. Dena Y. Clary
Mableton, Georgia

EASY CREAM PUFFS

1/2 c. shortening
1 c. boiling water
1 c. all-purpose flour
4 eggs
1 recipe custard

Measure shortening into saucepan; add boiling water. Boil until shortening melts. Add flour, all at once, stirring vigorously. Cook and stir until mixture forms a ball. Remove from heat. Add eggs, one at a time, beating until smooth after each addition. Drop by heaping tablespoonfuls onto greased shallow baking pan. Round dough with spoon, leaving a pointed center. Bake in preheated 450-degree oven for 10 minutes. Reduce temperature to 400 degrees; bake for 25 minutes longer. Cool; slit on side and scoop out centers. Fill with custard filling. Dust with confectioners' sugar or top with frosting or sauce.

Mrs. Lynnell Holland
Chiloquin, Oregon

ECLAIRS SUPREME

1/3 c. margarine
1 tsp. sugar
1/2 tsp. salt
1 c. flour
4 eggs
1 pkg. vanilla pudding mix
1 1/2 c. milk
1/2 tsp. brandy flavoring

2 c. miniature marshmallows
3 bananas, sliced
1 10-oz. jar chocolate topping

Combine margarine, 1 cup water, sugar and salt in saucepan; blend well. Bring to a boil. Add flour, stirring thoroughly. Place over low heat, stirring constantly, until mixture forms a ball. Remove from heat. Add eggs, one at a time, beating until smooth after each addition. Shape into 3 x 1-inch rectangles on ungreased baking sheet. Bake in preheated 400-degree oven for 40 minutes or until lightly browned. Cool. Prepare pudding mix according to package directions using 1 1/2 cups milk. Stir flavoring into pudding, blending well. Cover top with waxed paper; chill. Fold in marshmallows and banana slices. Slice eclairs in half and scoop out any soft dough. Fill with cream filling; chill for 1 hour. Spread chocolate topping over eclairs.

Mrs. Judith Bowers
Batavia, Ohio

DANISH PUFF

Butter
2 c. sifted flour
1 tsp. almond extract
1 1/2 tsp. vanilla extract
3 eggs
1 1/2 c. powdered sugar
2 tbsp. milk

Cut 1/2 cup butter into 1 cup flour. Add 2 tablespoons cold water to make dough. Divide dough into 2 parts. Pat each part out into 3 x 12-inch rectangle on ungreased cookie sheet. Bring 1/2 cup butter and 1 cup water to a boil. Add almond extract and 1 teaspoon vanilla extract. Remove from heat; add remaining flour all at once, beating vigorously. Add eggs, one at a time, beating well after each addition. Spread over rectangles. Bake in preheated 350-degree oven for 1 hour. Cool. Combine 2 tablespoons butter, powdered sugar, remaining 1/2 teaspoon vanilla extract and milk; beat until smooth. Spread over pastry. Garnish with chopped walnuts.

Mrs. Wealthy Crawford
Canfield, Ohio

APPLE DANISH

Flour
Salt
1 c. vegetable shortening
Milk
1 egg yolk, beaten
6 c. peeled sliced apples
1 1/2 c. sugar
1 tsp. cinnamon
1/4 c. butter or margarine
1 egg white, lightly beaten
1 1/2 c. powdered sugar
1 tsp. vanilla extract

Mix 3 cups flour and 1/2 teaspoon salt; cut in shortening. Combine 1/2 cup milk and egg yolk; add to flour mixture. Mix well. Roll out half the mixture on floured surface to fit 11 x 16 x 1/2-inch jelly roll pan; place in pan. Arrange apples on crust. Combine sugar, 2 tablespoons flour and cinnamon; sprinkle over apples. Dot with butter. Roll out remaining pastry; place over cinnamon mixture. Brush pastry with egg white. Bake in preheated 375-degree oven for 45 minutes. Combine powdered sugar, 1/8 teaspoon salt, vanilla extract and 2 to 3 tablespoons milk for glaze. Spread over top while warm.

Mary Yevin
Granite City, Illinois

EASY STRUDEL

1 1/4 c. margarine
Sifted flour
3 egg yolks
2 tbsp. vinegar
1/4 c. water
1 c. fine bread crumbs
7 cooking apples, chopped fine
1/2 c. sugar
1 tsp. cinnamon

Cut 1 cup margarine into 2 cups flour until mixture is size of peas. Add egg yolks, vinegar and water; mix well. Form into ball; divide into 3 parts. Chill for at least 2 hours. Roll out 1/3 of the dough very thin on floured pastry cloth; sprinkle with 1/3 of the bread crumbs. Arrange 1/3 of the apples over bread crumbs. Combine 1 tablespoon flour, sugar and cinnamon; sprinkle 1/3 of the mixture over apples. Dot with 1/3 of the remaining margarine. Roll as for jelly roll; place on baking sheet. Bake in preheated 350-degree oven for 30 minutes. Repeat with remaining dough and remaining ingredients.

Bettye L. Robinson
La Puente, California

MAKE-AHEAD PIE CRUST

5 c. all-purpose flour
1 1/2 tsp. salt
2 1/4 c. vegetable shortening
1 egg
2 tbsp. white vinegar

Combine flour and salt in large mixing bowl; cut in shortening with pastry blender until mixture is of cornmeal consistency. Beat egg; add 1 cup cold water and vinegar. Pour slowly into flour mixture, stirring with a fork until particles are moistened. Divide pastry into 3 balls; wrap securely in plastic wrap. Refrigerate until ready to use.

Rose Schauer
Midland, Michigan

ORANGE JUICE PASTRY

1 3/4 c. flour
6 tbsp. sugar
Pinch of salt
1/2 c. shortening
1/4 c. orange juice

Sift flour, sugar and salt together. Cut in shortening, using 2 knives or pastry blender, until of cornmeal consistency. Sprinkle in orange juice gradually; toss to form a soft ball. Divide dough for 2-crust pie, using larger portion for bottom crust.

Mrs. Martelle Mayfield
Monroe, Louisiana

EXTRA SPECIAL LEMON TARTS

3 c. flour
1 tsp. salt
1 1/4 c. shortening
1 tsp. vinegar
7 eggs
1 c. soft butter or margarine
2 c. sugar
Juice of 3 lemons
Grated rind of 1 lemon

Sift flour and salt into bowl; cut in shortening until consistency of coarse cornmeal. Combine 5 tablespoons cold water, vinegar and 1 egg in bowl; beat well. Stir into flour mixture. Form into ball; chill. Roll out on floured board; cut and fit into tart tins. Prick pastry generously. Bake in preheated 425-degree oven for 10 to 12 minutes or until golden brown. Beat remaining 6 eggs slightly. Mix butter, sugar, eggs, lemon juice and rind in heavy saucepan. Bring to a boil, stirring constantly; remove from heat. Chill until thickened. Fill tart shells with lemon mixture; top with whipped cream or dessert topping, if desired. Filling will keep in refrigerator for 2 weeks. Yield: 36 tarts.

Mrs. William Cornish
Vanderbilt, Michigan

CALIFORNIA WALNUT MAPLE TARTS

1/2 c. butter
3/4 c. (firmly packed) light brown sugar
1/2 c. maple syrup
3 eggs, lightly beaten
1/4 c. heavy cream
1 1/4 c. chopped California walnuts
1/2 tsp. vanilla
8 unbaked tart shells

Heat butter, brown sugar and syrup in saucepan just to boiling point. Mix eggs, cream, walnuts and vanilla together; stir in hot syrup mixture gradually. Mix well; pour into tart shells. Bake in preheated 375-degree oven for 20 minutes or until golden brown and custard is set. Let cool. Garnish with fluffs of whipped cream; top with walnut halves, if desired.

Photograph for this recipe below.

JAZZ PIES

Flour
1 tsp. salt
1 1/2 c. shortening
3 eggs
1 tbsp. vinegar
5 tbsp. cold water
1 c. cooked raisins
1 c. sugar
1 c. chopped walnuts
1/2 c. melted butter

Combine 3 cups flour and salt in bowl; cut in shortening until mixture is consistency of small peas. Combine 1 egg, vinegar and water; beat well. Mix with flour mixture. Roll out between 2 sheets of waxed paper. Set aside. Combine raisins, sugar, walnuts, butter, 1 tablespoon flour and remaining 2 eggs in bowl; mix well. Cut 12 circles of pastry; fit into muffin cups. Wrap remaining pastry securely; store in refrigerator for future use. Spoon filling into pastry-lined muffin cups. Bake in preheated 400-degree oven for 25 minutes. Yield: 1 dozen.

Mrs. Linda Wells
Imperial Beach, California

MRS. MOORE'S TARTS

1 c. sugar
Flour
1 tsp. salt
1 c. milk
5 egg yolks, beaten
1 c. raisins
1 c. chopped dates
1/2 c. chopped walnuts
1/2 c. shortening
Whipped cream

Combine sugar, 1 tablespoon flour and 1/4 teaspoon salt in saucepan; stir in milk and egg yolks. Add raisins, dates and walnuts; blend well. Cook over medium heat, stirring constantly, until thickened. Remove from heat; cool. Sift 1 1/2 cups flour and remaining 3/4 teaspoon salt into bowl; cut in shortening until consistency of large peas. Sprinkle with 3 tablespoons water, 1 tablespoon at a time, blending lightly until dough forms ball. Roll out on lightly floured board to 1/8-inch thickness; cut into 2 1/2-inch rounds. Line 1 3/4-inch muffin cups with pastry rounds; prick bottoms and sides with fork. Bake in preheated 450-degree oven for 10 minutes or until lightly browned; cool. Spoon raisin filling into shells; top with whipped cream.

Mrs. Raymond B. Moore
Alden, Iowa

ROSY APPLE DUMPLINGS

2 1/2 c. flour
1 tsp. salt
2/3 c. shortening
1 3/4 c. sugar
1 1/2 tsp. cinnamon
3 apples
4 tbsp. butter
1 tbsp. cinnamon candies

Combine flour and salt in bowl; cut in shortening until particles are size of small peas. Add about 7 tablespoons water gradually, tossing with fork to form a soft dough. Roll out on floured surface to 10 x 15-inch rectangle; cut in 5-inch squares. Combine 3/4 cup sugar and cinnamon in bowl. Peel apples; cut in halves. Remove cores. Place apple half in center of each pastry square with cavity up. Sprinkle about 2 tablespoons sugar mixture over apple half. Fold each corner of pastry to center; press 4 corners together to seal. Place in casserole about 2 inches deep. Combine butter, remaining 1 cup sugar, 2 cups water and cinnamon candies in saucepan; bring to a boil. Stir until sugar is dissolved and candy is melted. Pour syrup over dumplings. Bake in preheated 400-degree oven for 20 to 25 minutes or until golden brown.

Mrs. Julia A. Walter
Jupiter, Florida

APPLE FLIPS

2 c. sifted flour
1 tsp. salt
Shortening
1/3 c. ice water
2 c. stewed dried apples, drained
1/4 c. sugar

2 tbsp. melted margarine
Confectioners' sugar

Sift flour and salt together into bowl; cut in 1/3 cup shortening until crumbs are size of peas. Add water gradually until soft dough forms. Roll out pastry to 1/8-inch thickness on lightly floured pastry cloth; cut into 5-inch rounds. Coffee can top may be used for cutter. Combine apples, sugar and margarine; place 1 1/2 tablespoons mixture on each pastry round. Moisten edge of pastry with water. Fold in half; seal edges by pressing together with tines of fork. Prick tops 2 or 3 times with fork. Place shortening in frying pan to depth of 2 inches; heat to 360 degrees. Slide 3 or 4 pies into hot fat, using spatula. Fry for 2 to 3 minutes or until golden brown on underside. Turn; brown tops. Lift out; drain on absorbent paper. Sprinkle with confectioners' sugar. Serve warm or cold, as desired.

Sister Tabitha Kaup
Omaha, Nebraska

PEACHY PERFECT PIES

Vegetable shortening
3 c. flour
1 egg
5 tbsp. ice water
1 tbsp. vinegar
1 No. 2 can sliced peaches
1 tbsp. sugar
1 1/2 tbsp. cornstarch
1 tbsp. lemon juice
1 tbsp. butter
Few grains of salt
1/4 tsp. almond extract

Cut 1 1/2 scant cups shortening into flour until evenly distributed. Beat egg, water and vinegar together until well mixed; toss into shortening mixture, using fork, until all particles are moistened. Let stand in refrigerator for 30 minutes. Drain peaches; reserve syrup. Combine sugar and cornstarch in saucepan; pour in 1 1/4 cups reserved syrup slowly, stirring to mix well. Cook over low heat until thick, stirring constantly. Remove from heat. Add lemon juice, butter, salt and almond extract; stir until butter is melted. Stir

in peaches; let stand until cool. Turn out pastry on floured board; roll out to desired thinness. Cut into rounds using teacup. Place a small amount of peach filling in each round; fold over and seal edges with tines of fork. Melt enough shortening in electric skillet to measure 1/2 inch; heat to 370 degrees. Fry pies for 10 minutes or until golden brown on each side. Remove from skillet; drain well on absorbent toweling.

Joan A. Bradshaw
San Antonio, Texas

CHERRY TURNOVERS

1 3-oz. package cream cheese
Sugar
1 tbsp. fresh lemon juice
1 3/4 c. tart cherries, drained
1/4 c. cherry juice
2 tbsp. cornstarch
2 tsp. almond extract
4 drops of red food coloring
3 c. flour
1 tsp. salt
1 1/4 c. vegetable shortening
1 egg, beaten
1 tbsp. vinegar
4 tbsp. cold water
Milk or beaten egg white

Soften cream cheese; stir in 3 tablespoons sugar and lemon juice. Chill thoroughly. Combine cherries, cherry juice, 3/4 cup sugar, cornstarch, 1/2 teaspoon almond extract and food coloring in saucepan; cook over medium heat until thick, stirring constantly. Let cool. Combine flour and salt; cut in shortening. Add egg, vinegar, water and remaining 1 1/2 teaspoons almond extract; mix well. Divide in half; roll out on floured surface. Cut into 5 or 6-inch circles. Place 1 teaspoon cheese filling in center of each circle; top with 1 tablespoon cherry filling. Fold over. Moisten edges with cold water; press together with fork. Brush with milk; place on ungreased cookie sheet. Bake in preheated 425-degree oven for 20 to 25 minutes. Yield: 12-14 turnovers.

Mrs. Cecilia Holcomb
Garber, Oklahoma

Dessert Favorites

A list of favorite American desserts immediately reflects not only the great American love for sweets, but also the rich Old World heritage from which our favorite desserts have developed. Of course, there are some truly American desserts, including strawberry shortcake, pound cake, cheesecake, angel food cake, brownies and chocolate chip cookies. But, the overwhelming list of delights that please the American palate each day includes the recipes for the hundreds of sweets and confections brought to this country by Old World cooks.

Finely granulated and refined white sugar as we know it today was not readily or cheaply available to the people settling the American frontier. Quickly though, honey, maple syrup and molasses became indispensable staples in the household larders. Getting syrup from maple trees and honey from the beehives, a common "appliance" around the settlers' homes, the frontier cooks wasted no time in developing dessert dishes for their families.

Without the culinary knowledge of Scandinavian and European people, we would be without many of the fancy, sweet breads, cobblers, jelly rolls, coffee cakes, ice creams and many types of delightful cookies, doughnuts, kuchens and tortes. Instead, America has it all — its own plus all the best from other countries — and Americans eat more sweets than the people of any other country.

Dessert is always a treat at the end of a meal, because no matter how full the diners are, they will almost always relish a little dessert! This is especially true when the dessert balances in flavor and texture with the rest of the meal. And, because dessert ingredients often include eggs, fruits and cheese or other dairy products, they are also nutritious and provide energy for growing children and active adults alike.

Americans like to make desserts as well as they like to eat them. In fact, making cakes, cookies, candies and other sweets long ago became a part of the family holiday custom in America. The unmistakable smell of sweets baking in the kitchen, any time of the year, still brings back childhood memories of some holiday season long ago. To almost every adult, this arouses the appetite almost beyond description.

Cakes, probably the most popularly enjoyed dessert of all, are also the most versatile. They can be flavored in almost any way, shaped into almost any figure, decorated to fit most any occasion and go well with a long list of toppings, ice creams, punches and other sweets.

Although there is a great variety of cake mixes on grocery store shelves, it is still well worth the extra time it takes to make a cake "from scratch." And, it is not just the personal attention that makes a homemade cake taste better. Even though commercial preparations, by necessity, are comprised of ingredients that cannot spoil (therefore lacking whole eggs, whole milk and butter), the shopper has no way of knowing how long the mix has been on the shelf. So, not only are

homemade cakes usually cheaper, they contain absolutely fresh ingredients, and are therefore more flavorful.

Cookies are almost inseparable from the Christmas season, but are certainly not limited to that! They can be made into so many colorful, fanciful shapes that even the plainest dough becomes delightful. Another positive point in favor of cookies is that both the dough and the cookies can usually be prepared in advance and refrigerated or frozen until time for use.

Cookies are also a perfect gift to send through the mail. What better way could there be to share a special occasion with a far-away relative than to send home-baked cookies! Package them with care to preserve their freshness and to keep them from crumbling. Wrap the cookies in moisture-proof material in pairs with their backs together. Between packages of cookies to be mailed in the same box, place popcorn or marshmallows, so that the boxes will not get jumbled. After covering the mailing container in brown paper, tie it with string and mark it "Fragile, Handle with Care." It is always exciting to receive a gift in the mail, and there could hardly be a more enjoyable gift than homemade cookies.

Of all the frozen and chilled desserts, ice cream is probably the most loved, especially the homemade hand and electrically churned varieties. Many restaurant and ice cream parlor chains across America are famous for their many flavors, making this cool, nutritious dessert available to everyone.

Homemade ice cream, with the ritual, anticipation and bustle surrounding its preparation has, over the past generations, become a favorite family tradition for hot-weather gatherings. George Washington and Thomas Jefferson both enjoyed this smooth, sweet confection and probably, as long as there is hot weather and dessert lovers, ice cream will continue to hold an unshakable popularity on American tables.

Chilled desserts incorporate a wide variety of ingredients, including gelatins, pudding mixtures, fruits, nuts, whipped cream and other dairy products. For this reason, chilled desserts give cooks a wide and appealing choice of simple or elegant, heavy or light desserts. But, the best advantage chilled desserts offer the cook is that they can be made well in advance and still be fresh and delicious when served. This leaves the oven and range free for other cooking — quite a boon for the busy homemaker!

Because fudge, divinity, pralines and peanut brittle are among candy lovers' favorites, candymaking, like baking cakes and cookies, is another favorite holiday task for families to enjoy. Actually, with the right tools, plenty patience and some practice, making candy becomes fund and very rewarding.

Proper utensils include a large kettle, a double boiler, rubber spatulas, measuring cups and spoons, wooden spoons and, most important, an accurate candy thermometer. The cold water test may be used if a thermometer is not available, although this test is only dependable when used by more experienced candymakers. The cold water test for candy is as follows: 1/2 teaspoon of candy syrup, when pressed between the thumb and forefinger in a cup of cold water (at sea level), has reached the *soft-ball stage* (234-240°F) when it can be picked up, but flattens; the *firm-ball stage* (242-248°F) has been reached when it holds shape until pressed; the *hard-ball stage* (250-268°F) has been reached when it holds shape, though pliable; the *soft-crack stage* (270-290°F) has been reached when it separates into hard, not brittle, threads; and, the *hard-crack stage* (300-310°F) has been reached when it separates into hard, brittle threads.

Minimize overcrystallization by first, heating the liquid that the sugar is to be dissolved in and stirring in the sugar thoroughly, dissolving it well before putting it on the heat; secondly, in the first few minutes of cooking, keep the pan well covered and this will allow the steam to wash the sugar crystals from the side of the pan. Then uncover the pan to allow for evaporation.

Americans have recently begun to shun desserts in their diets because they are "too fattening" or because they have "too many carbohydrates" and not enough nutritive value. But, like any other food, desserts, in moderation, are important in a well-balanced diet. In this section are the Home Economics Teachers' favorite recipes for all of these, and who knows more about good nutrition and good taste?

AFTERDINNER MINTS

1 egg white
1 tbsp. cream
1 tsp. vanilla extract
3 drops of oil of peppermint
Food coloring
1 box powdered sugar
1 1/2 tsp. soft butter or white
   shortening

Combine egg white, cream, vanilla, oil of peppermint and desired food coloring. Stir well. Add box of sugar all at once; mix thoroughly. Work in the butter, adding more sugar if needed to make of firm consistency. Shape into small balls. Arrange balls on waxed paper; press each ball with tines of fork dipped in additional powdered sugar or cornstarch. Let stand overnight to form a crust, then pack in tins with waxed paper between each layer. May be frozen and kept several months.

Shirley Andersen
Dalton, Nebraska

ARIZONA CREAMS

3 c. sugar
1 lg. can evaporated milk
1 tbsp. butter
1 c. chopped nuts

Caramelize 1 cup sugar until light brown. Add milk slowly, stirring constantly until mixed. Stir in remaining 2 cups sugar. Cook to 236 degrees on candy thermometer or to soft-ball stage. Remove from heat; add butter. Place pan in cold water; beat until thickened. Add nuts; beat until stiff. Pour into buttered 8 x 8-inch cake pan; cool. Cut into squares.

Gloria R. McHenry
Mesa, Arizona

CHOCOLATE-ALMOND TOFFEE

1 c. (packed) brown sugar
1 c. sugar
1/3 c. white corn syrup
1/2 c. water
1/8 tsp. salt
1/3 c. butter
1 6-oz. package semisweet
   chocolate chips, melted
1/2 c. toasted almonds, chopped

Combine sugars, syrup, water and salt in heavy saucepan; blend thoroughly. Place over medium heat; cook, stirring, until sugar is dissolved and mixture is boiling moderately. Cook to 245 degrees on candy thermometer or to firm-ball stage. Add butter; cook to 290 degrees or hard-crack stage. Pour into lightly oiled 9 x 9-inch pan. Cool until hard. Spread with half the melted chocolate; top with half the almonds. Let cool until chocolate is set. Loosen candy from pan; turn out on flat surface. Spread remaining chocolate on other side; sprinkle with remaining almonds. Let cool; break into pieces.

Darlene M. Johnson
New Richmond, Wisconsin

BUTTERMILK FUDGE

1 tsp. soda
1 c. buttermilk
2 c. sugar
2 tbsp. corn syrup
1/2 c. margarine
1 c. nuts

Blend soda and buttermilk, stirring well. Pour sugar into large boiler; add buttermilk mixture, corn syrup and margarine. Bring to a boil; cook to 240 degrees on candy thermometer or to medium soft-ball stage. Remove from heat; beat well. Stir in nuts. Pour candy into buttered dish or drop by spoonfuls onto waxed paper.

Ruth Stovall, State Dept. of Ed.
Montgomery, Alabama

MILLION-DOLLAR FUDGE

4 1/2 c. sugar
1 lg. can evaporated milk
1/2 c. butter or margarine
3 6-oz. packages chocolate chips

1 1/2 tsp. vanilla extract
2 c. broken nuts

Combine sugar and milk in saucepan; bring to a boil. Boil, stirring constantly, for 10 minutes. Melt butter and chocolate chips together in top of double boiler over hot water. Add milk mixture gradually to chocolate mixture, beating constantly. Remove from heat; beat vigorously until candy loses its gloss. Add vanilla extract and nuts. Pour into 8 x 12-inch buttered pan. Cool; cut into squares. Yield: 5 pounds.

June Elizabeth Rector
Abingdon, Virginia

PINEAPPLE FUDGE

1 c. evaporated milk
3 c. sugar
2 tbsp. butter or margarine
1 c. crushed pineapple, well drained
2 tsp. lemon juice

Combine milk, sugar and butter. Heat slowly to boiling point. Add pineapple; cook over medium heat to 235 degrees on candy thermometer or to soft-ball stage, stirring constantly to prevent burning. Cool. Add lemon juice. Beat until candy loses gloss. Turn into buttered pan. Mark in squares. Garnish with pecan halves, if desired. Cool completely.

Louise Bollinger
Sweetwater, Texas

EASY CHRISTMAS DIVINITY

3 c. sugar
3/4 c. light corn syrup
3/4 c. water
2 egg whites
1 3-oz. package strawberry or
    lime-flavored gelatin
1 c. chopped nuts
1/2 c. shredded coconut (opt.)

Combine sugar, corn syrup and water in saucepan; bring to boiling point. Reduce heat; cook to hard-ball stage. Beat egg whites until fluffy. Add dry gelatin gradually, beat-

ing until stiff peaks form. Pour syrup slowly into egg white mixture, beating constantly until candy holds shape and loses gloss. Stir in nuts and coconut; pour quickly into 9-inch buttered pan. Let stand until firm. Dip knife blade into hot water; cut candy as desired.

Mrs. Marjorie H. Kirby
North Little Rock, Arkansas

HOLIDAY CREAMY CARAMELS

1/2 c. butter
2 c. sugar
3/4 c. light corn syrup
Dash of salt
2 c. cream
1 tsp. vanilla extract
1 1/2 c. chopped nuts

Combine butter, sugar, corn syrup, salt and 1 cup cream in saucepan; bring to boiling point. Add remaining 1 cup cream slowly; cook to hard-ball stage. Add vanilla extract and nuts; pour into buttered pan. Cool; turn out onto flat surface. Cut and wrap. Do not substitute margarine for butter.

Cynthia Atkins
Buffalo, Kansas

ORANGE SNOWBALLS

2 3/4 c. vanilla wafer crumbs
1/4 c. melted margarine
3 c. powdered sugar
1 c. chopped nuts
1/4 c. undiluted frozen orange juice
2 tbsp. soft margarine
Milk
Flaked coconut

Mix crumbs, melted margarine, 1 cup sugar, nuts and orange juice; shape into small balls. Mix soft margarine and remaining 2 cups powdered sugar; add enough milk for spreading consistency. Roll snowballs in milk mixture; roll in coconut. Let dry. Store in airtight container. Confection improves after several days of storing. Yield: 3 1/2 dozen.

Mrs. Willie Mae Cornwell
Waco, Texas

PEANUT CLUSTERS

1   6-oz. package chocolate chips
2/3 c. sweetened condensed milk
1 tsp. vanilla extract
1 1/2 c. salted Spanish peanuts

Melt chocolate chips in double boiler; remove from heat. Add milk, vanilla and peanuts; mix well. Drop by spoonfuls onto buttered cookie sheet or waxed paper. Yield: 1 1/2 dozen.

Mary Lou Meyer
Aviston, Illinois

PEANUT BRITTLE

1 1/2 c. sugar
1/2 c. white Karo syrup
1/4 c. water
2 c. shelled peanuts
1 tsp. soda
1/4 tsp. salt

Combine sugar, syrup and water; bring to a boil. Stir peanuts in gradually so that mixture continues to boil. Keep at rolling boil until peanuts pop and turn brown. Remove from heat; stir in soda. Add salt. Pour on a well-greased platter. Cool. Break into pieces when cold.

Mrs. Billye Tingle
Brooklyn, Mississippi

SUGARED NUTS

2 c. sugar
1/2 c. water
5 tbsp. white corn syrup
8 lg. marshmallows
1 tsp. vanilla extract
2 c. chopped nuts

Mix sugar, water and corn syrup in saucepan; cook to 240 degrees on candy thermometer or to medium soft-ball stage. Add marshmallows; stir until melted. Add vanilla and nuts; stir until thickened. Pour out on waxed paper; separate with fork. Yield: 24-30 pieces.

Joan Wilf
Walnut Ridge, Arkansas

PARTY POPCORN BALLS

1 c. sugar
1/3 c. light corn syrup
1/3 c. water
1/4 c. butter
3/4 tsp. salt
3/4 tsp. vanilla extract
3 qt. popped popcorn

Mix sugar, corn syrup, water, butter and salt in saucepan. Cook, stirring, until the sugar is dissolved. Cook, without stirring, to 270 to 290 degrees on candy thermometer or to soft-crack stage. Add vanilla; stir just enough to mix. Place popcorn in large bowl. Pour syrup over popcorn slowly; mix well. Wet hands slightly; shape popcorn mixture into balls. Yield: 12 medium balls.

Bonnie O'Connell
Tracy, Minnesota

ANGEL FOOD CAKE

1 c. cake flour
1 1/2 c. confectioners' sugar
1 1/2 c. egg whites
1 1/2 tsp. cream of tartar
1 c. granulated sugar
1/8 tsp. salt
1 tsp. vanilla
Icing

Sift cake flour and confectioners' sugar together 3 times. Beat egg whites until foamy. Add cream of tartar; beat until stiff but not dry. Add granulated sugar gradually; mix in salt and vanilla. Sift flour mixture over egg whites; fold in carefully. Spread batter in tube pan. Bake in preheated 325-degree oven for 1 hour and 5 minutes or until cake tests done. Let cool; spread Icing over cake.

Icing

2 c. sugar
3/4 c. water
2 egg whites
1/4 tsp. cream of tartar

Cook sugar and water together to 238 degrees on candy thermometer or to soft-ball stage. Beat egg whites and cream of tartar until stiff. Add sugar syrup slowly to egg whites; beat to spreading consistency.

Mrs. Kathleen K. Horne
Big Stone Gap, Virginia

BANANA LAYER CAKE

2 1/4 c. sifted all-purpose flour
1 1/4 c. sugar
2 1/2 tsp. baking powder
1/2 tsp. soda
1/2 tsp. salt
1/2 c. shortening
1 1/2 c. mashed ripe bananas
2 eggs
1 tsp. vanilla
Speedy Banana Frosting

Sift flour, sugar, baking powder, soda and salt into large mixing bowl. Add shortening, 1/2 cup mashed bananas and eggs; beat for 2 minutes with electric mixer at medium speed. Scrape down bowl and beaters. Add remaining 1 cup mashed bananas and vanilla; beat 1 minute longer. Spread batter in 2 greased 8-inch round layer pans. Bake in preheated 375-degree oven for 25 minutes or until cake tests done. Remove layers to cool; frost with Speedy Banana Frosting.

Speedy Banana Frosting

1/4 c. butter or margarine
1 lb. confectioners' sugar
1/2 c. mashed ripe bananas
1/2 tsp. lemon juice

Cream butter until soft and fluffy. Add half the sugar; beat until well blended. Add mashed bananas and lemon juice; mix well. Add remaining sugar; beat until frosting is light and fluffy. Yield: 2 cups frosting.

Mrs. Maggie Beth Watts
Era, Texas

GINGERBREAD

3 1/2 c. flour
1 tbsp. ginger
2 tsp. cinnamon
2 tsp. nutmeg
1 c. shortening
1 1/2 c. (packed) brown sugar
2 eggs
1 c. molasses
1 tsp. soda
1 c. hot water

Sift flour, ginger, cinnamon and nutmeg together. Cream shortening. Add sugar; cream thoroughly. Add eggs; beat well. Stir in molasses. Dissolve soda in hot water. Add flour mixture to sugar mixture alternately with water; mix well. Pour into 9 x 12-inch pan. Bake in preheated 350-degree oven for about 30 minutes or until cake tests done. Remove from pan. Cut into squares to serve. Top with whipped cream, if desired.

Odessa Smith, State Supvr.
Home Ec. Ed., Louisiana Dept. of Ed.
Baton Rouge, Louisiana

ORANGE CANDY SLICE CAKE

1 c. butter
2 c. sugar
4 eggs
1 1/2 c. buttermilk
1 tsp. soda
1/4 tsp. salt
4 c. flour
1 lb. dates, chopped
1 lb. orange candy slices, halved
2 c. mixed nuts, chopped
1 sm. can frozen orange juice
   concentrate, thawed
1/2 c. (packed) light brown sugar

Cream butter and sugar together. Add eggs, one at a time, beating well after each addition. Add 1 cup buttermilk; mix well. Add soda to remaining 1/2 cup buttermilk; add to egg mixture. Combine salt and flour; stir into egg mixture. Stir in dates, orange candy slices and nuts; blend well. Line tube pan with well-greased brown paper; pour in batter. Bake in preheated 275-degree oven for 2 hours and 30 minutes or until cake tests done. Combine orange juice concentrate and brown sugar; mix well. Pour over hot cake. Let cake cool in pan before removing.

Mrs. Dorothy A. Foster
Mathews, Virginia

CHOCOLATE POTATO CAKE

1/2 lb. potatoes, peeled
1/2 c. milk
2 c. sifted flour
2 tsp. baking powder
1/2 tsp. salt
1 c. shortening
2 c. sugar
4 eggs
1 tsp. vanilla extract
1 1/2 oz. unsweetened chocolate, melted
Whipped cream
Chocolate frosting

Cook potatoes in small amount of boiling water in covered saucepan until tender. Drain well. Shake pan over low heat to dry contents thoroughly. Force hot potatoes through ricer or sieve. Combine 1 cup sieved potatoes with milk; set aside to cool. Sift flour, baking powder and salt together. Cream shortening; beat in sugar gradually until light and fluffy. Add eggs, one at a time, beating well after each addition. Mix in vanilla extract and chocolate. Add dry ingredients in 4 parts and potato mixture in 3 parts alternately to creamed mixture. Beat only until smooth after each addition. Spread batter in 2 greased and waxed paper-lined 9-inch layer cake pans. Bake in preheated 350-degree oven for 45 minutes or until cake tests done. Remove from oven.

Let stand in pans 10 minutes. Remove from pans; cool. Fill with whipped cream; frost with favorite chocolate frosting.

Photograph for this recipe on this page.

CHOCOLATE CAKE

1 pkg. sweet cooking chocolate
1/2 c. shortening
1 c. butter
3 c. sugar
5 eggs
1 tsp. lemon flavoring
1 tsp. vanilla extract
3 c. flour
1 tsp. baking powder
1/2 tsp. salt
1 c. milk
1 c. chopped almonds
Vanilla ice cream
Apricot halves
Sliced toasted almonds
Chocolate curls

Melt chocolate over hot water. Cream shortening and butter in large mixing bowl. Add sugar gradually; cream well. Add eggs, one at a time, beating well after each addition. Stir in flavorings. Sift flour, baking powder and salt together; add to sugar mixture alternately with milk. Stir in chopped almonds; pour into large greased ring mold or bundt pan. Bake in preheated 350-degree oven for 1 hour and 15 minutes or until done. Cool for 10 minutes; remove from mold. Cool. Place on cake plate. Fill center of cake with ice cream. Garnish with apricots, sliced almonds and chocolate curls.

Photograph for this recipe on page 272.

RED VELVET CAKE

2 1/2 c. sifted flour
1 1/2 c. sugar
1 tsp. soda
1 tsp. cocoa
1 c. buttermilk
1 1/2 c. Crisco oil or Wesson oil
1 tsp. vinegar
2 eggs
1   1-oz. bottle red food coloring

1 tsp. vanilla
1 tsp. butternut flavoring

Sift dry ingredients together. Add remaining ingredients in order listed; mix thoroughly. Grease and flour layer cake pans; spread batter in pans. Bake in preheated 350-degree oven for 25 minutes or until cake tests done. Remove from pans; let cool.

Filling and Frosting

1/2 c. margarine
1   8-oz. package cream cheese
1 box confectioners' sugar
1/2 tsp. vanilla
1 c. chopped toasted nuts

Let margarine and cream cheese soften to room temperature; cream well. Add sugar; beat until creamy. Add vanilla and nuts; spread on cake.

Ruth Stovall, State Dept. of Ed.
Montgomery, Alabama

SOUR CREAM POUND CAKE

3 c. sifted flour
1/4 tsp. soda
1 c. butter or margarine, softened
3 c. sugar
6 eggs
1 c. sour cream
1 tsp. vanilla or lemon extract

Sift flour and soda together twice; set aside. Cream butter; add sugar slowly, beating constantly. Cream well. Add eggs, one at a time, beating well after each addition. Stir in sour cream. Add flour mixture, 1/2 cup at a time, beating constantly. Stir in vanilla extract; turn batter into well-greased and floured 10-inch tube pan. Bake in preheated 325-degree oven for about 1 hour and 30 minutes or until cake tests done. Place pan on rack to cool for 5 minutes. Loosen cake around edge of pan and edge of tube with dull side of knife, pressing toward pan rather than toward cake to protect crust. Turn cake onto rack to cool completely. Serve plain. Wrap whole or cut cake in several thicknesses of clear plastic or aluminum foil to freeze.

Jean Bugg
Highland Home, Alabama

SOUTHERN FRUITCAKE

Flour
1 tsp. baking powder
1 tsp. allspice
2 tsp. apple pie spice
2 c. butter
2 1/4 c. sugar
1/2 c. honey
2 tbsp. lemon juice
12 eggs, well beaten
1 tbsp. almond extract
1 1/2 c. strawberry preserves
1 c. fig preserves
2 lb. candied red cherries, chopped
2 lb. candied green pineapple, chopped
2 lb. candied yellow pineapple, chopped
2 lb. dates, chopped
1/2 lb. figs, chopped
1/2 box white raisins
1 box seeded raisins
1 lg. coconut, grated
1/2 lb. orange peel, chopped
1/2 lb. black walnuts, chopped
3/4 lb. English walnuts, chopped
4 c. pecans, chopped
1/2 lb. almonds, chopped
1/2 c. bourbon

Sift 4 1/2 cups flour, baking powder and spices together. Cream butter until smooth. Add sugar gradually; cream until fluffy. Add honey and lemon juice to eggs; mix well. Add to creamed mixture. Stir in flour mixture, a small amount at a time, mixing well. Stir in almond extract, strawberry preserves and fig preserves. Dredge fruits, peel and nuts with flour; add to batter. Add bourbon, as needed, to thin batter. Grease and line 1 large tube pan and 2 loaf pans with brown paper. Bake in preheated 250-degree oven for at least 3 hours or until cakes test done. Fruitcakes may be decorated with almonds, pineapple and cherries, if desired.

Mrs. Suanne Lett Black
Montgomery, Alabama

APPLE-CINNAMON ROLL

3 c. flour
2 tbsp. baking powder
1 tsp. salt
2 tbsp. sugar
1/2 c. shortening
1 1/8 c. milk
3 tbsp. butter, softened
3 1/2 c. chopped tart apples
3 tbsp. lemon juice
3/4 c. (packed) brown sugar
2 tsp. cinnamon

Sift flour, baking powder, salt and sugar together in mixing bowl; cut in shortening. Add milk all at once; stir until ingredients are just dampened. Turn out on floured board; knead to mix well. Roll out in rectangle 1/4 inch thick; brush with softened butter. Combine apples, lemon juice, brown sugar and cinnamon; arrange over pastry. Roll up as for jelly roll. Cut into 1-inch slices; place on well-buttered baking pan. Bake in preheated 450-degree oven for 10 minutes. Reduce oven temperature to 350 degrees; bake for 25 minutes longer. Serve hot with cream or sauce, if desired.

Betty Henderson
Sandy, Utah

CHOCOLATE CREAM ROLL

5 eggs, separated
Powdered sugar
1 tbsp. cake flour
3 tbsp. cocoa
1 tsp. vanilla
1 c. whipping cream, whipped and
    sweetened
Sauce

Line greased jelly roll pan with waxed paper; grease waxed paper. Beat egg yolks until light and fluffy. Add 1 cup powdered sugar, flour and cocoa; beat until well mixed and light. Fold in beaten egg whites and vanilla. Pour batter into prepared pan, smoothing gently. Bake in preheated 350-degree oven for 12 to 15 minutes or until done. Remove from oven; invert on towel sprinkled lightly with powdered sugar. Remove waxed paper quickly; roll up in towel, starting at narrow end. Let cool. Unroll; spread with whipped cream. Roll again. Cut into 6 portions; top with small amount of Sauce to serve.

Sauce

1/2 c. milk
1/2 c. sugar
1 tbsp. flour
1 tbsp. cocoa

Combine all ingredients in saucepan; cook over low heat until thickened, stirring constantly. Let cool.

Marjorie L. Benesh
Mandan, North Dakota

OLD-FASHIONED JELLY ROLL

3/4 tsp. baking powder
1/4 tsp. salt
4 eggs, at room temperature
3/4 c. sugar
3/4 c. sifted flour
1 tsp. vanilla
Powdered sugar
1 c. tart red jelly

Line 15 x 10-inch jelly roll pan with greased brown paper. Mix baking powder, salt and eggs together. Add sugar; beat until mixture becomes thick and light. Fold in flour and vanilla; turn into prepared pan. Bake in preheated 400-degree oven for 13 minutes or until cake tests done. Turn cake out on towel dusted with powdered sugar. Remove paper; cut off crisp edges of cake. Roll up cake and towel together; let cool for 10 minutes. Unroll; spread cake with jelly. Roll again.

Mrs. Fern Ruck
Rangely, Colorado

BAKED CUSTARD

4 eggs, well beaten
1/2 c. sugar
1/4 tsp. salt
4 c. milk, scalded

1/2 tsp. vanilla extract
Nutmeg

Combine eggs, sugar and salt in bowl; stir in milk slowly. Stir in vanilla. Pour into custard cups; sprinkle with nutmeg. Place in pan of hot water. Bake in preheated 350-degree oven for 30 to 40 minutes or until knife inserted in center comes out clean. Serve warm or cold. Yield: 10 servings.

Jewell West
Crowder, Oklahoma

BANANA PUDDING

Sugar
2 tbsp. flour
1/4 tsp. salt
2 c. milk
3 eggs, separated
1 tsp. vanilla extract
1 med. box vanilla wafers
4 to 6 bananas, sliced

Combine 1/2 cup sugar, flour and salt in top of double boiler. Mix milk and slightly beaten egg yolks; stir into sugar mixture. Cook over boiling water, stirring, until mixture coats spoon; stir in vanilla. Line baking dish with half the vanilla wafers; add half the bananas. Pour 1/2 of the custard over bananas; repeat layers. Beat egg whites until soft peaks form. Add 6 tablespoons sugar gradually, beating constantly; beat until stiff peaks form. Spread over pudding, sealing to edge of baking dish. Bake in preheated 425-degree oven for 5 minutes or until lightly browned. Serve hot or cold. Yield: 6-8 servings.

Mrs. Ruby C. Phillips
Dist. Supvr., Home Economics Education
Montevallo, Alabama

COCONUT CUSTARD

3 eggs, slightly beaten
1/4 c. sugar
1/4 tsp. salt
2 c. milk, scalded
1/2 tsp. vanilla extract

Nutmeg to taste
1 c. shredded coconut

Combine eggs, sugar and salt in bowl; stir in milk slowly. Stir in vanilla, nutmeg and coconut. Pour into custard cups or small casserole; place in pan of hot water. Bake in preheated 325-degree oven for 30 to 40 minutes or until knife inserted in center comes out clean. Serve warm or cool. Yield: 6 servings.

Mrs. Betty Kirschten
Rosebud, Montana

BREAD PUDDING WITH ORANGE SAUCE

5 c. day-old bread crumbs
5 c. milk
1/4 c. sugar
2 eggs, well beaten
1 tsp. vanilla extract
1/3 c. raisins
Orange Sauce

Place bread crumbs in 2-quart casserole; pour milk over bread crumbs. Let stand until bread crumbs are moist and mixture is at room temperature. Add sugar, eggs and vanilla; stir well. Fold in raisins. Bake in preheated 350-degree oven for about 1 hour and 30 minutes or until knife inserted in center comes out clean. Serve warm with Orange Sauce.

Orange Sauce

1/2 c. sugar
1 tbsp. cornstarch
1 c. boiling orange juice
2 tbsp. butter
1 1/2 tbsp. lemon juice
Dash of nutmeg
Dash of salt

Mix sugar and cornstarch in saucepan; add orange juice gradually, stirring constantly. Bring to a boil; cover. Reduce heat; cook for 5 minutes, stirring occasionally. Remove from heat; stir in remaining ingredients.

Margaret Allen Shanks
Orrville, Alabama

STEAMED CHOCOLATE PUDDING AND FOAMY SAUCE

1 egg
1/2 c. sugar
2 sq. unsweetened chocolate, melted
2 c. sifted flour
1 tbsp. baking powder
1/2 tsp. salt
1 c. milk
Foamy Sauce

Combine egg, sugar and chocolate in bowl; beat with rotary beater until mixed. Sift dry ingredients together; add to egg mixture alternately with milk. Pour into greased 1-quart mold; cover. Steam for 1 hour and 30 minutes; serve warm with Foamy Sauce.

Foamy Sauce

2 tbsp. butter
1 c. powdered sugar
1 egg
1 tsp. vanilla extract
1 c. whipping cream, whipped

Cream butter and sugar in bowl. Add egg; beat until smooth. Add vanilla; blend in whipped cream.

Margaret M. Taylor
Pocatello, Idaho

DATE-PINEAPPLE PUDDING

1 c. sifted flour
1 c. sugar
1 tsp. baking powder
1/4 tsp. salt
1 c. chopped dates
1 c. crushed pineapple
1/4 c. milk
2 c. water
1 c. (packed) brown sugar
1 tbsp. butter

Sift flour, sugar, baking powder and salt together into large bowl; stir in dates, pineapple and milk. Pour into greased 13 x 9 x 2-inch baking pan. Combine water, brown sugar and butter in saucepan; bring to a boil. Boil for 1 minute; pour over pudding.

Bake in preheated 350-degree oven for 35 minutes or until done.

Mrs. Iris Hendershot
Warfordsburg, Pennsylvania

ENGLISH PLUM PUDDING

1 8-oz. jar maraschino cherries
6 eggs, well beaten
2 c. (packed) brown sugar
1/2 c. milk
3 c. flour
1 c. bread crumbs
1/4 tsp. cloves
1 tsp. nutmeg
2 tsp. cinnamon
1 lb. seedless raisins
1 lb. seeded raisins
1 lb. currants, chopped
1 lb. mixed candied fruits, chopped
3/4 lb. ground beef suet
1/2 c. chopped pecans
2 tbsp. fresh lemon juice
Hard Sauce

Drain cherries; reserve juice. Chop cherries. Mix eggs and sugar in bowl until well blended; stir in reserved cherry juice and milk. Mix flour, bread crumbs and spices in large bowl; stir in cherries, raisins, currants and mixed fruits. Add egg mixture; stir well. Add suet, pecans and lemon juice; mix well. Place in well-greased molds; cover. Steam for 3 hours and 30 minutes to 4 hours; serve with Hard Sauce.

Hard Sauce

1/2 c. butter
2 c. confectioners' sugar
1 tsp. vanilla extract

Cream butter until very light; add confectioners' sugar gradually. Stir in vanilla.

Faye S. Sutherland
Hodgenville, Kentucky

GRATED POTATO PUDDING

1 c. sugar
3/4 c. butter

4 eggs, well beaten
2 c. grated sweet potatoes
2 c. milk
1 c. corn syrup
1 tsp. vanilla extract

Blend sugar and butter in bowl. Add eggs; mix thoroughly. Add potatoes, milk, corn syrup and vanilla; blend. Pour into casserole. Bake in preheated 300-degree oven for 1 hour or until knife inserted in center comes out clean. Serve warm or cold with whipped cream or ice cream, if desired. Yield: 8 servings.

Mrs. Yvonne McCoy
Naples, Texas

LEMON CUSTARD PUDDING

1/2 c. flour
1/2 tsp. baking powder
1/4 tsp. salt
1 c. sugar
3 eggs, separated
1/4 c. lemon juice
2 tsp. grated lemon rind
2 tbsp. melted butter
1 1/2 c. milk

Sift flour, baking powder, salt and 1/2 cup sugar together. Beat egg whites until soft peaks form. Beat until stiff peaks form, adding remaining 1/2 cup sugar gradually; set aside. Beat egg yolks; stir in lemon juice, lemon rind, butter and milk. Add flour mixture gradually; fold in meringue. Spoon mixture into buttered 2-quart baking dish. Bake in preheated 350-degree oven for 45 minutes; cool. Chill for 1 hour. May be served with whipped cream, if desired.

Mary Roscoe
Edison, New Jersey

CHEESECAKE WITH CHERRY TOPPING

1 1/2 c. graham cracker crumbs
1/2 c. butter or margarine, melted
1 c. sugar
1 8-oz. package cream cheese
1 pt. creamed cottage cheese

1 tbsp. lemon juice
2 eggs, lightly beaten
1 tsp. vanilla extract
1 can cherry pie filling

Combine crumbs, butter and 1/2 cup sugar; press on bottom and side of 12-inch spring-form pan. Chill. Mix cream cheese and cottage cheese together until well blended. Add lemon juice and eggs; mix well. Beat in remaining 1/2 cup sugar and vanilla until smooth. Pour into crust. Bake in preheated 375-degree oven for 25 minutes or until set. Let cool. Spread cherry pie filling over top of cheesecake; serve.

Dorothy Miller
Casstown, Ohio

PINEAPPLE CHEESECAKE

1 1/2 c. graham cracker crumbs
1 1/3 c. sugar
1 tsp. cinnamon
1/2 c. butter or margarine, melted
1 No. 2 can crushed pineapple
2 env. unflavored gelatin
4 eggs, separated
2 tsp. grated lemon rind
1/4 tsp. salt
1 tbsp. lemon juice
2 12-oz. cartons small-curd cottage cheese
1 tbsp. vanilla extract
2 c. heavy cream, whipped

Combine crumbs, 1/3 cup sugar, cinnamon and butter; mix well. Press half the mixture in 9-inch pan. Drain pineapple; reserve juice. Soften gelatin in 1/2 cup reserved pineapple juice. Combine slightly beaten egg yolks, remaining 1 cup sugar, lemon rind, salt and 2 tablespoons reserved pineapple juice in top of double boiler; cook for 5 to 8 minutes or until thickened. Remove from heat; stir in gelatin until dissolved. Add lemon juice, pineapple, cottage cheese and vanilla; mix well. Fold in whipped cream and stiffly beaten egg whites; pour into crust. Sprinkle remaining crumb mixture over top; chill for at least 5 hours or overnight.

Wilma A. Talkington
Wheeler, Texas

BLUEBERRY-CREAM CHEESE SQUARES

1/4 c. cornstarch
1/2 c. sugar
1/2 c. water
3 c. blueberries, rinsed and drained
1 13 1/2-oz. package graham cracker crumbs
3/4 c. melted butter or margarine
2 8-oz. packages cream cheese
1 1/2 c. sugar
2 tsp. vanilla extract
1 9-oz. package frozen whipped topping, thawed

Combine cornstarch, sugar, water and blueberries in saucepan. Cook over medium heat, stirring, until thickened; cool. Combine cracker crumbs and butter; press half the crumbs into bottom of foil-lined 13 x 9 x 2-inch pan. Mash cream cheese until soft; beat in sugar and vanilla gradually. Fold in whipped topping; drop by spoonfuls over crumbs mixture. Spread gently with spatula. Spread blueberry filling evenly over cheese mixture; spread with remaining cheese mixture. Sprinkle with remaining crumbs mixture; chill overnight. Use foil to remove dessert from pan. Place dessert on platter; cut into squares. Yield: 15 servings.

Photograph for this recipe above.

STRAWBERRY CHEESECAKE

32 graham cracker squares
1/2 c. butter, melted
1 lb. cream cheese, softened
Sugar
2 eggs, slightly beaten
1 tsp. vanilla extract
2 c. sour cream
1 box frozen sliced strawberries, thawed
2 tbsp. cornstarch

Crush graham crackers; mix with butter. Press mixture in springform pan. Combine cream cheese, 1/2 cup sugar, eggs and vanilla; mix until creamy. Pour into crust. Bake in preheated 350-degree oven for 20 minutes or until set. Let cool. Combine sour cream and 5 tablespoons sugar; beat with electric mixer for 2 minutes. Pour over cream cheese filling. Bake in preheated 450-degree oven for 5 minutes. Let cool. Drain strawberries; reserve juice. Combine 1/2 cup sugar, cornstarch and reserved juice in saucepan; cook until thick, stirring constantly. Let cool. Stir in strawberries; spread over cheesecake. Chill until ready to serve.

Mrs. Imogene Abernathie
Williamsville, Illinois

GOURMET CHEESECAKE

1 box zwieback, crushed
Sugar
3 tbsp. butter, melted
1 tbsp. cinnamon
6 eggs, separated
1 1/2 lb. cream cheese, softened
1/2 c. sifted flour
1 1/2 c. sour cream
1 1/2 tbsp. lemon juice
1 tsp. vanilla extract

Combine zwieback crumbs, 3 tablespoons sugar, butter and cinnamon; mix well. Reserve part of the mixture for topping; press remaining mixture on bottom and side of greased springform pan. Beat egg whites until frothy. Add 3/4 cup sugar gradually; beat until stiff peaks form. Combine egg yolks, 3/4 cup sugar, cream cheese, flour, sour cream, lemon juice and vanilla; beat until smooth. Fold egg whites into cheese mixture; pour into crust. Top with reserved crumb mixture. Bake in preheated 325-degree oven for 1 hour. Let cheesecake cool in oven for 1 hour. Remove from oven; let cool before serving.

Mrs. Mary Ann Yelovich
Union, Wisconsin

LEMON SQUARES

1 c. confectioners' sugar
1/4 tsp. salt
1 c. flour
Butter or margarine
1 c. sugar
1/2 tsp. baking powder
2 eggs, lightly beaten

4 tbsp. lemon juice
Grated lemon rind to taste

Combine 1/4 cup confectioners' sugar, 1/8 teaspoon salt and flour; mix well. Work in 1/2 cup butter. Press mixture in 8-inch square pan. Bake in preheated 350-degree oven for 15 minutes. Remove from oven. Combine sugar, baking powder and remaining 1/8 teaspoon salt. Blend in eggs, 2 tablespoons lemon juice and lemon rind. Spread over baked mixture. Return to oven. Bake for 20 minutes longer. Remove from oven; cool completely. Combine remaining 3/4 cup confectioners' sugar, remaining 2 tablespoons lemon juice and 1 tablespoon butter for glaze. Spread over lemon mixture. Cut into squares to serve.

Ruth McRae Carlson
Washington, D. C.

FRUITCAKE DROP COOKIES

1 lb. white raisins
1 lb. candied pineapple, diced
1/4 lb. candied red cherries, diced
1/4 lb. candied green cherries, diced
1 1/2 lb. chopped pecans
3 1/2 c. sifted cake flour
1/2 c. butter
1 c. (packed) brown sugar
4 eggs
1 tsp. soda
1/2 tsp. nutmeg
3 tbsp. sour milk
1 tsp. vanilla extract

Combine raisins, pineapple, cherries and pecans; sprinkle with 1/2 cup flour. Mix well. Cream butter and sugar together until fluffy. Add eggs, one at a time, beating well after each addition. Sift remaining 3 cups flour with soda and nutmeg; add alternately with milk to creamed mixture, beating well after each addition. Stir in vanilla extract and fruit mixture until well blended. Drop from teaspoon onto greased baking sheet. Bake in preheated 350-degree oven for about 15 minutes or until brown. Yield: 7 dozen.

Mrs. Mabel Flanagan
Bogue Chitto, Mississippi

BROWNIES

2/3 c. sifted flour
1/2 tsp. baking powder
1/4 tsp. salt
1/3 c. butter or shortening
2 sq. unsweetened chocolate
2 eggs
1 c. sugar
1/2 c. broken walnuts
1 tsp. vanilla extract

Sift flour with baking powder and salt. Melt butter and chocolate together in double boiler over hot water. Beat eggs well; add sugar gradually, beating well. Beat in chocolate mixture. Add flour mixture; mix until well blended. Stir in walnuts and vanilla extract. Spread in greased 8 x 8 x 2-inch pan. Bake in preheated 350-degree oven for about 25 minutes. Cool in pan. Cut in squares.

Mrs. Mary Ann Calhoun
Woodbury, Georgia

PEANUT BUTTER COOKIES

3/4 c. shortening
3/4 c. (packed) brown sugar
3/4 c. sugar
2 eggs, beaten
1 c. peanut butter
2 1/2 c. flour
1 tsp. soda
1/2 tsp. salt

Cream shortening until fluffy. Add sugars; beat until sugars are dissolved. Add eggs; beat well. Blend in peanut butter. Combine flour, soda and salt; add to peanut butter mixture. Mix until well combined. Roll into 1-inch balls; place on ungreased cookie sheet. Flatten balls with tines of fork in crisscross fashion. Bake in preheated 350-degree oven for 10 minutes. Cool on rack. Store in tightly covered container.

Deanna Patin
Marksville, Louisiana

SUPERB WALNUT COOKIES

1/2 c. shortening
1/2 tsp. salt
1 tsp. vanilla extract
1 c. sugar
2 eggs, well beaten
3/4 c. flour, sifted
3/4 c. chopped walnuts

Cream shortening, salt and vanilla in bowl. Add sugar gradually; cream well. Add eggs; mix thoroughly. Add flour and walnuts; mix well. Drop from teaspoon onto greased baking sheet; flatten with bottom of glass dipped in additional flour. Bake in preheated 325-degree oven for 12 to 15 minutes. Yield: 30 cookies.

Photograph for this recipe on page 202.

GINGERSNAPS

3/4 c. shortening
1 c. sugar
1/4 c. molasses
1 egg, well beaten
2 c. flour
2 tsp. soda
1 tsp. cinnamon
1 tsp. ginger
1 tsp. cloves

Cream shortening and sugar together thoroughly. Add molasses and egg; mix well. Sift remaining ingredients together; add to creamed mixture. Beat until smooth. Shape into walnut-sized balls; roll in additional sugar. Place 2 inches apart on greased baking sheet. Bake in preheated 350-degree oven until edges are browned. Store in airtight container. These cookies improve with age.

Mrs. H. L. Burleson
Swan Quarter, North Carolina

OATMEAL COOKIES

3/4 c. shortening
1 c. sugar
2 eggs, beaten
2 c. sifted flour
1/4 tsp. salt
1 tsp. cinnamon
1/2 tsp. allspice

1/2 tsp. cloves
1/2 tsp. nutmeg
3/4 c. sour milk
1 tsp. soda
1/2 c. raisins or chocolate chips
1/2 c. chopped walnuts
2 c. oatmeal

Cream shortening and sugar; add eggs, one at a time, beating well after each addition. Combine flour, salt and spices in separate bowl. Combine milk and soda. Add flour mixture alternately with milk mixture to creamed mixture. Add raisins, walnuts and oatmeal. Drop by teaspoonfuls onto greased cookie sheets. Bake in preheated 400-degree oven for 15 minutes or until browned. Yield: About 40 cookies.

Mary Jean Kearsley
Fruita, Colorado

ROLLED SUGAR COOKIES

1 c. shortening
2 c. sugar
4 eggs
2 tbsp. cream
4 c. flour
4 tsp. baking powder
1/8 tsp. salt
1 tsp. vanilla extract

Cream shortening and sugar together. Add eggs, one at a time, beating well after each addition. Blend in cream. Sift flour with baking powder and salt; add creamed mixture. Mix well; add vanilla extract. Chill for 20 minutes. Roll out very thin; cut with cookie cutter. Place on baking sheet. Bake in preheated 400-degree oven for about 10 minutes or until edges are browned. Yield: 3 dozen.

Carrie Hinton
Wiggins, Mississippi

SNICKERDOODLES

2 3/4 c. sifted flour
3 tsp. baking powder
1/2 tsp. salt
1 c. soft butter
1 3/4 c. sugar
2 eggs
4 tsp. cinnamon

Sift flour, baking powder and salt together. Cream butter; add 1 1/2 cups sugar gradually, creaming until fluffy. Blend in eggs. Add dry ingredients gradually; mixing well. Chill in refrigerator. Shape dough into small balls, using 1 tablespoon dough for each ball. Combine remaining 1/4 cup sugar and cinnamon; roll balls in sugar mixture. Place about 2 inches apart on ungreased baking sheets. Bake in preheated 400-degree oven about 10 minutes. Store in covered container. Yield: 5 dozen.

Artie G. Bell
Washington, D. C.

SPICED APPLESAUCE DROPS

1/2 c. shortening
1 c. sugar
1 egg
2 c. sifted all-purpose flour
1 tsp. baking powder
1/4 tsp. cloves
1/2 tsp. soda
1/2 tsp. salt
1/2 tsp. cinnamon
1 c. chopped dates
1 c. chopped nuts
1 c. unsweetened applesauce

Cream shortening; beat in sugar gradually. Add egg; beat until light and fluffy. Sift dry ingredients together. Mix 1/2 cup flour mixture with dates and nuts. Add remaining flour mixture alternately with applesauce to egg mixture. Stir in floured fruit and nut mixture. Drop from teaspoon onto greased baking sheet. Bake in preheated 350-degree oven for about 15 minutes or until tops spring back when pressed with finger.

Thyra Krauss
Concordia, Kansas

PARTY TORTE

1 1/8 c. egg whites
1 1/2 tsp. vanilla extract
1 tsp. vinegar
2 c. sifted sugar
2 c. heavy cream
1 c. drained crushed pineapple
3/4 c. maraschino cherries, cut in
quarters

Beat egg whites, vanilla and vinegar in bowl until soft peaks form. Add sugar, 1 tablespoon at a time, beating until stiff peaks form and sugar is dissolved. Spread in 2 brown paper-lined 9-inch round layer pans. Bake in preheated 350-degree oven for 1 hour and 15 minutes; cool in pans. Remove from pans; remove brown paper. Whip heavy cream until stiff; fold in pineapple and cherries. Place 1 meringue layer on cake plate; spread whipped cream mixture over layer. Add remaining meringue layer; spread whipped cream mixture over top and side of torte. Cut into wedges to serve. Yield: 12 servings.

Loretta Sawin
Chapman, Kansas

BUTTERSCOTCH NUT TORTE

6 eggs, separated
1 1/2 c. sugar
1 tsp. baking powder
2 tsp. vanilla extract
1 tsp. almond extract
2 c. graham cracker crumbs
1 c. broken nutmeats
1 pt. whipping cream
3 tbsp. powdered sugar

Beat egg yolks well; stir in sugar, baking powder and extracts. Beat egg whites until soft peaks form; fold into sugar mixture. Fold in crumbs and nutmeats. Line two 9-inch layer pans with waxed paper; pour in cake batter. Bake in preheated 325-degree oven for 30 to 35 minutes; cool. Remove waxed paper. Beat whipping cream until stiff, adding powdered sugar gradually.

Spread on layers; place layers together. Spread remaining whipped cream around side of torte.

Sauce

1 c. (packed) brown sugar
1/4 c. butter
1/4 c. water
1 tbsp. flour
1/4 c. orange juice
1 egg, well beaten
1/2 tsp. vanilla extract

Mix all ingredients in saucepan; bring to a boil. Cook, stirring frequently, until thickened. Cool; pour over torte.

Bobbie Jean Pope
Holly Pond, Alabama

CHOCOLATE TORTE

2 env. unflavored gelatin
2 4-oz. packages chocolate fudge
pudding and pie filling mix
1/4 c. sugar
2 c. water
3 1/3 c. Carnation evaporated milk
1/4 c. lemon juice
2 8 or 9-in. cake layers, split
crosswise into 4 layers
Sliced blanched almonds
Stemmed red maraschino cherries
Chocolate curls

Mix gelatin, pudding mix and sugar together in saucepan; stir in water and 2 cups evaporated milk. Cook, stirring, until mixture comes to a boil. Cool until mixture mounds when dropped from a spoon. Chill remaining evaporated milk in refrigerator tray for 10 to 15 minutes or until ice crystals form around edges of the tray. Whip for 1 minute or until stiff. Add lemon juice and whip for 1 minute or until very stiff. Fold into chocolate mixture. Spoon over cake layers and stack. Chill until firm. Garnish torte with almonds, cherries and chocolate curls.

Photograph for this recipe on page 231.

CHOCOLATE DOBOSCH TORTE

1/2 tsp. salt
5 eggs
1 c. sugar
1 1/2 tsp. vanilla extract
1 1/2 c. pancake mix
1 pt. whipping cream
1/4 c. cocoa
1/4 c. sifted powdered sugar
2 sq. semisweet chocolate, shaved
1/4 c. toasted slivered almonds

Line three 8-inch round cake pans with waxed paper. Add salt to eggs; beat for about 4 minutes or until thick and lemon colored. Add sugar, a small amount at a time, beating well after each addition. Add 1 teaspoon vanilla and pancake mix; stir until smooth. Pour into prepared pans. Bake in preheated 350-degree oven for 15 minutes or until cake tests done. Invert onto wire rack; cool for 15 minutes. Remove from pans; peel off paper. Cool. Slice each layer in half crosswise. Combine cream, remaining vanilla and cocoa in mixing bowl; chill thoroughly. Whip until frothy. Add powdered sugar gradually; whip until stiff. Place layer of cake on serving plate; spread with 1/4 of the whipped cream mixture. Sprinkle with 1 tablespoon shaved chocolate. Add another layer of cake; spread with 1/4 of the whipped cream mixture. Sprinkle with 1 tablespoon chocolate. Repeat with remaining 2 layers, whipped cream and chocolate, sprinkling chocolate around edge of top layer. Sprinkle almonds in center of top layer.

Alma R. Frerichs
Grants Pass, Oregon

AMBROSIA

1 doz. oranges
1 med. fresh coconut
1 1-lb. 13-oz. can crushed pineapple

Peel oranges; remove sections over bowl in order to obtain all juice. Remove seeds from orange sections. Punch holes in coconut; drain milk from coconut. Reserve coconut milk for ambrosia, if desired. Remove hull and brown covering of coconut; grate coconut fine. Combine coconut, coconut milk, orange pulp and juice and pineapple. Sugar may be added if mixture is not of desired sweetness. Chill. Place in sherbet dishes; garnish with red or green cherries or mint leaves. Yield: About 20 servings.

Hazel P. Lowe
Chatham, Virginia

APPLE WHIP

6 med. Washington State apples, pared,
    cored and quartered
1/3 c. sugar
1/8 tsp. salt
1 tsp. vanilla extract
6 tbsp. caramel, maple or dark corn syrup
    or honey
Soft Vanilla Custard

Place apples in 2-quart saucepan. Cook, covered, in as small amount of water as possible until tender. Mash to form thick puree. Add sugar, salt and vanilla extract. Pour 1 tablespoon caramel syrup in each of six 6-ounce custard cups, swirling syrup around cup to coat entire surface. Spoon apple mixture into cups; place in pan of hot water. Cover. Bake in preheated 350-degree oven for 15 to 20 minutes. Serve cold with Soft Vanilla Custard. Washington golden delicious or winesap apples are suggested for this recipe.

Soft Vanilla Custard

1/4 c. sugar
1/4 tsp. salt
2 eggs, lightly beaten
1 1/2 c. milk
1 tsp. vanilla extract

Combine sugar, salt and eggs in top of double boiler; blend in milk. Cook over hot water, stirring constantly, until mixture coats a spoon. Remove from heat; stir in vanilla extract. Let cool. Yield: 2 cups custard.

Photograph for this recipe on page 193.

POMMES SAUTE

3 tbsp. butter or margarine
4 c. chopped unpared Wash. State apples

Melt butter in skillet. Add apples; saute for 5 to 10 minutes or until pink and soft, stirring occasionally. Washington golden delicious or winesap apples are suggested for this recipe.

Photograph for this recipe on page 193.

CINNAMON-FRUIT COBBLER

2 c. buttermilk biscuit mix
Sugar
3 tbsp. melted butter
1/2 c. milk
1/4 tsp. cinnamon
1 16-oz. can sliced peaches
1 13 1/4-oz. can pineapple tidbits
4 tsp. cornstarch
1/4 tsp. almond extract
Light cream or half and half

Mix biscuit mix and 1 tablespoon sugar in bowl. Add 2 tablespoons butter to milk; stir into biscuit mixture with fork until thoroughly blended. Roll out on lightly floured surface to 9-inch square; brush with remaining melted butter. Combine 2 tablespoons sugar and cinnamon; sprinkle over dough. Roll as for jelly roll; wrap and chill. Drain peaches and pineapple, reserving 1 1/2 cups syrup. Combine 1/3 cup sugar and cornstarch in 2-quart saucepan; stir in reserved syrup gradually. Cook over medium heat, stirring constantly, until thickened and clear. Add fruits and almond extract; bring to a boil. Turn into shallow 2-quart baking dish. Cut biscuit roll into 6 or 8 slices; place on top of fruit mixture. Bake in preheated 350-degree oven for 30 to 35 minutes or until done. Serve warm with cream.

Photograph for this recipe on page 98.

SUMMER BASKET WITH STRAWBERRIES

4 egg whites
1 1/4 c. confectioners' sugar
3/4 c. whipping cream
1/4 tsp. vanilla extract
3 tbsp. sugar
1 qt. whole strawberries

Beat egg whites until foamy. Add confectioners' sugar gradually, beating until stiff peaks form. Draw two 6 1/2-inch circles on brown paper; grease circles well. Place paper on baking sheet. Place meringue in pastry tube; force meringue through tube to fill 1 circle for bottom of basket. Begin to fill circle from outside and move toward the center in spiral movement until circle is completely covered. Form thick ring on outline of remaining drawn circle; do not fill in. Draw 2 more circles on another sheet of paper. Grease circles; place paper on another baking sheet. Force meringue through tube around the edge of circles to form thick rims; reserve remaining meringue for filling. Place 1 baking sheet on lower rack of preheated 225-degree oven and remaining baking sheet on higher rack. Bake for 20 minutes. Reverse baking sheets on racks; bake for 25 minutes longer. Cover with foil if meringue browns too fast. Remove from oven; loosen meringues from paper. Place on cooling racks. Place solid-filled meringue layer on ovenproof platter; spread with part of reserved meringue. Add rings, spreading the meringue between each ring to hold basket together. Return to the oven; bake for 5 to 10 minutes longer. Whip cream until soft peaks form. Add vanilla and sugar gradually, beating until stiff peaks form. Arrange strawberries and whipped cream in alternate layers in basket.

Photograph for this recipe on page 203.

FRESH PEACH COBBLER

1/2 c. butter
1 c. all-purpose flour
2 tsp. baking powder
1 1/2 c. sugar
3/4 c. milk
4 or 5 lg. fresh peaches
1/2 c. water

Melt butter in baking dish. Mix flour, baking powder, 1 cup sugar and milk; pour into the baking dish. Peel and slice peaches; arrange over batter. Sprinkle remaining 1/2 cup sugar over peaches. Pour water over peaches. Bake in preheated 350-degree oven for 50 minutes.

Mrs. James Hilderbrand
Mena, Arkansas

CHERRY-APPLE DESSERT

2 2/3 c. sifted all-purpose flour
1 1/4 tsp. salt
1 c. vegetable shortening
6 1/2 tbsp. water
1 8-oz. jar red maraschino cherries
1/3 c. (firmly packed) light brown sugar
1/3 c. finely chopped walnuts
3/4 tsp. cinnamon
6 med. tart apples
Cream or milk
2 tbsp. sugar
Cherry Praline Sauce

Combine flour and salt in bowl; cut in shortening until mixture is uniform, but coarse. Sprinkle with water; toss with fork, then press into ball. Roll out on lightly floured surface to 14 x 21-inch rectangle; cut into six 7-inch squares. Drain cherries; reserve syrup for sauce. Chop 1/2 jar cherries coarsely; drain on paper towels. Reserve remaining cherries for sauce. Combine chopped cherries with brown sugar, walnuts and 1/4 teaspoon cinnamon. Pare and core apples; place an apple on each pastry square. Fill each apple cavity with cherry mixture. Moisten edges of squares with cream. Bring opposite points of pastries up over apples; press together. Brush pastries with cream. Blend sugar with remaining 1/2 teaspoon cinnamon; sprinkle over pastries. Place pastries on ungreased baking sheet. Bake in preheated 400-degree oven for 30 to 35 minutes or until brown. Serve with Cherry Praline Sauce.

Cherry Praline Sauce

1 c. sugar
Reserved maraschino cherry syrup
Reserved maraschino cherries

Spread sugar evenly over bottom of large saucepan. Place over very low heat; let stand undisturbed until sugar melts and forms light, golden liquid. Mix 3/4 cup water and 1/4 cup reserved cherry syrup in another saucepan; bring to a boil. Stir into caramelized sugar slowly and cautiously; cook, stirring, until sugar dissolves and clear, thick syrup is formed. Add reserved whole cherries; serve warm or cold. Any leftover sauce may be used on pancakes, custard, fruit or ice cream.

Photograph for this recipe on page 212.

RICH STRAWBERRY SHORTCAKE

2 c. flour
2 tbsp. sugar
3 tsp. baking powder
1/2 tsp. salt
1/2 c. margarine
1 egg, beaten
2/3 c. light cream
Soft butter
3 to 4 c. sweetened strawberries
1 c. heavy cream, whipped

Sift dry ingredients together into bowl; cut in margarine until mixture resembles coarse crumbs. Combine egg and light cream; add all at once to margarine mixture, stirring just until dry ingredients are moistened. Turn out on floured surface; knead gently for 30 seconds. Pat or roll out 1/2 inch thick. Cut 6 rounds with floured 2 1/2-inch cutter; place on ungreased baking sheet. Bake in preheated 450-degree oven for about 10 minutes. Split shortcakes; spread butter on bottom layers; add layer of strawberries. Place top layers over strawberries; add layer of strawberries. Top with whipped cream. Other fruits may be used instead of strawberries.

Mrs. Suzanne Le Blanc
Saugerties, New York

CHOCOLATE REFRIGERATOR DESSERT

2 c. vanilla wafer crumbs
1 c. chopped nuts
1/2 c. melted butter or margarine
1 c. whipping cream
3 tbsp. sugar
Pinch of salt
1 bar German's chocolate
2 tbsp. water
1 tsp. vanilla extract

Mix crumbs, nuts and butter. Pat 1/2 of the mixture into bottom of 9 x 6-inch loaf dish or pan. Whip cream until stiff, adding sugar and salt gradually. Melt chocolate in water over boiling water; stir in vanilla. Fold into whipped cream. Spread over crumb mixture; sprinkle remaining crumb mixture on top. Chill overnight. Slice to serve. Yield: 6 servings.

Mrs. Charlotte J. Callihan
Snow Hill, North Carolina

FRENCH CREAM

1/2 lb. vanilla wafers
1/2 c. butter
1 c. powdered sugar
2 eggs
1/2 pt. whipping cream
2 tbsp. sugar
1/2 c. chopped nuts
1 c. maraschino cherries

Crush vanilla wafers; place half the crumbs in 8-inch square pan. Cream butter, powdered sugar and eggs together until light and fluffy; spoon over crumbs. Whip cream until stiff, adding sugar gradually; fold in nuts and cherries. Pour over creamed mixture; sprinkle remaining crumbs on top. Place in freezing compartment of refrigerator overnight. Yield: 8 servings.

Myrtle Keck
Nampa, Idaho

CHOCOLATE ICE CREAM

4 c. milk
3 eggs
1 tbsp. flour
3 sq. chocolate
4 c. cream
1/2 tsp. salt
2 c. sugar
3 tbsp. vanilla extract

Scald 2 cups milk. Beat eggs with flour and 1/2 cup milk; stir into scalded milk. Cook, stirring, until mixture coats spoon. Add chocolate; stir until melted. Stir in cream, remaining 1 1/2 cups milk and remaining ingredients. Place in 1-gallon freezer container;

freeze according to manufacturer's directions. Yield: 12 servings.

Mrs. Peter Alberda
Manhattan, Montana

HOMEMADE ICE CREAM

8 eggs
4 c. sugar
2 pt. whipping cream
7 c. milk
4 tsp. vanilla extract

Beat eggs slightly. Add sugar; beat well. Add cream; beat just until well mixed. Add milk and vanilla; mix well. Pour into freezer can; freeze according to manufacturer's directions. Yield: 1 gallon.

Mrs. Jean Lewis
Platteville, Colorado

ORANGE SHERBET

3 c. orange juice
1 c. (or more) sugar
Lemon juice to taste
2 1/2 qt. milk

Mix orange juice, sugar and lemon juice; stir in milk. Pour into 1-gallon freezer container; freeze according to manufacturer's directions.

Mrs. Dorothy S. Samson
Lakeport, California

PEARS DE MENTHE

2 qt. vanilla ice cream, softened
1/2 c. green creme de menthe syrup
1 1-lb. 13-oz. can pear halves, chilled

Spoon ice cream into large mixing bowl. Swirl creme de menthe syrup through ice cream with rubber spatula, being careful not to overmix. Spoon ice cream mixture into 3 or 4 ice trays; freeze for about 4 hours or until firm. Drain pears, reserving juice. Arrange pears in large serving dish; mound scoops of ice cream on top. Pour reserved syrup over ice cream; serve at once.

Mrs. Yvonne Lindrum
Montebello, California

ORANGE CHRISTMAS BREADS

2 c. Florida orange juice
1/2 c. butter or margarine
2/3 c. sugar
1 tbsp. grated orange rind
1 tsp. salt
1 tsp. cinnamon
1 tsp. ginger
1 tsp. nutmeg
2 pkg. dry yeast
1/4 c. warm water
2 eggs, beaten
8 c. sifted all-purpose flour
1 c. light raisins
2 c. chopped mixed candied fruits
1 c. chopped nuts
Orange Glaze
Halved candied red cherries
Pieces of citron
Quartered candied green cherries
Candied fruits

Heat orange juice until hot, but not boiling. Combine butter, sugar, orange rind, salt and spices in large bowl. Pour orange juice over butter mixture; cool to lukewarm. Sprinkle yeast over warm water; stir until dissolved. Add to butter mixture. Add eggs; mix well. Beat in 4 cups flour; stir in raisins, candied fruits and nuts. Blend in enough remaining flour to make soft dough. Turn out onto floured surface; knead until smooth. Form into ball; place in a greased bowl. Grease surface of dough lightly; cover. Let rise in warm place for 2 to 3 hours or until doubled in bulk. Turn out onto lightly floured surface; punch down. Knead lightly; divide into 3 equal parts. Roll out 1/3 of the dough 1/4 inch thick on lightly floured surface; cut out 24 stars with 3-inch star cutter. Place on greased baking sheet; let rise in warm place for 30 to 45 minutes or until doubled in bulk. Bake in preheated 325-degree oven for 20 minutes. Shape 1/3 of the dough into rope about 30 inches long; form into tree shape on greased baking sheet. Start with 1 end of rope; make stem and base of tree. Continue folding rope into progressively shorter loops, ending with curl at top. Let rise in warm place for about 45 minutes or until doubled in bulk. Bake in preheated 325-degree oven for 45 minutes. Divide remaining 1/3 of the dough into 3 equal parts; shape each part into thin rope about 24 inches long. Braid ropes, twisting ends to seal; place on greased baking sheet. Let rise in warm place for about 45 minutes or until doubled in bulk. Bake in preheated 325-degree oven for 45 minutes. Drizzle breads with Orange Glaze while still warm. For Christmas tree, ornaments may be simulated by surrounding halved candied red cherries with pieces of citron. For star at top, use quarters of candied green cherries. Decorate braid by sprinkling additional grated orange rind over glaze. Decorate stars with candied fruits. To use stars as Christmas tree ornaments, make hole in 1 point with cake tester or skewer; make loop with red ribbon.

Orange Glaze

2 1/2 c. confectioners' sugar
2 tbsp. soft butter or margarine
3 tbsp. Florida orange juice
1 tbsp. grated orange rind

Blend all ingredients in bowl until smooth.

Photograph for this recipe on page 236.

BANANA BREAD

1/2 c. cooking oil
1 c. sugar
3 bananas, mashed
3 eggs, well beaten
2 c. flour
1 tsp. soda
1/8 tsp. salt
2 tbsp. buttermilk
1 c. chopped nuts

Combine oil and sugar; beat until creamy. Add bananas and eggs; mix well. Sift flour, soda and salt together; add alternately with buttermilk to banana mixture, blending well. Stir in nuts. Pour into medium-sized oiled loaf pan. Bake in preheated 350-degree oven for 1 hour or until loaf tests done.

Myrtle Brookshire
Mountain City, Tennessee

PINEAPPLE COFFEE CAKE

1 1/2 c. sifted flour
Sugar
2 tsp. baking powder
3/4 tsp. salt
1 egg, beaten
1/4 c. melted shortening
1 c. pineapple juice
1 tsp. cinnamon
1 tbsp. butter or margarine, melted
1/3 c. drained crushed pineapple

Sift flour, 1/3 cup sugar, baking powder and salt into bowl. Combine egg, shortening and pineapple juice; stir into flour mixture, beating until smooth. Spread in 9-inch baking pan. Combine 1/2 cup sugar, cinnamon, butter and pineapple. Spread over batter in pan. Bake in preheated 350-degree oven for 35 minutes or until cake pulls away from side of pan. Cool slightly before serving.

Mrs. Glen Ruder
North Adams, Michigan

PRUNE AND APRICOT COFFEE CAKE

3/4 c. dried prunes
3/4 c. dried apricots
Sifted all-purpose flour
2 tsp. baking powder
1/2 tsp. salt
2/3 c. (firmly packed) light brown sugar
1 tbsp. cinnamon
3/4 c. shortening
3/4 c. sugar
2 eggs
3/4 c. milk
1 tsp. vanilla extract
6 tbsp. butter or margarine, melted
1/3 c. chopped pecans or walnuts

Combine prunes and apricots with enough hot water to cover; let stand for 5 minutes. Drain; chop fine. Sift 2 cups flour with baking powder and salt into bowl. Combine brown sugar, 1 tablespoon flour and cinnamon in bowl; mix well. Combine shortening and sugar in large bowl of electric mixer; beat at medium speed until light and fluffy.

Beat in eggs, one at a time, beating well after each addition. Combine milk and vanilla extract. Add flour mixture and milk mixture alternately to creamed mixture, beginning and ending with flour mixture. Mix at low speed until just combined. Fold in prune mixture gently with rubber spatula. Spread 1/3 of the batter in greased and floured 9-inch tube pan. Sprinkle with 1/3 of the brown sugar mixture, then with 2 tablespoons butter. Repeat layers twice. Sprinkle top with pecans. Bake in preheated 350-degree oven for 55 minutes or until cake tester inserted in center comes out clean. Let cool in pan on wire rack for about 25 minutes. Remove from pan. Serve warm.

Elizabeth L. Stokes
Sulligent, Alabama

FEATHERWEIGHT PANCAKES

3 eggs, separated
1/4 tsp. salt
1/4 c. all-purpose flour
3/4 c. cottage cheese

Beat egg yolks until light; stir in salt, flour and cottage cheese. Fold in stiffly beaten egg whites. Drop by small spoonfuls onto hot, greased griddle. Cook until golden on both sides. Serve at once with butter and hot maple syrup.

Janet Schmidecamp
Chadwick, Illinois

SOUR CREAM COFFEE CAKE

1 c. margarine
1 1/4 c. sugar
2 tbsp. brown sugar
2 eggs
1 tsp. vanilla extract
1 tsp. cinnamon
1 c. sour cream
2 c. flour
1 1/2 tsp. baking powder
1/2 tsp. soda
1/4 tsp. salt
1 c. chopped pecans

Combine margarine and sugars; cream until smooth. Add eggs, vanilla extract and cinnamon; beat until well blended. Add sour cream; beat until smooth. Sift flour, baking powder, soda and salt together; add to sour cream mixture. Stir until all ingredients are well mixed. Add pecans. Pour into slightly oiled 9-inch angel food cake pan. Bake in preheated 350-degree oven for 50 minutes. Turn upside down on tube until cooled. Ice if desired. Keeps indefinitely.

Margaret S. Killian
Normal, Illinois

CRANBERRY ORANGE LOAF

2 1/2 c. sifted flour
3/4 c. sugar
3 tsp. baking powder
1 tsp. salt
1/2 tsp. soda
1 tsp. cinnamon
1/2 c. milk
1 egg, beaten
2 tbsp. melted shortening
1 1/2 c. ground cranberries
1/2 c. chopped nuts
1 tbsp. grated orange peel
1/4 c. orange juice

Sift first 6 ingredients together. Combine milk, egg and shortening; stir in cranberries, nuts, orange peel and juice. Add to flour mixture, stirring only until moistened; turn into loaf pan. Bake in preheated 350-degree oven for 40 minutes or until loaf tests done.

Mrs. Judith A. Anderson
Tuscola, Illinois

ORANGE-NUT BREAD

1 orange
1 c. raisins
1 egg, beaten
2 tbsp. melted butter
2 c. flour
1/2 c. sugar
1 tsp. baking powder
1/2 tsp. soda
1/4 tsp. salt
1/2 c. chopped nuts

Squeeze juice from orange; add enough hot water to juice to measure 1 cup liquid. Grind orange rind with raisins; pour juice over raisin mixture. Add egg and butter; mix well. Sift flour, sugar, baking powder, soda and salt together; add to raisin mixture. Mix until well blended. Stir in nuts. Pour into greased loaf pan. Bake in preheated 350-degree oven for 1 hour.

Sandra M. Cuchna
La Farge, Wisconsin

SOUR CREAM TWISTS

1 pkg. dry yeast
3/4 c. lukewarm sour cream
1 egg, beaten
2 tbsp. soft shortening
3 tbsp. sugar
1/8 tsp. soda
1 tsp. salt
3 c. sifted flour
2 tbsp. soft butter
1/3 c. (packed) brown sugar
1 tsp. cinnamon

Dissolve yeast in 1/4 cup warm water in mixing bowl. Stir in sour cream. Add egg and shortening; mix well. Sift sugar, soda, salt and flour together; mix into sour cream mixture. Turn out on lightly floured board; knead until smooth. Roll into 24 x 6-inch rectangle; spread with butter. Combine brown sugar and cinnamon; sprinkle over half the dough. Fold buttered side over brown sugar mixture. Cut into 24 strips, 1 inch wide. Hold strip at both ends and twist in opposite directions. Place 2 inches apart on greased baking sheet. Let rise in warm place for 1 hour or until indentation remains when touched lightly with finger. Bake in preheated 375-degree oven for 12 to 15 minutes or until browned. Frost warm twists with white icing, if desired.

Mrs. Ruth J. Romesberg
Rockwood, Pennsylvania

Foreign Food Favorites

Foreign foods have been cooked, served and enjoyed by Americans for years. In fact, many foreign dishes such as spaghetti and chow mein are eaten so often in this country that we tend to forget where these delicious entrees originated. Probably, many of the foods that are favorites in our homes today are prepared by recipes brought from the Old World. Carefully guarding these recipes as they were handed down from generation to generation, our ancestors realized the importance of preserving their heritage.

Although new methods of cooking were developed here, they were greatly influenced by the cooking art of the British, French, Greeks, etc. For example, grandma's potato dumplings were first steamed in Germany and mother's delicious lasagna came directly from Italy. True foreign foods, once considered rare and exotic, are certainly not unusual sights in this country. Since the development of modern transportation, Americans have become some of the most well-traveled people anywhere. Having learned to appreciate tastes of foreign lands, they are constantly searching for ways to duplicate the flavors enjoyed during their journeys. Because each country's cuisine is different, it is important to understand what foods are at the base of each.

Old-fashioned British cooking is a down-to-earth way of preparing food. The regional specialties that abound in all five of the countries depend upon what is produced in a particular area. For example, potatoes are essential to the diet of those in Ireland; lamb is often one of the main courses in Wales; scrumptious baked goods are enjoyed in Scotland and the most popular food in England is beef. Family books of handwritten recipes combining British legacy, countryside and character have passed from mother to daughter for years. However, cooking in the British Isles, as a whole, is centered around home-grown fruits and vegetables prepared simply and flavorfully.

Dependent upon other countries for the development of its cuisine, Canada has distinctively combined the cooking of France, England and America. Primarily an agricultural country, Canada is famous for numerous foods including maple syrup, blueberries, apples, summer squash and doughnuts. Its people derive great pleasure from good food, preferring home cooking to any other.

The French, known as the best cooks in the world, have an innate love for good foods. Due to the abundance of locally grown products, they use only the finest, freshest foods available in the preparation of each dish. Some of these include olives, figs, oranges, apples and fish. Many of the most distinctive dishes have been passed from generation to generation by the males of a family rather than the females. These chefs believe that the real art of French cooking is perfectly blending each and every ingredient and also preparing great sauces for almost all foods.

Hearty, rich and filling, German cooking mainly consists of breads, pota-toes, pork, dried fruit, and root and winter vegetables. Gourmets all over the world cherish the infinite varieties of the famous German bread that has been made by hand for centuries. Probably the most notable part of German cooking is their tendency to add a sour or a sweet-and-sour taste to so many foods.

Greece's deliciously robust national cookery is relatively simple, based on a desire for moderation and perfection. While agricultural methods are primitive and crop yields are typically low, olive trees and citrus groves flourish here. The basic ingredient in Greek cooking is olive oil. However, many herbs and spices are also used. Most famous for their pastries, the Greeks are also experts at preparing salads, fresh vegetables and lamb.

The age-old Italian ability to work with what nature provides lends Italian cooking its unique personality. A combination of sophistication and variety, it is identified by the use of numerous kinds of pasta and cheese, wines, delicious antipasti, artful fish, fowl and meat dishes, sumptuous soups and lavish desserts. It is no wonder that Italy is considered the mother of Continental cooking.

Spicy, colorful and unique are words which best describe the cooking of Mexico. While the staple food of the Mexicans is the tortilla, boiled black beans, tamales, tacos and enchiladas are also quite an important part of their diets. Many of their recipes have been handed down from the ancient Indians, including those for delicious drinks and sauces made from the cacao beans. Quite fond of chocolate, Mexicans often cook fowl and meats in spiced chocolate sauces.

Middle Eastern specialties have become well-known throughout the world. One of the most prominent Middle Eastern dishes is the shish kabob. This method of roasting or grilling meat on skewers first began in Lebanon. Many Turkish, Jewish and Arabian dishes, though not as famous, are equally delightful. The foods found in the greatest abundance throughout these countries are fresh fruits of all kinds, figs in particular, melons and berries.

Throughout the years, the cuisine of Mid-Europe has been strongly influenced by other countries. Modern Hungarian cooking, however, does have a character all its own, using lard, onions, paprika and sour cream extravagantly. Czechoslovakia, on the other hand, has long been famous for its unusual cakes and puddings. Because Mid-Europe's fields are rich, its people are practically self-sufficient in their production of food.

The art of oriental cooking is treated with a great deal of respect, for the Chinese chef must earn this place of honor. A typical meal consists of meat, fish, vegetables, and soup, plus the famous bowl of rice served with every meal. Since grain crops grow well here, noodles, cereals and bean products are the foods most readily available.

Scandinavia boasts of a cuisine more highly developed than anywhere else in the world. Large meals unsurpassed in beauty, variety, freshness and flavor are found throughout Sweden, Denmark and Norway. Lush garden vegetables, dairy products straight from the farm and freshly caught fish are just a few of the taste-tempting foods that are cooked here.

True Latin American cooking features an abundance of flavors that cannot be equalled. Nowhere does the populace enjoy chili peppers the way Latin Americans do. However, this land's greatest influence on the outside world is coffee. Due to geographical barriers, each country from Venezuela to Argentina has a specialty all its own.

Food in Spain is exotic and very delicious. While many dishes are highly seasoned with garlic and olive oil, mild foods are more often the rule. One of the most important foods in Spain is bread. Always a part of the basic Spanish meal, bread is usually accompanied by potatoes, beans, olives and cheese and wine — Spain being unequalled in its quality of Sherry.

Home Economics Teachers' favorite recipes for foods from all of these foreign countries are awaiting you in the following section. As we celebrate our own country's glory in this its two hundredth year, let us not forget the contributions made by our foreign neighbors.

British Isles

ANGELS ON HORSEBACK

Large oysters
Strips of bacon, cut in halves

Simmer oysters in their own juice until edges just curl. Drain; wrap each oyster in 1/2 strip of bacon. Fasten with toothpick. Broil until bacon is crisp. May be served on toast, if desired.

Eloise B. Hawkins
Walterboro, South Carolina

BASIC WELSH RAREBIT

2 tbsp. butter
3 c. grated Cheddar cheese
1/2 tsp. dry mustard
1/4 tsp. salt
Dash of cayenne pepper
1/2 tsp. Worcestershire sauce
2 egg yolks
1/2 c. light beer
4 slices hot buttered toast

Melt butter and cheese over boiling water, stirring constantly, using a wooden spoon. Add seasonings, stirring constantly. Mix egg yolks and beer together; pour slowly into cheese mixture, stirring constantly. Cook, stirring, for 10 minutes or until thick and smooth. Do not allow to boil. Pour over toast; serve immediately. Yield: 4 servings.

Mrs. M. Bellopede
Victoria, British Columbia, Canada

FAMILY-STYLE CORNISH PASTY

4 c. flour
2 tsp. salt
1 1/2 c. lard
7/8 c. cold water
2 eggs
2 lb. sirloin steak, cut into 1/2-in. cubes
6 med. potatoes, quartered and sliced
6 med. onions, chopped
1/2 c. suet, chopped

Salt and pepper to taste
1/4 c. butter

Sift flour and salt together; cut in lard. Beat cold water and eggs together; stir into flour mixture. Roll out half the pastry into rectangle to fit 9 x 15 x 2 1/2-inch baking pan; place in pan. Mix steak cubes, vegetables and suet together; add salt and pepper. Place in lined pan; dot with butter. Cover with top crust. Seal carefully; cut slits in top. Bake for 20 minutes in preheated 400-degree oven. Reduce oven temperature to 350 degrees; bake for 1 hour and 30 minutes longer. Cut into squares to serve. May serve with coleslaw, beets and chili sauce, if desired.

Mrs. Marian Ahlgrimm
Mineral Point, Wisconsin

ENGLISH CRUMPETS

2 cakes yeast
4 c. lukewarm water
4 c. sifted flour
1 tbsp. salt
Butter

Dissolve yeast in lukewarm water. Add flour and salt; beat well. Cover; let rise in warm place for about 1 hour or until doubled in bulk. Beat down. Place greased muffin rings on greased hot griddle; fill muffin rings 1/2 full with dough. Cook over low heat until well risen and brown on under side. Turn rings and dough; cook until brown on other side. Serve crumpets with butter.

Mrs. Daisymae Eckman
Pawnee City, Nebraska

ENGLISH TRIFLE

6 thick slices pound cake
1 c. sherry
1/2 c. raspberry jam
18 to 24 ladyfingers
5 egg yolks
2/3 c. sugar
1/3 c. flour
Dash of salt
2 c. milk
1 tbsp. butter

1 1/2 tsp. vanilla
Whipped cream
Candied cherry halves

Arrange cake slices in serving dish; pour 1/2 cup sherry over cake. Spread jam over top. Dip ladyfingers in remaining sherry; arrange over cake slices. Beat egg yolks well. Combine sugar, flour and salt; beat into egg yolks. Heat milk in saucepan; stir gradually into egg yolk mixture. Return to saucepan; cook, stirring, until thickened. Add butter and vanilla; let cool. Spread over ladyfingers, covering well. Chill thoroughly. Top with whipped cream and cherry halves to serve.

Mrs. E. B. Spinks
Raymondville, Texas

IRISH SODA BREAD

3 c. sifted self-rising flour
2 tbsp. sugar
1/2 tsp. soda
1 tsp. caraway seed
1 1/2 c. milk
1/2 c. melted margarine or oil
3/4 to 1 c. raisins

Sift flour, sugar and soda together into mixing bowl; stir in caraway seed. Combine milk, margarine and raisins; add all at once to flour mixture, stirring only until flour is moistened. Turn into greased 4 1/2 x 8 1/2-inch pan. Bake in preheated 400-degree oven for 40 to 45 minutes or until cake tester inserted in center comes out clean. Remove from pan immediately; cool on rack. Serve warm or cool. Yield: 1 loaf.

Mrs. Hazel Johnson
Lake City, Tennessee

Canada

CANADIAN SAVORY EGGS

1 c. grated Cheddar cheese
2 tbsp. butter
1/2 c. cream
1 tsp. prepared mustard
1/2 tsp. salt
1/4 tsp. pepper
6 eggs, slightly beaten

Sprinkle cheese in 9 x 9 x 1 3/4-inch pan; dot with butter. Mix cream, mustard, salt and pepper; pour half the mixture over cheese. Pour eggs over cream mixture; add remaining cream mixture. Bake in preheated 325-degree oven for 25 minutes; serve at once. Yield: 6 servings.

Shirley Anne Shompbe
Chetecamp, Nova Scotia, Canada

France

CREME VICHYSSOISE

4 green onions, chopped
1 med. onion, chopped
6 tbsp. butter
4 med. potatoes, peeled and quartered
1 qt. water
4 chicken bouillon cubes
4 c. light cream
Salt and pepper to taste
1 pt. sour cream

Cook onions in butter in saucepan until tender. Add potatoes, water and bouillon cubes; bring to a boil. Cook over medium heat for 30 minutes. Mash. Add cream, salt and pepper; bring to a boil. Cool; stir in sour cream. Chill until cold; serve. Yield: 6 servings.

Mrs. Earl Ellis
New Summerfield, Texas

CHICKEN-MUSHROOM SPREAD

2 tbsp. butter
1/4 lb. mushrooms, chopped
1 1/2 c. ground cooked chicken or turkey
1/3 c. ground blanched almonds
1 tsp. salt
1/4 tsp. freshly ground pepper
1/4 c. mayonnaise

Melt butter in skillet; saute mushrooms in butter for 5 minutes. Cool. Combine with chicken, almonds, salt, pepper and mayonnaise; blend well.

Mrs. S. J. Ziegler
Long Branch, New Jersey

SAVARIN CREME CHIBOUST

1/2 c. milk
1/4 c. butter or margarine
1/2 c. sugar
1/2 tsp. salt
1 pkg. dry yeast
1/4 c. warm water
2 eggs, beaten
1/2 tsp. grated lemon peel
2 1/2 c. sifted all-purpose flour
3/4 c. toasted chopped filberts
1 8-oz. jar red glace cherries, chopped
Rum-Flavored Syrup
Apricot Glaze
12 glace cherries, halved
Creme Chiboust
Whipped cream (opt.)
6 glace cherries, quartered (opt.)

Scald milk; stir in butter, sugar and salt. Cool to lukewarm. Sprinkle yeast over warm water in large bowl; stir until dissolved. Blend in milk mixture. Add eggs, lemon peel and flour; beat vigorously for 5 minutes. Cover; let rise in warm place for about 1 hour and 30 minutes or until almost doubled in bulk. Stir down; beat in filberts and chopped cherries. Turn into well-greased 9-inch ring mold. Cover; let rise for about 1 hour or until doubled in bulk. Bake in preheated 350-degree oven for 50 minutes. Turn out onto deep platter; pour some of the hot Rum-Flavored Syrup over savarin immediately. Repeat until all syrup is absorbed; cool. Glaze ring with some of the warm Apricot Glaze. Arrange cherry halves in design over glaze; spoon remaining glaze over cherries. Cool. Fill center of ring with Creme Chiboust. Decorate with whipped cream and quartered glace cherries.

Rum-Flavored Syrup

1 c. water
3/4 c. sugar
1 long strip orange peel
1 long strip lemon peel
2 tsp. rum extract

Mix water, sugar, orange peel and lemon peel in saucepan; bring to a boil. Remove from heat; stir in rum extract. Discard orange and lemon peel. Keep syrup hot.

Apricot Glaze

1/2 c. strained apricot preserves
2 tbsp. sugar

Combine preserves and sugar in saucepan. Cook over high heat, stirring constantly, for 2 to 3 minutes or until mixture coats spoon with light film. Keep warm.

Creme Chiboust

3 eggs, separated
Sugar
1/4 c. flour
1 c. milk
1/2 tsp. vanilla extract
1/4 tsp. rum extract
1 env. unflavored gelatin
1/4 c. water
1 c. heavy cream

Blend egg yolks and 1/2 cup sugar thoroughly; mix in flour. Bring milk to a boil in saucepan; stir in vanilla and rum extracts. Add to sugar mixture gradually, stirring constantly. Return mixture to saucepan; bring to a boil, stirring constantly. Remove from heat. Soften gelatin in water; stir into sugar mixture until dissolved. Stir in cream. Beat egg whites until stiff. Add 1/4 teaspoon sugar; beat well. Add cream mixture gradually, beating constantly. Chill for at least 1 hour and 30 minutes. Beat creme before serving in savarin.

Photograph for this recipe on page 246.

FRENCH ONION SOUP WITH WINE

6 lg. yellow onions, thinly sliced
2 tbsp. butter or margarine
1 tbsp. olive oil
6 c. beef stock or bouillon
1/3 c. white or red wine
Salt and pepper to taste
6 slices buttered toasted French bread
Grated Parmesan cheese

Place onions in butter and oil in heavy 4-quart saucepan; cover. Cook over low heat for 15 minutes, stirring frequently. Pour in beef stock and wine; simmer for 30 minutes. Stir in salt and pepper. Ladle soup into individual bowls; top each serving with a slice of bread. Sprinkle each toast slice with cheese. Yield: 6 servings.

Mrs. Marie Edmunds
Bonners Ferry, Idaho

BEEF CHATEAUBRIAND

1 3 to 4-lb. beef tenderloin
1 1/2 tsp. salt
1/2 tsp. pepper
1 tsp. garlic salt
1 tsp. monosodium glutamate
1 pkg. dry French salad dressing herbs
1 c. corn oil
1/2 c. wine vinegar

Remove membranes from outside of tenderloin. Rub tenderloin with salt, pepper, garlic salt, monosodium glutamate and salad herbs. Place in shallow baking dish. Mix oil and vinegar; brush over tenderloin. Marinate from 4 to 6 hours, turning tenderloin several times. Pour marinade into small pan. Broil tenderloin until brown on both sides, basting with marinade. Insert meat thermometer in tenderloin. Bake in preheated 350-degree oven to desired doneness. Slice diagonally about 3/4 inch thick before serving. Yield: 6 servings.

Mrs. Elizabeth F. Smith, Area Supvr.
Home and Family Life Ed.
Big Spring, Texas

COQ AU VIN

2 2 1/2-lb. fryers, disjointed
1/4 c. cognac
1/3 c. flour
1 tsp. salt
1/4 tsp. pepper
1/4 tsp. butter
1 tbsp. salad oil
2 1/2 c. Burgundy
Sprig of parsley
1/2 tsp. peppercorns
1 bay leaf
Sprig of thyme
1 clove of garlic, crushed
1/4 lb. salt pork
6 sm. onions
1/2 lb. fresh mushroom caps

Place chicken pieces in large skillet. Pour cognac over chicken; ignite. Cover skillet to extinguish flame. Mix flour, salt and pepper; dredge chicken with flour mixture. Add butter and salad oil to skillet; cook chicken in skillet until lightly browned. Remove chicken to baking dish. Add 1 1/2 cups water to drippings in skillet; heat, stirring, until browned particles are loosened. Pour over chicken; add Burgundy. Tie parsley, peppercorns, bay leaf and thyme in cheesecloth; add to chicken. Add garlic; cover. Bake in preheated 325-degree oven for 30 minutes. Simmer salt pork in 1/2 cup water for 5 minutes; drain and dice. Saute salt pork in skillet with onions and mushrooms for several minutes; add to chicken. Cover; bake for about 2 hours longer or until chicken and vegetables are tender. Serve chicken and vegetables on hot platter with the wine sauce. Two 4-ounce cans button mushrooms may be used instead of fresh mushrooms. Yield: 6-8 servings.

Ann Whitaker
West Point, Mississippi

QUICHE LORRAINE

2/3 c. sifted flour
1/3 c. cornmeal
1/2 tsp. salt
1/3 c. shortening
2 to 4 tbsp. cold water

Sift flour with cornmeal and salt into bowl; cut in shortening until mixture resembles coarse crumbs. Add water, 1 tablespoon at a time, mixing with fork until ingredients hold together. Form into ball. Roll out on lightly floured board or canvas to form 13-inch circle; fit loosely into 9-inch pie plate. Trim crust, allowing 1/2 inch beyond rim. Fold edge under; flute.

Filling

1/2 lb. sliced bacon
1/4 c. finely chopped onion
1 c. grated Swiss cheese
4 eggs, beaten
1 pt. half and half or light cream
3/4 tsp. salt
1/8 tsp. nutmeg
Dash of cayenne pepper

Cook bacon in skillet until crisp. Remove from skillet; drain, then crumble. Pour off all drippings except 1 tablespoon from skillet. Saute onion in the skillet until tender. Sprinkle cheese on bottom of pie crust. Combine onion and bacon; sprinkle over cheese. Combine eggs, half and half, salt, nutmeg and cayenne pepper; beat until thoroughly mixed. Pour into pie crust. Bake in preheated 400-degree oven for 10 minutes. Reduce oven temperature to 350 degrees; bake for 30 minutes longer or until knife inserted 1 inch from edge comes out clean. Let stand for 10 minutes before serving. Yield: 4-6 servings.

Mrs. Jean Henkle
Rockford, Ohio

QUICHE DE CRABE

All-purpose flour
1 tsp. sugar
1 tsp. salt
Butter
4 eggs
1 egg white, slightly beaten
2 tbsp. minced shallot or green onion
1 lb. crab meat
1 c. shredded Swiss cheese
1 c. light cream
Dash of pepper
Dash of nutmeg

Sift 1 1/3 cups flour, sugar and 1/2 teaspoon salt into bowl; cut in 1/2 cup butter. Beat 1 egg slightly; stir into flour mixture. Form into ball; wrap tightly with waxed paper. Chill for several hours or overnight. Roll out pastry on floured surface; place in 9-inch pie pan. Flute edge. Brush inside with beaten egg white; let dry. Saute shallot in 1 tablepoon butter until tender; stir in crab meat and 1 tablespoon flour. Sprinkle half the cheese in pie shell; spread crab meat mixture over cheese. Sprinkle remaining cheese on crab meat mixture. Beat 3 remaining eggs slightly; stir in cream, remaining 1/2 teaspoon salt, pepper and nutmeg. Pour over cheese. Bake in preheated 400-degree oven for 10 minutes. Reduce oven temperature to 350 degrees; bake for 40 minutes longer or until knife inserted in center comes out clean. Two 6 1/2-ounce cans crab meat, drained, may be used instead of fresh crab meat. Yield: 6 servings.

Emily T. Duley
Upper Marlboro, Maryland

RATATOUILLE

2 c. yellow squash, cut into 1/2-in. cubes
1 1/2 tsp. salt
3 cloves of garlic, minced
1/3 c. salad oil
1/3 tsp. cumin or comino seed
2 c. peeled eggplant, cut into 1/2-in. cubes
1/2 tsp. oregano
3 med. onions, sliced
2 green peppers, cut into strips
1/2 tsp. marjoram
3 med. tomatoes, sliced
1/3 tsp. dillseed

Place squash in greased 2 1/2-quart casserole; sprinkle with 1/3 of the salt, garlic and oil. Add cumin seed. Add eggplant; sprinkle with half the remaining salt, garlic and oil. Add oregano. Add onions, then green peppers; sprinkle with marjoram and remaining salt, garlic and oil. Cover. Bake in preheated 350-degree oven for 1 hour. Add tomatoes; sprinkle with dillseed. Bake, uncovered, for 15 minutes longer. Yield: 6 servings.

Mrs. Emma Lou Leftwich
Mount Pleasant, Texas

GALETTE CREOLE CALAS

1/2 c. rice
1/2 pkg. yeast
3 eggs, beaten
1/2 c. sugar
3 tbsp. flour
1/2 tsp. nutmeg
Vegetable oil
Powdered sugar

Pour rice into 3 cups rapidly boiling water in saucepan; cook until tender. Drain, then chill and mash. Dissolve yeast in 1/2 cup warm water. Add to rice; mix well. Let rise overnight. Add eggs, sugar and flour to rice mixture; beat thoroughly. Let rise for 15 minutes; stir in nutmeg. Drop by large spoonfuls into deep, hot oil. Fry until golden brown; drain. Sprinkle with powdered sugar.

Mrs. Allen S. Lawrence
Sinton, Texas

Germany

DELICIOUS SAUERBRATEN

1 3-lb. round steak, 2 1/2 to 3 in. thick
1 tbsp. salt
1/2 tsp. pepper
2 onions, sliced
1 carrot, sliced
1 stalk celery, chopped
4 cloves
4 peppercorns
1/2 c. red wine vinegar
2 bay leaves
3 1/2 c. water
2 tbsp. fat
4 tbsp. butter
3 tbsp. flour
1 tbsp. sugar
5 gingersnaps, crushed

Wipe steak with a damp cloth; sprinkle with salt and pepper. Place in earthenware, glass or enamelware bowl. Add onions, carrot, celery, cloves, peppercorns, vinegar, bay leaves and water. Cover; refrigerate for 4 days, turning occasionally. Remove steak from marinade; dry with paper towels. Strain and reserve marinade. Heat fat and 1 tablespoon butter in heavy casserole. Add steak; sear over high heat until browned. Add marinade; bring to a boil. Cover; cook over low heat for 3 hours. Melt remaining butter in small skillet; stir in flour and sugar until smooth. Cook, stirring, until roux browns. Stir carefully into simmering marinade. Cover; simmer for 1 hour longer. Remove steak to warm serving platter; add gingersnap crumbs to marinade. Cook, stirring, until smooth and thickened. Serve with steak. Yield: 8 servings.

Mrs. Dorothy M. Hardin
Lebanon, Illinois

BAVARIAN NOODLES

1 12-oz. package noodles, cooked and drained
1 16-oz. carton cottage cheese
1 c. sour cream
1 c. thinly sliced green onions
1/2 c. milk
2 tsp. salt
1 tsp. monosodium glutamate
1/4 tsp. pepper
1/8 tsp. cayenne pepper

Mix all ingredients together carefully; pour into 2-quart casserole. Bake, covered, in preheated 350-degree oven for 1 hour or until heated through and bubbly. Yield: 8 servings.

Mrs. Ray A. Waters
Texarkana, Arkansas

HAZELNUT TORTE

7 eggs, separated
3/4 c. powdered sugar
1/8 tsp. cinnamon
1 tsp. lemon juice
Grated rind of 1/2 lemon
1/2 c. dried bread crumbs
1 c. finely ground hazelnuts
1/4 tsp. salt
Sweetened whipped cream

Beat egg yolks and powdered sugar until very light; fold in cinnamon, lemon juice, lemon rind, bread crumbs and hazelnuts. Beat egg whites and salt until stiff but not dry; fold into mixture gently. Grease and line three 9-inch cake pans with waxed paper. Spread batter in prepared pans. Bake in preheated 350-degree oven for 30 minutes or until cake tests done. Let cake age for 1 day. Spread whipped cream between layers and on top; garnish with chopped hazelnuts, if desired.

Mrs. R. W. McMartin
Marietta, Georgia

Greece

BAKLAVA

1 c. sugar
1 1/2 c. honey
Grated peel of 1 orange
1 tsp. cinnamon
1 1/2 lb. blanched toasted almonds,
    finely chopped
1 1/2 c. sweet butter, melted
1 lb. phyllo

Combine 1/2 cup sugar, 1/2 cup water, honey, orange peel and cinnamon in saucepan; bring to a boil. Simmer for about 15 minutes; cool. Mix almonds with remaining 1/2 cup sugar. Brush a 10 x 14-inch baking pan with butter. Line pan with 3 sheets phyllo, brushing each sheet with butter. Sprinkle lightly with almond mixture; repeat layers, alternating 2 sheets of buttered phyllo and the almond mixture to a depth of 1 inch, ending with phyllo. Cut into 1 x 1 1/2-inch triangles. Bake in preheated 325-degree oven for 50 minutes or until golden brown. Remove from oven; cut through pastry diamonds again completely. Pour cooled honey syrup mixture over top while hot. Yield: 48 servings.

Mrs. Virginia Pope
San Angelo, Texas

Italy

EGGS FLORENTINE

4 eggs, hard boiled
2 c. cooked spinach
1/8 c. grated Parmesan cheese
1 c. hot cream sauce
1 c. dry bread crumbs
Butter

Cut eggs in halves. Arrange spinach in casserole; place eggs on top in circle. Reserve a small amount of cheese for topping; stir remaining cheese into cream sauce. Pour hot sauce over eggs and spinach. Sprinkle with bread crumbs; dot with butter. Top with reserved cheese. Bake in preheated 450-degree oven until browned and bubbly. Yield: 4-6 servings.

Roma E. Wood
Cambridge, Nebraska

RISOTTO

2 1/2 c. consomme
1 c. white rice
1/2 c. chopped green pepper
1/2 c. chopped onion
1/2 c. drained sliced mushrooms
1/2 c. sliced pepperoni
1 tbsp. oil
3 1/2 c. canned tomatoes
1 tsp. salt
6 oz. shredded mozzarella cheese

Bring consomme to a boil; add rice. Cover; cook over low heat for about 25 minutes or until liquid is absorbed. Saute green pepper, onion, mushrooms and pepperoni in oil in saucepan. Add tomatoes and salt; simmer, uncovered, for 20 minutes. Stir rice into tomato mixture. Place half the mixture in 10 x 6 1/2 x 2-inch baking dish. Sprinkle with half the cheese. Repeat layers. Bake in preheated 350-degree oven for 20 minutes or until bubbly. Yield: 4-6 servings.

Janet Malone
Loveland, Colorado

CHICKEN CACCIATORE

1   2 1/2 to 3-lb. fryer, disjointed
1/4 c. olive oil
2 med. onions, sliced
2 c. tomatoes
1   8-oz. can seasoned tomato sauce
1 tsp. salt
1 tsp. crushed oregano
1/4 tsp. pepper
1/2 tsp. celery seed
2 bay leaves
1 can mushrooms

Brown chicken in hot olive oil; remove from skillet. Add onion slices; cook until tender but not brown. Combine tomatoes, tomato sauce, salt, oregano, pepper, celery seed and bay leaves for sauce. Return chicken to skillet; pour sauce over chicken. Cover; simmer for 45 minutes. Stir in mushrooms. Cook, uncovered, for 20 minutes or until chicken is tender and sauce is thick, turning occasionally. Skim off excess fat; remove bay leaves. Yield: 4-6 servings.

Mrs. Bobbie K. Troutman
Rosiclare, Illinois

CIOPPINO CINZANO

2 tbsp. olive or salad oil
3/4 c. chopped onion
1/2 c. chopped green pepper
2 med. garlic cloves, crushed
1 c. Cinzano Asti Spumante wine
1   28-oz. can tomatoes
1 1/2 tsp. salt
1/4 tsp. rosemary, crushed

1/4 tsp. thyme, crushed
Dash of cayenne pepper
1 1/2 doz. hard-shelled littleneck clams
1 lb. striped bass fillets, cut into
   serving pieces
1 lb. shelled, deveined fresh shrimp

Heat oil in a Dutch oven or large saucepan. Add onion, green pepper and garlic; saute over medium heat, stirring occasionally, for about 5 minutes or until onion and pepper are tender. Add wine, undrained tomatoes, salt, rosemary, thyme and cayenne pepper. Bring to a boil; reduce heat to low. Cover; simmer for 15 minutes. Increase heat to medium high. Add clams; cook, uncovered, for 5 minutes, stirring occasionally. Add bass and shrimp. Cook, uncovered, for about 5 minutes or until shrimp turn pink and bass flakes easily when tested with fork, stirring occasionally. Garnish with chopped parsley. Serve immediately in soup bowls. Yield: 6 to 8 servings.

Photograph for this recipe on page 240.

ITALIAN SPAGHETTI

1 1/2 lb. ground beef
1/2 lb. ground sausage
4 onions, cut up
1 clove of garlic, cut up
2 cans tomato paste
Salt and pepper to taste
1 tsp. sugar
1/2 tsp. oregano
Dash of Tabasco sauce
1 c. grated Parmesan cheese
2 qt. drained tomatoes
Cooked long spaghetti

Saute beef and sausage in skillet until browned. Saute onions and garlic in Dutch oven in small amount of fat until browned. Add tomato paste, salt, pepper, sugar, oregano, Tabasco sauce, cheese and tomatoes; mix well. Add beef mixture; simmer for 3 hours. Serve over spaghetti. Yield: 10-12 servings.

Mrs. Delbert Hlavinka
Mayville, North Dakota

STUFFED MANICOTTI

1 lb. ground beef
1/4 c. olive oil
1/2 c. chopped onion
1 clove of garlic, minced
2 6-oz. cans tomato paste
2 c. water
2 tbsp. chopped parsley
4 tsp. basil
2 tsp. oregano
Salt and pepper
1 tsp. thyme
1 tsp. marjoram
3/4 lb. ricotta cheese
1/3 c. grated Parmesan cheese
1 beaten egg
2 tbsp. chopped parsley
8 oz. manicotti
Romano cheese

Saute beef in hot oil until browned. Add onion, garlic, tomato paste, water, parsley, basil and oregano; mix well. Stir in 1 1/2 teaspoons salt and a dash of pepper. Simmer, uncovered, for about 45 minutes, stirring occasionally. Combine thyme, marjoram, ricotta cheese, Parmesan cheese, egg and parsley in mixing bowl; mix well. Season with salt and pepper. Cook manicotti in boiling salted water until tender; drain and rinse in cold water. Stuff manicotti with cheese mixture. Pour half the beef mixture into 11 x 7-inch baking dish; arrange manicotti in layer over sauce, overlapping slightly. Top with remaining sauce. Sprinkle with Romano cheese. Bake in preheated 350-degree oven for 25 to 30 minutes or until heated through and bubbly. Yield: 6-8 servings.

Doris SanFilippo
Tustin, California

VEAL PALAZZO

12 thin slices veal cutlet
12 thin slices ham
12 thin slices Swiss cheese
2 tbsp. butter
Salt and pepper to taste
1/2 c. white or rose wine
2 tbsp. tomato paste
1 bay leaf
1/2 tsp. basil

Top pieces of veal with ham and cheese. Roll up; secure with picks or heavy thread. Saute veal rolls in butter in skillet until browned. Sprinkle with salt and pepper. Stir in wine, tomato paste, bay leaf and basil; cover. Simmer for 15 minutes or until tender. Yield: 6 servings.

Mrs. Frankie B. Skeels
Alexandria, Louisiana

Mexico

CHILI CON QUESO

1 lg. onion, chopped
1 garlic clove, minced
2 tbsp. bacon drippings
1 8-oz. can tomatoes and green chilies
1 tbsp. flour
1 lb. Velveeta cheese, cut into cubes
Chili powder to taste
Dash of Worcestershire sauce
Dash of Tabasco sauce (opt.)

Saute onion and garlic in bacon drippings in saucepan until onion is tender. Drain 2 tablespoons liquid from tomatoes and green chilies; reserve. Add remaining tomatoes and green chilies to onion mixture; bring to a boil. Mix flour and reserved juice; stir into tomato mixture. Add cheese, chili powder, Worcestershire sauce and Tabasco sauce; cook, stirring, until cheese is melted. Serve with tortilla chips, tostados or corn chips.

Mrs. Brenda Hager
Waynesville, Ohio

NACHOS

10 tortillas
2 c. grated Cheddar cheese
1 sm. can jalapeno peppers

Cut each tortilla into 4 pieces; fry in deep, hot fat until crisp. Remove from fat; drain on absorbent toweling. Sprinkle cheese on each tortilla piece. Drain jalapeno peppers; cut into thin strips. Place 1 strip jalapeno pepper on each tortilla; place tortillas on baking sheet. Broil until cheese melts.

Mrs. Emily Bierschwale
Junction, Texas

Middle East

COLD MARINATED EGGPLANT

1 sm. eggplant
1/2 c. chopped celery
1/3 c. chopped pimento
1 sm. clove of garlic, minced
2 tbsp. chopped capers
2 tbsp. chopped parsley
1/8 tsp. dillweed
1/4 tsp. oregano
1/2 tsp. salt
1/8 tsp. pepper
1/3 c. salad oil
1/3 c. vinegar

Trim stem from eggplant; place in pan of boiling salted water. Cook until tender. Drain; cool. Peel and cut into 2-inch lengths. Combine remaining ingredients; mix well. Add eggplant. Cover tightly; store in refrigerator for several hours for flavors to blend. Serve cold. Yield: 6 servings.

Janell Bullard
Glenmora, Louisiana

Middle Europe

ARMENIAN RICE

1 bunch green onions, chopped
1/2 green pepper, diced
1/2 c. butter or margarine
2 c. long grain rice
2 1/2 tsp. salt

1/4 tsp. pepper
2 cans beef consomme
2 c. water

Saute onions and green pepper in butter. Stir in rice; saute until browned. Add salt, pepper, consomme and water; bring to a boil. Place in large greased casserole; cover. Bake in preheated 350-degree oven for 1 hour and 30 minutes to 2 hours. Do not uncover during baking. Diced pimento, sliced mushrooms or almonds may be added, if desired. Yield: 8 servings.

Mrs. Phyllis McFarland
Salem, Oregon

KOLACHE

1 c. scalded milk
1/2 c. shortening
3/4 c. sugar
1 tsp. salt
1 env. dry yeast
1/4 c. warm water
3 eggs, beaten
4 1/2 c. flour
2/3 c. cooked prunes
2/3 c. cooked apricots
1 sm. can crushed pineapple
1 1/2 tbsp. quick-cooking tapioca

Combine milk, shortening, 1/2 cup sugar and salt in bowl; cool to lukewarm. Dissolve yeast in warm water. Add to milk mixture; stir well. Add eggs; mix well. Add flour; mix until smooth. Knead lightly on floured board. Place in greased bowl; cover. Let rise until doubled in bulk. Shape dough into balls about 1 1/2 inches in diameter; press flat. Let rise until doubled in bulk. Make large indentation in center of each roll; place rolls on baking sheet. Combine remaining 1/4 cup sugar and remaining ingredients in saucepan. Cook over low heat, stirring, until thick. Drop by teaspoonfuls in centers of rolls; let rise until light. Bake in preheated 325-degree oven for 12 to 15 minutes or until lightly browned. Yield: 2 1/2 dozen rolls.

Mrs. Mary Witt
Buffalo, Wyoming

CHICKEN PAPRIKAS

1/2 c. chopped onion
1 clove of garlic, minced
1/4 c. oil
1 tbsp. salt
1/2 tsp. pepper
1 tbsp. paprika
1   3 to 4-lb. chicken, disjointed
1 c. sour cream

Saute onion and garlic in oil in skillet; add salt, pepper and paprika. Add chicken; brown lightly. Add 1 1/2 cups water; cover. Cook slowly for 1 hour and 30 minutes. Water should cook down; add more only if needed. Remove chicken; stir in sour cream just before serving. Pour over chicken. This dish may be served with dumplings, if desired. Yield: 6 servings.

Mrs. Gladys Heter
Langdon, Kansas

Orient

CHINESE CHICKEN WINGS

12 chicken wings
3 tbsp. butter or margarine
1 sm. onion, sliced
1   8 1/2-oz. can pineapple chunks
Orange juice
1/4 c. soy sauce
2 tbsp. brown sugar
1 tbsp. vinegar
1 tsp. ginger
1/2 tsp. salt
1/2 tsp. mace
1/2 tsp. Tabasco sauce
1/4 tsp. dry mustard
1 1/2 tbsp. cornstarch

Fold tips of wings under to form a triangle. Melt butter in large skillet; add wings and onion. Cook for about 10 minutes or until wings are brown on both sides. Drain pineapple; reserve chunks. Measure syrup; add enough orange juice to measure 1 1/4 cups liquid. Blend in soy sauce, brown sugar, vinegar, ginger, salt, mace, Tabasco sauce and dry mustard; pour over chicken. Cover; simmer for about 30 minutes or until tender, basting top pieces with liquid occasionally.

Remove wings to hot platter. Add a small amount of cold water to cornstarch; blend slowly into liquid in skillet. Add pineapple chunks. Bring to a boil, stirring constantly. Pour over wings. Serve with steamed rice.

Photograph for this recipe on page 255.

RICE-CASHEW CASSEROLE

1 med. onion, diced
1 sm. green pepper, diced
3 tbsp. butter
1 1/4 c. rice
1 sm. can mushrooms
2 cans consomme
1 sm. package cashew nuts

Saute onion and green pepper in butter in skillet until onion is tender. Add uncooked rice; stir until mixed. Add mushrooms and consomme. Pour into casserole; cover. Bake in preheated 350-degree oven for 1 hour. Stir in cashew nuts just before serving. Four beef bouillon cubes dissolved in 2 cups boiling water may be substituted for consomme.

Mrs. Marietta McIntire
Buena Park, California

FORTUNE COOKIES

3/4 c. soft butter or margarine
2 c. sugar
1 tsp. vanilla extract
3 eggs
1 c. sifted flour

Cream butter and sugar in bowl until fluffy; blend in vanilla. Add eggs, one at a time, beating well after each addition; beat in flour. Grease and flour cookie sheets. Drop 6 rounded teaspoons dough on each cookie sheet at least 2 inches apart. Bake in preheated 375-degree oven for 15 to 20 minutes or until edges are well browned. Remove from oven; loosen carefully with wide spatula. Keep pan warm. Fold each cookie in half gently, wrapping fortune inside and keeping top of cookie on outside; pinch points together. Yield: 5 dozen.

Mrs. Virginia B. McCarthy
Berryville, Arkansas

SHRIMP TEMPURA

3 or 4 drops of yellow food coloring
3/4 c. water
1 c. sifted flour
2 tsp. baking powder
2 tbsp. sugar
1 tsp. salt
1 1-lb. box frozen shrimp
Cooking oil

Combine food coloring and water. Combine flour, baking powder, sugar and salt. Stir in colored water until batter is just mixed. Clean shrimp, leaving tails. Slit along back, being careful not to cut through. Cut slits in 3 places at edges to prevent curling. Sprinkle shrimp lightly with additional salt. Place on paper towels. Dip shrimp in batter, holding each by the tail. Fry in hot deep oil until browned. Batter may also be used to make tempura sweet potatoes, string beans, carrots, celery, fish and meat. Yield: 4 servings.

Juliette Miranda
Newberg, Oregon

CHINESE SNOW PEAS WITH WATER CHESTNUTS

1 tbsp. salad oil
1 tsp. soy sauce
1 med. clove of garlic, minced
1 5-oz. can bamboo shoots
1 5-oz. can water chestnuts
1 8-oz. package frozen Chinese snow
   peas, thawed
1 chicken bouillon cube
1 tsp. cornstarch

Heat oil in skillet. Add soy sauce and garlic; cook over low heat until garlic is brown. Drain bamboo shoots and water chestnuts; slice water chestnuts. Add peas and drained vegetables to garlic mixture; cook, stirring, over high heat for 1 minute. Dissolve bouillon cube in 1/4 cup boiling water; add to pea mixture. Cover; cook over medium heat for 2 minutes. Combine cornstarch and 1 teaspoon cold water; stir into pea mixture. Cook, stirring constantly, over high heat for

1 minute or until sauce thickens. Yield: 4 servings.

Mrs. Dorothy Shirley
Live Oak, California

RUMAKI

1 lb. chicken livers
1 5-oz. can water chestnuts, sliced
12 to 14 bacon slices, cut in half
10 scallions, sliced thin lengthwise
1/2 c. soy sauce
1/4 tsp. ground ginger
1/2 tsp. curry powder

Slice chicken livers into three pieces each; fold each piece over water chestnut slice. Wrap a strip of bacon and scallion slice around liver-chestnut core, pinning each kabob with a toothpick. Combine soy sauce, ginger and curry. Marinate kabobs for 2 hours in soy sauce mixture. Drain. Place on broiler pan. Broil in preheated broiler, turning frequently, until bacon is crisp. Serve on picks.

Mrs. Dallas Sturlaugson
Maddock, North Dakota

Portugal

PORTUGUESE RISOIES

2 tbsp. oil
2 6-oz. frozen South African rock
   lobster tails, thawed
1 sm. onion, chopped
2 tbsp. chopped parsley
1/3 c. instant mashed potato granules
2 eggs, well beaten
Salt to taste
1 11-oz. package pie crust mix

Heat oil in skillet. Cut away underside membrane of lobster tails with scissors. Remove lobster meat; chop. Add lobster meat to hot oil; saute until lobster meat loses translucency. Add onion and parsley; saute over low heat for 2 minutes. Stir in instant potato granules; cool. Reserve 3 tablespoons egg to brush tops of risoies. Stir remaining egg into lobster mixture; stir in just enough water to hold ingredients together. Season with salt. Prepare pie crust mix according to package directions; roll out on floured surface to 1/8-inch thickness. Cut crust into twelve 4-inch rounds. Top each round with 1 tablespoon lobster filling; brush edges of rounds with water. Fold crust over filling to shape a half moon; crimp edges with tines of fork. Place risoies on greased cookie sheet; brush with reserved egg. Bake in preheated 400-degree oven for 15 to 20 minutes or until well browned. Risoies may be fried in 1 1/2-inch deep fat at 360 degrees. Fry 3 or 4 at a time for 2 to 3 minutes on each side; drain on absorbent paper. Serve hot. Yield: 12 risoies.

Photograph for this recipe on page 35.

Russia

RUSSIAN SOLIANKA

1/4 c. butter or margarine
1 onion, sliced
1 peeled cucumber, chopped
2 tomatoes, chopped
8 c. chicken broth
2 6-oz. frozen South African rock
   lobster tails, thawed
1 8-oz. can minced clams, undrained
2 gherkins, thinly sliced
12 pitted ripe olives, sliced
1 tbsp. capers
1 tbsp. chopped fresh dill
Salt and pepper to taste

Melt butter in large saucepan. Add onion, cucumber and tomatoes; saute for about 5 minutes. Stir in chicken broth. Cut away underside membrane of uncooked lobster tails with scissors. Insert fingers between shell and lobster meat at heavy end of tail; work lobster meat loose from shell, removing meat in 1 piece. Cut lobster meat into 1-inch thick crosswise slices. Add lobster

meat, clams, gherkins, olives, capers and dill to soup mixture; heat until soup bubbles. Season with salt and pepper. Garnish with sprigs of fresh dill. Each serving may be topped with spoons of thick sour cream, if desired. Yield: 6 servings.

Photograph for this recipe on page 35.

Scandinavia

SWEDISH ROCK LOBSTER MACARONI

1 8-oz. package med. noodles
1 c. elbow macaroni
2 6-oz. frozen South African rock
   lobster tails
1/4 c. butter or margarine
1/2 c. flour
3 c. chicken broth
2 c. half and half
1/4 c. white wine
Salt and pepper to taste
1 c. grated sharp Cheddar cheese
1/4 c. dry bread crumbs
1/4 c. melted butter or margarine

Cook noodles and macaroni according to package directions; drain well. Mix noodles and macaroni in 3-quart casserole. Drop frozen lobster tails into boiling, salted water. Bring to a boil; boil for 5 minutes. Drain immediately; drench with cold water. Cut away underside membrane with scissors; pull out lobster meat in 1 piece. Cut lobster meat into 1/2-inch crosswise slices; add to noodles mixture. Melt butter in saucepan; stir in flour. Stir in chicken broth and half and half gradually; stir in wine. Cook over low heat, stirring, until smooth and thickened; season with salt and pepper. Pour sauce evenly over casserole; mix gently. Combine remaining ingredients in bowl; mix with fingers until crumbly. Sprinkle crumbs around edge of casserole. Bake in preheated 350-degree oven for 35 to 40 minutes or until well browned and bubbly. Yield: 6 servings.

Photograph for this recipe on page 35.

SWEDISH PANCAKES

2 eggs, beaten
2 c. milk
2 tbsp. melted butter
1 c. sifted all-purpose flour
1/4 tsp. salt
1/4 tsp. sugar

Combine eggs, milk and butter; beat well. Sift dry ingredients together; add gradually to milk mixture, beating constantly. Pour 3 tablespoons batter for each cake onto hot griddle; bake until top is bubbly and edges look cooked. Turn and cook until remaining side is brown. Fill with jelly, preserves or fruit. Roll in confectioners' sugar or serve with butter and syrup. Yield: 16-18 pancakes.

Photograph for this recipe above.

SWEDISH CANAPES

1 8-oz. package cream cheese, softened
1 tbsp. horseradish
6 slices crisp bacon, crumbled
Dash of salt
Garlic salt to taste
Thin crisp toast or crackers

Mash cream cheese; stir in horseradish, bacon, salt and garlic salt. Spread on toast; garnish with paprika or sliced olives, if desired.

Mrs. Don Dubbe
Sturgis, South Dakota

SCRAMBLED EGGS WITH CRAB MEAT-MUSHROOM SAUCE

1 6 1/2-oz. can king crab meat, drained
1/2 c. undiluted cream of mushroom soup
1/4 c. light cream
1 tsp. lemon juice
2 tbsp. sherry (opt.)
4 eggs
1/4 c. milk
Salt and pepper to taste
2 tbsp. butter or margarine

1 tbsp. finely chopped parsley
Toast triangles

Remove all cartilage from crab meat. Combine soup and cream in small saucepan; bring to a boil, stirring constantly. Stir in crab meat, lemon juice and sherry; heat through. Cover; keep warm. Place eggs, milk, salt and pepper in medium bowl; beat with rotary beater until combined. Melt butter in medium skillet over low heat. Pour in egg mixture; lift cooked portion gently with spatula, letting uncooked portion flow to bottom of skillet. Cook to desired doneness; remove to heated serving platter. Sprinkle with parsley. Surround eggs with toast; serve with crab meat sauce. Yield: 2-3 servings.

Mrs. Sue Purcell
New Deal, Texas

South American

SHRIMP SOUFFLE

3 c. milk
1 c. flour
Pinch of salt
1/2 c. chopped walnuts
1/4 lb. American cheese, grated
1 tbsp. butter, melted
2 1/2 lb. shrimp, cooked and cut up
6 eggs, separated

Stir milk into flour gradually in saucepan until smooth; add salt, walnuts, cheese and butter. Stir in shrimp and beaten egg yolks. Cook over low heat, stirring constantly, until slightly thickened. Fold in stiffly beaten egg whites. Place in a casserole. Bake in preheated 350-degree oven until souffle rises and is slightly brown. Yield: 6-8 servings.

Mrs. Doris Balbach
Warren, Illinois

SEVICHE

1/2 lb. whitefish, diced
Lemon or lime juice
1 med. onion, chopped

1 med. tomato, chopped
1/2 green pepper, chopped
1 hot pepper, chopped
1/2 c. vinegar
1/8 c. cooking oil
Oregano to taste
Catsup to taste

Place fish in shallow dish; cover with lemon juice, coating well. Let stand for 1 hour. Combine onion, tomato, green pepper and hot pepper. Combine vinegar, oil and oregano in saucepan; simmer for about 5 minutes. Cool. Drain lemon juice from fish; place fish in serving bowl. Add onion mixture and vinegar mixture. Stir in catsup. Chill well; serve with crackers. Yield: 4 servings.

Mrs. Billie Garner
Hurst, Texas

Spain

TRADITIONAL GAZPACHO

1 clove of garlic, split
1/2 tsp. salt
2 tbsp. olive oil
5 ripe tomatoes, chopped
1 onion, chopped
1/4 tsp. pepper
1/4 tsp. paprika
1 1/2 tsp. vinegar
1 1/2 c. cold water or bouillon
1/4 c. dry bread crumbs
Croutons
Chopped cucumber
Chopped green pepper

Crush garlic. Add salt, olive oil, tomatoes, onion, pepper, paprika, vinegar and water; let stand for 1 hour. Put through a food mill or force through a coarse strainer. Add more salt, if needed. Stir in bread crumbs. Pour into 4 soup bowls or 6 bouillon cups; place ice cube in each bowl. Sprinkle with croutons, cucumber and green pepper. Serve immediately. Yield: 4-6 servings.

Alice Eavey Britt
Chesapeake, Virginia

Holiday Favorites

Almost all people in the world have a calendar full of unique celebrations peculiar to their culture. The Germans have their beer fests, the Japanese celebrate the seasons, while the Spanish celebrate Holy Week in Seville and a bullfight fiesta in Pamplona. The Scandanavians, who have long, dark winter days, celebrate the sun: the Norwegians on January 21, the Swedes in June and the Finns on May Day.

The United States, as the melting pot for so many of these people, has its own outstanding series of holidays, too. From Friendship Day in August, all through the year to Independence Day on July 4, there is one or more days in each month set aside for commemoration of some event or some person.

Some of these commemorative days have been family affairs for decades. In our modern, mobile society, with family members often scattered far afield, sons and daughters, relatives and in-laws travel many long miles to be with the rest of their family on important occasions — maybe for the first time in a year. They travel in happy anticipation, full of expectations about the people they will see, the stories they will hear and the familiar, appetizing foods that they will get to enjoy again.

Christmas is probably the most loved holiday in all the year, with more gaiety, bustle, anticipation and excitement than at any other time. Boxes full of sparkling decorations get pulled from the attic, furniture is moved back to make room for the tree and the smell of myriad home-baked goodies pervades every room in the house.

Christmas entertaining, the planned and spontaneous events alike, is always a success because happiness is in the air, decorations are up and plenty of special food is on hand. A rich batch of hot chocolate or eggnog can be whipped up in no time, and the traditional Christmas Eve Wassail Bowl waits in the house to welcome carolers and friends. Christmas dinner is the high point of the whole season. Family members gather around the table to bless the birthday of Jesus Christ and to enjoy the love and friendship they share. The table is laden with favorite holiday meats such as turkey and dressing, ham, stuffed goose or rib roast and Yorkshire pudding. Favorite vegetables include creamed onions, peas and mushrooms, rutabagas, asparagus and sweet potato souffle. The meal ends with special desserts like Lane cake, German chocolate cake, ambrosia, Charlotte russe and fruitcake. A family meal at this time of the year is important because it brings everyone together for a happy reason, and it gives children and adults both warm memories to carry with them for the rest of their lives.

Thanksgiving comes at a quiet time, in the fall of the year. The summer is over, the harvests are in and the end of a busy year beckons. The leaves are turning gay colors and falling in bright, crackling array onto the ground, and there is an unseen energy in the autumn air. In the midst of all this, families gather together to give thanks for the bounty and blessings of another year.

The traditional menu for the Thanksgiving dinner is reminiscent of the foods that the Pilgrims gave thanks for in October of 1621, after that first grueling year in their new land. Although Thanksgiving then was hardly the grand feast it has since become, the bounty of the new land did offer pumpkins, wild turkey and game, cranberries, corn, beans and fish. Our repast of turkey and dressing, cranberry salad and pumpkin pie reflects the meal that the Pilgrims shared with their Indian friends. But the modern Thanksgiving Dinner has also come to reflect the bounty of our modern age. Todays menus include broccoli, avocados, domestic and imported wines, and fruits and desserts that the Pilgrims would never know of. Thanksgiving should continue to be celebrated in this way, because it reminds us of our rich and humble heritage, and helps us to look to the future with anticipation and thanksgiving.

Many of our customary holidays are religious in nature and origin, and Easter is one holiday that has remained that way, more so than any of the others. The Easter season is also the harbinger of spring, as are the traditional Easter foods, lamb and eggs. Little girls get new dresses in soft, spring colors, and young boys squirm uncomfortably in brand new suits. The table shines with bright spring flowers. After church services, families come home to a delicious Easter meal of roast lamb or baked ham and stuffed eggs, made from the brightly colored eggs left by the Easter bunny. Pear or carrot salad, spinach, eggplant or fresh garden peas accompany the meat. White and yellow cakes sprightly decorated with pastel-tinted coconut and sugar cookies cut into seasonal shapes serve as dessert.

The Fourth of July is a true celebration in every sense of the word. Not just families, but entire communities gather together and have parades, firework displays and speeches. They attend picnics and family reunions featuring swimming, sack races, tug of war, horseshoes, and of course, delicious foods appropriate for hot weather and hungry people. Typical Fourth of July foods include barbecue, baked, chilled ham slices, hearty potato salad, juicy tomato slices, and unforgettable homemade ice cream served with sweet, fresh delicious fruit.

For most areas, Labor Day marks the end of summer and all its activity. In order to get in a little more vacation fun, families get in their cars and travel to the beaches, the lakes and the mountains, loaded with all they need, including plenty of food. Because so much of the activity is centered outdoors, foods that can be made ahead or cooked over charcoal are the favorites. Onions, carrots and corn are wrapped in aluminum foil and roasted in the coals while fresh fish, chicken, shish kabobs or hamburgers cook above. Fruit salads and baked beans often accompany the meal, while brownies, apple pie or strawberry shortcake often serve as dessert.

With horns blowing, bells ringing and balloons popping, friends and families gather together to bring in the New Year. Father Time is featured at New Year's parties, along with delicious and festive hors d'oeuvres, fondues, snacks and punches. After the strains of Auld Lang Syne die down, partygoers return home for a short night's sleep and awaken the next day to a traditional New Year's Day meal.

Halloween, that spooky night filled with goblins, ghosts, witches and black cats is a good time to give an imaginative party. Both children and adults can escape for awhile into a make believe world of weird costumes, eerie decorations and scary stories. It is also a good time to serve unique party refreshments like popcorn balls, candy apples, spicy punch, chips, dips and doughnuts.

Valentine's Day comes in the deep of winter, and what better way to break the monotonous days than to set one aside for romance! It is the perfect time to surprise loved ones with a special Valentine's Day meal that says I Love You. Decorate the table with the symbolic colors and shapes, and serve a heart-shaped gelatin salad or aspic. Say I Love You for dessert, with a pink-frosted angel food cake decorated with candy hearts.

Saint Patrick's Day, as well as Washington's and Lincoln's birthdays are also traditional commemorative days that suggest their own menu and decorating themes. In this section, Home Economics Teachers want to help you make the most out of each and every holiday.

New Year's

HOT ONION APPETIZERS

1/2 c. butter
1/2 pkg. dry onion soup mix
1   10-count pkg. refrigerator biscuits

Melt butter in electric skillet at 150 degrees. Add soup mix; stir well. Cut biscuits into quarters; place in skillet. Cover skillet. Cook at 275 degrees for about 20 minutes or until brown, turning once. Reduce heat to lowest setting; keep warm. Serve hot with toothpicks. Shake package of soup mix before measuring.

Betty Hagberg
Chisago City, Minnesota

LIVER PATE

1 med. onion
1/2 lb. liver, cut in strips
1/4 c. butter
1 tsp. salt
1/2 tsp. pepper
1 tbsp. red wine
2 hard-cooked eggs, separated

Cut onion into eighths. Saute onion and liver in butter until liver is just done, stirring frequently; place in blender container. Add salt, pepper, wine and egg whites; cover. Process at high speed until smooth, scraping side of blender container with rubber spatula frequently. Place in serving bowl. Blend egg yolks until chopped fine; sprinkle over pate.

Mrs. Kathleen Burns
Mahtomedi, Minnesota

WINTER TOSSED SALAD

1 red onion
4 oranges
1 head iceberg lettuce
1/2 sm. head curly endive
Juice of 1 lemon
1/4 tsp. garlic salt
1 tbsp. grated Parmesan cheese
2 tbsp. light salad oil
Salt and pepper to taste

Peel onion; slice and separate into rings. Peel and section oranges. Combine iceberg lettuce, endive, onion rings and orange sections in large bowl. Toss gently. Combine lemon juice, garlic salt, Parmesan cheese, salad oil, salt and pepper in jar. Cover; shake to mix well. Pour over salad; toss and serve. Yield: 8 servings.

Mrs. Doris W. Larke
Peoria, Illinois

OLD ENGLISH PRIME RIB

2 tbsp. Worcestershire sauce
1 tsp. paprika
1 tsp. monosodium glutamate
Salt and pepper to taste
Choice prime or standing rib roast,
    1/2 lb. per serving
Ice cream salt

Combine Worcestershire sauce, paprika, monosodium glutamate, salt and pepper; rub into roast. Line heavy roasting pan with aluminum foil; cover with layer of ice cream salt. Dampen salt lightly with water until just moist. Place roast on salt in standing rib position. Cover roast completely with ice cream salt; repeat dampening procedure. Do not cover. Bake in preheated 500-degree oven for 12 to 20 minutes per pound, depending on degree of doneness desired. Remove from oven. Crack salt with mallet; pull salt sections away from meat. Brush all salt particles from roast. Place roast on serving platter; cut into serving portions.

Mrs. Estella Hottel
Dimmitt, Texas

CURRIED OYSTER CASSEROLE

2 c. Uncle Ben's long grain and wild
    rice
1/2 c. melted butter
4 doz. oysters
Salt and pepper to taste
1 can cream of chicken soup
1 c. light cream
1 1/2 tbsp. onion powder

3/4 tsp. thyme
1 tbsp. curry powder
1/4 c. hot water

Cook rice according to package directions; combine with butter. Place half the rice in casserole; add half the oysters. Season with salt and pepper; repeat layers. Combine soup, cream, onion powder, thyme, curry powder and hot water in saucepan; heat through. Pour over oysters. Bake in preheated 300-degree oven for 45 minutes.

Mrs. Virginia O. Savedge
Eastville, Virginia

WINE POTATOES

5 or 6 lg. potatoes
Salt and pepper to taste
1/2 c. cubed Cheddar cheese
1/2 c. minced white onion
1 can golden mushroom soup
1/2 c. white cooking wine

Pare and slice potatoes; arrange half the slices in a greased casserole. Season with salt and pepper. Sprinkle 1/2 of the cheese and 1/2 of the onion over potatoes. Spoon half the soup over top, then pour half the wine over soup. Repeat layers; cover casserole. Bake in preheated 400-degree oven for 1 hour. Remove cover; bake for 15 minutes longer.

Mrs. Nora Foster
St. Joseph, Missouri

EGGNOG CAKE

1 doz. macaroons
1 lg. angel food cake
1/2 lb. butter
Powdered sugar
5 egg yolks, beaten
1 c. chopped toasted almonds
Bourbon
Rum
1/2 tsp. almond extract
1 c. heavy cream, whipped

Toast and grind macaroons. Slice cake horizontally into 4 layers. Cream butter and 1 3/4 cups powdered sugar thoroughly. Add egg yolks; mix well. Stir in 3/4 cup almonds, 1/3 to 1/2 cup bourbon, 2 to 3 tablespoons rum, almond extract and macaroons. Spread between layers of cake; place layers together. Cover; refrigerate overnight. Add 2 tablespoons powdered sugar to whipped cream slowly; stir in 2 teaspoons rum or bourbon. Frost cake with cream mixture; garnish with remaining 1/4 cup almonds. Refrigerate until served. Yield: 15-20 servings.

Nancy McLain
Commerce, Texas

Lincoln and Washington's Birthday

SOUR CREAM MEAT PIES

1 1/2 c. lean hamburger
1 c. finely chopped mushrooms
1 lg. onion, finely chopped
3 tbsp. butter
1 1/2 c. sour cream
1 1/2 tsp. salt
1/4 tsp. pepper
2 c. flour
1 tbsp. sugar
1/2 c. shortening
1 egg, separated

Saute hamburger, mushrooms and onion in butter until hamburger is lightly browned. Remove from heat; stir in 1/2 cup sour cream, 1/2 teaspoon salt and pepper. Mix flour, remaining salt and sugar in bowl; cut in shortening. Mix egg yolk and remaining sour cream. Add to flour mixture; mix well. Roll out on floured surface; cut into circles with sour cream carton. Place 1 heaping teaspoon filling in middle of each circle of pastry. Fold over; seal edges. Mix egg white with 1 tablespoon water; brush over pies. Place on baking sheet. Bake in preheated 400-degree oven for 15 to 20 minutes. Chopped, cooked roast may be substituted for hamburger. Yield: 1 1/2 dozen.

Mrs. Judy Stetson
Alberta, Canada

BY GEORGE CHERRY LOGS

1 env. unflavored gelatine
6 tbsp. sugar
2 eggs, separated
1 c. milk
1/2 c. maraschino cherry syrup
1 tsp. vanilla extract
1 c. heavy cream, whipped
1/2 c. chopped maraschino cherries
Grated sweet cooking chocolate

Combine gelatine and 2 tablespoons sugar in medium saucepan. Beat egg yolks, milk and syrup together; stir into gelatine mixture. Place over low heat; cook for about 5 minutes or until gelatine dissolves, stirring constantly. Remove from heat; stir in vanilla extract. Chill, stirring occasionally, until mixture mounds slightly when dropped from spoon. Beat egg whites in medium bowl until soft peaks form. Add remaining sugar gradually; beat until stiff but not dry. Fold in gelatine mixture, cream and cherries; turn into eight 6-ounce metal juice cans. Chill until firm. Dip cans in warm water; loosen sides with sharp knife to unmold. Sprinkle chocolate over piece of waxed paper; place cherry roll on chocolate. Roll to coat sides by lifting ends of paper; tranfer carefully to dessert plate with large spatula. Repeat with remaining rolls. Garnish with additional cherries, if desired. Yield: 8 servings.

Photograph for this recipe on page 260.

MINUTEMAN BROCCOLI CASSEROLE

2   10-oz. packages frozen broccoli
     spears
1 can cream of mushroom soup
2 eggs, well beaten
1 c. grated sharp cheese
1 med. onion, chopped fine
1 c. mayonnaise
1/2 pkg. Pepperidge Farm stuffing mix
Butter

Cook broccoli according to package directions; drain. Place in casserole. Combine soup, eggs, cheese, onion and mayonnaise; pour over broccoli. Sprinkle with stuffing mix; dot with butter. Bake in preheated 350-degree oven for 25 to 30 minutes or until bubbly. Yield: 5-6 servings.

Mrs. Frances VanLandingham
Snow Hill, North Carolina

SOURDOUGH BISCUITS

1 c. Starter
3 tbsp. soft shortening
Pinch of soda
Flour

Place Starter in large mixing bowl; add shortening. Stir soda into 1/4 cup warm water; add to Starter mixture quickly. Add enough flour to form stiff dough. Roll out on lightly floured board; cut with biscuit cutter. Place in greased baking pan; let rise for 20 to 30 minutes. Bake in preheated 400-degree oven for 15 minutes or until done.

Starter

1 pkg. yeast
Sugar
1 tbsp. salt
Sifted flour

Sprinkle yeast over 1/2 cup warm water; stir until dissolved. Place in large mixing bowl. Add 1 tablespoon sugar, salt, 2 cups warm water and 2 cups flour; mix well. Cover; let stand for 3 days, stirring daily. Add 1 cup warm water, 1 1/2 cups flour and 1 teaspoon sugar to Starter after a portion has been used. Cover; let stand at room temperature. Stir daily to keep Starter active.

Mrs. Pat Bandy
Stephenville, Texas

DOUBLE CHERRY PIE

2 c. frozen pitted tart cherries
1 c. frozen pitted dark sweet cherries
1/4 c. sugar
2 1/3 tbsp. quick-cooking tapioca
1 1/2 tbsp. cornstarch
Pastry for 2-crust pie
1 tsp. lemon juice

Thaw cherries; drain, reserving juices. Mix sugar, tapioca and cornstarch in saucepan; add 2/3 cup reserved tart cherry juice and 1/3 cup reserved sweet cherry juice. Mix well. Cook over high heat until thickened; cool. Line 9-inch pie pan with half the pastry. Add cherries and lemon juice to tapioca mixture; pour into pastry-lined pie pan. Cover with remaining pastry; make slits in top with knife. Bake in preheated 425-degree oven for 30 to 35 minutes or until browned. Bake on lowest oven shelf for brown undercrust.

Jo Nita Schwarz
Miles, Texas

Valentine's

SAVORY BUTTERED SHRIMP APPETIZERS

1 clove of garlic, minced
2 tbsp. lemon juice
Basil and rosemary to taste
1/2 tsp. salt
1/4 tsp. pepper
Tabasco sauce to taste
1 c. melted butter or margarine
2 lb. shrimp, peeled and deveined

Combine seasonings and butter. Place shrimp in shallow pan. Broil for 5 minutes. Spoon butter sauce over shrimp; broil for 5 to 8 minutes longer. Serve immediately. Yield: 8 servings.

Mrs. Susan McAlexander
Abernathy, Texas

EASY VEAL CORDON BLEU

8 3-oz. tenderized veal steaks
4 thin slices ham
4 slices Swiss or Monterey Jack cheese
1 egg
1 tbsp. water
Salt and pepper to taste
Garlic salt and onion salt to taste
1 c. cracker crumbs
1/2 c. vegetable oil
1 c. medium white sauce

1 c. sliced mushrooms
1 tbsp. grated onion

Layer 1 veal steak, 1 slice ham, 1 slice cheese and top with another veal steak for each of 4 stacks; trim edges of ham and cheese to make slices smaller than steaks. Press edges together securely. Beat egg with water. Dip steak stacks into egg mixture. Sprinkle with salt, pepper, garlic salt and onion salt; roll in crumbs. Heat oil in heavy frypan. Fry on each side until golden brown; transfer to casserole. Bake in preheated 325-degree oven for 30 minutes or until done. Combine white sauce, mushrooms and onion in saucepan; cook, stirring, for about 3 minutes or until bubbly. Serve over veal steak stacks.

Mrs. Dorothy Wuertz
Los Angeles, California

PINK MERINGUE HEARTS

3 egg whites
1 tsp. vanilla
1/4 tsp. cream of tartar
Dash of salt
1 c. sugar
Red food coloring
1 qt. vanilla ice cream
1 pt. fresh strawberries, sliced and
    sweetened

Beat egg whites with vanilla, cream of tartar and salt until frothy. Add sugar, a small amount at a time, beating until stiff peaks form and sugar is dissolved. Add enough food coloring to make a delicate pink tint. Cut heart pattern from 4 1/2-inch square of paper. Cover baking sheet with brown paper; draw 6 hearts on brown paper from pattern. Spread meringue over each heart shape, making 1/4-inch thick layer. Pipe rim about 3/4 inch high with pastry tube. Bake in preheated 275-degree oven for 1 hour. Turn off heat; let meringues dry in oven for 1 hour for crisper meringues. Fill meringues with scoops of vanilla ice cream; top with strawberries. One 10-ounce package frozen strawberries, thawed, may be substituted for fresh strawberries.

Mrs. Kay Nemetz
Brussels, Wisconsin

DELICIOUS STUFFED MUSHROOMS

24 med. mushrooms
2 tbsp. butter
1 tbsp. minced onion
1/2 c. herb-seasoned stuffing mix
1/4 c. chopped almonds
4 strips fried bacon, drained and crumbled
1/4 tsp. salt
Chicken broth

Wash and dry mushrooms. Remove and chop stems. Heat butter. Add mushroom stems and onion to butter; saute until tender. Combine stuffing mix, almonds, bacon and salt; stir in enough broth to moisten. Fill mushroom caps; place in shallow baking dish. Bake in preheated 350-degree oven for 8 to 10 minutes or until heated through.

Margenia F. Keeton
Burkesville, Kentucky

St. Patrick's Day

BAKED CORNED BEEF WITH PEPPERED CABBAGE

1   3 to 4-lb. corned beef brisket
3/4 c. sugar
1/2 tsp. ginger
1/2 tsp. cloves
1/2 tsp. dry mustard
1 tbsp. honey
1 med. head white cabbage, grated
1/4 c. butter
2 tbsp. sour cream
Dash of salt
1 tsp. freshly ground pepper

Boil beef brisket in enough water to cover for 2 to 3 hours or until tender. Remove from water; trim off excess fat. Place in roasting pan. Mix sugar, ginger, cloves, mustard and honey; spread over beef. Bake in preheated 325-degree oven for 25 to 30 minutes. Saute cabbage in butter for 2 to 3 minutes or until tender-crisp, stirring constantly. Stir in sour cream; season with salt and pep-

per. Serve with corned beef. Yield: 6 servings.

Margery Juk
Warren, Michigan

HOT BROCCOLI DIP

3 stalks celery, finely chopped
1/2 lg. onion, chopped
1 sm. can mushrooms, drained
Margarine
1 pkg. frozen chopped broccoli
1 can mushroom soup
1 6-oz. roll garlic cheese spread

Saute celery, onion and mushrooms in small amount of margarine until onion is tender. Cook broccoli according to package directions; drain well. Combine celery mixture, broccoli and soup; mix well. Melt cheese in double boiler; stir in broccoli mixture. Place in fondue pot; serve with cubes of French bread, if desired.

Mrs. Jane Silvey
Ft. Worth, Texas

ST. PATRICK'S DAY SCONES

1 1/2 c. sifted flour
3 tsp. baking powder
1/2 tsp. salt
Sugar
1/3 c. shortening
1/2 c. quick-cooking rolled oats
2/3 c. milk
1 tsp. melted butter
Cinnamon to taste

Sift flour, baking powder, salt and 2 tablespoons sugar into mixing bowl; cut in shortening. Add oats and milk; stir just until blended. Form dough into ball. Divide into 3 parts; press each part into a circle. Spread each circle with melted butter; sprinkle with 1 teaspoon sugar and cinnamon. Arrange on cookie sheet. Bake in preheated 450-degree oven for 12 to 15 minutes or until well browned.

Mary Bray
Clinton, New York

Recipes on pages 279 and 280.

Recipes on pages 280, 281 and 284.

CREAMY CHEESE POTATOES

1 1/4 c. milk
1   8-oz. package cream cheese, softened
1 tbsp. snipped chives
1/2 tsp. instant minced onion
1/4 tsp. salt
4 c. cubed cooked potatoes
Paprika

Blend milk with cream cheese in medium saucepan; place over heat. Stir in chives, onion and salt. Add potatoes; stir carefully to coat. Turn into 1 1/2-quart casserole; sprinkle with paprika. Bake in preheated 350-degree oven for 30 minutes.

Jane A. Bower
Crescent City, California

Easter

BUNNY SALAD

Lettuce leaves
5 pear halves, chilled
10 raisins
5 red cinnamon candies
10 blanched almonds
Cottage cheese

Place lettuce leaves on plate; arrange pears on lettuce, cut side down, with narrow end of each pear toward center of plate. Place 2 raisins on each pear half for eyes; place 1 cinnamon candy on each half for nose. Use 2 almonds for ears; shape tail with 1 spoon cottage cheese.

Hazel Pielemeier
Loogootee, Indiana

SAVORY FRESH HAM ROAST

2 tsp. salt
1 tsp. pepper
1 tsp. paprika
1/4 tsp. garlic salt
1 tsp. rosemary leaves
1 tbsp. steak sauce

Recipe on page 125.
Recipe on page 220.

1   12-lb. fresh pork ham, boned
1/3 c. chopped parsley
1/3 c. chopped black olives
1/3 c. chopped green onions
3 canned pimentos, chopped

Combine salt, pepper, paprika, garlic salt, rosemary leaves and steak sauce; rub half the mixture on inside of pork. Combine remaining ingredients; stuff pimento mixture inside pork. Tie securely. Score fat and skin; rub remaining salt mixture on outside of pork. Place roast, fat side up, on rack in shallow baking pan. Roast in preheated 325-degree oven to 185 degrees on meat thermometer or for 4 hours and 30 minutes.

Karen L. LeClair
Olivet, Michigan

EASY EASTER BREAD

1 pkg. yeast
1/4 c. warm water
1   3-oz. package instant lemon pudding
   mix
1/4 c. margarine, softened
1/2 tsp. salt
3/4 c. scalded milk
4 to 4 1/2 c. flour
4 eggs
Multicolored sprinkles

Dissolve yeast in warm water. Mix pudding mix, margarine and salt in bowl; pour milk over pudding mixture. Mix until margarine is melted and pudding is dissolved; cool to lukewarm. Add 1 1/2 cups flour; mix well. Beat in yeast and 3 eggs with electric mixer; add enough remaining flour gradually to make soft dough. Turn out on floured surface; let rest for 10 minutes. Knead for 10 minutes; place in greased bowl. Let rise for 1 hour. Divide into 6 equal parts; shape each part into rope. Make 2 braids, using 3 ropes for each; place in circle in 2 greased 9-inch round cake pans. Let rise for 1 hour in warm place. Beat remaining egg with 1 tablespoon water; brush on braids. Shake sprinkles over braids. Bake in preheated 375-degree oven for 25 minutes or until bread tests done.

Mrs. Charlotte Van Arum
Rochester, New York

FRESH COCONUT CAKE

3/4 c. butter
3 c. sugar
4 eggs, separated
3 c. flour
3 1/2 tsp. baking powder
1 tsp. vanilla extract
1 c. milk
3 egg whites
1 coconut, grated fine

Cream butter with 2 cups sugar until light and fluffy; add beaten egg yolks. Sift flour and baking powder together; add vanilla extract to milk. Add flour mixture to butter mixture alternately with milk, beginning and ending with the flour mixture. Fold in 4 stiffly beaten egg whites carefully. Divide batter into 3 greased and floured cake pans. Bake in preheated 350-degree oven for 30 minutes or until done. Let cool. Beat remaining 3 egg whites until soft peaks form; add remaining 1 cup sugar gradually, beating constantly. Beat until stiff. Reserve part of coconut to decorate top and side of cake; fold remaining coconut into egg white mixture. Stack layers together with frosting; frost side and top of cake. Sprinkle reserved coconut on top of cake; pat onto side.

Ruth F. Thompson
El Paso, Texas

Fourth of July

CHEESE TIDBITS

1 c. margarine, softened
2 c. grated sharp Cheddar cheese
2 c. flour
2 c. Rice Krispies
1/4 tsp. red pepper
1/2 tsp. salt

Combine all ingredients; mix well. Form into small balls; place on cookie sheet. Press down with fork in crisscross fashion. Bake in preheated 325-degree oven for 20 minutes.

Mrs. Ruth M. Wilson
Beaumont, Texas

STRAWBERRY-LEMONADE PUNCH

1   12-oz. can frozen pink lemonade
     concentrate
1   6-oz. can frozen orange juice
     concentrate
1   10-oz. package frozen sliced
     strawberries
1 qt. bottle ginger ale, chilled
Vodka (opt.)

Reconstitute lemonade and orange juice according to package directions. Add strawberries; refrigerate until ready to serve. Pour lemonade mixture into punch bowl; add ginger ale slowly. Add desired amount of vodka; stir well.

Mrs. Jane K. Marsh
Delta, British Columbia, Canada

FREEZER ICE CREAM

2 sm. packages vanilla pudding mix
Milk
3 c. sugar
1 tbsp. vanilla extract
1/2 tsp. salt
6 eggs, well beaten

Prepare pudding mix according to package directions, using 3 cups milk; cook until thickened. Add sugar gradually; add vanilla and salt. Add pudding mixture to eggs, beating constantly; pour into freezer container. Add milk until container is 2/3 full. Freeze according to manufacturer's directions. Cream may be substituted for milk used to fill container, if desired. Yield: 1 1/2 gallons.

Jean Searcy
Silver Lake, Kansas

FIRECRACKERS FOR AN
OLD-FASHIONED FOURTH

1 recipe potato salad
12 slices boiled ham
Parsley

Place 2 rounded tablespoons potato salad in center of each slice of boiled ham. Roll up;

secure with toothpicks. Stick a small sprig of parsley in one end of each roll for a fuse.

Mrs. Phyllis Fry
Orrville, Ohio

VANILLA FLAG CAKE

2 1/2 c. all-purpose flour
2 tsp. baking powder
1/4 tsp. salt
1 1/2 c. butter or margarine, softened
2 c. sugar
6 eggs, separated
2 tbsp. vanilla extract
2 tbsp. lemon juice
Vanilla Cream Cheese Frosting
Fresh blueberries
Fresh strawberries, sliced

Combine flour, baking powder and salt; set aside. Cream butter and 1 cup sugar in the large bowl of an electric mixer until light and fluffy. Beat in egg yolks, 2 at a time, until mixture is well blended. Blend in flour mixture gradually with electric mixer at low speed until just blended. Blend in vanilla ex-tract and lemon juice. Beat egg whites until soft peaks form; add remaining 1 cup sugar gradually. Beat until egg whites are stiff but not dry. Fold egg white mixture into cake batter just until blended. Pour into greased and lined 13 x 9 x 2-inch baking pan. Bake in preheated 325-degree oven for 1 hour or until cake tester inserted in center comes out clean. Cool cake in pan or rack for 10 min-utes. Remove from pan to rack; cool com-pletely. Frost top and sides of cake with Vanilla Cream Cheese Frosting. Decorate top of cake with blueberries and strawberries to resemble the American flag.

Vanilla Cream Cheese Frosting

1 8-oz. package cream cheese, softened
1 tbsp. vanilla extract
1 tbsp. milk
1 1-lb. package confectioners' sugar

Combine cream cheese, vanilla extract and milk; beat until blended. Add confectioners' sugar gradually; beat until creamy.

Photograph for this recipe above.

Labor Day

GREEN BEANS IN SOUR CREAM DRESSING

1 onion, thinly sliced
3 cans Blue Lake beans, drained
1 can water chestnuts
1 tbsp. salad oil
1 tbsp. vinegar
Coarsely ground pepper to taste
Salt to taste
1 c. sour cream
1/2 c. mayonnaise
1 tsp. lemon juice
1/4 tsp. dry mustard
1 tbsp. horseradish

Place onion slices over beans in container. Drain and slice water chestnuts; place over onion slices. Add oil, vinegar, pepper and salt; refrigerate for 1 hour or longer. Drain well. Combine remaining ingredients; season with salt. Add to bean mixture; mix well. Refrigerate for at least 12 hours before serving.

Mrs. Martha Dunlap
Corsicana, Texas

FISH IN BEER BATTER

1 c. flour
1 c. beer
1 egg, beaten
1 tsp. salt
1 tsp. baking powder
Fish
Shortening or butter

Combine flour, beer, egg, salt and baking powder in bowl; beat lightly. Dip fish into batter to coat well. Fry in hot shortening until brown.

Mrs. Marilyn Fritch
Wauwatosa, Wisconsin

POTATO SCALLOP LYONNAISE

5 or 6 potatoes, sliced
2 c. grated Cheddar cheese
1 lg. onion, sliced
Salt and pepper to taste
Margarine
1 1/2 tbsp. flour
Milk

Arrange a layer of potatoes in 2-quart casserole; sprinkle with a layer of cheese. Spread with layer of onion. Season with salt and pepper; dot with margarine. Sprinkle with flour. Repeat layers until all ingredients are used. Pour in enough milk to cover potatoes; cover. Bake in preheated 350-degree oven for 1 hour. Uncover; bake for 30 minutes longer or until potatoes are tender. Yield: 6 servings.

Mrs. Carolyn Martin
Eau Gallie, Florida

HUSH PUPPIES

1 c. cornmeal
1/2 c. all-purpose flour
1 1/2 tsp. baking powder
1 tsp. garlic salt
1/2 tsp. salt
1 egg, beaten
1 c. milk
Oil

Sift cornmeal, flour, baking powder, garlic salt and salt together in bowl. Add egg and milk to cornmeal mixture; stir until well mixed. Let stand for 5 minutes; add more milk, if needed. Drop by small spoonfuls into hot oil in skillet. Fry until golden brown; drain on paper toweling.

Margaret Hefner Peden
Raeford, North Carolina

LABORER'S BLUEBERRY CAKE

1/2 c. butter
1 c. flour
1 c. sugar
1/4 tsp. salt
1 tbsp. baking powder
2/3 c. milk
1 can blueberry pie filling

Melt butter in baking dish. Combine remaining ingredients except pie filling; pour into baking dish. Pour pie filling over top of flour mixture; do not stir. Bake in preheated 350-degree oven for about 45 minutes or cake tests done.

Mary R. Abney
Bay Springs, Mississippi

Halloween

FLYING WITCH CAKE

1 pkg. yellow cake mix
2 eggs
Orange food coloring
3 sq. unsweetened chocolate
3 tbsp. sugar
1 pkg. orange butter frosting
1 1/2 tsp. butter

Mix cake mix with 1 1/4 cups water and eggs; reserve 1 cup batter. Add enough food coloring to remaining batter for desired shade. Melt 1 1/2 squares chocolate in double boiler. Add sugar and 3 tablespoons water; mix until sugar is dissolved. Blend into reserved batter. Spoon batters alternately into 2 greased and floured 8-inch square pans; marbleize with knife. Bake in preheated 350-degree oven for about 30 minutes or until done. Cool in pans on racks for 10 minutes. Remove from pans; cool on racks. Prepare orange butter frosting according to package directions; spread between layers and on top and sides of cake. Cut paper pattern of witch; trace outline of witch on frosting with tip of knife. Melt remaining chocolate with butter in double boiler; spread within outline.

Mildred Taylor Marsh
Orlando, Florida

GOBLIN'S PERKY PUNCH

Candy pumpkins
Candy corn
1   46-oz. can orange fruit drink
1   46-oz. can pineapple juice
2   1-lb. 13-oz. cans apricot nectar
1/4 c. lemon juice
1 qt. Seven-Up

Place 1 pumpkin and several pieces of candy corn alternately in each section of ice cube tray; fill with water. Freeze overnight. Chill remaining ingredients. Mix orange drink, pineapple juice, apricot nectar and lemon juice in punch bowl; add Seven-Up just before serving. Add prepared ice cubes to punch; serve punch in cups with ice cube in each cup.

Mrs. Judy Vrklan
Arlington, Minnesota

MOLASSES-POPCORN BALLS

1 c. light corn syrup
1 c. molasses
1 tsp. vinegar
1 tsp. soda
1 tbsp. hot water
4 qt. popped popcorn

Mix corn syrup, molasses and vinegar in saucepan; cook until mixture forms brittle ball when dropped into cold water. Dissolve soda in hot water; stir into molasses mixture. Pour over popcorn; mix well. Form into balls of desired size.

Mrs. Eunice Cole Salomonson
Loveland, Colorado

HALLOWEEN TREATS

1 c. sugar
1 c. light corn syrup
1 c. peanut butter
6 c. Rice Krispies
1 c. chocolate chips
1 c. butterscotch chips

Mix sugar and corn syrup in 3-quart saucepan; cook over moderate heat until mixture begins to bubble. Remove from heat; stir in peanut butter and Rice Krispies. Press into buttered 13 x 9 x 2-inch pan; let harden. Mix chocolate and butterscotch chips in top of double boiler; place over hot water until melted, stirring to blend. Spread over cereal mixture; chill. Cut into 2 x 1-inch bars. Yield: 48 bars.

Opal Pruitt
Buda, Illinois

FRUIT-O-LANTERN CAKE

1   18 1/2-oz. package yellow cake mix
1/2 c. flaked coconut
2   16 or 17-oz. cans apricot halves,
    drained
1/2 c. apricot preserves
1 1/2 tsp. lemon juice
1/4 tsp. grated lemon peel
White frosting, whipped cream or topping
4 lg. green gumdrops

Prepare cake mix according to package directions, using 2 greased and floured 9-inch layer cake pans. Sprinkle coconut over batter in 1 pan. Bake both layers according to package directions; let cool for 10 minutes. Remove each layer from pan; cool on wire racks. Wrap and freeze cooled plain layer for future use. Place coconut cake, coconut side up, on serving plate. Place apricot halves on cake close together, cut side down. Combine preserves, lemon juice and lemon peel in small saucepan; cook over low heat until mixture is warm, stirring occasionally. Spoon part of the mixture over apricots on cake; spread remaining mixture on side of cake. Pipe frosting on apricots to make triangle eyes, triangle nose and smiling mouth for Jack O'Lantern face. Secure gumdrops on wooden skewer; insert in side of cake to resemble a pumpkin stem. Chill until ready to serve.

Photograph for this recipe above.

Thanksgiving

SPINACH-BROCCOLI BUFFET CASSEROLE

2   10-oz. packages frozen chopped
    spinach
2   10-oz. packages frozen chopped
    broccoli
2 c. sour cream
1 env. dry onion soup mix
Salt to taste
1/2 c. grated Cheddar cheese

Cook spinach and broccoli according to package directions; drain well. Combine sour cream and soup mix; stir in spinach and broccoli. Season with salt. Place in casserole; cover. Bake in preheated 325-degree oven for 40 minutes. Remove from oven; top with cheese. Bake, uncovered, until cheese melts.

Elaine Hillyer
Bellevue, Washington

ORANGE SWEET POTATOES

1 can sweet potatoes
1 unpeeled orange, cut in 1/4-in. slices
2/3 c. sugar
1 tbsp. cornstarch
1/4 tsp. salt
1 c. orange juice
2 tbsp. butter

Drain sweet potatoes; slice. Arrange sweet potato slices and orange slices in alternate layers in casserole. Combine remaining ingredients in saucepan; simmer, stirring constantly, until thickened. Pour over potatoes; cover. Bake in preheated 400-degree oven for 25 minutes. Uncover; bake for 20 minutes longer.

Mrs. Frances A. Feltham
Stroudsburg, Pennsylvania

CRESCENT ROLLS

4 3/4 to 5 1/4 c. all-purpose flour
2 pkg. dry yeast
1/2 c. sugar
1 1/2 tsp. salt
1/2 c. butter, softened
1/2 c. hot water
1 c. warm milk
2 eggs
1 1/2 c. quick or old-fashioned rolled
    oats
Melted butter

Combine 2 cups flour, dry yeast, sugar and salt in large bowl; stir well to blend. Add softened butter. Add water and milk all at once; beat with electric mixer at medium speed for 2 minutes, scraping bowl occasionally. Add eggs and 1 cup flour; beat with electric mixer at high speed for 1 minute or until thick and elastic, scraping bowl occasionally. Stir in oats and enough remaining flour to make soft dough. Turn out on lightly floured board or canvas; knead for about 10 minutes or until smooth and satiny. Cover with plastic wrap, then a towel. Let rest on board for about 20 minutes; punch down. Divide dough into 3 equal parts. Roll out each part to 14-inch circle; cut each circle into 12 pie-shaped wedges. Brush with melted butter; roll up tightly, beginning at wide end. Place on buttered cookie sheets, point side down; curve to form crescents. Brush with melted butter. Cover loosely with plastic wrap. Refrigerate for 2 to 48 hours. Remove from refrigerator; uncover. Let stand for 10 minutes. Puncture any surface bubbles with toothpick. Bake in preheated 375-degree oven for 18 to 20 minutes; brush with melted butter. Yield: 3 dozen.

Photograph for this recipe on page 269.

PUMPKIN BREAD WITH TOPPING

3 c. sugar
1 c. oil
4 eggs
2 c. mashed pumpkin
3 1/2 c. flour
2 tsp. soda
1 1/2 tsp. salt
1 tsp. cinnamon
1 tsp. nutmeg
1 c. nuts (opt.)
1 pkg. Dream Whip
1 c. drained crushed pineapple

Beat sugar, oil, eggs, 2/3 cup water and pumpkin together. Sift dry ingredients together; beat into egg mixture. Stir in nuts. Pour into 2 small well-greased and floured loaf pans. Bake in preheated 350-degree oven for 1 hour. Cool; turn out of pans. Prepare Dream Whip according to package directions; stir in pineapple. Slice bread; serve each slice with dollop of pineapple topping. Batter may be baked in 4 well-greased and floured 1-pound coffee cans, filling 1/2 full.

Mrs. Patsy Evans
Bridge City, Texas

BUTTER-BASTED TURKEY WITH SAUSAGE-CORN BREAD DRESSING

1 1/2 lb. bulk pork sausage
2 c. chopped celery
1/4 c. chopped onion
1/4 c. butter
1 recipe Corn Bread, coarsely crumbled
8 c. dry bread cubes
1 tsp. sage
1/2 tsp. pepper
2 eggs, beaten
1 3/4 c. water
1 16 to 18-lb. turkey
Melted butter

Crumble sausage; cook in skillet, stirring frequently, until brown. Drain off excess fat. Saute celery and onion in butter until tender. Combine Corn Bread, bread cubes, sausage, sage and pepper in very large bowl. Add celery mixture; mix lightly. Add eggs and water gradually; toss lightly. Stuff about 2/3 of the dressing into body cavity and neck region of turkey. Place turkey in roasting pan. Bake in preheated 325-degree oven for about 6 hours and 30 minutes or until done, basting frequently with melted butter. Place remaining dressing in 2-quart casserole; cover. Bake during last 45 minutes of baking time.

Corn Bread

1 1/2 c. enriched cornmeal
1 1/2 c. all-purpose flour
1/2 tsp. salt
4 tsp. baking powder
2 eggs
1 1/2 c. milk
1/4 c. soft butter

Sift dry ingredients together into bowl. Add eggs, milk and butter; beat with rotary beater for about 1 minute or until smooth. Do not overbeat. Pour into buttered 9-inch square baking pan. Bake in preheated 425-degree oven for about 25 minutes or until golden brown. Prepare Corn Bread 1 or 2 days in advance; cover.

Photograph for this recipe on page 269.

Christmas

SYLLABUB

1 qt. heavy cream
1 c. milk
1 c. sugar
1 tsp. vanilla extract
1/4 c. sherry

Have all ingredients cold. Place all ingredients in large bowl; beat with egg beater until frothy. Serve immediately. Yield: About 20 servings.

Marion P. Elkin
Beulaville, North Carolina

GLORIOUS PUNCH

1 46-oz. can pineapple juice
2 6-oz. cans frozen lemonade
   concentrate
4 c. cranapple juice
1 8-oz. jar maraschino cherries
2 oranges, sliced
Red food coloring
1 qt. ginger ale or sparkling water,
   chilled

Combine pineapple juice, lemonade concentrate, cranapple juice, cherries with syrup and oranges in large bowl; add enough food coloring for desired color. Chill. Combine punch and ginger ale in punch bowl. Unmold Sherbet Ring by dipping mold in warm water; float ring in fruit punch.

Sherbet Ring

1 pt. raspberry sherbet
1 pt. lemon sherbet
Mint or mistletoe leaves
2 c. cranapple juice, chilled

Form 4 scoops each of raspberry and lemon sherbets, using small ice cream scoop; freeze for Sherbet Ring. Arrange leaves in bottom of 4 1/2-cup ring mold; place balls of sherbet alternately in mold. Pour 1 cup cranapple juice over sherbet; freeze. Add remaining juice; freeze until firm.

Photograph for this recipe on page 270.

YULETIDE HAM-CHEESE BALL

2 8-oz. packages cream cheese
1/2 lb. sharp cheese, shredded
2 tsp. grated onion
2 tsp. Worcestershire sauce
1 tsp. lemon juice
1 tsp. mustard
1/2 tsp. paprika
1/2 tsp. salt
1 2 1/4-oz. can deviled ham
2 tbsp. chopped parsley flakes
2 tbsp. chopped pimento
2/3 c. chopped pecans

Soften cream cheese in large bowl. Add sharp cheese, onion, Worcestershire sauce, lemon juice, mustard, paprika, salt, deviled ham, parsley flakes and pimento; mix well. Chill until nearly firm. Shape into ball; roll in pecans. Wrap in foil; refrigerate overnight. Sprinkle with additional paprika; slice to serve.

Mrs. Margaret Byram
Belmont, Mississippi

HOLIDAY CRANBERRY-ORANGE RELISH

2 oranges
1 pkg. cranberries
2 c. sugar

Quarter oranges; remove seeds. Grind oranges and cranberries together; stir in sugar. Cover; refrigerate for several hours before serving. Yield: 6-8 servings.

Mrs. Mae Van Petett
Tompkinsville, Kentucky

HOLIDAY SANDWICH LOAF

1 2-lb. loaf unsliced tinted
   sandwich bread, chilled
Softened butter

Ham Filling

1 c. ground cooked ham
1/3 c. sour cream
1/4 c. chopped walnuts
1/4 c. pickle relish
3/4 tsp. prepared horseradish
1/4 tsp. crushed basil leaves

Cheese Filling

1 1/2 c. shredded Cheddar cheese,
   at room temperature
1/4 c. butter, at room temperature
1/4 c. dry sherry
1/2 tsp. salt
1/8 tsp. cayenne pepper
Dash of ground ginger

Turkey Filling

1 c. chopped cooked turkey
1 8 1/2-oz. can crushed pineapple,
   well drained
1/3 c. sour cream
1/2 tsp. celery salt

Frosting

2 8-oz. packages cream cheese,
   at room temperature
1/3 c. sour cream

Remove crusts from bread. Cut bread into 4 slices lengthwise about 3/4 inch thick; spread 3 slices with butter. Combine ham, sour cream, walnuts, pickle relish, horseradish and basil leaves in small mixing bowl for Ham Filling. Chill. Blend cheese, butter, sherry, salt, cayenne pepper and ginger in small mixing bowl for Cheese Filling. Chill. Combine turkey, pineapple, sour cream and celery salt in small bowl for Turkey Filling. Chill. Top 1 bread slice with Ham Filling; spread second slice with Cheese Filling. Spread Turkey Filling on third slice; reassemble loaf, topping with plain fourth slice. Cover with damp towel or protective wrap; chill thoroughly. Frost sandwich about 1 hour before serving. Place cream cheese and sour cream in small mixing bowl for Frosting; beat until fluffy. Spread on sides and top of chilled sandwich loaf. Swirl sides and top of loaf with serrated knife; garnish top and sides with flowers made from radish slices and green pepper slices. Chill. Yield: 24 servings.

Photograph for this recipe on page 270.

GOOSE WITH FRUIT STUFFING

2 c. pitted prunes
Sherry
1   12-lb. goose
Salt and pepper to taste
2 c. white raisins
2 fresh pears
2 pkg. frozen peaches, thawed
2 c. dried apple rings, cut in half
2 c. dried apricots
1 c. dry or toasted bread crumbs
1/2 tsp. ginger
1/2 tsp. cinnamon
8 whole cloves
1/4 tsp. nutmeg
3/4 c. apricot brandy
Green or red grapes

Place prunes in bowl; add enough sherry to cover. Soak overnight. Sprinkle goose inside and out with salt and pepper. Rinse raisins in hot water. Peel pears; remove cores. Dice pears. Add fruits to prunes and sherry; stir in bread crumbs and spices. Stuff into cavity of goose; truss. Place goose, breast side up, in roasting pan. Bake in preheated 325-degree oven for 4 hours, draining off fat occasionally. Bake for 45 minutes longer, basting goose with brandy frequently. Place grapes in pan; bake for 15 minutes longer, basting goose and grapes with brandy frequently. Place goose on platter; place grapes around goose. Serve with rice. Yield: 8 servings.

Mary Alice Bird
Detroit, Michigan

HOLIDAY PEAS

1   4-oz. can mushroom stems and pieces
1   10-oz. package frozen green peas
1 sm. onion, chopped
1/2 c. chopped celery
3 tbsp. butter
1   2-oz. jar pimentos, drained and
    chopped
1/2 tsp. salt
1/8 tsp. pepper

Drain mushrooms, reserving liquid. Cook peas according to package directions, substituting reserved liquid for equal amount of water; drain. Cook onion and celery in but-ter in saucepan until soft. Add mushrooms and pimentos; heat thoroughly. Add peas and seasonings; heat through.

Lettie Ann Boggs
Orrville, Ohio

CHRISTMAS DINNER ROLLS

2 pkg. yeast
1 c. warm water
2 c. hot water
3/4 c. oil
1/4 c. honey
2 tsp. sea salt
2 eggs, beaten
6 c. unsifted whole wheat flour

Dissolve yeast in warm water in large bowl. Add remaining ingredients except flour; mix well. Add flour gradually; mixture will be sticky, but do not knead. Chill overnight. Shape into rolls; place in greased pan. Bake in preheated 425-degree oven for about 10 minutes.

Susan McAlexander
Abernathy, Texas

WHITE FRUITED FUDGE

2 c. sugar
1 c. light cream
1/4 c. butter
1/4 c. light corn syrup
1/2 tsp. salt
1 c. miniature marshmallows
1 tsp. vanilla extract
1/2 c. pecan halves
1/3 c. chopped red candied cherries
1/3 c. chopped green candied cherries

Combine sugar, cream, butter, syrup and salt in large heavy saucepan. Bring to a gentle boil over low heat. Cook, stirring constantly, until sugar melts. Continue cooking, stirring occasionally, until mixture reaches 238 to 240 degrees on candy thermometer or to soft-ball stage. Remove from heat; stir in marshmallows and vanilla extract. Stir until marshmallows melt and candy starts to lose gloss. Stir in pecan halves and fruits. Stir until candy starts to set. Pour into buttered 8-inch square pan. Cool; cut into squares.

Photograph for this recipe on page 283.

CHOCOLATE NUT CARAMELS

2 c. sugar
1/2 tsp. salt
1 c. light cream
1 c. butter
1/2 c. light corn syrup
2 2-oz. squares unsweetened chocolate
1 tsp. vanilla extract
1 to 1 1/2 c. pecan halves

Combine sugar, salt, cream, butter, syrup and chocolate in large heavy saucepan. Bring to a gentle boil over low heat. Cook, stirring frequently, until syrup reaches 248 degrees on candy thermometer or to the firm-ball stage. Remove from heat; cook for 5 minutes. Stir in vanilla extract and pecan halves. Pour into buttered 8-inch square pan. Cool. Cut into 1-inch squares; wrap in waxed paper. Yield: 64 caramels.

Photograph for this recipe on page 283.

PETITS FOURS

3/4 c. butter
1 1/2 c. sugar
3 eggs
1 tsp. vanilla extract
3 c. sifted all-purpose flour
1 tbsp. baking powder
1 tsp. salt
1 1/2 c. milk
1/2 c. water
1/2 c. light corn syrup
1 tsp. lemon extract
2 or 3 drops of yellow food coloring
2 1-lb. boxes confectioners' sugar
Red cinnamon candies
Green candied cherries, sliced

Cream butter in mixing bowl. Add sugar gradually; beat until light and fluffy. Beat in eggs, one at a time; stir in vanilla. Sift flour, baking powder and salt together; add to creamed mixture alternately with milk. Spread evenly in buttered and floured 15 1/2 x 10 1/2 x 1-inch jelly roll pan. Bake in preheated 350-degree oven for 25 to 30 minutes or until done; cool in pan on wire rack for 10 minutes. Remove from pan; finish cooling on wire rack. Cover with towel. Cut into diamond shapes when ready to frost. Combine water, corn syrup, lemon extract and food coloring in top of double boiler; place over boiling water. Add sugar gradually; heat until mixture is of dipping consistency, stirring frequently. Reduce heat; keep warm while dipping cake. Stick a 2-tine kitchen fork in bottom of each piece of cake; dip and turn cake in icing until top and sides are coated. Add small amount of hot water and stir well if icing becomes too thick for dipping. Slip frosted cake off of fork with spatula; place on wire rack, frosted side up, until hardened. Decorate each piece of cake with 3 cinnamon candies and slices of candied cherries. Cake made day before frosting is easier to handle. Practice dipping technique on triangles of cake left over after cutting. Cake may be frosted, wrapped in protective wrap and frozen. Defrost at room temperature in wrapping. Yield: 24 petits fours.

Photograph for this recipe on page 270.

CRANBERRY-NUT BREAD

1 egg
3/4 c. sugar
1 c. sour cream
2 1/4 c. all-purpose flour
1 tsp. baking powder
1 tsp. soda
1 tsp. salt
3 tbsp. grated orange peel
1/2 c. chopped walnuts
1 c. coarsely chopped cranberries

Beat egg in large mixing bowl. Add sugar; mix well. Stir in sour cream carefully. Sift flour, baking powder, soda and salt together; add to creamed mixture, stirring just until moistened. Add orange peel, walnuts and cranberries; turn into buttered 9 x 5 x 3-inch loaf pan. Bake in preheated 350-degree oven for 55 minutes to 1 hour or until done. Turn out of pan onto wire rack; cool.

Photograph for this recipe on page 270.

Special Occasions

CHAMPAGNE PUNCH

1 1/2 c. sugar
2 c. lemon juice
2 qt. sauterne, chilled
1 qt. champagne, chilled

Dissolve sugar in lemon juice; pour into punch bowl. Add sauterne; pour in champagne. May garnish with lemon slices, if desired.

Fern Alexander
Big Spring, Texas

COCKTAIL MIX

1   1-lb. box Wheat Chex
1 med. box Cheerios
1 lb. margarine or butter
1 lb. mixed nuts or pecans
1 med. box pretzel sticks
1 tbsp. celery salt
1 tbsp. onion salt
1 tbsp. garlic salt

Place all ingredients in large roaster or baking pan. Bake in preheated 250-degree oven for 2 hours, stirring every 30 minutes. Cool. Store in covered containers; may be kept indefinitely. Yield: 100 servings.

Mrs. Geraldine M. Beveridge
Beaufort, North Carolina

BRIDGE CLUB SURPRISE SNACK

1   5-oz. jar cheese-bacon spread,
    softened
4 tsp. butter, softened
Dash of Worcestershire sauce
Dash of Tabasco sauce
3/4 c. flour
1 jar stuffed olives
Paprika to taste

Beat cheese spread and butter together until fluffy. Add sauces; mix well. Stir in flour to make a dough-like consistency. Shape about 1 teaspoon dough around each olive. Place on ungreased cookie sheet. Bake in pre-

heated 400-degree oven for 12 to 15 minutes. Sprinkle with paprika.

Mrs. Frances VanLandingham
Snow Hill, North Carolina

ANNIVERSARY FRUIT CUP

2 c. watermelon balls
2 c. honeydew melon balls
2 c. cantaloupe balls
2 c. fresh pineapple cubes
2 c. seedless grapes or peach cubes
Lemon juice
Pink champagne or ginger ale

Mix fruits together gently; arrange in parfait glasses. Sprinkle each serving with several drops of lemon juice. Fill glasses with champagne; garnish each glass with a mint sprig. Yield: 8-10 servings.

Patricia Shradel Mundy
Perry, Iowa

MINIATURE CREAM PUFFS

6 tbsp. butter
3/4 c. water
3/4 c. sifted all-purpose flour
3 eggs
1   12-oz. can chicken, chopped
1 c. chopped celery
1 c. mayonnaise
1 tbsp. Good Seasons onion salad dressing
    mix
1/4 c. lemon juice

Place butter and water in saucepan; bring to a boil. Reduce heat; add flour all at one time, stirring rapidly. Cook, stirring, until mixture thickens and leaves side of pan. Remove from heat. Add eggs, one at a time, beating well after each addition. Beat until mixture is satiny. Drop from teaspoon onto ungreased baking sheets. Bake in preheated 425-degree oven for 20 to 30 minutes or until brown; cool. Place chicken in mixing bowl. Add remaining ingredients; mix well. Fill cream puffs with chicken mixture. Yield: 4 1/2 dozen.

Mrs. Taylor Cowan, III
Knoxville, Tennessee

CREPES FLORENTINE

1 3/4 c. flour
1 1/2 tsp. salt
3 eggs, beaten
3 1/2 c. milk
1/4 c. butter
1 tsp. dry mustard
1 tsp. Worcestershire sauce
1 10-oz. package frozen chopped spinach
2 c. cooked diced chicken
1 c. sharp American cheese, shredded

Sift 1 1/2 cups flour and 1/2 teaspoon salt together. Combine eggs and 1 1/2 cups milk. Add to flour mixture; beat until smooth. Pour enough into hot, lightly buttered 6 or 7-inch skillet to cover bottom of skillet; cook until browned on both sides. Remove from skillet. Cook remaining batter; separate each crepe with sheet of waxed paper. Keep warm. Melt butter in saucepan; blend in remaining 1/4 cup flour, mustard, remaining 1 teaspoon salt and Worcestershire sauce. Add remaining 2 cups milk; cook, stirring constantly, until thick. Cook spinach according to package directions; drain. Blend 3/4 cup sauce with chicken and spinach. Fill each crepe with 1 heaping tablespoon filling; roll up. Place crepes in shallow 13 x 9-inch baking dish, seam side down. Pour remaining sauce over crepes; top with cheese. Bake in preheated 350-degree oven for 20 minutes or until heated thoroughly.

Mrs. Mary Jane Kline
Rockville, Maryland

CONFETTI RICE

1/4 c. butter or margarine
1 1/4 c. long grain rice
2 cans consomme or broth
1 tsp. salt
3/4 c. chopped green onions
3/4 c. chopped carrots
3/4 c. chopped celery
1/2 c. sliced almonds

Melt butter in large frying pan. Add rice; cook, stirring occasionally, for about 5 minutes or until heated but not brown. Add

consomme and salt; bring to a boil. Turn into 1 1/2-quart casserole; cover. Bake in preheated 375-degree oven for about 20 minutes. Stir in vegetables and almonds; cover. Bake for 10 minutes longer or until vegetables are crisp-tender. Yield: 8 servings.

Patricia Rovey
Buckeye, Arizona

FLOWERING PLUM CORNISH HENS

4 Cornish hens, split
1 tsp. seasoned salt
2 lg. oranges, sliced
1/4 c. margarine, melted
1/4 c. diced onion
1 tsp. ginger
1 tsp. Worcestershire sauce
1 1/2 tsp. prepared mustard
1/3 c. chili sauce
1/4 c. soy sauce
1 6-oz. can frozen lemonade, thawed
1 1-lb. can purple plums, drained and
    pureed
1/4 c. shredded coconut

Sprinkle hens with seasoned salt. Arrange orange slices in shallow roasting pan; place hens, skin side up, over oranges. Bake in preheated 350-degree oven for 45 minutes. Combine margarine, onion, ginger, Worcestershire sauce, mustard, chili sauce, soy sauce, lemonade and plums in saucepan; blend well. Simmer, stirring frequently, for 15 minutes. Pour plum sauce over hens. Bake for 20 minutes longer, basting frequently. Arrange hens on heated platter; top with pan drippings. Sprinkle with coconut. Yield: 4-6 servings.

Mrs. Francis Baratz
Waterford, Connecticut

CRAB LOUIS LUNCHEON

1 lb. crab meat
1 head lettuce, shredded
1/2 tsp. salt
1 cucumber, sliced
4 tomatoes, sliced
3 hard-cooked eggs, sliced
1 c. mayonnaise

3 tbsp. catsup
2 tbsp. chopped sweet pickle
1 tbsp. lemon juice

Remove bits of shell and cartilage from crab meat. Place lettuce in large, shallow salad bowl; sprinkle with salt. Arrange crab meat over lettuce. Place overlapping alternate slices of cucumber, tomatoes and eggs around edge of bowl. Combine mayonnaise, catsup, pickle and lemon juice; spread over crab meat. Chill. Yield: 6 servings.

Mrs. Viola Gracey
Snyder, Texas

STRAWBERRY ROLL

5 egg whites
1/2 tsp. cream of tartar
Powdered sugar
3 egg yolks, beaten
1/2 c. all-purpose flour
1/2 tsp. vanilla
1 pt. fresh or frozen strawberries, sliced
1 c. whipping cream, whipped and sweetened

Beat egg whites until frothy. Add cream of tartar; beat until stiff. Beat in 3/4 cup powdered sugar gradually; beat in egg yolks, flour and vanilla. Pour into greased jelly roll pan. Bake in preheated 325-degree oven for 20 minutes or until cake tests done. Turn out on towel sprinkled with powdered sugar; roll up towel and let cool. Unroll; arrange strawberries over cake. Spread with whipped cream. Roll up again. May frost with favorite butter frosting flavored with strawberries, if desired.

Mrs. Audrey Bowers
Duncan, South Carolina

ELEGANT RASPBERRY CHIFFON PIE

1   10-oz. package frozen raspberries
4 eggs, separated
1 tbsp. lemon juice
3/4 c. sugar

1 1/2 env. unflavored gelatin
1/2 c. heavy cream
1/8 tsp. salt
1 baked 9-in. pie shell

Thaw frozen raspberries. Place egg whites in small mixing bowl. Combine egg yolks, lemon juice and 1/2 cup sugar in saucepan. Soften gelatin in 1/4 cup water. Cook egg yolk mixture, stirring constantly, until slightly thickened and mixture coats spoon. Add softened gelatin to egg mixture; stir until dissolved. Add raspberries; stir well. Chill until mixture begins to thicken. Whip cream until stiff. Beat egg whites and salt until soft peaks form; beat in remaining 1/4 cup sugar gradually. Beat until stiff peaks form. Fold egg whites and whipped cream into raspberry mixture. Pile lightly into pie shell. Chill until set.

Mrs. Gwendolyn Murphy
Yorktown Heights, New York

APRICOT HORNS

1 lb. butter
1 lb. creamed cottage cheese
4 c. (about) sifted flour
1 lb. dried apricots
3 3/4 c. sugar
1 1/2 c. ground walnuts
3 egg whites, beaten
Powdered sugar

Blend first 3 ingredients together by hand until stiff dough is formed. Shape into 1-inch balls; refrigerate overnight. Cook apricots according to package directions until tender. Drain, then puree. Stir in 2 cups sugar; cool. Mix walnuts and remaining 1 3/4 cups sugar. Roll out pastry balls on floured surface into 3-inch rounds, rolling 5 or 6 at a time; place 1 teaspoon apricot on each round. Shape into horn. Dip into egg whites; dip into walnut mixture. Place on greased baking sheet. Bake in preheated 375-degree oven for 12 minutes or until lightly browned; sprinkle with powdered sugar. May be frozen. Yield: 10 dozen.

Mrs. Marlys Bierman
Lansford, North Dakota

ABBREVIATIONS, SUBSTITUTIONS AND COOKING GUIDES

WHEN YOU'RE MISSING AN INGREDIENT . . .

Substitute 1 teaspoon dried herbs for 1 tablespoon fresh herbs.

Add 1/4 teaspoon baking soda and 1/2 cup buttermilk to equal 1 teaspoon baking powder. The buttermilk will replace 1/2 cup of the liquid indicated in the recipe.

Use 3 tablespoons dry cocoa plus 1 tablespoon butter or margarine instead of 1 square (1 ounce) unsweetened chocolate.

Make custard with 1 whole egg rather than 2 egg yolks.

Mix 1/2 cup evaporated milk with 1/2 cup water (or 1 cup reconstituted nonfat dry milk with 1 tablespoon butter) to replace 1 cup whole milk.

Make 1 cup of sour milk by letting stand for 5 minutes 1 tablespoon lemon juice or vinegar plus sweet milk to make 1 cup.

Substitute 1 package (2 teaspoons) active dry yeast for 1 cake compressed yeast.

Add 1 tablespoon instant minced onion, rehydrated, to replace 1 small fresh onion.

Substitute 1 tablespoon prepared mustard for 1 teaspoon dry mustard.

Use 1/8 teaspoon garlic powder instead of 1 small pressed clove of garlic.

Substitute 2 tablespoons of flour for 1 tablespoon of cornstarch to use as a thickening agent.

Mix 1/2 cup tomato sauce with 1/2 cup of water to make 1 cup tomato juice.

Make catsup or chili with 1 cup tomato sauce plus 1/2 cup sugar and 2 tablespoons vinegar.

CAN SIZE CHART

8 oz. can or jar	1 c.	1 lb. 4 oz. or 1 pt. 2 fl. oz. or No. 2 can or jar	2 1/2 c.
10 1/2 oz. can (picnic can)	1 1/4 c.	1 lb. 13 oz. can or jar or No. 2 1/2 can or jar	3 1/2 c.
12 oz. can (vacuum)	1 1/2 c.		
14-16 oz. or No. 300 can	1 1/4 c.	1 qt. 14 fl. oz. or 3 lb. 3 oz. or 46 oz. can	5 3/4 c.
16-17 oz. can or jar or No. 303 can or jar	2 c.	6 1/2 to 7 1/2 lb. or No. 10 can	12-13 c.

SUBSTITUTIONS

1 square *chocolate* (1 ounce) = 3 or 4 tablespoons cocoa plus 1/2 tablespoon fat.
1 tablespoon *cornstarch* (for thickening) = 2 tablespoons flour (approximately).
1 cup sifted *all-purpose flour* = 1 cup plus 2 tablespoons sifted cake flour.
1 cup sifted *cake flour* = 1 cup minus 2 tablespoons sifted all-purpose flour.
1 teaspoon *baking powder* = 1/4 teaspoon baking soda plus 1/2 teaspoon cream of tartar.
1 cup *bottled milk* = 1/2 cup evaporated milk plus 1/2 cup water.
1 cup *sour milk* = 1 cup sweet milk into which 1 tablespoon vinegar or lemon juice has been stirred; or 1 cup buttermilk.
1 cup *sweet milk* = 1 cup sour milk or buttermilk plus 1/2 teaspoon baking soda.
1 cup *canned tomatoes* = about 1 1/3 cups cut-up fresh tomatoes, simmered 10 minutes.
3/4 cup *cracker crumbs* = 1 cup bread crumbs.
1 cup *cream, sour, heavy* = 1/3 cup butter and 2/3 cup milk in any sour milk recipe.
1 cup *cream, sour, thin* = 3 tablespoons butter and 3/4 cup milk in sour milk recipe.
1 cup *molasses* = 1 cup honey.

METRIC CONVERSION CHARTS FOR THE KITCHEN

VOLUME

1 tsp.	=	4.9 cc
1 tbsp.	=	14.7 cc
1/3 c.	=	28.9 cc
1/8 c.	=	29.5 cc
1/4 c.	=	59.1 cc
1/2 c.	=	118.3 cc
3/4 c.	=	177.5 cc
1 c.	=	236.7 cc
2 c.	=	473.4 cc
1 fl. oz.	=	29.5 cc
4 oz.	=	118.3 cc
8 oz.	=	236.7 cc

1 pt.	=	473.4 cc
1 qt.	=	.946 liters
1 gal.	=	3.7 liters

CONVERSION FACTORS:

Liters	X	1.056	=	Liquid quarts
Quarts	X	0.946	=	Liters
Liters	X	0.264	=	Gallons
Gallons	X	3.785	=	Liters
Fluid ounces	X	29.563	=	Cubic centimeters
Cubic centimeters	X	0.034	=	Fluid ounces
Cups	X	236.575	=	Cubic centimeters
Tablespoons	X	14.797	=	Cubic centimeters
Teaspoons	X	4.932	=	Cubic centimeters
Bushels	X	0.352	=	Hectoliters
Hectoliters	X	2.837	=	Bushels

WEIGHT

1 dry oz.	=	28.3 Grams
1 lb.	=	.454 Kilograms

CONVERSION FACTORS:

Ounces (Avoir.)	X	28.349	=	Grams
Grams	X	0.035	=	Ounces
Pounds	X	0.454	=	Kilograms
Kilograms	X	2.205	=	Pounds

EQUIVALENT CHART

3 tsp. = 1 tbsp.	16 oz. = 1 lb.	4 c. sifted flour = 1 lb.
2 tbsp. = 1/8 c.	1 oz. = 2 tbsp. fat or liquid	1 lb. butter = 2 c. or 4 sticks
4 tbsp. = 1/4 c.	2 c. fat = 1 lb.	2 pt. = 1 qt.
8 tbsp. = 1/2 c.	2 c. = 1 pt.	1 qt. = 4 c.
16 tbsp. = 1 c.	2 c. sugar = 1 lb.	A Few Grains = Less than 1/8 tsp.
5 tbsp. + 1 tsp. = 1/3 c.	5/8 c. = 1/2 c. + 2 tbsp.	Pinch is as much as can be taken
12 tbsp. = 3/4 c.	7/8 c. = 3/4 c. + 2 tbsp.	between tip of finger and thumb.
4 oz. = 1/2 c.	2 2/3 c. powdered sugar = 1 lb.	Speck = Less than 1/8 tsp.
8 oz. = 1 c.	2 2/3 c. brown sugar = 1 lb.	

WHEN YOU NEED APPROXIMATE MEASUREMENTS . . .

1 lemon makes 3 tablespoons juice
1 lemon makes 1 teaspoon grated peel
1 orange makes 1/3 cup juice
1 orange makes about 2 teaspoons grated peel
1 chopped medium onion makes 1/2 cup pieces
1 pound unshelled walnuts makes 1 1/2 to 1 3/4 cups shelled
1 pound unshelled almonds makes 3/4 to 1 cup shelled
8 to 10 egg whites make 1 cup

12 to 14 egg yolks make 1 cup
1 pound shredded American cheese makes 4 cups
1/4 pound crumbled blue cheese makes 1 cup
1 cup unwhipped cream makes 2 cups whipped
4 ounces (1 to 1 1/4 cups) uncooked macaroni makes 2 1/4 cups cooked
7 ounces spaghetti make 4 cups cooked
4 ounces (1 1/2 to 2 cups) uncooked noodles make 2 cups cooked.

MAKE 1 CUP OF FINE CRUMBS WITH . . .

28 saltine crackers
4 slices bread
14 square graham crackers
22 vanilla wafers

Index

PHOTOGRAPHY CREDITS: Frozen Southern Vegetable Council; North American Blueberry Council; Pickle Packers International, Inc.; The California Apricot Advisory Board; Louisiana Yam Commission; National Macaroni Institute; Spice Islands; The Spanish Green Olive Commission; National Cherry Growers and Industries Foundation; Carnation Evaporated Milk Division; Schieffelin & Company; American Dairy Association; Accent International; Tabasco; Knox Gelatine, Inc.; Sunkist Growers; Campbell Soup Company; The American Spice Trade Association; Vanilla Information Bureau; Washington State Apple Commission; National Livestock and Meat Board; United Fresh Fruit and Vegetables; National Dairy Council; Charcoal Briquet Institute; The Florida Citrus Commission; DIAMOND Walnut Growers, Inc; Ruth Lundgren, Ltd.; South African Rock Lobster Service Corporation; Angostura-Wuppermann Corporation.